The Economist Looks at Society

Gustav Schachter
Northeastern University

Edwin L. Dale, Jr.
New York Times

XEROX

XEROX COLLEGE PUBLISHING, Lexington, Massachusetts / Toronto

CONTRIBUTING AUTHORS

Alan B. Batchelder
Kenyon College

Juanita M. Kreps
Duke University

Simon Rottenberg
University of Massachusetts

Oscar T. Brookins
State University College of
New York

Niles M. Hansen
The University of Texas
at Austin

Harold M. Goldstein
Northeastern University

Marsha Goldfarb
Yale University

Marshall I. Goldman
Wellesley College

Bruce Cohen
Northeastern University

The Economist Looks at Society

Arnold Raphaelson
Temple University

William H. Miernyk
West Virginia University

Christopher Green
McGill University

Peter L. Bernstein
CBWL-Hayden, Stone Inc.

Richard Sherman
The Ohio State University

Richard Thorn
The University of Pittsburgh

Richard Ward
R. L. Hines Associates, Inc.

Library
Fashion Institute of Technology
227 WEST 27th STREET
NEW YORK, N.Y. 10001

PICTURE CREDITS

XEROX ® is a trademark of Xerox Corporation.
Copyright © 1973 by Xerox Corporation.
All rights reserved. Permission in writing must be obtained
from the publisher before any part of this publication may
be reproduced or transmitted in any form or by any means,
electronic or mechanical, including photocopy, recording,
or any information storage or retrieval system.
ISB Number: 0 – 536 – 00950 – 3
Library of Congress Catalog Card Number: 72 – 91029
Printed in the United States of America.

Preface

Suppose we were to ask the question why a bank vice president sitting behind a desk earns upwards of $25,000 a year while a waitress in a restaurant drags herself home exhausted each working night and earns only $4,000.

But also, suppose, it requires looking at a set of tough charts and grasping some unfamiliar ideas in order to answer the question of why the bank vice president earns more than the waitress.

Those two "supposes" are what this book is about. They are applied to an amazing variety of common human problems: hunger, crime, traffic jams, migrant workers, black poverty, discrimination against women, national defense and how much should be spent on it, why there are slums, and pollution.

Economists don't necessarily have "solutions" to these problems. But they are pretty good at identifying the problems accurately and throwing away phony solutions. For example, did you ever think that society would be, and will be, better off to allow *some* crime rather than to try to eradicate crime completely? See Chapter 10.

The purest environmentalist will hate this book; he wants to stop all pollution, period. The economist has doubts (Chapters 6 and 7). The "back to nature" school is certain that outmigration from rural areas of the United States is a tragedy, but perhaps that school has not thought the problem through (Chapter 5).

Economists, like all decent Americans, are against discrimination on the basis of race or sex. But they can measure its effects a bit better than most, and sometimes they can make a distinction between out-and-out prejudice on the one hand, and low productivity on the other (Chapters 2 and 3).

Are poor people poor because of things like "exploitation"? In part, maybe. But, with some effort, it is possible to see that the real reason is something called "marginal average product," which most people who demonstrate on the streets have never heard of (Chapter 1).

Economists have been given credit, rightly, for evolving a set of ideas on how the central government should manage its finances— called monetary and fiscal policy— to keep industrial nations like ours prosperous without serious inflation. Politicians, from presidents to parliaments, have sometimes erred, and the economists have not been the fount of all wisdom. But the fact is that the industrial world of the United States, Western Europe and Japan in the quarter-century since World War II has experienced astonishing prosperity, with interruptions (usually called "recessions" now) that are very mild compared to former times.

This book does not involve *that* contribution of economic thought, of which Lord Keynes of England and too many Americans to mention are the heroes. That part a student will learn through his regular textbook, and it is an important story.

This book involves something else: whether some of the principles of economics can help governments and people solve smaller, more "homely" problems like dirty air and traffic jams. The economists, it turns out, often come up with non-obvious solutions, or at least non-obvious explanations of why the problem exists. The extraordinary set of economic incentives, disincentives and other motivations that create clogged city streets make up a good example (Chapter 9).

Economists are good, also, at exploding myths— such as the myths about defense spending (Chapter 17). An implicit in this book is something economists have always agreed on: "There is no such thing as a free lunch." It is just a way of saying that total resources in any society— a difficult word usually meaning money— are always limited. We cannot solve everything at once, certainly not with money, and all of us cannot have everything we want.

But we can understand better and sometimes even avoid wrong paths in our eager effort to solve problems that trouble all of us. Alas, making the right choices, if they are possible at all, requires knowledge and often a difficult mental exercise. Like a free lunch, there is no such thing as simpleminded analysis or solution that is worth anything.

When the economist looks at society, he does not propose a Utopia. He, perhaps more than most people, doubts that Utopia is possible at all. But he can clear some of the mist surrounding our problems and possibly make the path to a solution a little more visible. That is the purpose of this book.

January 1973

To the Instructor

The Economist ... is intended as an unusual and challenging supplement for use in a basic course in Economics. Each chapter is intended to: (1) present to the student a current social or economic problem, (2) discuss fully the economic issues involved in the causes of and solutions to this problem, (3) acquaint the student with techniques of economic analysis as they apply to the problem, and (4) allow the student to assess the economic issues involved in each problem and to appreciate the difficulty of identifying *one* cause and *one* solution to the problem.

Unlike the usual readings book, *The Economist Looks at Society* is not a collection of articles. Each chapter of this volume is an original piece of work, written expressly for this book, according to a prescribed length, level, and format, by a specialist in one of twenty areas of national concern covered in the book. While the organization is not meant to parallel that of the standard text or course, the level of each chapter is such that the student can easily grasp the economic issues involved and economic principles introduced. Each chapter serves as a case study, designed to teach and reinforce economic principles by applying them to a complex issue. A detailed cross reference of basic principles and appropriate chapters to assign appears in Appendix C.

This book is due to so many people that it would be impossible to list them all here. The authors would like to thank especially Herman Epstein (Brandeis University), who in 1967 experimented with teaching freshman biology through original research papers; Harold Goldstein and Bruce Cohen (Northeastern University), who along with Gustav Schachter in the following year attempted and developed a few problem cases to replace the research-oriented papers used in the experiment and the normative textbook; Marshall Goldman (Wellesley College), Robert Lakachman (State University of New York at Stonybrook), Paul Hohenberg (Cornell University), Lawrence Ritter (New York University), and Richard Sherman (The Ohio State University) for their valuable comments on the outline and chapters.

At Xerox College Publishing the authors gratefully acknowledge the encouragement and enthusiasm of Ted Caris, the company's young and innovative president. In addition to Ted Caris, William Frohlich and Dana Andrus were most understanding and cooperative. Ms. Andrus deserves more than commendation, because without her patient mediation this book could not have been published.

To Sylvia Goldberg and Dianne Genovese go special acclaim for handling the maze of communications, drafting and redrafting, and for their struggling with a most illegible handwriting. Yet, the real mastermind behind this publication to begin with was Francine N. Schachter, who dreamed up the entire idea. She is first to receive thanks.

Contents

Part 1

When the
Individual
Suffers

1 *Poverty*

In *I Am Curious (Blue)*, Lena, the young Swedish heroine, badgers a doctor:[1]

> Some people are very poorly endowed by nature. They're clumsy and backward and haven't got the brains needed for education. Others get an entirely different deal from the start. They can study, they have the chance to do so, they have parents, they have everything behind them, helping them and pushing them on. Should they be *rewarded* for that? So that later on they get better, more interesting jobs, higher salaries, and a better position in society? Is that fair? Should it be that way?

Lena thinks it should be otherwise. The doctor disagrees. Irritated by the doctor's opinions, Lena is further incensed because they are shared by Swedish students:[2]

> They thought it was damn natural that those who had the brains to learn should earn a lot more than others. And they didn't seem to care a bit if we got an education-conscious society that rewards the eggheads and makes it hard for everyone else.

The Statistics of Poverty

In America, as in Sweden, income differences are large. Many Americans receive high incomes, but even more receive low incomes. The Social Security Administration has established income criteria to distinguish between the poor and the nonpoor. The Census Bureau used these criteria to count the number of poor in America in 1970, and it found that there were 25.5 million of them in that year.

---

[1]Vilgot Sjoman, *I Am Curious (Blue)* (New York: Grove Press, 1970), p. 51. Reprinted by permission of Grove Press, Inc. Copyright © 1970 by Grove Press, Inc.
[2]*Ibid.*, p. 49.

The Census Bureau then calculated the total income of those 25.5 million poor Americans in 1970. Finally, it calculated the lowest income the poor would have had to have received to have kept themselves just barely out of poverty. The difference between actual income and the income the poor needed to be out of poverty was $11.1 billion.

So this was the size of America's poverty problem in 1970: (1) 25.5 million Americans were poor; and (2) the total income of the poor was at least $11.1 billion below the minimum income that would have held them just above the poverty level.

Though many Americans are still poor, the extent and severity of American poverty are falling. The Census Bureau has counted the number of poor Americans each year since 1959. Because prices were lower in the years before 1970, income lines distinguishing poor from nonpoor were lower each year before 1970. Using income criteria appropriate to 1959 prices, the Census Bureau counted 38.8 million poor Americans in 1959.

The Census Bureau calculated the total 1959 income of those 38.8 million poor Americans and then calculated the minimum total income that would have held them out of poverty. The difference between those two totals was $13.7 billion.

The 1970 poverty problem was, therefore, a change from the 1959 poverty problem, which was that: (1) there were 38.8 million poor Americans; and (2) a $13.7 billion "poverty gap" existed.

Millions of Americans were poor in 1959; millions were poor in 1970. But between 1959 and 1970, many millions moved up and out of poverty. This chapter will consider: (1) the reasons so many Americans were poor in 1970; and (2) the trends that have already reduced and that in the future will continue to reduce the number of Americans living in material poverty.

Solutions to American Poverty. Poverty can be reduced in either of two ways: (1) by taking from people who are not poor and giving to the poor, or (2) by increasing total output and therefore income, with part of the increases going to the poor.

If the nation's population and total output are the same in 1974 as in 1973, poverty can be reduced in 1974 only by taking away from the nonpoor. Under this assumption of an unchanged national output, the poor can be better off in 1974 only if the nonpoor become worse off. This, incidentally, would be one consequence of a policy of "zero growth," as advocated by some.

In contrast, if the 1974 population equals the 1973 population, while 1974 national output is up, part of the *increase* in per capita output may go to the poor. In this case, the nonpoor need not be made worse off for the poor to become better off in 1974.

These generalizations can help one to see why seemingly simple "solutions" may be unacceptable to the general public. For example, some urge curing poverty simply by giving poor people the money they need.

That is possible. The federal government could print extra currency and give it to the poor in 1974. The poor could then buy more than they had been able to buy in 1973 (though the increased money stock and the resulting extra spending would raise prices). What would be the effect of such a program on the nonpoor?

If 1974 output equaled 1973 output, any extra output gained by the former poor would just about equal output lost by the nonpoor. The mechanism for this transfer of income would be inflation. The nonpoor, who would lose by such a program, would have cause to oppose it.

Conditions Determining the Extent of Poverty. Poverty can be *reduced* by increasing output per capita or by taking from the nonpoor and giving to the poor. Poverty *results* in the first place from two causes: (1) a low ratio of output to population; and (2) the way output is divided among the population.

America's output-to-population ratio has long been large and in 1971 was:

$$\frac{\text{Total output}}{\text{Total population}} = \frac{\$1,050,000,000,000}{210,000,000} = \$5,000$$

In any country where that ratio is large, most people will *not* be poor.

India's output-to-population ratio was small, about $200, in 1970. With output small relative to population, poverty cannot be eliminated. Divide output evenly among all Indians and every Indian would be poor. Because Indian output is divided unevenly, a small minority are not poor, and the majority are a little poorer than otherwise.

The world is in the same position as India; if world output were divided evenly among Americans, Indians, and all other nationalities, *everyone* would be poor by American standards. No political revolution, no change in the way world output is divided, can eliminate poverty this year or for many years to come.

Because world output is divided unequally, most Americans, Australians, and Swedes are not poor. An equal division of world output would make the present poor only a little less poor and would leave everyone sharing poverty equally. World poverty can be eliminated only by an increased world output-to-population ratio.

As noted, America's output-to-population ratio is large and is growing larger. American poverty is, therefore, the result of the way output is divided among Americans.

The next section will consider the reasons why America's output-to-population ratio is large and growing. The section immediately following describes the way American output is divided and the reasons why that division leaves many poor.

Ratio of Output to Population

Most Americans are *not* poor precisely because America's annual output is so large relative to total U.S. population. In 1971, output per American was worth $5,000. In 1940, in 1971 prices, it was worth $2,400. By 1976, even in 1971 prices, it will be worth well over $6,000.

America has long been and will long continue to be in a highly favorable position respecting output and population. The reason the national figures are so favorable will be easier to understand after a look at a simple example involving small numbers in output-to-population ratios.

The simple example can be a corn farm comprising 1,000 cultivated acres and a large collection of tools. If, during 1974, only one man is employed to plant, tend, and harvest corn, the farm will produce 20,000 bushels of corn. But if, during 1974, not one, but two men are employed, the farm will produce 38,000 bushels of corn. In sentences, the figures blur; in Table 1.1, they make sense.

Table 1.1   1974 Possibilities for the Total Product and Average Product of Labor on a 1,000-Acre Corn Farm

Number of farm workers	Total product (bu. of corn)	Average product of labor (bu. of corn)
0	0	0
1	20,000	20,000
2	38,000	19,000
3	54,000	18,000
4	68,000	17,000
5	80,000	16,000
6	90,000	15,000

The figures represent mutually exclusive production possibilities; that is, if, during 1974, four persons work the land, seven cannot. Therefore, most of these numbers can never happen; only one possibility can ever be realized.

Figure 1.1 translates Table 1.1 into a sketch. The dots of Figure 1.1 are the average product possibilities of Table 1.1. The dashed line through the dots shows labor's average product possibilities if some part-time employees bring total employment to 2.5 or 3.12 or 4.98 workers. The dashed line to the right of the dots shows average product for seven or more laborers.

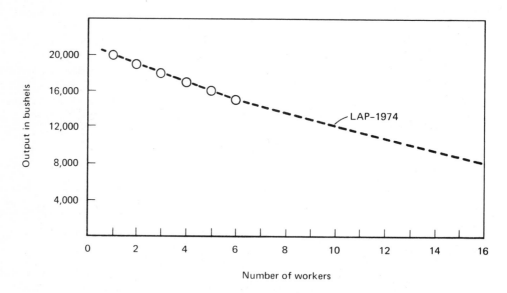

FIGURE 1.1   Average product of labor, 1974 possibilities.

This farm is fictitious, its numbers arbitrary, but the general principle is almost universally true: Average product is smaller the larger the number of laborers working with a fixed quantity of capital and land. This principle shows up in the diminishing figures of the right-hand column of Table 1.1 and in the downward sloping curve of Figure 1.1.

The corn example is trivial, but Figure 1.1 can be taken to represent labor's 1974 average product possibilities in the United States as a whole. Thus the "4" along the base can represent 40,000,000 workers. Still, the line slopes down. *Should* American "labor's average product" curve for 1974 (abbreviated LAP-1974) slope down? Does that make sense? Yes, it does, because the size of the United States and of its stock of buildings and machinery will be some particular amount for 1974. Given those fixed amounts of capital and land and given technology, the larger the labor force, the smaller will be labor's potential average product.

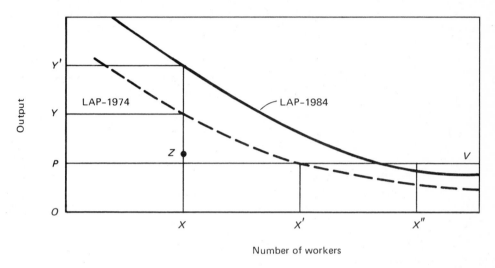

FIGURE 1.2 Average product of labor, 1974 and 1984 possibilities.

Figure 1.2 draws the connection between national poverty and LAP. The horizontal line, *PV,* is drawn at a height such that for any sized labor force, a labor average product of *OP, equally* divided among the entire population, would leave everyone just below the poverty line.

Given LAP-1974, a labor force of *OX,* fully employed and working at maximum efficiency, would realize an average product, *OY.* Everyone, depending on how output was divided, *could* be nonpoor.

But if a labor force of *OX* were fully employed at less than full efficiency, or if many in a labor force of *OX* were unemployed, realized average product would be only *XZ.* However output is divided within a nation, the extent of poverty is likely to be greater with an average product of *XZ* than with an average product of *OY.* In the United States between 1959 and 1960 and again between 1969 and 1970, unemployment rose, labor's realized average product fell, and poverty grew.

Because labor's potential average product is smaller the larger the labor force is, the size of a nation's labor force is critical in determining realized average product. If the population was so large that the labor force was *OX'* instead of *OX,* then, given the size of the nation and its stock of capital, labor's average product could not exceed *OP.* Even an equal division of output would leave everyone poor.

The U.S. labor force is small relative to the location of its LAP curve; most resources are fully employed most of the time; therefore, realized average product is well above *OP*. In Brazil, China, and Egypt, the labor force is large relative to LAP; realized average product cannot be much above *OP*; therefore, most people must be poor.

Americans today are lucky to have a population more like *OX* than *OX'*. They are also lucky because every year (1) the nation's stock of structures and machinery grows larger; (2) the education and training of the labor force improves; and (3) applied technology is improved. Each of these changes continually raises labor's average product, as from LAP-1974 to LAP-1984 in Figure 1.2. Such an increase permits an increase of realized average product from *OY* to *OY'* if population and labor force remain constant. But if population growth raised the 1984 labor force to *OX''*, realized average product could not reach *OP*. Most people would have to be poor.

Over the past 200 years, the growth of LAP relative to population has been *the single most important cause* of the reduction in poverty in Europe, Japan, and America. LAP has been lifted by improved education, improved technology, and accumulating physical capital.

The latter changes have also lifted the LAP curve in Latin America. But North America's population and labor force rise 1.5 percent a year; Latin America's rises 3 percent a year, almost as fast as its LAP curve rises. Consequently, the extent of Latin American poverty falls only very little each year.

Most Americans are not poor because U.S. technology, education, and physical capital stock are large relative to population size. Fewer Americans are poor each year because the LAP curve rises more rapidly than does population. But why should any Americans be poor in the 1970's?

Meritocracy and Marginal Analysis

In meritocracies, most output is divided among individuals in proportion to each individual's contribution to the value of production. At present, meritocracy tends to prevail wherever labor's average product is large, as in the United States, Japan, East Germany, France, Czechoslovakia, and Russia.

The corn farm can next be used to show how meritocracy firms behave when dividing output "in proportion to each individual's contribution to the value of production." Table 1.2 tells about the corn farm's mutually exclusive 1974 average *and* marginal production possibilities.

A "margin" is the difference between two adjacent totals. Table 1.2 derives marginal product figures from total product figures. For example, if two rather than three workers are employed during 1974, total product will be 38,000 instead of 54,000 bushels; the difference, the "marginal product" between two and three workers, is 16,000 bushels.

Down Table 1.2's "marginal product" column, the figures decline. For some farms and factories the first figures in the marginal product column would rise; but eventually, in every marginal product column, the figures decline because: The larger the quantity of labor combined with a fixed quantity of capital and land, the smaller labor's marginal product will be.

Given this nearly universal rule, how many people will an employer hire? The profit-seeking employer's rule is, "I'll hire another worker if he adds more to my

Table 1.2   1974 Possibilities for the Total Product, Marginal Product, Marginal Revenue Product, Total Labor Cost, and Marginal Labor Cost on a 1,000-Acre Corn Farm

Number of farm workers	Total product (bu. of corn)	Marginal product (bu. of corn)	Marginal revenue product	Total labor cost	Marginal labor cost
0	0			0	
1	20,000	20,000	$10,000	$6,000	$6,000
2	38,000	18,000	9,000	12,000	6,000
3	54,000	16,000	8,000	18,000	6,000
4	68,000	14,000	7,000	24,000	6,000
5	80,000	12,000	6,000	30,000	6,000
6	90,000	10,000	5,000	36,000	6,000

total revenue than he adds to my total cost." The comparison requires dollar figures. Two assumptions can be made for the corn farm: (1) that corn sells for 50¢ a bushel; and (2) that many workers are available for $6,000 a year apiece.

The "marginal revenue product" column of Table 1.2 converts bushels of corn into dollar value by multiplying 50¢ a bushel. For example, as between two and three workers, marginal product is 16,000 bushels; therefore, marginal revenue product is 16,000 × 50¢ = $8,000. Marginal revenue product tells how much each prospective worker would — if hired — add to the employer's total revenue.

Each "marginal labor cost" in Table 1.2 is the difference between two adjacent total labor cost figures; for example, total labor cost is $18,000 for three workers, $24,000 for four workers; so marginal labor cost between three and four workers is $6,000. Marginal labor cost tells how much each prospective worker would — if hired — add to the employer's total costs.

Figure 1.3 uses dots to represent the marginal revenue product (hereafter MRP) and marginal labor cost (hereafter MLC) figures of Table 1.2. Dashed lines connect the dots to indicate marginal values if the employer changes from one to another fractional number of workers, for instance, from 1¾ to 2¾ workers.

Figure 1.3 shows the comparisons the employer makes when deciding how many workers to hire. MRP = $10,000 and MLC = $6,000 if one person is hired. Since one employee would add more to total revenue than to total cost, the profit-seeking employer would hire at least one person. MRP = $9,000 and MLC = $6,000 when a second person is hired; thus the profit-seeking employer would hire at least two people. Whenever MRP exceeds MLC, a profit-seeking employer would hire; this would clearly be the case for each of four workers on the corn farm.

A fifth worker would add MRP = $6,000 to total revenue and MLC = $6,000 to total cost, so would not affect total profit. Assuming employers prefer bigger to smaller operations, a fifth worker would be hired. But a sixth worker would add MRP = $5,000 to total revenue, MLC = $6,000 to total cost, thus cutting total profit by $1,000. Therefore, no sixth person would be hired. Marginal analysis shows this corn farmer maximizing profit by hiring in such a way that MRP = MLC — in this case, five workers.

In this situation, how do wages compare with each worker's contribution to the value of output? The answer is that "meritocracy results in wages that equal that contribution."

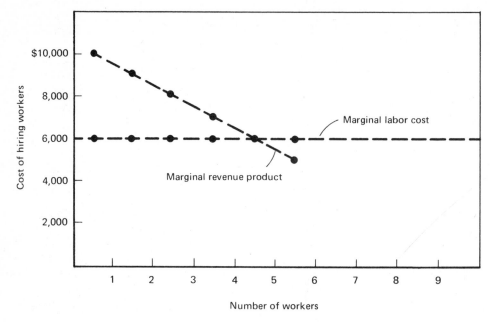

FIGURE 1.3 Marginal revenue product and marginal labor cost,
1974 possibilities.

Five workers are hired on the corn farm; the fifth worker's MRP is $6,000. He is paid $6,000. Each of the five is assumed to be equal in work performance to all the others. If any one of the five does not work, output would be 12,000 bushels, or $6,000, less. In this sense, each, when paid $6,000, is paid the value of his contribution to production.

It is important to note here the significance of the assumption that corn sells for 50¢ a bushel. If the price were $1, the marginal revenue product of each worker would be twice as much, and employers would find it worthwhile to hire more workers at higher wages. In the vast mix of preferences exercised by consumers, corn happens to be "worth" only 50¢ a bushel and thus corn workers have a wage of $6,000 in this example. American society places a "price" on plumbing about double what it places on corn, and thus employers find that it pays to hire plumbers at $12,000 a year.

One plumbing firm and one corn farm are insignificant, but the general principle is important. Profit-maximizing employers determine the size of their labor force by enlarging until the last worker included adds to total revenue just what he or she adds to total cost. At that point, wages *equal* the worker's contribution to the value of total output. Employers would prefer to pay less, employees would prefer to receive more, but self-interest impels employees to work and employers to hire, with each worker paid the value of his or her contribution to production.

Because employers need to utilize different skills — or nonskills — a different downward sloping MRP curve serves as the demand curve for each kind of labor. In each different labor market, if labor were well informed and freely mobile and if monopoly and government controls were absent, each worker's wage would equal his or her contribution to the value of total production.

The different curves for each different kind of labor are crucial to understanding income inequality and, to some extent, poverty. The marginal revenue product of a bank vice-president is, say, $25,000; hiring one more vice-president will add to the bank's loans and otherwise increase earnings by $25,000, but no more than $25,000. That is why the bank vice-president is paid $25,000. The marginal revenue product of a waitress is only $4,000 in some towns, less in others; and that is why a waitress is paid only $4,000. The waitress may think she "deserves" $10,000 for the hard work she does, but she does not add $10,000 worth of revenue to the restaurant.

One can imagine a hypothetical town, however, where most of the younger women have left and the older ones do not want to work, and yet people still like to eat in restaurants. The shortage of waitresses would require the owners to pay higher wages to induce anyone to take the job. Restaurant prices would then rise to the point where there would eventually be fewer customers. The marginal revenue product for waitresses in this case might be $7,000, though they would be doing work no different from that done by the same kind of women in a town 50 miles away.

Thus, the marginal revenue product curve for different types of labor — which determines the wage — varies for many reasons. A situation could be imagined in which garbagemen earned $25,000 because there were so few of them. But generally, as we shall see, the marginal revenue product of each person depends upon his own personal qualities and education in the context of his society.

Every producer needs physical capital as well as labor. Each firm has a downward sloping MRP curve for capital, and each firm "hires" capital until its MRP equals marginal *capital* cost. Thus each unit of capital, like each worker, tends to be paid the value of its contribution to production.

In practice, firms do not know the exact location of their MRP curves. Because American markets constantly change, most MRP curves are constantly in motion. Because of these changes and this ignorance, few people are paid exactly what they contribute to production value. Nevertheless, *most American incomes tend to equal their contributions to production.* This is meritocracy, where people who contribute capital and skilled labor to production earn large incomes, where people who contribute very large amounts of capital to production earn very large incomes, and where people who contribute little to production receive little income.

Ability to Contribute to Production

Individuals contribute to production with their labor and with their financial, and hence physical, capital. Incomes differ in large part because people differ in the quantity and quality of labor and capital they can contribute to production. Differences among individuals in the quantity and quality of the capital and labor they can sell are largely a matter of luck.

People lucky enough to inherit and retain much capital can avoid poverty with income earned by their inherited capital. People who can save will acquire title, either directly as with shares of stock or indirectly as through savings accounts, to America's growing stock of physical capital. Both lucky heirs and savers can earn income on their physical capital. People without physical capital must depend on their labor.

Differences among individuals in the quality of their labor are also largely a matter of luck. Why the differences? Let "intelligence" mean potential or actual ability with marketable value. "Intelligence" thereby embraces ditch digging, poetry writing, corporate management, cooking — a great variety of activities, each with its own MRP or labor curve, a low curve for ditch diggers, a much higher curve for corporate management.

The Role of Intelligence. In terms of potentiality and realization, three categories of intelligence can be distinguished:

Intelligence A: potential at the moment of conception.
Intelligence B: potential immediately after birth.
Intelligence C: performance ability at any point during an individual's life, and thus the marginal value of the person's labor.

America's economic system could operate so that everyone conceived with equal Intelligence A grew up with equal Intelligence C and earned equal incomes from their labor. Then, meritocracy income differences would be based only on differences in inherited capital and on differences in genetic Intelligence A.

Since Intelligence C depends on genes plus all experience, including education, how would education be distributed in this system? Marginal analysis would guide the way.

When an individual receives an education, he and society receive some total benefit, he and society bear some total cost. The costs include the resources used to instruct (teachers' time and capital and labor embodied in books and school buildings) and the loss of output occurring while students are learning instead of producing. The benefits include material and psychic returns to the individual plus the advantages other people receive from the education of that one person.

A little more education involves more (marginal) benefits and more (marginal) costs. So long as marginal benefits exceed marginal costs, a little more education for an individual is justified. Americans would derive maximum satisfaction from education if every person were educated to the point where the marginal benefits from that person's education just equalled the marginal costs (assuming those marginal costs and benefits could be calculated). Conceptually, medical care could be allocated in a similar manner.

If this educational and medical system prevailed along with meritocracy, everyone conceived with equal Intelligence A would be born with equal Intelligence B, would (except for disease and accidental injuries) grow up to have equal Intelligence C, and would receive equal incomes for the use of their labor.[3] Poverty would be the result of having the bad luck to inherit little property and only modest Intelligence A.

The latter misfortune might be only the result of being born in the wrong century. Intelligence A has many facets. An individual with exceptionally superior Intelligence A as a tracker might become a tribal chief if born in 12,066 B.C.; born in America in 1930, he might never be able to earn his way out of poverty. A man born in 1930 unable to earn an above-poverty income in 1973 might, if born in 2930 A.D., find that his Intelligence A would permit him to become a chief.

---

[3]If Jules and Jim are equally adept at physics, but Jules does not want to work hard (or at all), his Intelligence C will rank below Jim's in market value. "Intelligence" measures what one can *and will* put into the marketplace.

Nongenetic Determinants of Intelligence. Intelligence C is not just a matter of the luck of inheritance of Intelligence A. Between conception and the first week of extrauterine life much can happen to erode productive potential. When pregnant women used thalidomide, babies conceived as normal were born deformed. Malnourished mothers bear lighter babies than well-fed mothers. German measles, other illnesses, maternal mental trauma, and clumsy delivery can also cause babies conceived with equal Intelligence A to be born with unequal Intelligence B.

Psychologists have not yet reached definitive conclusions respecting the effects of malnutrition on the learning ability of babies' brains. Without doubt, children learn less in school when malnourished than when adequately fed. Perhaps they "could" do better, but they don't when hungry.

Intelligence C begins building in bassinet and playpen, at play with peers, at the dinner table. Home life, family, friends, and neighborhood make a difference. Most bankers' sons are better prepared for the executive suite and other high-paying jobs by their home life than are most janitors' sons.

Among school districts, among schools within a district, among teachers within a school, the quality of education varies enormously. In August 1971, California's Supreme Court concluded that school systems financed principally through property taxes denied students the equal protection of the law as guaranteed by the Constitution because property tax receipts vary so much from one school district to another. If the Supreme Court of the United States upholds that ruling, interschool differences may be reduced. By providing more money per pupil to poor districts than to rich districts, federal aid to education has already reduced interschool differences. But for the foreseeable future, quality will continue to vary widely among schools.

Many blacks, Indians, Puerto Ricans, and Mexican-Americans possess inferior educations because of past discrimination by white-dominated school boards and legislatures. These people have a lower Intelligence C than their majority-group peers who had no greater Intelligence B.

Some individuals fail to raise their Intelligence C because they are ignorant of career opportunities or of educational opportunities. In general, the lower the parents' income, the less information their children have respecting careers, educational opportunities, and even short-run jobs. People who are less informed about the market acquire less Intelligence C than people who are better informed, even when both start from equal Intelligence B.

Differences in nutrition, in home life, or in schooling result in differences in Intelligence C for people born with equal Intelligence B. As a result, individuals who might have risen to higher Intelligence C end with low Intelligence C and, therefore, with incomes below the poverty line.

Inequality of Rewards for Equal Intelligence. Many factors operate to bring unequal money incomes to people with equal Intelligence C. One such factor is the psychic "income" associated with many jobs. Some people choose life in Appalachia, in monasteries, or near their parents because the extra psychic income resulting from these choices exceeds the money income foregone because of their refusal to make geographic, occupational, or educational changes that would bring higher money incomes. Some people who could apply high Intelligence C to earning an above-poverty income prefer poverty to change.

Discrimination continues to restrict the employment of minorities. Consequently blacks and some others are restricted to poverty incomes while majority-group whites of *equal* Intelligence C earn above-poverty-level incomes. Discrimination, both against minorities and women, will be discussed in greater detail in Chapters 2 and 3.

Labor union monopolies add to poverty. Plumbers' and electricians' and doctors' unions exclude blacks as well as some whites who would do the work for lower wages than those prevailing. When unions exclude, the prices of the products they make or of the services they sell are forced up. The workers excluded swell labor supplies in other markets, thus lowering wages there, and sometimes even driving them below the poverty level. Thus union exclusion can depress the real incomes of excluded workers whose Intelligence C equals that of better paid union members.

Ignorance of the labor market leaves many people poor who might otherwise become nonpoor if they could only learn about and/or get to the jobs open to workers of their Intelligence C. Americans continue to lean heavily on friends and relatives for job information — and misinformation.

But even a known job opening must be reached. Some large black ghettos have no bus service. Lacking cars, the poor — black and white — may be unable to get to where the jobs are. In any case, daily transportation costs and moving costs deter movement. As a result, some Americans fail to learn about or to get to jobs that would lift them out of poverty.

Some people with Intelligence C who could earn above-poverty incomes are left poor because family obligations keep them from working. This is most often the case for women with small children, though others with sick or infirm relatives are similarly affected. The question begged in such cases is, "Would society be better off by making arrangements permitting these people to work, or by leaving them home and giving them a bigger share of output through welfare or other government transfer payments, or by leaving the status quo unchanged?"

Some Americans choose low or zero earnings because America's welfare system imposes a 100 percent tax on earnings. For example, if a family is receiving $2,500 a year from Aid to Families with Dependent Children and if a family member takes a part-time job paying $1,000 a year, the AFDC payments in many states drop $1,000.

If *any* extra costs for travel or clothing or food are required by the job, the family in the above case is *worse* off if a member works. Better then not to sell one's Intelligence C unless the wage is well above the level of the AFDC payments.

Bad luck can bring poverty when physical or mental illness takes away Intelligence C. Old age can bring poverty when people retire, though transfer payments reduce that effect. In 1970, about 4 million elderly people were held above the poverty line by Social Security payments.

Being able and willing to work is not enough. Jobs must be available, and dips in aggregate demand associated with recessions throw many people out of work and into poverty, though unemployment compensation tends to limit this result. When aggregate demand falls or slows its rate of increase, the number of job opportunities slows its usual year-to-year rise or the number of American jobs may even fall. The American labor force grows persistently; when aggregate demand falls, unemployment and part-time employment must rise. Individual incomes fall; poverty grows. The dip in aggregate demand between 1969 and 1970 added 1,233,000 Americans to the poverty list. On the other hand, 8 million Americans left poverty during the 1964 – 66 upward surge in aggregate demand.

Recessions, illness, old age, family obligations, immobility, ignorance about opportunities, discrimination, psychic income all operate so that among individuals with the same Intelligence C, some earn above-poverty incomes while others earn below-poverty-level incomes. As we have seen, other and equally inportant factors operate so that individuals conceived with equal Intelligence A grow up to unequal Intelligence C. And we must remember that some of the difference starts all the way back with unequal Intelligence A.

Marginal analysis has indicated: (1) that most Americans earn what they contribute to the total value of production, and (2) that Americans are poor when they contribute (because of ill luck in inheritance or because of barriers to the development of or application of Intelligence C) little to the value of production. These considerations are reflected in recent American statistics on poverty.

Defining the Poor

By what criteria are the poor to be distinguished from the nonpoor? Each year, the Census Bureau counts the number of poor Americans. Census takers could ask people, "Are you poor or not poor?" The answers could then be collected, but interpretation of them would hardly be objective because respondents differ widely in judging the meaning of the term "poor."

Instead of soliciting self-classification, the Census Bureau uses poverty criteria calculated by the Social Security Administration (hereafter abbreviated SSA). The SSA assumes that:

1. "Poverty" concerns the relation between material "needs" and the means to meet those needs.
2. Needs vary with family size, members' ages and sex, and farm-nonfarm location.
3. The poor, as shown by consumer surveys, devote one-third of their expenditures to food.
4. The Department of Agriculture has accurately calculated the cost of "minimally nutritious diets" for various family categories.

The SSA defines 124 nonfarm family categories, each different in the size, sex, or age of its members. The SSA uses Department of Agriculture calculations of food costs for a minimally nutritious diet for each family category and for a man or woman living alone and multiplies by three. This calculation produces an income poverty criterion for individuals and for each family category. For example, in 1970, a nonfarm family of four, with a male head under age 65 and with two children under 18, was judged "poor" if its income was less than $3,970 but "nonpoor" if its income was $3,970 or more. For every farm family, the income poverty criterion was 85 percent of the figure for an otherwise identical nonfarm family; this was on the assumption that farm families have smaller cash needs (most grow some food) than nonfarm families.

The income poverty criteria were lower for each year before 1970 because prices were lower. For example, the income poverty criterion for the four-person nonfarm family mentioned above was $3,745 in 1969 and $3,555 in 1968.

In 1970, the Census Bureau found that 25,522,000 people, or 12.6 percent of all

Americans, were poor according to SSA income poverty criteria. The breakdown by age and race was as follows:

	Among the 25,522,000 poor Americans	Among all 203,200,000 Americans
Were under age 18	41%	35%
Were over age 65	18%	10%
Were black	30%	11%

In short, most poor Americans (41 percent + 18 percent = 59 percent) are poor simply because they are either too young or too old to work and because they have no relatives able to lift them out of poverty.

Discrimination in education and in employment, accumulated throughout American history, holds the "incidence" of poverty (the number of poor in a category as a percentage of all people in a category) relatively high for minority groups. Thus, in 1970, 9.9 percent of white Americans, but 33.6 percent of black and 50 percent of red Americans were poor.

Child-care obligations keep many Americans poor even though government transfers to such families have grown rapidly in recent years. In 1969, 1.1 of the 1.3 million families headed by a woman aged 25 to 64 had children under age 6. Nevertheless, 543,000 of these 1.1 million women worked at least part-time part of the year.

Ill health is also a big factor in keeping many Americans poor. In 1969, 1.9 million poor families were headed by a man aged 25 to 64; yet .3 million of these men were unable to work during that year because they were ill or disabled. In 1969, 1.3 million poor families were headed by a woman aged 25 to 64; .1 million of these women were unable to work during 1969 because they were ill or disabled.

Modest education has limited the Intelligence C of many Americans. Of the .84 million poor male family heads aged 25 to 64 who worked year round during 1969, .45 million had eight or less years of formal schooling; .12 million were high school dropouts.

Many Americans with modest Intelligence C work — yet remain poor. In 1969, 1.6 million families headed by a healthy man aged 25 to 64 were poor. Of these, .84 million of the men worked full-time year round, while .62 million worked part of the year. In 1969, 1.2 million families headed by a healthy woman aged 25 to 64 were poor. Of these, .14 million of the women worked full-time year round, while .47 million worked part of the year.

Youth, old age, ill health, family obligations, limited Intelligence A, limited education — these are the principal causes of poverty in America. As the Intelligence C of the poor — or former poor — is improved, as physical capital accumulates, as technology improves, America's average and marginal physical product curves are raised, individuals become more productive, and the number of American poor falls. Also, as rising average product makes the society more affluent, government transfers from the nonpoor to the poor are increased and the severity of poverty and the number of poor are decreased.

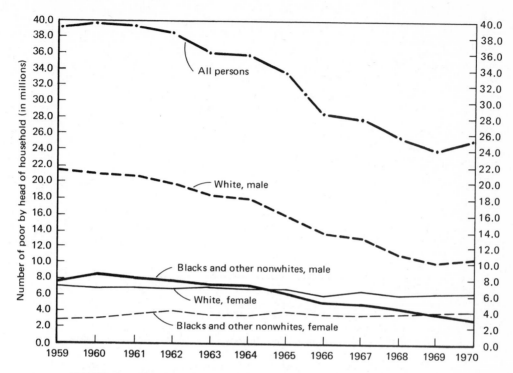

FIGURE 1.4 Number of persons below the poverty level, classified by sex and race of head of the family, 1959–1970. [Source: U.S. Department of Commerce, Bureau of the Census, *Current Population Reports, Series P-60,* No. 77 (May 7, 1971), p. 44.]

The Decline of American Poverty

Figure 1.4 shows the drop in the number of poor Americans from 40 million in 1959 to 25.5 million in 1970. Figure 1.4 also shows, by sex and color of the head of the household, the decline in the number of poor families headed by men but the growth in the number of poor families headed by nonwhite women.

Figure 1.5 takes a longer view and shows the decline in the number of poor and in the *incidence* of poverty in America between 1948 and 1970. The poverty counts during this period allowed for price changes, but otherwise used the same SSA "needs" criteria in each of the 23 years.

Over those years, rising government transfer payments have lifted many people out of poverty. More important, technological change and capital accumulation *raised the marginal product of labor* in almost every labor market, while education allowed most of the population to move from labor markets with relatively low to labor markets with relatively higher marginal physical product curves for labor. What becomes of the people who leave poverty? Do they join a growing mass of people clinging just above the poverty line, or do they mount an escalator carrying most people further up the income scale each year? The SSA has established "near-poverty" income criteria, which are one-fourth higher than the SSA poverty income criteria.

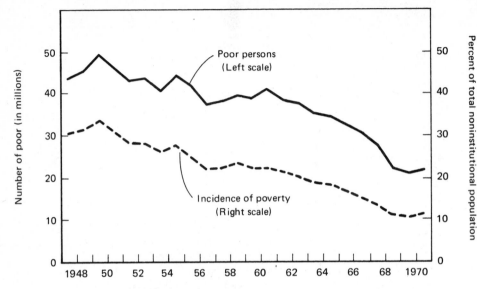

FIGURE 1.5 Number of poor persons and incidence of poverty
(poor persons as a percent of the total noninstitutional population),
1948 – 1970. [Sources: U.S. Department of Labor, *President's Economic Report: 1969* (Washington, D. C.: U.S. Government Printing
Office, 1969), p. 154; and U.S. Department of Commerce, Bureau of
the Census, *Current Population Reports*, Series P-60, No. 77 (May 7,
1971), p. 44.]

Between 1960 and 1969, the number of near-poor households fell from 4.3 to 3.5
million; the number of near-poor persons fell from 15.8 to 10.6 million (the numbers
stayed about the same during 1970). The number of poor Americans fell from almost
40 million in 1960 to 24.3 million in 1969. In general, people moving from poverty to
near-poverty were on an up escalator; as millions moved from poverty to near-
poverty, *more* millions moved up to above near-poverty.

The Role of Exploitation and Technological Change

"Exploitation" and technological unemployment are sometimes cited as causes of
poverty. They have not been mentioned in this chapter before because they are relatively unimportant in America.

Economists have several precise definitions of "exploitation," but one is not
needed here. It is enough to recognize that significant "exploitation" can occur only
when workers have no alternative jobs. Workers can't be "exploited" if they can tell
the boss to, "Keep your job and . . . ."

During the past century, sharecroppers have been exploited because landowners
and sheriffs kept them tied to the land. Some sharecroppers remain subjugated, but
each year fewer and fewer remain to be victimized. Nevertheless, many former
sharecroppers and others in small towns continue to receive exploitation wages
because geography and ignorance of distant job alternatives — or other elements of
Intelligence C — keep them dependent upon one or two local employers.

Technological change, whether "automation" or some other innovation, does put people out of work — *but* most only temporarily. Some years ago, the fictional Boat Builders' Brotherhood, the Seamen's Protective Association, and the Donkey and Camel Drivers' Alliance (Triple B, the SPA, and the DCDA) rallied together to protest imminent technological change. They warned that the new technology would put thousands out of work and would make mass unemployment chronic. But government rejected their protests, the wheel was introduced, unemployment rose only briefly, and mass unemployment has not yet appeared. Instead, the wheel raised labor's average and marginal product curves and made everyone better off.

As in the ancient world, so today. People want more than they have. Technological change permits them to have more. Our unlimited wants provide the aggregate demand that — to the extent government monetary and fiscal policy do not interfere — keeps the economy near full employment.

Technological innovations do throw people out of work, though more often innovations simply slow the growth of jobs in a specific firm. Where there are actual layoffs, in most cases most such people move to other jobs within a few months. But a few of the people laid off, most often the older people, are dropped into poverty by their inability to move or adapt to other work. This is why 20 percent of persons living on farms but only 11.7 percent of persons living off farms were poor in 1970. Elderly and other immobile farm residents have been slow to adjust to technological changes that permit only middle-sized and large farms to be profitable.

Concluding Observations

In India, most people are poor because the population is large relative to the nation's stock of capital and natural resources. Consequently, most people must remain poor.

In America, the population is small relative to the nation's stock of capital and natural resources. Consequently, most people can be nonpoor, and those who are poor are so because of the way in which America's large output is divided.

In large part, American meritocracy divides output on the basis of the formula: "To each according to the value of his labor and capital contributions to production." At the time of conception, ability distribution among Americans is, presumably, a bell-shaped curve:

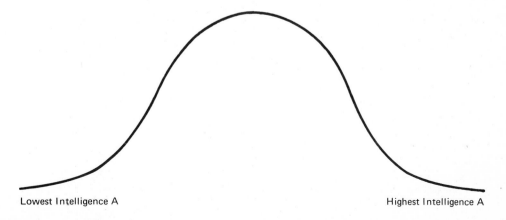

Lowest Intelligence A   Highest Intelligence A

The distribution of people with high Intelligence A tails off about the same way as does the distribution of people with low Intelligence A.

If Intelligence A turned into Intelligence C at the same rate for everyone, and if all income were divided on the basis, "to each according to his contribution to production," the distribution of income among Americans would be (except for income based on property inheritance and property accumulation) a bell-shaped curve. Poverty would be the lot only of people unlucky enough to inherit little property and low Intelligence A.

In practice, most of those unlucky people are poor. But America's income distribution is not bell-shaped. Rather, the bump is on the left, and the curve tails off far to the right:

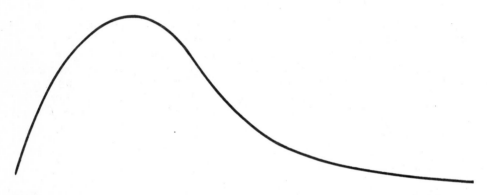

Lowest incomes   Highest incomes

The right-hand tail results because a few are very lucky. The bump occurs so far left because many born with reasonably high or average Intelligence A earn lower incomes than others conceived with equal Intelligence A. This happens (1) partly because babies with equal Intelligence A do not all attain equal Intelligence B; (2) partly because babies with equal Intelligence B do not all achieve equal Intelligence C; (3) partly because discrimination, family obligations, geographic immobilities, ill health, and dips in aggregate demand keep some people from full use of their Intelligence C; and (4) partly because of unequal property inheritance.

American poverty is, therefore, the result of (1) bad luck in property and genetic inheritance, (2) failure to achieve high enough Intelligence C, or (3) inability to apply one's Intelligence C.

In any particular year, the extent of poverty in America is much reduced by transfer programs, such as welfare, that shift command over some output from those who earn more to those who earn little or nothing: to children, the blind, the disabled, the unemployed, the aged. *Most* of these transfers are made within families; for example, some income goes to buy food for the children. Governments also effect large income transfers. Without family and government transfers, many Americans would be poor who are not now poor. Many who are now poor would be even poorer.

Over the past 200 years, the incidence and severity of American poverty have been falling. Increased government transfers from nonpoor to poor have accomplished part of these reductions. *But* growth in the output-to-population ratio has been by far the chief cause of the decline of poverty in America.

The trend will continue. America will continue to accumulate physical capital more rapidly than population. Technology will continue to improve; so the average physical product of labor and the marginal physical product of each kind of labor will continue to rise.

The children of each generation's poor will be better educated than their parents. Poor parents working in labor markets with low marginal physical product will see their children earning above-poverty incomes in labor markets with high marginal physical product.

Consequently, wages and salaries will continue to rise for nearly everyone — for the poor, the near-poor, and most others. One may speculate that government transfers were very small in the past because the nonpoor were a minority and had relatively little to give away through taxation, that government transfers grew as the nonpoor became a majority and became increasingly well-to-do, and, finally, that government transfer payments will grow in the future as the nonpoor majority becomes increasingly productive and thus better able to help the minority who are poor.

In the long run these trends may abolish poverty (though not inequality) in America. But right now, millions of Americans remain poor because they contribute little to the value of production. As Lena asked, "Is that fair? Should it be that way?"

Most Americans accept income differences based on differences in productive contributions. Nonpoor Americans differ regarding the poor. The trend is toward fewer poor, but one person may feel impatient to speed that trend, while another may feel that already too much is being done for the poor. The long-run trend toward fewer poor can be either hurried along or slowed (1) by changes in programs of income transfer from nonpoor to poor, (2) by changes in programs that raise the Intelligence C of the present poor (adults and children), and (3) by changes in programs that increase the opportunities (for example, by reducing discrimination) for individuals of equal Intelligence C to earn equal incomes. The next chapter will consider such programs in detail.

SUGGESTIONS FOR FURTHER READING

Bagdikian, Ben H. *In the Midst of Plenty: The Poor in America.* New York: Signet (paperback), 1964. This little book puts flesh on the poverty statistics with a dozen dramatic vignettes, each illustrating a different "cause" of poverty.

Batchelder, Alan. *The Economics of Poverty.* 2nd ed. New York: John Wiley & Sons (paperback), 1971. Elaborates upon the content of this chapter and considers the variety of private and governmental activities that effect change in the extent of poverty in America.

Bell, Carolyn S. *The Economics of the Ghetto.* New York: Pegasus (paperback), 1970. In general, ghetto incomes are low for the same reasons that incomes are low for people outside ghettos. This book cogently summarizes and interprets income statistics, causes of poverty, and the economics of proposed reforms. Scarcity, opportunity costs, and cost-benefit analysis are stressed.

Bowen, Ian. *Acceptable Inequalities: An Essay on the Distribution of Income.* Montreal: McGill-Queens, 1970. Rejects perfect equality, but argues for reductions in inequalities among and within countries. Favors market forces to determine primary income distribution among workers, larger transfers, and "reform" respecting inheritance, capital gains, and windfall profits.

Harrington, Michael. *The Other America: Poverty in the United States.* Baltimore: Penguin Books (paper-back), 1963. The first popular post-World War II book respecting poverty in America. A best seller. Written to tell the nonpoor majority that millions were poor through no fault of their own.

Kotz, Nick. *Let Them Eat Promises: The Politics of Hunger in America.* Garden City, N. Y.: Doubleday Anchor (paperback), 1971. Concerned with the number of Americans, especially children and the elderly, who are hungry and with federal programs that help some people who would otherwise go hungry.

Miller, Herman P. *Rich Man, Poor Man.* 2nd ed. New York: Thomas Y. Crowell, 1971. A comprehensive presentation of recent income statistics. The commentary assumes that rational efforts to improve income distribution will follow from knowledge of the facts.

Scoville, James, ed. *Perspectives on Poverty and Income Distribution.* Lexington, Mass.: D.C. Heath (paperback), 1971. A collection of 25 articles respecting income, wealth, taxes, causes of poverty, and programs that change the incidence of poverty.

Zimpel, Lloyd and Range, Daniel. *Business and the Hardcore Unemployed; A Management Guide to Hiring, Training, and Motivating Minority Workers.* New York: Frederick Fell, 1970. A realistic, inform-ative, and very well-written report about business and the hardcore unemployed.

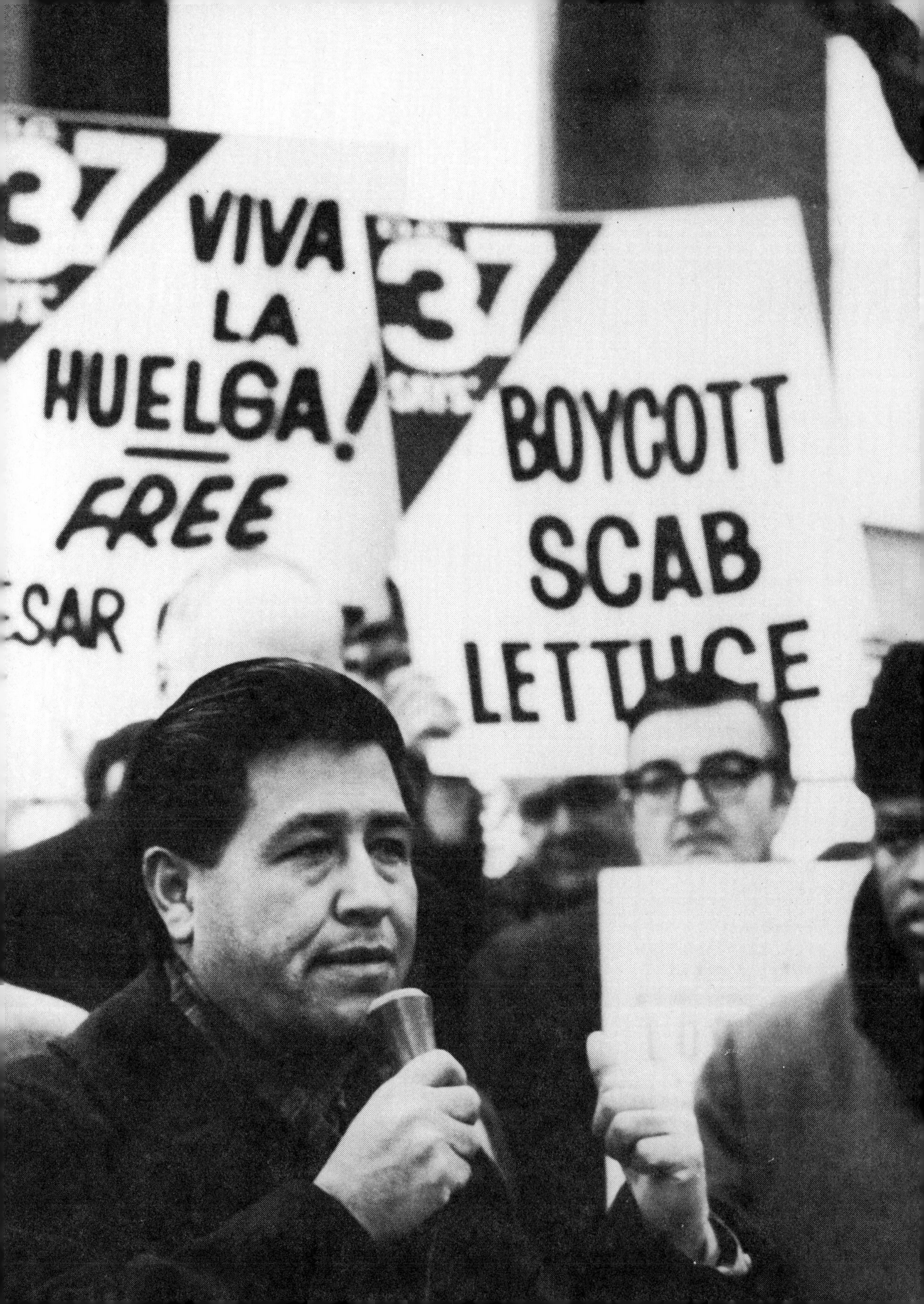
VIVA
LA
HUELGA!
FREE
BOYCOTT
SCAB
LETTUCE

2 Discrimination: Race

One of America's most pressing contemporary socioeconomic problems is not new, for in a real sense the United States was founded on discrimination. Initially, the settlement of North America by Europeans was undertaken as an escape from religious persecution; yet the settlers who sought refuge here perpetrated something close to genocide upon native-born Americans. After abortive attempts to enslave the American Indian, the settlers began importing captives from Africa as slaves. The brutalization of the Indians and Africans had a long-lasting debilitating and dehumanizing influence on American character as a whole, and largely determined the present socioeconomic status of Indians and blacks. Pursuing what they claimed to be "manifest destiny," Americans expanded westward and there, in the Southwest, encountered Mexicans whom they also systematically relegated to inferior positions. In its ascendancy to world power, the United States next acquired Puerto Rico, and these people too were subjected to discriminatory practices. Thus, when one speaks of racial discrimination in the United States, it is usually in reference to the four largest minority groups: blacks, Chicanos, Puerto Ricans, and Indians.

Defining Economic Discrimination

In our analysis, "discrimination" will refer to any of several instances wherein individuals receive less than the market value of their resources (including their labor), or must pay a price greater than the market value of a good.[1] It also includes those instances where persons are barred from participation in the marketplace for reasons other than their ability or willingness to pay the going market price, or are barred from the market even

---

[1]This definition excludes many nonmarket transactions — for example, government provision of goods and services such as education — that may be more important than market factors. Much nonmarket economic discrimination will eventually manifest itself in the marketplace; for example, inferior education shows up later in the form of lower wages.

though they are willing to accept the market price offered for resources and goods of a given quality. We also consider it discrimination if the actual return to a resource or product is less than that paid to other owners of resources and products of the same quality in a given market at the same time.

Since we are concerned with race and economic status in the United States, generally we shall say racial economic discrimination exists whenever race is a determinant of the economic opportunities available to an individual. A society can be termed racist when the set of alternatives available to segments within that society is determined, even in part, by ethnic and racial factors. A key to understanding the economics of racism and discrimination is the recognition of this dualistic structure.

Why concern ourselves with the economics of discrimination? It is, of course, true that many Americans do not. However, the events of recent years suggest that the very future of our society may depend on whether minorities are accorded equal rights and opportunities.

A crucial factor in understanding and correcting the situation is the recognition of discrimination as a multifaceted problem. Minorities are caught up in a vicious cycle in which they have little economic power because they have little political power. Gains in economic power are likely to be transitory unless educational and political gains are also forthcoming. But economic gains are still important. Economic power provides an individual with the ability to exercise control over those aspects of his life that are dependent on purchasing power; it may not guarantee educational or political gains and opportunities, but it is necessary for permanent improvement.

Racism is institutionalized when its practice is so ubiquitous, so automatic, and so deeply imbedded in a society's fabric that instances of exploitation and discrimination are not even perceived as such. Once the practice of racism is institutionalized, its detection and measurement become difficult for the simple reason that detection depends on the observer's willingness to reject the existing system and its values to begin with. All too frequently, economists analyze the market and institutional patterns without questioning their origins. Yet if we analyze a situation without understanding its historical origins, we are overlooking a vital link in the chain of understanding. Such an approach may be able to detect discrimination, but it almost always understates its magnitude.

Economics has generally concerned itself exclusively with exploitation by pointing out only what inequalities exist. It is as if economists were saying, "Yes, we have a racist society, but let us see if and how much it is exploitative." As an example, one could conclude that there are no economic effects of discrimination in an *apartheid* society, because so long as the market system operates in the two segments there can be no observed discrimination or exploitation. Of course, this conclusion is possible only if we take as given the *apartheid* conditions; the next step is to acknowledge that *apartheid* is itself a mode of discriminating.

Empirical evidence shows that minorities have economic problems that are different in kind and magnitude from those of whites. The major portion of economic, social, educational, and political status differences can ultimately be traced to racial factors. Differences in occupational status and income level as between the majority and minority groups provide a relatively simple and straightforward measure of the extent of economic discrimination. If members of a group are systematically concentrated at the lower end of the occupational ladder and of income distribution, then we say that they are victims of discrimination.

The Economic Status of Minorities in the United States

Racial discrimination persists in the twentieth century and is reflected in the socioeconomic plight of minorities. Industrialization of the economy shifted minorities from agricultural day labor to urban industrial and service work, where they were (and remain) concentrated in unskilled, low-paying jobs. But apart from that generality, since each region of the country offers different economic opportunities, an aggregative appraisal of the opportunities open to minorities can be misleading. The geographical location of minorities and their patterns of mobility have been shaped by historical accident, relative economic growth, and prevailing racial attitudes.

Native Americans. Of all minority groups, American Indians have been the most restricted and abused. During the course of the nineteenth century, they were forced onto reservations — mostly west of the Mississippi River — that were largely arid, infertile lands. Unlike other minorities in the United States, their subordinate socioeconomic position is the result of colonial conquest.

1871 marked the beginning of forced assimilation and the weakening of the Indian's own social and economic organizations as the official U.S. policy toward its Indian population. Previously, the quasi-official policy had been the takeover of the Indians' most important economic resource — land — while leaving the tribes essentially alone in their organization. Subsequent to 1871 policies called for private ownership of commonly held lands, a land allotment scheme that reduced Indian-held land from 138 million acres in 1887 to 47 million in 1914,[2] and finally an educational policy that removed children from their tribal schools and placed them in white-run schools where the teaching of Indian culture was prohibited. The result of these policies was the demoralization and subjugation of the Indian and his transformation into a ward of the nation.

The Indian is the poorest of all minorities in the United States, having an estimated annual average income of only $1,500 and an unemployment rate that was as high as 40 percent in 1966.[3] These figures compare with the national averages of $2,598 and 3.8 percent for the same year. Although age, occupations, and geographical distribution affect these figures, it is still true that the greatest proportion of the difference is due to older racism, together with attitudes stemming from Indian culture itself.

Unlike the majority of blacks and Puerto Ricans in the United States, most Indians are rural residents. Of the 552,000 Indians enumerated in the 1960 census, approximately 70 percent lived in rural areas. This pattern contrasts dramatically with the spatial distribution of Puerto Ricans, more than half of whom live in New York City alone, with most of the remainder in other metropolitan areas, to yield an urban concentration exceeding 90 percent. It is clear that we must deal with rural economic opportunities in any discussion of the economic welfare of Indians; for other groups, the problem is much more an urban one.

---

[2]Cited in C. F. Marden and G. Meyer, *Minorities in American Society* (New York: Van Nostrand Reinhold Company, 1965), p. 363. Taken from Ward Shepherd, "Land Problems of an Expanding Indian Population," in Oliver La Farge (ed.), *The Changing Indian* (Norman: University of Oklahoma Press, 1942), p. 11.
[3]*Ibid.*

Indians, to an even greater extent than other minorities, have had a difficult time in American society and undoubtedly will face many more difficulties before they are accepted and acculturated. Their cultural and economic background is so different from that of the dominant culture that they are in effect faced with a choice between being annihilated or segregated, at least for the time being. Acculturation is perhaps an unrealistic alternative, considering that southern European immigrants to America, who were more akin to the dominant Anglo-Saxons than are Indians, were accepted only after a long and arduous struggle. Separatism would seem to be a viable alternative at this point in time, though it remains to be shown that an ethnic minority can prosper under such as arrangement. Indian progress may also depend on the headway other groups are able to make.

Chicanos. Mexican-Americans are the second largest ethnic minority in the United States; a 1972 Census Bureau report places their number at 5.3 million. The population is quite young and consists of large families. In 1960, their median age was 20 years, compared to a median of 30 for whites, and the ratio of families with more than four children was twice that of whites. They are heavily concentrated in the southwestern states where they comprise 12 percent of the population, so our descriptions will be based on conditions existing in the Southwest.

Emigration from Mexico continues to provide a significant proportion of the total Mexican-American population; in 1960, 45 percent were either foreign-born or born of foreign parents.[4] Since a large share of this migration comes in search of better economic opportunities than in Mexico and since the immigrants do not ordinarily have command of the English language, they are usually in a poor bargaining position.

Unlike the American Indian, Mexican-Americans have never been restricted to reservations, but they have experienced considerable *de jure* as well as *de facto* residential segregation from both whites and other nonwhites. Such laws and practices served to reduce the economic opportunities of all nonwhites, of course.

The schooling gap is often a significant, fundamental cause of the chronically depressed economic state of Chicanos and other minorities. This gap has two measures associated with it: the number of years of formal schooling and the level of achievement on standardized tests. They are interrelated and strongly influenced by an individual's perception of potential economic returns from schooling. Education is an *investment*,[5] and since minorities expect lower returns per year of school than do whites, rational decision rules indicate that a lower investment is a sensible decision. This reduction takes the form of fewer years of schooling and less diligence in study.

When income data are adjusted for both age and level of formal schooling, Mexican-American males show higher earnings than males of comparable age and education in any other minority group. Although their overall earning potential is way below that of whites, this finding indicates that each additional year of schooling is

[4]See Leo Grebler, Joan W. Moore, and Ralph C. Guzman, *The Mexican-American People: The Nation's Second Largest Minority* (Glencoe, Ill.: The Free Press, 1970), p. 29.
[5]An *investment* means that the stock of *capital* is increased. Capital is a man-made or created economic factor used in producing economic goods and services. Investments are made with the idea that the *investor* will receive income from them. Here we assume that education is not for education's sake but is valued because it may raise one's income.

more valuable to Chicanos than it would be to any other minority. It provides evidence that, other things being equal, education is an apparently viable avenue for Mexican-Americans to pursue in their attempt to achieve economic equality with whites.

Black Americans. Despite modest gains, blacks remain far behind whites in most economic categories. Blacks are three times more likely to live in poverty, twice as likely to be unemployed, and three times as likely to die in infancy or at birth. Eighty percent of blacks live in cities, both North and South, and though urban poverty is less than the remaining black rural poverty, about one-quarter of the blacks in cities have incomes below the poverty line, and more than that in some individual cities.[6] The best evidence available indicates that these gaps are firmly rooted in the history of the black enslavement. The economic history of black Americans provides vivid confirmation that the effects of discrimination are long-lasting. Considering the deprivation blacks have suffered, it is remarkable that they have made the progress they have, but much more is needed.

Differences between blacks and whites with respect to levels of performance and opportunity are one set of measures used to assess the cost of discrimination. This indicator is easily obtained, but it has some serious drawbacks. A major shortcoming is that it focuses only on the more obvious, materialistic aspect of discrimination. In addition, it is unable to distinguish causes from effects, for example, whether the level of income determines education or vice versa. There have been several attempts to estimate the costs of discrimination. The one thing they all have in common is that they place the cost rather high. Table 2.1 provides some recent data.

Table 2.1   Some Estimates of the Costs of Discrimination

A. Percent below poverty level, 1968	
whites	10%
nonwhites[a]	35%
B. Occupancy of substandard housing, 1968	
whites	6%
nonwhites[a]	24%
C. Income loss per nonwhite,[a] 1960	$1000/year
D. Human capital cost per nonwhite[a] 1960	$10,000
E. Cost of wage discrimination to nonwhites[a] 1965	$12.8 billion
F. Cost to economy, 1965	
GNP growth losses	3.7%
dollars GNP loss	$23 billion

Source: Items A and B, U.S. Departments of Labor and Commerce, *The Social and Economic Status of Negroes in the U.S., 1969,* BLS Report No. 375 (GPO, 1970), Item C, Paul M. Siegel, "On the Cost of Being a Negro," *Sociological Inquiry,* Winter 1965. Item D, Barbara Bergmann, "Investment in Human Resources of Negroes," U.S. Joint Economic Committee, *Federal Programs for the Department of Human Resources,* Vol. 1, Part II, *Manpower and Education* (GPO, 1968). Items E and F, Council of Economic Advisers, *Staff Memorandum,* March 26, 1965; reprinted in John F. Kain, *Race and Poverty,* 1969, pp. 58 – 59.

[a] Refers to blacks only.

---

[6]U.S. Bureau of the Census, *U.S. Census of Population: 1970* (Washington, D.C.: U.S. Government Printing Office, 1972).

Items A and B indicate the implicit costs borne by nonwhites in the form of poverty (low incomes) and poor housing. These are direct private costs which do not suggest the costs to society as a whole. Items C, D, and E tell much the same thing, but in money terms. Finally, Item F represents a first approximation to the cost of discrimination borne by the entire economy as measured in lost income, output, and growth.

In measuring the economic position of blacks and other minorities relative to whites, it is important to distinguish between absolute gaps and relative gaps. For example, between 1960 and 1970 the median income of nonwhite families rose somewhat more rapidly than the income of white families, with the result that nonwhite median income was 64 percent of white income in 1970, up from 55 percent in 1960. This represents undeniable progress. However, even with a smaller percentage rise in income, the absolute dollar increase in white income was larger in the decade than for the median nonwhite family, because the smaller percentage was applied to a higher starting point. Thus median white family income in 1970 was $10,236, or $3,720 higher than median nonwhite income. In 1960, median white income was $7,664, or $3,428 higher than median nonwhite income. The absolute dollar gap thus actually widened slightly.

While it is true that blacks have lower levels of education and training, level of education is not sufficient to explain the occupational and income gaps between blacks and whites. The black who has a college training is able to earn no more than a white with some high school training. Even after one takes account of educational and geographic factors, a large unexplained difference remains which, for the most part, must be attributed to the effects of discrimination.

Puerto Ricans. Puerto Rico has been a territory of the United States since the Spanish-American War, but immigration to the mainland is of relatively recent origin, coming mostly since 1950. The pattern of migration has been such that Puerto Ricans are heavily concentrated along the East Coast. Approximately 80 percent of the total Puerto Rican population resides in New York City, largely in the district commonly referred to as "Spanish Harlem." Perhaps 10 percent live in Florida, primarily in Miami, with most of the remainder stretched out along the northern half of the eastern seaboard. From an estimated population of 301,000 in 1950 and 569,000 in 1953, the 1969 population was estimated at 1.5 million, representing a fourfold net increase in 20 years. This increase in migration to the mainland is motivated primarily by the desire to improve economic opportunities and status.

Puerto Ricans comprise 17 percent of all Spanish-speaking people in the United States, ranking second behind Mexican-Americans. Relative to the general population, Spanish-Americans are an average of eight years younger. The median number of years schooling for Spanish-speaking Americans in 1969 was 8.5 years, as compared with 12.0 years for the total population. Income statistics show that the average income of Spanish-speaking residents was $5,600, or 70 percent of the U.S. total, in 1969; however, the Puerto Rican level was below this. The Spanish unemployment level was 6 percent, or 1.7 times the general level, in November 1969. Generally, Puerto Ricans fare worse than other Spanish-speaking residents.

Some Aspects of the Economics of Discrimination

Is Economic Growth — General Prosperity — the Answer? There is no doubt that when the economy is booming, employment opportunities improve for nonwhites, simply because employers find no other labor available. In a sense, these conditions of "tight" labor markets tend to create, not simply use, nonwhite labor resources. Even if an employer has all kinds of prejudice about blacks, he will find himself gladly trying to train a black machinist if there is no one else to be found.

The story of World War II in this respect is often overlooked. The labor market was so tight that there were shortages everywhere. A huge number of blacks migrated to northern industrial cities, mainly because of the good wages to be found. This has left many problems, but its successes are important, too. Today, in the United States, just under 30 percent of the black families have incomes of $10,000 a year or more — middle-class incomes. Many of those families got their start in the tight labor market of the early 1940's.

As will be noted in other chapters, there are problems — above all, inflation, which can hurt many of the poor — in running the economy at such a boom level as to give minorities relatively easy access to job opportunities. The boom of the late 1960's, apart from the inflation that accompanied it, gave rise to additional doubts.

It is true that the overall black unemployment rate dropped in the late 1960's to about 7 percent, still twice the white rate but much better than it had been when the economy was relatively slack. Yet *within* that rate there was a grave problem. At the height of the boom, the unemployment rate among teenage blacks was upward of 25 percent. Part of this was accounted for by black teenagers who were still in school but counted themselves as looking for jobs and unable to find them. Part of it was accounted for by the new problem of labor mobility in our urban society, in which a perfectly capable black teenager in Harlem, for example, cannot get a job because the new jobs are opening up in the suburbs; and he has no reasonably cheap way of getting there.

Part of the answer, too, undoubtedly lies in discrimination, though it cannot be specified in the statistics. But here we come to the vicious circle. The late 1960's were a time when given various civil rights acts of Congress and a somewhat greater disposition on the part of the white majority to recognize the wrongs of the past, a fair number of large businesses tried to go out of their way to hire blacks. They needed the labor anyway. But many of them soon professed themselves "discouraged": the new laborers did not show up on time, or soon quit, or had high rates of absenteeism. Insofar as these perceptions were true, the reason was the long story of the past. But it is quite possible — a matter for sociologists, not economists — that the white employers were certain in advance that they would find these characteristics.

In any event, boom and low overall unemployment (a national unemployment rate of about 3.5 percent in 1968 and during most of 1969) produced real employment gains for minorities in the late 1960's as in World War II, and helped to close a little the income gap. Minority poverty declined. But the boom did not solve the problem.

Discrimination and Efficiency. Suppose a black girl and a white girl each applies for a job as a receptionist or typist, and the black girl happens, by training or native ability, to be the better qualified. But also suppose that the white employer, because of an ingrained set of prejudices, hires the white girl almost instinctively. He finds, though he does not admit it, that fewer letters are typed per hour or fewer phone calls handled efficiently per hour. In short, there are higher costs and lower productivity if the white hired is less capable than the potential nonwhite employee, in any occupation. This kind of "exclusion" principle in the labor market will be examined in a later chapter in connection with practices sometimes followed by labor unions.

The result is the same. The "ins" *do* get easier access to jobs and higher incomes, but overall efficiency in the economy is less.

A dilemma here must be faced. Anti-discrimination laws have the potential to eliminate this kind of discrimination, which really harms everyone concerned. But in a society with several million employers, most of them small despite the image of a "big business" economy, such laws are very difficult to enforce. Apart from that, the underlying problem goes back, again, to the vicious circle. It remains true that if nonwhites have received less training and education than whites, the case of the more efficient black girl is likely to be the exception rather than the rule. All too many of the minority jobseekers will be unable to meet minimal job qualifications, even ones that are not designed purposely to keep out minorities. White "monopoly power" in some labor markets will exist for this reason even if there is no overt discrimination.

Product Markets. It is only recently that the concept of "dual markets" has begun to be perceived by economists and even by congressional investigators. We have always assumed that in the United States there was essentially a national market: that the price for the same can of spinach or refrigerator would be about the same everywhere, allowing only for such things as different transport costs. But it turns out that, to some extent, there is in fact a dual market with different prices — one for inner city minorities and a lower one for everyone else. There are higher prices for the same can of spinach and higher interest rates for instalment purchases of the refrigerator in the minority market than elsewhere.

To sellers, this seems quite rational. A supermarket owner will cite more pilferage, higher insurance costs, less reliable labor, and the like, in the market whose customers are mainly from minority groups. Supermarket chains have argued seriously that their choice is either to charge higher prices in these stores or close them altogether. The bank or finance company will cite much higher delinquency on loans in these areas to "justify" their higher interest rates.

But this argument is not very appealing to the law-abiding, hard-working minority family who finds that, among all the other discriminations found through life, it has to pay more for the same pound of hamburger than a white family a half a mile away.

Once again, it is a vicious circle. And once again, part of the explanation is discrimination — a set of decisions by white majority owners of retail and other facilities based in part on their long-held prejudices. How much of the difference is "justified" and how much is prejudice is almost impossible to disentangle. But the fact is that there are dual markets within the same, supposedly free and mobile, market system.

Discrimination and Housing. Somehow the free market system has made it not only possible but sometimes profitable for minority-occupied slums to be created. Why? The answer is highly complex, covering such matters as local property taxes, rent controls in some places (which is not a free market), and the movement of business and industry — and hence jobs — away from central cities. It is important to remember that slums exist in such places as London and Paris and Rome where there is little or no racial problem.

But race and discrimination have played a major role in the creation of slums in U.S. cities. As population migration occurred, landlords have found it profitable to rent to minorities in the first instance and then, when whole sections became minority-occupied, have found that there is little significant additional return to them from investing in maintenance and repairs. Essentially, this is because the free market has not worked, and it has not worked because of discrimination. A black family in Harlem with a landlord who will not make repairs finds itself, unless it is comparatively very well-off, shut off from other decent housing. Free consumer choice, the essence of the free market, has been curtailed for noneconomic reasons.

It is a case of what economists call a market imperfection. There may be a balanced supply and demand in the nation for steel or wheat or nylon stockings, and the price or supply of these products will respond to changing demand; but in a given urban housing market the freedom of choice of the consumer is in practice limited and the seller, the landlord, quite understandably makes what profit he can. As slums reach the ultimate state of deterioration, or tenants cannot or will not pay the rent, even the landlords ultimately lose.

Once again — and the economics of discrimination must repeat the point *ad nauseum* — it is the vicious circle.

We must repeat that the problem of slums goes beyond the issue of racial discrimination alone. Family living habits — whether the slum dwellers be white or nonwhite — have something to do with it, for example. But it is obvious that if a black or Chicano family is barred, in practice, from buying or renting some part of the available supply of housing, there is a market imperfection, from which many consequences follow. Both local and federal laws and regulations have endeavored to abolish racial segregation of housing, certainly for minority families who have the means to buy or rent better-grade housing, and there has been some progress. But it is slow.

Solutions

To the extent that *racial* attitudes create *economic* results, the solution lies in a change of the racial attitudes, and laws to help force that change where necessary. The economist as economist has little to contribute here.

But economists have been deeply involved in the development of various possible strategies for ending or diminishing poverty itself — regardless of race — and in developing other means to aid the disadvantaged, such as "black capitalism" and subsidized housing.

The Income Strategy for Ending Poverty. Broadly speaking, there are two possible "battle plans" with which to fight a war on poverty. One is known as the "services strategy" and is the one tried — with little success to date — by the government. It involves providing a wide variety of service-type aids to the poor, ranging from occupational training to special help for inner-city school systems. The aim is to "upgrade" individuals, and the results have been discouraging.

Economists have come increasingly to prefer what is called an "income strategy." This would simply distribute sizeable cash grants to poor families on the assumption that they can start, with that early assurance, the long climb upward. The cash grants would be devised in such a way that they diminish but do not disappear as earned income rises, so that there remains an incentive to work. This is a complex issue, involving major governmental costs, and it will be discussed later. What can be said here is that, insofar as historic discrimination is a major cause of poverty, it may be preferable to attack poverty quickly and directly rather than relying only on the slow process of changing racial attitudes or "training" the poor. It should be added, however, that the problem of discrimination would remain if poverty, in the simple sense of income, were abolished. What if a black or Chicano family has more cash than before but is not permitted into nearby decent housing or finds its working-age members denied jobs for which they are qualified?

Black Capitalism. This is a rather vague term but generally it means a system of subsidies and other aids from the government, or sometimes from the larger private businesses and banks, to help members of minority groups who want to start or expand or maintain businesses of their own. Black ownership of business is disproportionately small, by any test, when measured against the black proportion of the population.

The government's main efforts, which began in earnest only at the beginning of the decade of the 1970's, have included various methods of guaranteeing loans or providing loans at below-market interest rates, establishment of "Minority Small Business Investment Companies" which can invest equity capital in minority enterprises, and a number of types of counseling services for minority businessmen. It is too early to say whether this effort will produce significant results in increasing entrepreneurship among minorities. Some of the early efforts were failures, as the new businesses simply did not succeed. But failure for new enterprises is common among whites, too. At the very least, the program is a small effort to right past wrongs by singling out minority businesses for special help.

Housing Subsidies. This issue will be taken up in a later chapter. It arises here because, in practice, so many of the low and lower-middle income families that benefit from these programs are in fact nonwhite families.

By 1971 about one-quarter of all the new housing units constructed had a federal government subsidy of some kind (quite apart from the long-standing program of mortgage insurance by the Federal Housing Administration, which is not a direct subsidy and has aided mainly suburban housing). The subsidies keep down interest rates, and hence monthly payments, for those lower-income families who are being helped to purchase their homes, and keep down rents for those who rent. As we shall note later, the programs have run into major difficulties. But the key issue here is *location*. A number of suburban communities, though by no means all, have resisted the location of subsidized units within their boundaries on ill-disguised racial grounds. And yet there is now overwhelming evidence that the chief growth of jobs is outside the central cities.

A solution that has attracted many economists is a counterpart of the income strategy for the cure of poverty. It is called "housing allowances." Low-income families would be given cash grants for housing and then would have the opportunity to seek better housing wherever they could find it. Reinforced by anti-discrimination laws and regulations in the real estate industry, this could allow the market system to commingle the population more than now and, probably even more important, could allow minorities to locate where the jobs are.

Many black and other minority families, of course, *want* to live with members of their own group or have no job-related need to move. Again, a housing allowance — though it would require some kind of "means test" to determine who qualifies and would be costly to taxpayers — would preserve individual freedom of choice while creating an effective market demand for better housing.

SUGGESTIONS FOR FURTHER READING

The data on Chicanos were largely taken from Grebler et al.; those on Indians came from Marden and Meyer and the USDA's *Rural Indian Americans in Poverty*. The sources for blacks are Kain, Thurow, and the two reports of the Department of Labor. The primary source for Chicanos and Puerto Ricans is the Bureau of the Census, *Current Population Reports*.

Grebler, Leo; Moore, Joan W.; and Guzman, Ralph C. *The Mexican-American People: The Nation's Second Largest Minority*. Glencoe, Ill.: The Free Press, 1970. A series of essays on the sociology, politics, and economics of Mexican-Americans. Probably the most comprehensive and detailed study available.

Kain, John F., ed. *Race and Poverty: The Economics of Discrimination*. New York: Prentice-Hall, 1969. A collection of articles originally published in professional and popular journals. They range from general treatments to detailed economic and sociological studies of a technical nature.

Liebow, Eliot. *Tally's Corner*. Boston: Little, Brown and Company, 1967. An excellent treatment of the ill effects discrimination can have on social structure and organization.

Marden, C.F. and Meyer, G. *Minorities in American Society*. New York: Van Nostrand Reinhold Books, 1965. A general sociological analysis of minority groups.

Myrdal, Gunnar. *An American Dilemma*. New York: Harper & Row, Publishers, 1944. The classic study of antiblack discrimination in the U.S. by an eminent Swedish economist-sociologist. It remains the most comprehensive and detailed study available.

Thurow, Lester C. *Poverty and Discrimination*. Washington, D.C.: The Brookings Institution, 1969. An econometric study of the first class, perhaps the definitive study to date. Highly technical economics and statistics in areas, but Chapter 7 provides an excellent treatment for the noneconometrician.

U.S. Bureau of the Census. *Current Population Reports*, Series P-20, No. 213, "Persons of Spanish Origin in the U.S., November 1969." Washington, D.C.: Government Printing Office, 1971.

U.S. Department of Agriculture. *Rural Indian Americans in Poverty*, Agricultural Economic Report No. 167. Washington, D.C.: U.S. Government Printing Office, 1969. A brief descriptive and statistical report on the plight of the American Indian.

U.S. Department of Labor. *Social and Economic Conditions of Negroes in the United States, 1969*. Washington, D.C.: U.S. Government Printing Office, 1970. Also published for 1970. A brief descriptive tabular presentation of recent changes in the socioeconomic status of blacks. It covers all major areas, including education, employment, and income.

3 Discrimination: Sex

Until World War II it was fairly unusual for women, especially married women, to work. A married woman pursuing a career while her husband was also earning a living wage was the exception to the rule. A woman's function was to raise a family and keep house. This view of women apparently began to change during the 1940's, when the general mobilization of males and an intense need for labor for the war effort made it necessary and even patriotic to employ women. Since that time long periods of economic prosperity, greater educational attainments by women, smaller families, and the never-ending flow of labor-saving devices like processed foods and mechanical household cleaning devices have lessened the amount of time a woman needs to spend in the house maintaining her family and at the same time raised her expectations about her ability to get a job.

The result is that the average young woman today is far more likely to work for a significant number of years — even when she is married and raising children — than her mother ever was. In fact, in 1969 over a third of all those who were employed "full time" (35 or more hours per week) were females, and more than two out of every five women who worked in 1969 worked both a regular workweek and at least 50 weeks that year. Thus, women have come to play an important part in the work force. But they are far from achieving equality of job conditions with men; in 1969 women earned only 21.8 percent of all job income. And while *all* women received a small share of income relative to their numbers in the labor force, black women have fared even worse than white women.

White women aged 16–64 make up 44.8 percent of the population of working age. But — partly because some do not want to work — they comprise only 30.9 percent of the labor force; more important, they receive only 19.7 percent of the earnings of the labor force at work. Black women constitute 6 percent of the working-age population and 4.6 percent of the labor force, but they earn only 2.1 percent of the job income. Thus, relative to their size in the population, both black and white women hold fewer than their share of the jobs and receive an even smaller share of the wages, salaries, and earnings from employment.[1]

In this chapter we will investigate several aspects of the emergence of women as a significant factor in the labor force and as a group whose wages are so low relative to men's that they appear to be the victims of sex discrimination. The approach will be analytical. Rather than stating polemical conclusions without first thoroughly considering the facts, we will present a series of well-documented facts and then try to explain why and how they have been produced. Without such careful analysis, we might incorrectly diagnose discrimination where it does not exist, or fail to diagnose the real roots of discrimination where it does exist.

The figures on job income quoted above are only one indication that women are unequally treated in the labor force. As another bit of evidence, working women obtain many fewer full-time jobs than do men; men are half again as likely to hold a full-time job, at least 50 weeks of the year, as are women. One explanation for this disparity, too, is the existence of discrimination.

But there are other possible explanations as well. First, women may have fewer jobs than men because many women prefer not to work. Women may prefer not to work for relatively objective reasons: they are bearing or raising children and must therefore stay at home; or for relatively subjective reasons: they can afford not to work and prefer leisure for homemaking or community activities to the benefits of paid employment. Second, the wages of working women may be less than those of working men if the average employed woman is less qualified than the average employed man. Each of these three explanations — discrimination, preference, and skills — has some validity in explaining employment differences between men and women. Furthermore, none of the three explanations is independent of the other two. Women who do not plan to work for any appreciable period of time have less reason to acquire skills by formal education and less opportunity to develop saleable skills on the job than persons who expect to work permanently. Since the fewer the skills, the lower the salary a worker can expect to earn, women with little preparation for jobs may feel that the gain from working is worth less than the extra time they gain from having no job commitment. In addition, women's preferences regarding work and higher education are partially the result of social norms as to women's proper place; if employers perceive that as a group women have little long-term desire to work, they will tend to discriminate against women. Finally, lack of skills will limit the choice of jobs open to a woman. She will be less likely to take a job, other things being equal, if she views her employment options as unpleasant or uninteresting. Hence the three basic explanations for women's inferior status in the labor market may all reinforce one another.

Are women discriminated against? To begin answering this question, we must first recognize that the word "discrimination" has no single, unambiguous meaning. Discrimination can exist in many forms, and it is entirely possible that a situation which looks like discrimination from one point of view will not seem to be discrimination from another. By introducing ideas from economic analysis, we can clarify more

---

[1]Population and employment percentages are from U.S. Department of Labor, *Manpower Report of the President, 1971* (Washington, D.C.: U.S. Government Printing Office, 1971), Tables B-14 and E-4. Job income percentages are calculated from *Current Population Survey*, Series P-60, No. 75, Table 61.

precisely what might be meant by discrimination against women. There are both narrow and broad definitions. Narrowly defined, discrimination exists when equally productive men and women are paid different wages for "the same job." It is this type of discrimination that we will discuss first.

Table 3.1   Occupational Earnings by Sex (1960)

(1)	Ratio of median income in occupation to median for total male labor force [a]		Ratio of median female to male income	Ratio of median female to male education level
	(2)	(3)	(4)	(5)
Occupation	Male	Female		
TOTAL	1.00	0.59	0.59	1.09
Professional Workers				
Dancers and Dancing Teachers	0.83	0.61	0.73	1.00
Dietitians and Nutritionists	0.76	0.68	0.89	1.04
Librarians	1.01	0.77	0.76	0.97
Musicians and Music Teachers	1.03	0.29	0.28	0.99
Nurses	0.84	0.71	0.85	1.02
Recreation and Group Workers	1.00	0.78	0.78	0.97
Social and Welfare Workers	1.04	0.87	0.84	0.99
Religious Workers	0.77	0.49	0.64	0.82
Elementary Teachers	1.03	0.85	0.83	0.97
Teachers, n.e.c.[b]	1.10	0.74	0.67	0.98
Therapists and Healers	0.97	0.83	0.86	0.98
Clerical Workers				
Library Attendants and Assistants	0.55	0.54	0.98	0.96
Physicians' and Dentists' Office Attendants	0.68	0.53	0.78	1.00
Bank Tellers	0.84	0.63	0.75	0.98
Bookkeepers	0.89	0.64	0.72	0.98
File Clerks	0.75	0.59	0.79	0.98
Office-machine Operators	0.96	0.68	0.71	0.99
Payroll and Timekeeping Clerks	1.00	0.73	0.73	0.99
Receptionists	0.77	0.57	0.74	1.00
Secretaries	1.05	0.71	0.68	0.99
Stenographers	1.02	0.70	0.69	1.00
Typists	0.80	0.64	0.80	1.00
Telephone Operators	1.07	0.67	0.63	0.99
Cashiers	0.78	0.53	0.68	1.00
Clerical Workers, n.e.c.[b]	0.99	0.66	0.67	1.00
Sales Workers				
Demonstrators	[c]	0.50	[c]	1.01
Hucksters and Peddlers	0.82	0.16	0.20	1.18

Source: Valerie Kincade Oppenheimer, *The Female Labor Force in the United States, Population Monograph Series No. 5* (Berkeley: University of California Press, 1970), pp. 100 – 101.

[a] Wage and salary workers in the civilian labor force who worked 50 – 52 weeks in 1959.
[b] n.e.c.-not elsewhere classified.
[c] Base not large enough to compute a median.

Unequal Pay For Equal Work

A good indication of the striking discrepancies in income received by men and women for similar work is contained in Table 3.1. Columns 2-4 contain data showing the median[2] earnings of females compared to the median earnings of males in 27 different occupations. Together, these occupations contain 42 percent of all female workers, 71 percent of all women in professional and technical work, and virtually all women in clerical positions. In each of these occupations, *at least 51 percent of the workers were female.*

In *none* of these occupations is median female income greater than median male income. Further, no occupation shows a median female income as large as the average male income for all occupations together. Columns 2 and 3 indicate, for each occupation, by what percentage the income earned by the median male or median female employed in that occupation in 1960 exceeded or fell short of the income earned by the median male employed in the entire United States labor force. It can be seen that, for males, over a third of these jobs are relatively well-paying; but in none of them do females earn even as much as the average for all the males in the labor force. In column 4 we get a direct comparison of the earnings of females and males in the same occupation. Males always earn more "for the same job"; in only one occupation, that of library attendants and assistants, do women earn about as much as males do. Over all occupations in this sample, the median female earns only 59 percent of the median male's earnings.

But observing that there are unequal incomes for the same job is not the same thing as establishing that discrimination has caused the whole differential. There are many reasons why men might be paid more on average than women for the same job. We will suggest several possible explanations.

Differences in Educational Attainments. One explanation involves differences in educational attainments. One of the most reliable predictors of an individual's income level is the level of education he or she has attained. Education can influence a person's income in at least two ways. First, by acquiring education, a person obtains knowledge and skills which are directly usable in the job for which he is being hired. A person who has learned how to type and take shorthand in school is far more likely to be able to get a job as a secretary than one who has not. Second, employers often assume that job applicants who are relatively well educated possess certain other desirable traits. More education may be interpreted to indicate self-discipline, maturity, ability to learn new skills, or ability to get along with superiors. Thus more schooling in an applicant may be presumptive evidence to the employer that the applicant is more skilled and has more desirable character traits than someone with less schooling. If men have more education than women performing the same job, we should then not be surprised that men tend to receive higher incomes. Does the evidence support this hypothesis about educational attainments?

From Table 3.1, column 5, it appears that different amounts of education are never very significant in explaining wage differences, except perhaps for religious workers. In four cases, women are more highly educated; in 22 cases, there is less than a 3 percent difference in the amount of education attained by the two sexes. It does not

---

[2]A median is the middle component of a series. If Tom, Dick, and Harry have incomes of $6,000, $10,000, and $11,000, respectively, the median income is $10,000. The *mean* is the arithmetic average; in this example, the mean income would be $9,000.

appear plausible from this sample of occupations that men earn higher incomes because they have more education, and there is some evidence that men earn higher incomes than women even though women are at least as well educated in their professions.

Differences in Experience. Just as education may be one measure of the quality of labor, experience may be another. Thus, a second explanation for the differences in wages between men and women may involve differences in the amount of previous job experience each sex has had. All other things being equal, it is reasonable to expect that the more experience a worker has had, the better he should be at his job; since he is more productive, he should be paid more. To use this fact to help explain male-female wage differentials, we would have to argue that women on the average have less job experience than men. Is there any reason to suspect that this is so? We will show later that women do spend less time working — accumulating general job experience — than men do.[3] Thus pay differentials between the sexes for similar jobs may be due in part to real and defensible differences in the quality of the labor provided.

The Effects of a Woman's Life Cycle on Productivity. A third possible explanation is somewhat more complicated than looking at a worker's educational attainment and work experience; it has to do with the effects of a woman's life cycle on her productivity. Suppose women quit their jobs more frequently than men do. From the point of view of the employer, rarely is a worker as useful on the first day he is hired as he is when he has been on the job for a few weeks, months, or even years. During the time a worker is still "learning the ropes" — mastering procedures, learning his way around, getting to know what is expected of him on the job — he is actually in training for the job he has. Economists call the time spent learning the ropes "on-the-job training." Every job involves at least some training. This training might be a 15-minute talk, a two-week orientation, or a long apprenticeship, or simply an indefinite time during which the worker learns his job by doing it. Since the worker is producing less while he is still learning his job, the employer would prefer to pay the worker a very low wage during the training period and then give him a raise when he has mastered the job; but this system penalizes a worker who gets fired or quits before he has worked long enough to recoup his early low earnings. A reasonable compromise to protect the interests of both the employer and the worker would be one whereby the worker protected himself against being fired by demanding a wage during his period of training greater than the actual value of his work, and the employer protected himself against the worker's quitting his job earlier than the employer anticipated by giving the worker raises not commensurate with his increasing productivity later on. But how does this affect women? Suppose that employers know that women tend to quit their jobs more often than men do. If the job involves much on-the-job training, more frequent quitting means that on the average employers will have less time in which to recoup the cost of the training of the worker;

---

[3]Other factors besides education and experience could make one worker more productive than another. Differences in native ability, talent, motivation, or stamina could imply that one worker should be paid more than another. But there is no reason to expect that on the average women will have more or less talent, motivation, or even stamina (which is not the same as brawn) than men do. In any case, it is often impossible to determine which of two workers is more productive from available data, either because the data do not exist or because some important factors like motivation are impossible to measure.

once the worker quits, part of the employer's training costs are lost forever. So if women do quit more frequently than men, then women should earn less than men because women would then be less productive.

Actually, this explanation illustrates how hard it is to define the boundaries between discrimination and justifiable wage differences. We assumed that employers were correct in thinking that women quit more frequently. Suppose, however, that employers overestimate the rate at which women will quit (even if women do quit more often than men, they don't quit as often as employers expect them to). Then part of the wage differential *may* be justified by differences in male-female quit rates, but another part of it will be discriminatory, reflecting employers' misperceptions (prejudices) about female behavior.

The Truth About Quit Rates: A Brief Digression.   Do women actually quit their jobs more often than men? According to surveys of the Bureau of Labor Statistics,[4] quit rates are only very slightly higher for women: 26 per 1,000 as opposed to 22 per 1,000 for males. This means that in a "typical" year, any employer would have little reason to expect much difference in the rates at which his male employees and female employees quit. Furthermore, there is some evidence that women's quit rates have been falling relative to men's, so that in time differences will tend to disappear. Falling women's quit rates may be attributed to two causes: (1) there are more middle-aged women in the labor force (they will stay in until they retire); and (2) younger women are working longer into marriage and more of them are continuing to work after they have had children.[5]

In some types of jobs — for example, white-collar jobs in the government sector — it may appear that quit rates are higher for women employees than for male employees. But quit rates depend on a number of factors, one of which is that the higher the status of the job, the lower the quit rate, and this is as true for males as it is for females. Usually, lower-grade jobs — which have high quit rates — are disproportionately held by females, who have no seniority and may be quite young. Upper-level jobs are held by men, and there the quit rates are low. Therefore, if an employer sees women quitting at a higher rate than men, it may not be because they are female, but simply because they are in lower-status jobs "reserved" for women.

Why are these lower-status jobs "reserved" for women? Very possibly it is because employers believe that women quit more frequently. Employers may act on this belief not only by offering women lower wages, but also by refusing to hire women for certain types of jobs which demand "stability" or by refusing to promote women to jobs which carry both more responsibility and a higher income. This is one reason why women might tend to cluster in occupations different from those men are in. If men are typically hired in occupations where the development of skills

---

[4]Women's Bureau, *Facts About Women's Absenteeism and Labor Turnover* (Washington, D.C.: U.S. Government Printing Office, 1969), p. 2.

[5]Another reason given for offering women lower wages is that they are absent from work more than men because of illness or injury. In fact, in 1967, according to a Public Health Service study, women lost 5.6 days a year while men were absent 5.3 days, hardly a large difference. Women tended to be acutely ill slightly more than men, but men lost more time than women for chronic illnesses (for instance, heart trouble, arthritis, rheumatism, or orthopedic impairment). The total financial loss to the employers was about equal for men's absences and women's absences.

and experience is important, and women are reserved for jobs where either the experience component is not important or where the skills are learned before the woman takes the job (for example, learning typing and shorthand in high school), then observing wage differentials for the same job will clearly understate the difference in the level of male-female opportunity since the *distribution of occupations itself* favors males. We will discuss the distribution of men and women across occupations in the section on occupational typing.

Overly Broad Definitions of Job Categories. A fourth explanation might rationalize paying some people more than others for doing what appears to be the same job. It could be that the job categories which are used in statistical comparisons of the earnings of men and women "in the same job" are too broad, and that the jobs men and women actually do are in fact different.

The fact that women gather less experience and job training than men, largely because they spend less time in the labor force, means that when women enter the labor force, they will generally be assigned to jobs in the bottom half (the "less responsible" half) of that particular job category. For instance, the senior bookkeeper of a firm will probably be someone who, through many years at the firm, has gained great familiarity with the full range of the firm's operations. Persons whose employment is on the average of a shorter duration will never become senior bookkeepers. The women in the firm might indeed be bookkeepers, but they would be less likely than men to obtain as much seniority and, therefore, the higher prestige and salary levels within the occupation "bookkeeper."

Importance of Nonwage Compensation. The four explanations discussed so far relate to factors which affect employer demand for female labor. Other explanations of wage differences start from the supply side and point to reasons why women, much more often than men, may prefer jobs that offer good nonwage compensation but relatively low wages. Every job has costs and benefits associated with it other than the purely monetary return. For various reasons, different workers may prefer to work at companies offering lower pecuniary rewards because employment at these firms carries with it valuable nonpecuniary benefits. One firm may be more pleasant to work at or easier to get to than another, so that the latter firm may have to pay higher wages in order to compensate workers for unpleasant working conditions or transportation problems. A lower-paying firm may have more liberal maternity leave policies, more flexible hours, or may permit work to be done at home. These more flexible and convenient firms are providing something of value to their employees; assuming that workers at the flexible, convenient firms could get jobs at the higher-paying but less convenient firm, then these workers are not being discriminated against. Rather, they are simply foregoing current wages in order to receive other desirable benefits worth at least as much as the foregone wages.

So far we have given a series of reasons why the observed differences in pay between men and women may be attributed to several "nondiscriminatory" causes. Each of these factors probably explains some part of the wage differential between men and women, but they may not explain all of it. If we net out those factors determining the differences in workers' marginal productivities and those factors indicating trade-offs between current income and other benefits, we will still be left with a residual income differential. If this residual is greater than zero, then discrimination between the sexes is taking place.[6] Rather than just stating that a residual based on discrimination might exist, it would be very helpful to have good estimates of the size of this differential. There have in fact been attempts by economists to measure the size of the effect of discrimination, but these attempts have involved concepts of discrimination broader than — though including — the one discussed so far. The results of the most complete study to date will be briefly described after we present the broader concepts the study implicitly uses.

Occupational Stereotyping: "Woman's Work" in the Labor Force

Narrow discrimination — unequal pay for equal work — is hardly a complete or sufficient definition of discrimination. To see this, suppose that men and women in the same occupation always earn the same wage. Suppose further that there are two occupations, magicians and assistants. Magicians are paid $3 an hour, assistants only $1 an hour. Besides this, magicians have more fun. If 10 percent of working men but 100 percent of working women were assistants, we might well conclude that we were observing discrimination, even though there was equal pay for equal jobs.

Extent and Causes of Occupational Typing. There is a strong tendency for women to concentrate in particular occupations. In fact, some occupations like nursing and secretarial work are so largely "manned" by women that finding a man in such a position produces mild shock. This clustering phenomenon is sometimes called "occupational typing." The extent of occupational typing in a number of occupations is summarized in Table 3.2.

Table 3.2   Occupational Distribution by Sex[a] (1960)

	Number of persons in occupation	Percent female
1. Accountants and Auditors	476,826	16.9
2. Clergymen	201,836	2.3
3. Draftsmen	218,776	5.6
4. Engineers	871,582	b
5. Lawyers and Judges	213,058	3.5

Source: U.S. Bureau of the Census, *U.S. Census of Population: 1960*, Vol. I, Characteristics of the Population, Part I, United States Summary. (Washington, D.C.: U.S. Government Printing Office, 1964), Table 201.

[a] Includes all occupations in which there were more than 200,000 persons recorded.
[b] Less than 1 percent.

[6]An employer might discriminate against a well-qualified woman because he finds employing women distasteful or because he fears that hiring women will lower the productivity of his male workers or otherwise increase costs. There are several ways in which the employer might believe costs could be raised. He might believe that bringing women into an all-male operation would distract the men and thereby lower the men's productivity (even if it raised their morale). Coeducational army units might be delightful, but could be expected to cause serious discipline problems. Also, costs might be raised if the employer had to provide separate locker facilities. In addition, employers used to supervising males may fear that they will be less successful at supervising females. According to some sociologists, male workers in some occupations might feel very uncomfortable if women workers were present. For a good discussion of men's attitudes toward women coworkers, see Cynthia Fuchs Epstein, *Woman's Place* (Berkeley: University of California Press, 1971), Chapters 4 and 5.

Table 3.2   *(Cont.)*

	Number of persons in occupation	Percent female
6. Nurses	591,829	97.5
7. Physicians and Surgeons	229,590	6.8
8. Elementary Teachers	1,010,682	85.8
9. Secondary Teachers	520,567	47.1
10. Farmers	2,501,168	4.8
11. Store Buyers and Department Heads	237,582	23.1
12. Public Administration Officials and Administrators	201,019	19.2
13. Managers, Officials, and Proprietors-Salaried	2,593,448	13.2
14. Managers, Officials, and Proprietors-Self-employed	1,992,587	14.5
15. Bookkeepers	936,270	83.7
16. Cashiers	491,906	78.6
17. Mail Carriers	201,810	2.2
18. Office-machine Operators	318,089	74.3
19. Postal Clerks	218,097	18.7
20. Secretaries	1,492,964	97.2
21. Shipping and Receiving Clerks	294,624	8.5
22. Stenographers	276,015	95.7
23. Stock Clerks and Storekeepers	345,760	15.1
24. Telephone Operators	371,763	95.8
25. Typists	543,801	95.0
26. Insurance Agents, Brokers, Underwriters	369,230	9.8
27. Salesmen and Sales Clerks	3,888,635	40.9
28. Brickmasons, Stonemasons, Tilesetters	207,601	b
29. Carpenters	923,837	3.2
30. Electricians	355,522	b
31. Excavators	225,617	b
32. Foremen	1,199,055	6.8
33. Linemen and Servicemen (Telephone and Telegraph, Power)	278,188	2.0
34. Machinists	515,532	1.4
35. Mechanics and Repairmen	2,300,690	1.2
36. Painters (Construction and Maintenance)	416,040	2.0
37. Plumbers and Pipe Fitters	331,012	b
38. Stationary Engineers	275,515	b
39. Assemblers	686,754	45.3
40. Auto (and Parking) Attendants	377,824	2.0
41. Checkers (Manufacturing)	514,135	46.0
42. Deliverymen	438,002	2.6
43. Laundry and Dry Cleaning Operatives	412,042	71.9
44. Miners	330,739	b
45. Packers and Wrappers	491,695	61.1
46. Sewers and Stitchers	617,029	93.9
47. Truck and Tractor Drivers	1,662,723	b
48. Welders and Flame Cutters	386,622	4.7
49. Operatives	4,993,044	29.8
50. Babysitters	350,420	97.5
51. Private Household Workers	1,281,740	95.8
52. Hospital Attendants	408,587	73.7
53. Cooks	597,056	63.8
54. Hairdressers and Cosmetologists	306,179	88.7
55. Janitors	621,027	12.9

Table 3.2   (*Cont.*)

	Number of persons in occupation	Percent female
56. Kitchen Workers, n.e.c.	336,605	58.1
57. Practical Nurses	216,757	95.7
58. Protective Service Workers (Firemen, Policemen, etc.)	708,320	4.0
59. Waiters	896,273	86.7
60. Paid Farm Laborers	1,244,276	11.5
61. Gardeners	215,690	1.6
62. Laborers, n.e.c.	2,762,824	4.1

Why do women cluster in these occupations? First, employers attribute certain characteristics to women; these characteristics make women more desirable employees for some occupations and less desirable for others. As we saw earlier, employer perceptions that women have higher quit rates will imply to these employers that women should not be hired for jobs requiring large amounts of job specific training over long periods. Similarly, if women are perceived to have less physical strength, or ambition, this will exclude them from jobs where these characteristics are deemed important.

Second, women are more likely to obtain certain kinds of general skills than others (general skills being skills that are transferrable from one employer to another). The skills women obtain help determine the kinds of jobs they will get. Women are most likely to obtain skills like typing or bookkeeping and less likely to obtain the very specialized, very high levels of education required by engineering, law, medicine, or university teaching. They are also less likely to obtain specialized skills which can only be developed through long years on the job, such as the skills needed by plumbers, auto mechanics, or building inspectors. The attraction to women of skills obtainable in high school, and the lack of attraction of advanced-degree skills, can be partially explained. If a woman is conditioned by society to see her role primarily as raising a family, she will *anticipate* only intermittent periods of work. Thus, the "payoff" for extra years of training is lower than it is for men, who expect to work for many years. Therefore, while a man may choose his first jobs on the basis of how much useful experience they will provide for his later career, a woman is less likely to choose early jobs for their future value if she does not expect to be in the labor force for long.[7]

Third, if she decides to acquire skills, she must choose skills which do not deteriorate seriously from long years of nonuse. A skilled typist remains skilled, even without constant practice, but a physicist who goes away from the profession for five or six years to bear and raise children will have "out of date" skills when she tries to return to it. As Table 3.2 shows, most female occupations (1) can be learned in school rather than through experience alone, (2) do not require advanced degrees, (3) have low rates of deterioration of skills, or (4) have carryover value at home, such as teaching and nursing.

[7]See Juanita Kreps, *Sex in the Marketplace: American Women at Work* (Baltimore: The Johns Hopkins Press, 1971), pp. 43 – 45.

Occupational Typing and Social Norms. Besides employer perceptions and female skills, there are other factors which help to explain occupational typing. Social norms about what constitutes "feminine" or "nonfeminine" work may also play a part. Women may loathe even training for a job that has a masculine image, such as plumbing, although if they were trained, it is hard to see why they could not be as proficient as men. For most women, taking a job in a "female" occupation re-inforces her (and her family's) notions of feminine behavior. And working at a woman's job may have other nonwage advantages: she may be able to find work close to home, she may receive side benefits (for instance, discounts at stores where she is a salesperson), she may be able to get part-time work, which allows her to be home when the children return from school, and so forth.

Thus, occupational stereotyping is *not* a type of personal discrimination in which an employer with hiring or wage-setting power takes advantage of this power to underpay women. Rather, it is built into the structure of the labor market, and the system itself tends to perpetuate it.[8]

We have specified two important types of discrimination — unequal pay and occupational stereotyping. Underlying both are complex social attitudes about the place women ought to occupy; these attitudes produce particular employer perceptions and particular patterns of educational attainment, skill acquisition, and career mobility. Society's attitudes produce a situation in which women bear most of the costs of foregone careers in order to raise families. Education for men is conceived as preparing them for their life's work; education for women is all too often conceived as enhancing their prospects for a suitable marriage or as a sort of insurance policy should they have to support themselves or their families for any length of time. Where family resources are limited, education is provided for the boys rather than for the girls. This constraint on career choice and preparation, based on different male and female roles, is far more pervasive and more difficult to change than is narrowly-defined discrimination. Phenomena like occupational typing will begin to lessen in importance only as more young women — and their families — refuse to accept the limited choices society seems to offer them and start acquiring the education and skills that will enable them to go into male-dominated occupations.[9]

One of the best attempts to date to measure the wage losses due to discrimination is that made by Ronald L. Oaxaca.[10] Oaxaca is able to eliminate from the "gross" male-female wage differential the effects of such factors as different educational levels, differences between big-city and small-city wage levels, and so forth. In a sense, he has "cleansed" the total differential of a large number of factors that do not represent discrimination. What is left — the "cleansed" male-female differential — represents the results of narrow discrimination and occupational typing plus a

---

[8]Occupational typing does give women some protection against losing their jobs to men. As discrimination barriers lessen, females take more jobs in traditionally male occupations. It also means that men can move into occupations traditionally reserved for women.

[9]This is not to imply that government, the educational establishment, or business are powerless to help break the constraints. The aggressive recruiting of women into graduate professional schools, governmental equal opportunity regulations, and so forth can all help soften the constraint from the demand side. For one interesting suggestion, see John Kenneth Galbraith, Edwin Kuh, and Lester C. Thurow, "The Galbraith Plan to Promote the Minorities," *New York Times Magazine,* August 22, 1971.

[10]Ronald L. Oaxaca, *Male-Female Wage Differentials in Urban Labor Markets.* Princeton University, Industrial Relations Section, Working Paper Number 23, 1971.

few other variables not "washed out." Oaxaca finds that 69 percent of the wage differential between white males and white females is due to discrimination, while 94 percent of the wage differential between black males and black females is due to discrimination. Oaxaca believes that most of the remaining 31 percent white differential is due to the effects of part-time employment and childbearing.

Characteristics of Women's Participation in the Labor Force

In the first part of this chapter we speculated that the place of women in the labor force depended on three main factors: (1) their preferences as to work; (2) the level of their skills; and (3) the discriminatory attitudes they were likely to encounter. Naturally, if any of these factors change, women's role will also change. In fact, over the past two or three decades there have been large shifts in women's labor force activity. Do the shifts indicate that less labor market discrimination against women is taking place, or that women's work preferences have been altered? We will document and try to explain some of these shifts, and then point out their possible implications for change in the degree of discrimination.

Table 3.3   Labor Force Characteristics by Sex, 1947–1970

	Male			Female		
	Population (1,000's)	Labor force participation rates	Unemployment rates	Population (1,000's)	Labor force participation rates	Unemployment rates
1947						
Single	14,760	63.5%	9.1%	12,078	51.2%	3.1%
Married	33,389	92.6%	2.7%	33,458	20.0%	2.6%
Widowed Divorced Separated	4,201	65.7%	7.6%	9,270	37.4%	4.5%
1960						
Single	15,274	55.5%	12.6%	12,252	44.1%	6.0%
Married	40,205	88.9%	4.4%	40,205	30.5%	5.4%
Widowed, Etc.	4,794	59.3%	9.8%	12,150	40.0%	6.3%
1970						
Single	15,722	60.7%	9.1%	13,141	53.0%	7.1%
Married	45,055	86.9%	2.6%	45,055	40.8%	4.8%
Widowed, Etc.	5,416	54.2%	6.5%	15,065	39.1%	4.8%

Source: U.S. Department of Labor, *Manpower Report of the President, 1971* (Washington, D.C.: U.S. Government Printing Office, 1971), p. 234, Table B-1.

A measure of women's labor force activity is the rate of labor force participation, or in other words, the rate of women in the labor force to the female population of working age at any point in time. Table 3.3 presents labor force participation rates by sex for selected years between 1947 and 1970. The labor force participation rates of married women have increased dramatically from 20 percent in 1947 (and 16.7 percent in 1940) to 40.8 percent in 1970. By contrast, the labor force participation rate for widowed, divorced, and separated women has stayed essentially constant since 1947, hovering between 37.4 and 40.0 percent while the labor force participation of single women declined steadily through 1967, when a redefinition of the minimum age from 14 to 16 years artificially raised the labor force participation rate by nearly 10 percentage points. Since 1967, however, the participation rate of single women has increased by an average of nearly .8 percent a year. Thus, while many women may still leave the labor force when they marry, marriage per se is less important in deciding whether or not a woman works than it used to be.

Factors other than marital status may influence the participation rates of women: husband's income, age of the woman, educational attainment, and race all seem to have an effect. In addition, the growing availability of labor-saving devices in the home may give women more "free" time to work.

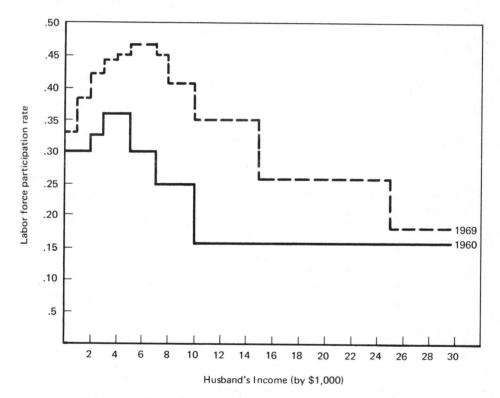

FIGURE 3.1 Labor force participation rates of married women by husband's income, 1960 – 1969. The data were tabulated by different investigators in separate studies, hence the income divisions are not the same. Husband's income is in the year *before* wife's participation rates were surveyed, that is, in 1959 and 1968. [Source: Juanita Kreps, *Sex in the Marketplace: American Women at Work* (Baltimore: The Johns Hopkins Press, 1971), pp. 21, 23. Reprinted with the permission of the author.]

Husband's Income. An overriding characteristic of married women's participation is that at any point in time, the higher her husband's income is, the less likely a wife is to work. There are two reasons for this. Many Americans think it improper for a wife to work if she does not have to; thus American society has condoned wives who do not want to work. If, in addition, her husband earns an "adequate" income, the woman and her family are less likely to feel they "need" the additional income she could bring home if she did work. Hence, a higher husband's income frees the wife to perform nonmarket ("leisure") activities such as spending more time at homemaking, raising a family, or being involved in community affairs. Figure 3.1 illustrates the results of two studies that summarize the general tendency for a wife to work less as her husband's income increases. There are, however, two peculiarities defying this point-in-time phenomenon.

First, the probability that a wife will work actually *increases* with the size of her husband's income, but only if the husband's income is less than around $5,000. There are some possible explanations for the increasing participation rates of wives in poor families. The very poorest families are likely to be living in rural areas or very poor urban areas, where there is an especially constraining lack of job opportunities for the husband. Families with slightly higher husbands' incomes may be in areas with more job opportunities for the wife as well.

Second, in comparisons over time, the participation rates of women have been increasing for *each* level of a husband's income. For example, the labor force participation rates of women whose husbands earned $5,000-$6,999 increased from 30 percent to 47 percent between 1960 and 1969.

Husbands' incomes have obviously risen over time. The general tendency found in the point-in-time data would lead us to believe that wives would work less, on the average, as their husbands' incomes rose. But as the preceding paragraph shows, the over-time data seem to go in the opposite direction. In fact, the over-time tendency dominates, so that rising husbands' incomes over time has been accompanied by a rise in average participation by married women.

How can we explain the second peculiarity and the overall rise in average participation? Increasing men's incomes have been part and parcel of an economywide increase in the overall demand for labor; the result has been that the economy's ability to absorb female labor has also increased, thereby pushing up the wages females can earn. If wages are going up, the opportunity cost to a woman of not working also goes up, so she is more likely to work. Hence, rising wages have increased both husbands' incomes and the tendency of women to take jobs. These rising wages undoubtedly explain at least part of the rise in participation.

Age. A second factor influencing whether a woman will decide to work or not is her age. Figure 3.2 presents women's participation rates for selected years by age category. Those over 65 years never had participation rates below 8.1 percent (in 1947) or above 10.9 percent (in 1956). The graph reveals several interesting facts about the age distribution of women's employment.

1. Up to about 1964 – 65, the labor force participation of women increased steadily from the teenage years until the early twenties, when their participation rates began to fall. But since 1965, female participation rates have increased through the mid-twenties, indicating that girls are now marrying later and thus working

longer, or getting more schooling, or continuing to work for some time after they are married.

2. Somewhere in the early to mid-twenties, the participation of women begins to fall off very sharply as girls drop out of the labor force to get married and raise families. Participation rates continue to decline until women are in their thirties, when the rates again begin to rise. This corresponds to the period when children have grown old enough to be in school during the day and the wife is unlikely to bear more children, so that she now has more free time available. There may be compelling reasons for the wife to work, since the family may have to finance the children's college educations or weddings, or pay off the mortgage on their own home, or even begin to save for retirement. By the 55 – 64-year-old age bracket, the second withdrawal of women from the labor market has begun, reflecting in part the fact that women on the average retire before men do.

3. The participation rates of younger women — those between 20 and 44 — have increased sharply since the mid-1960's. There are a number of possible explanations: birth rates have been declining, suggesting that women have fewer babies to care for; these women are more highly educated than women in the older age brackets, which also implies higher participation in the labor force; and general

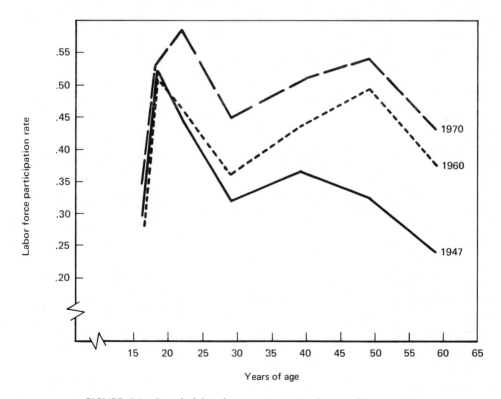

FIGURE 3.2 Female labor force participation by age. [Source: U.S. Department of Labor, *Manpower Report of the President, 1971* (Washington, D. C.: U.S. Government Printing Office, 1971), p. 205, Table A-2.]

prosperity has increased the number of jobs available in those occupations which women typically enter.

4. The work cycle of women has typically been subject to fairly predictable fluctuations; participation rises until the age of marriage, falls during the childbearing years, rises again in early middle age when bringing up children is no longer so time-consuming, and falls off again as women look to retirement. But there is some evidence that this cycle is now being smoothed out; fewer women are leaving the labor force when they are in their late twenties than was true a decade ago. If this trend continues, we can expect relatively fewer women to drop out and then reenter the labor force, and relatively more women to stay in the labor force during their childbearing years. This smoothing out of the cycle has important implications for the level of discrimination.

In our earlier discussion of discrimination, we saw that both employer attitudes and women's failure to gain specialized skills might contribute to the pattern of unequal wages and occupational typing. But if women are now spending more time in the labor force, this might have an effect both on employer attitudes and on the skills acquired by women. If women stay at their jobs longer, this should change employers' notions about the inevitability of women quitting their jobs frequently, and thus predispose employers to hire women on a more equal basis with men.

Further, a longer stint in the labor force means that it will be more possible (as well as profitable) for women to get the kind of specific training that leads both to a wider range of job options and to higher wages as employers anticipate a longer employment period in which to recoup the costs they incur while training female labor. Therefore, women's increasing participation rates in the labor force provide reason to hope that discrimination will lessen in the future as employers view the hiring and training of women as a better investment.

Education.   The more educated a woman is, the more likely she is to work. One important reason is purely economic: the more educated she is, the higher the wage she can expect to earn on a job. There are other reasons too: the more highly educated she is, the greater the range, interest, and status of the jobs available to her[11] and the less likely she is to be dominated by the conventional idea that a woman's place is in the home. In fact, education may itself imply the presence of a strong desire for a career. Some women may get a higher education because from adolescence they have had a strong desire to achieve, and for these women education is the same kind of investment that it is for men.

The percentage of women who have gone on to higher education has been increasing. Women now receive 42 percent of all bachelor's degrees — but only 13 percent of all doctoral degrees, which is still an improvement over the 1950's. Obviously, as women attain higher educational levels, employment for women in professions such as law and medicine should increase. Thus, at least in the professions, occupational typing can be expected to diminish somewhat.

Race.   While the participation of nonwhite women in the labor force has been consistently higher than that of white women, the rate of increase in white women's

---

[11]Compared to the jobs she would get with "less" education. Many women college graduates' jobs are less challenging than those their education prepared them for, usually as a result of occupational typing.

Table 3.4   Labor Force Participation Rates for Females by Race [a]

	White females	Nonwhite females
1948	31.3	45.6
1950	32.6	46.9
1955	34.5	46.1
1960	36.5	48.2
1965	38.1	48.6
1970	42.6	49.5

Source: U.S. Department of Labor, *Manpower Report of the President, 1971* (Washington, D.C.: U.S. Government Printing Office, 1971), pp. 207 – 208, Table A-4.

[a] For women aged 16 and over.

participation since 1948 has been much more rapid. Just under half the black women have worked as Table 3.4 shows; about 3 white females in 7 now participate in the labor force.

Occupational Typing.   On the basis of the sketchy data available, it does not appear that the rapid increase in female labor force participation has thus far led to a significant decline in the extent of occupational typing. Between 1950 and 1960, nearly 60 percent of the increase in female employment occurred in occupations which were mostly female in 1950. A third of the women were in occupations difficult to classify, so only 10 percent of the women entering the labor force since 1950 came into occupations which were predominantly male. The data for years since 1960 are much less precise, but it would appear that most growth in female employment has been among clerical workers and service workers, occupational groups in which women were already heavily represented. Economists will be better able to determine the extent of changes in occupational typing, if any have taken place, when the results of the 1970 census become available.

The Effect of Macroeconomic Policies on the Employment of Women

As we have already pointed out, recent changes in female labor force participation patterns indicate that improvement may be taking place in two ways — the changing patterns themselves may reflect changing societal attitudes, and the new patterns could be more conducive to greater skill acquisition by women and to more positive attitudes by employers toward women.

Suppose that the supply of women willing to work continues to increase rapidly. What effect is this likely to have on the structure of female employment, and on the employment of other groups? Perhaps the most crucial single determinant of the effect of increased willingness to work by women is the ability and determination of the government to achieve relatively full employment. If the government uses its monetary and fiscal policy tools to ensure a low level of unemployment, the economy will be able to absorb (and will welcome) the increase in labor supply represented by the women. If the government does not, there will be little growth in the number of jobs available, women — as well as men — will be less able to find jobs, and the jobs they do obtain may more often be at the expense of minority groups like blacks and older people.[12]

The lower the overall unemployment rate, the more likely it is that employer preferences for men will be overcome and that occupational typing will lessen. Why is this? In a "low unemployment" (tight) labor market, there are more jobs available than people available to fill them. Employers may prefer to hire white, prime-age males, but there are few available (they have all been snapped up by other employers). Thus, the employers who need labor must hire whomever is available. Women will be more often hired, and more often hired for the kinds of jobs that men would get in looser labor markets. Thus female job opportunity will increase, and job typing will lessen. The same goes, incidentally, for blacks and the young, who have relatively high unemployment rates.

Suppose the economy has had high unemployment rates for a long time and that these rates are to continue high. Suppose also that discrimination against women happens to be decreasing. In this world, women are likely to take jobs away from males; since the stock of jobs is relatively fixed, but employers suddenly perceive that women are good to hire at their relatively cheaper wages, women will get many of the vacancies that do arise. They will "take jobs away from" men. Such difficulties will be avoided only if a low unemployment rate is maintained.

Similarly, suppose demand for goods and services is "low" — so that unemployment rates are high — but that what demand there is is shifting toward industries with a high proportion of female jobs, such as the textile industry. Here, too, women will be hired at the expense of men. Again, this would be avoided if a low general unemployment rate were maintained.

Policies to Increase the Employment of Women

In this chapter we have generally assumed that the government makes no special efforts to promote the employment of women. We argued that if the government pursues expansionary monetary and fiscal policies, a useful by-product of the implied low unemployment rates will be better job opportunities for women. But we would expect the government to want low overall unemployment rates whether or not it was interested in increasing opportunities for women.

There are in fact a variety of government policies which could be used to try to increase directly the participation and employment of women. Legislation is one means of trying to insure equal pay for equal work and, to a lesser extent, of opening jobs to women either in occupations formerly closed to them or with firms previously unwilling to hire them; a constitutional amendment to achieve this was nearing ratification by the states in 1972. More child-care centers would free mothers of very young children to take jobs, and would in addition provide jobs for many women who would like to work, who enjoy children, and who might not

---

[12]The supply of female labor has been increasing steadily over the past decades. Even so, a higher overall unemployment level will tend to discourage female participation. When unemployment is higher, the probability of getting a job is lower, so fewer women search for jobs. This phenomenon is well documented in labor force participation studies. Thus, during a recession, because of this discouraged worker effect, female participation rates will be lower than they would be during prosperity, even though over the longer run female participation rates are increasing.

otherwise be able to find suitable jobs. High school girls could better prepare themselves to meet their future job needs if vocational guidance were improved and if curricula were modernized so as to attune students to areas where job opportunities were expanding.

One could conceive of other government policies that might also help: quota systems which set "floors" on the employment of women in different types of jobs, subsidies to firms which hired women in job slots previously available only to men, or enlarged scholarship programs or minimum quotas for women in professional schools. Each of these suggestions, however, carries with it important questions of effectiveness and equity: will any specific policy proposal designed to bring women into the labor force really do what it is intended to do?; will it be worth the costs of implementation?; who will end up paying for it? If firms are subsidized to hire women (by creating part-time career openings, for example), how will we know that the firm would not have hired an equivalent number of women anyway? Even the case of child-care centers is far from simple. Should the government subsidize them, perhaps through tax deductions, as some women's liberation organizations suggest and as Congress approved in 1971? Such subsidies must come out of tax revenues.[13] If the resulting child-care centers are used primarily by middle-class, relatively well-educated and affluent mothers who want to work, then it will be middle-class families with children who are the largest beneficiaries of the program. Yet the provision of subsidized child care to mothers whose families are below the poverty level — who pay no federal income tax and are not helped by a tax deduction — would permit these women to take jobs if they chose, and thus to raise their families' incomes. Besides the poverty reduction benefits, welfare rolls might even be reduced. The issue of child care is only beginning to emerge, but the realistic policy choice may involve helping some poor people while giving a very large subsidy to some members of the middle class, paid for by taxpayers from all income levels. In any event, the issue involves far more than simply the participation of women in the labor force.

SUGGESTIONS FOR FURTHER READING

Becker, Gary. *Human Capital.* New York: National Bureau of Economic Research, 1964. A pioneering study which presents a formal model of the relationship between on-the-job training and wages. Also presents estimates of the returns on high school and college education.

Bird, Caroline. *Born Female.* New York: David McKay, 1970. A discussion of the origins and consequences of discrimination against women. Covers sociological, legal, economic, and biographical aspects.

Bowen, William G. and Finegan, T. Aldrich. *The Economics of the Labor Force.* Princeton, N.J.: Princeton University Press, 1969. The most encyclopedic study of the labor force behavior of a large number of demographic groups. It builds on such earlier works as Mincer and Cain.

Cain, Glen. *Married Women in the Labor Force.* Chicago: University of Chicago Press, 1966. Cain builds on Mincer's earlier work with the use of additional data and develops results covering the behavior of nonwhite versus white wives.

Epstein, Cynthia Fuchs. *Woman's Place.* Berkeley: University of California Press, 1971. The socialization of women and its implications for their career decisions. Emphasizes women in the professions.

---

[13]Of course, the subsidy could also be paid for by cutting back other government spending or by increasing the size of the deficit. The student should consider "who pays" in these cases.

Fuchs, Victor. "Differences in Hourly Earnings Between Men and Women," *Monthly Labor Review*, May 1971, pp. 9 – 15. One reason why men earn more than women of equal educational attainment, race, age, and so forth is that they tend to work a longer workweek. This short article uses 1960 census data to show that even when the number of hours worked per week and many other variables are held constant, men earn higher *hourly* wages than women.

Kreps, Juanita. *Sex in the Marketplace: American Women at Work*. Baltimore: The Johns Hopkins Press, 1971. Examines in an interesting and lucid way factors affecting the supply of and demand for female workers, problems of women in the professions, and legal and cultural aspects of women's labor force participation.

Long, Clarence D. *The Labor Force Under Changing Income and Employment*. Princeton, N.J.: Princeton University Press, 1958. Another pioneering study of women in the labor force, made under the auspices of the National Bureau of Economic Research.

Mincer, Jacob. "Labor Force Participation of Married Women: A Study of Labor Supply," in National Bureau of Economic Research, *Aspects of Labor Economics*. Princeton, N.J.: Princeton University Press, 1962. One of the earliest important works on married women's labor force behavior. Mincer analyzes the effects of husband's income, age, education, number of children, and other variables on the labor force participation of women. The analysis, which is fairly technical, is both over time and across a large sample of women at a point in time.

Oppenheimer, Valerie Kincade. *The Female Labor Force in the United States*. Population Monograph Series, No. 5. Berkeley: University of California Press, 1970. Utilizes economic, demographic, and sociological data to attempt to explain the growth of female labor force participation. The approach is statistical and analytic, but not too technical.

U.S. Department of Labor. *Manpower Report of the President, 1971*. Washington, D.C: U.S. Government Printing Office, 1971. Contains discussions of current employment and income problems and their possible remedies. The statistical appendix is a valuable source of data on a variety of labor market variables.

U.S. Department of Labor, Women's Bureau. *Handbook of Women Workers, 1969*. Washington, D.C.: U.S. Government Printing Office, 1970. A very useful reference on women's employment, unemployment, income, education, and training. Also covers federal labor laws affecting women, women's political and legal status, women's organizations, and includes a bibliography.

U.S. Department of Labor, Women's Bureau. *Laws on Sex Discrimination in Employment*. Washington, D.C.: U.S. Government Printing Office, 1970. A summary of federal and state laws pertaining to women.

4 *Old Age*

A report made for the U.S. Senate's Special Committee on Aging posed a number of socially crucial questions.[1]

> Every American — whether poor or rich, black or white, uneducated or college-trained — faces a common aging problem: how can he provide and plan for a retirement period of indeterminate length and uncertain needs? How can he allocate earnings during his working lifetime so that he not only meets current obligations for raising children and contributing to the support of the aged parents but has something left over for his own old age?
>
> The economic situation of the aged today speaks ill of the solutions to this problem in the past. But people now old were hampered in their efforts to prepare for their future by two world wars, a major depression and lifetime earnings which were generally low. The important question persists: what are the prospects for the future aged?
>
> What do we intend for ourselves when aged and what are we to provide for those who are already old? How are older people, now and in the future, to share in our economic abundance?

Income distribution traditionally has been concerned with the allocation of income among those participating in the production of goods and services. The labor share of earned income consists of wages and salaries; property owners receive rent; entrepreneurs receive profit; and interest is received by the owners of capital. Income distribution questions of today, however, also have to do with the division of the national product as between workers and nonworkers. The latter group includes not only the

---

[1]*Economics of Aging: Toward a Full Share in Abundance*, p. 1. Prepared by a task force (Dorothy McCamman, Juanita M. Kreps, James H. Schulz, Agnes W. Brewster, and Harold L. Sheppard) for the Special Committee on Aging, U.S. Senate, 91st Congress, 1st Session, March 1969.

sick and disabled but the young and the old as well. Explanation for the economic dependency of persons who have not yet entered the labor force and of those who have retired from work is similar; in both cases, the lack of productive employment makes it necessary for the nonworkers to draw, in practice, on the output of the workers. Yet the arrangements by which the middle generation provides support for the two groups are quite different, and conflicts arise over the sources of financial support, the responsibilities of the members of each generation, and the claims each group can legitimately make on the national product.

Conflict is not new on the American scene: conflict between affluent and poor, black and white, male and female, conservative right and radical left — perhaps most of all, between young and old. Never mind the logic that such conflict ignores the existence, in some instances, of a vital center: the median-income recipient, the moderate-liberal voter, the middle-aged family head. Leave aside, too, the empirical evidence that the middle constitutes the majority, with extreme positions being taken only by relatively small proportions of the nation's population. Conflict is not necessarily generated by majorities, nor is it necessarily directed against majorities. Conflict can arise instead from real or supposed differences in two extremes, with the center's allegiance being very frequently courted, its interests almost inevitably jeopardized.

Intergenerational Conflict

The war between the generations is curious for at least two reasons. First, there would seem to be more grounds for consonance than for dissonance of interests among the generations; they are members of the same families — grandparents, parents, teenage sons and daughters — and they therefore share a common need for family stability and economic security, at the very minimum. Moreover, there is the commonality that all of us must move through each stage of life, the probability of premature death being fairly remote. So in contrast to other areas of dissent, such as racial issues — where once black, always black — there is no permanence to one's age. Clearly, the future of each age group is limited; as Kenneth Baulding has said, "the young become middle-aged, the middle-aged become old, and the old die." As a result, the support given any one group by another group is simply part of the intergenerational continuum of exchange. The support of the young will be repaid when those now young become middle-aged and those now middle-aged become old.

Second, the conflict apparently is not between the extremes of the age groups, but between generation 2 (parents) and generation 1 (youth) and between generation 2 and generation 3 (the aged), with some evidence that if we could skip the middle generation, the other two would get on splendidly. Grandparents and small children seem particularly fond of each other. One small boy explained to a young friend that a grandmother was "an old lady who sat in a rocking chair and kept your mother from hitting you."

Hence the notion of a struggle between these two extremes of the age continuum is farfetched. Rather, one quickly recognizes that the strong emotional and ideological conflicts so clearly evident in today's society are between the old and the middle-aged in some areas (the relinquishing of jobs and the remaining degree of the retirees' authority, for example) and between the young and the middle-aged in others (as in the case of age-related differences in attitudes toward work, the acquisition of material things, acceptance of certain religious beliefs, and so forth). The middle-aged thus have both the best and the worst of it — the key positions, authority, earning capacity, control of their own destinies and, to a large degree, the destinies of teenagers and retirees, but also the responsibility for supporting all three generations and for somehow resolving the intergenerational conflicts in such a way as to hold the society together.

The important problem area then is that of the middle-aged, one may argue. Indeed so. But it is the problems confronting the middle generation that are most often examined in economic analysis, since it is they who provide most of the human effort for production. In the allocation of the output, too, rewards are based on the quantity and quality of work rendered; therefore, our traditional analysis relates primarily to the incomes of generation 2. For the incomes of generations 1 and 3, who are supported either by public or private transfers, or directly by the family head, economists have no body of distribution theory. It is assumed that the young and the old are either workers or members of workers' families and that intrafamily support prevails.

Yet such has not been the case for some time, in part because of the lengthening of the periods regarded as youth and old age. For young men, the nonearning years have grown from an average of about 15 at the beginning of the century to approximately 20 at present. For older men, growth in the time span of retirement has also been roughly five years; only one in four males aged 65 or over is now in the work force (in contrast to the two out of three who worked at the turn of the century), despite the increase in life expectancy. There is an important difference in the two groups, however. Young people are expected to be busy acquiring an education so that they can earn a living, whereas the elderly are expected to be enjoying the free time they have already earned.

The dubious value of this free time can be understood only within the perspective of our traditional view of leisure.

Leisure in a Work-Oriented Society

> Mr. Creech, it is said, wrote on the margin of the Lucretius which he was translating, "Mem. — When I have finished my book, I must kill myself." And he carried out his resolution. Life . . . is a dreary vista of monotonous toil, at the end of which there is nothing but death, natural if it so happen, but if not, voluntary, without even a preliminary interval of idleness. To live without work is not supposed to enter into our conceptions.[2]

Twentieth-century views on leisure are often difficult to fathom. In contrast to Aristotle's belief that "the goal of war is peace, of business, leisure," the uneasy feeling that life with little work has little purpose seems to pervade much of today's thought. Contemporary writers often deplore the growing freedom from work, which provides "a great emptiness," devoid of meaning. Lacking training for leisure and having no strong interests or devotions, persons without work often lead dismal

---

[2]Leslie Stephen, "Vacation," reprinted from *Cornhill Magazine*, Vol. 20 (1869), in Eric A. Larrabee and Rolf Meyersohn, *Mass Leisure* (Glencoe, Ill.: The Free Press, 1958), pp. 281 – 290.

lives. The void created by leisure has thus replaced "... the days when unremitting toil was the lot of all but the very few and leisure was still a hopeless yearning."[3] In a less extreme form, concern is frequently voiced over the idleness forced upon youth because of lack of job opportunities, and upon the elderly because of early and compulsory retirement from work.

Time free of work is a luxury available to only a small proportion of the world's population. Retirement, the shortened workweek, and later entrance into the labor force are possible in developed economies because, as a result of higher productivity, a man can produce enough goods and services to meet his family's needs in fewer than 12 hours a day and over a work life much shorter than the one that used to begin at age 15 and end only with death. In less productive economies, it is not possible to subsist on the product of a short workweek, nor is it possible to keep children in school until age 18. Output per man-hour is so low that all persons have to work practically all their lives. Leisure in any form in those countries invites starvation.

Yet even in highly advanced economies, time is scarce and leisure limited. "In an economic as in a philosophical or poetical sense," wrote George Soule more than a decade ago, "time must now be regarded as the scarcest of all the categories of basic resources."[4] The notion of the scarcity of time has also been emphasized by Wilbert E. Moore, who notes that "in the world of commonsense experience the only close rival of money as a pervasive and awkward scarcity is time."[5]

Given the scarcity of time relative to its many alternative uses, the demand for leisure can be treated in the same manner as the demand for goods. Faced with the problem of allocating his time between leisure and goods, the individual will continue to work until the "advantages to be reaped by continuing seem no longer to overbalance the disadvantages."[6] According to what is called indifference analysis, the worker maximizes his satisfaction with that combination at which the marginal rate of substitution of leisure for wage-earned goods equals the ratio of the price of leisure to the price of wage-earned goods.

But time and money are not necessarily interchangeable; in many instances, groups of people — the unemployed, for example — may not be able to transform time into goods. Time may therefore have little or no value in economic terms and its utility as leisure, when all one's time is free of work, may be zero. The ability to exchange leisure for goods is also limited for a very large proportion of employed persons, whose annual hours of work are institutionally fixed and whose opportunities for moonlighting are practically nonexistent.

The desire of American workers for additional goods, despite our present levels of consumption, is alternately applauded and deplored, but it is obviously a fact of life. Industry in this country caters to the public taste for variety in style and form, and mechanical and electrical gadgets, household appliances, automobiles, and so on are readily available. As incomes rise, these goods rapidly become a part of the worker's standard of living; today's luxuries are tomorrow's necessities.

---

[3]Robert M. MacIver, *The Pursuit of Happiness* (New York: 1955). Chapter 6 is reprinted in Larrabee and Meyersohn, *Mass Leisure*, pp. 118 – 122.

[4]George Soule, *Time for Living* (New York: 1955), p. 99.

[5]Wilbert E. Moore, *Man, Time, and Society* (New York: Wiley and Sons, 1963), p. 4.

[6]Alfred Marshall, *Principles of Economics* (9th ed.; London: Macmillan Company, 1961), p. 527n. On the economics of time allocation, see G. S. Becker, "A Theory of the Allocation of Time," *Economic Journal*, Vol. 75 (September 1965), pp. 493 – 517.

The push for reduced working time, given these indications that workers generally prefer more goods to more leisure, can be explained on the basis of the belief that the total amount of work to be done is limited. In periods of unemployment this work must be spread among all job seekers either by reducing each worker's share of the total or by reducing the number of persons who work. Hence, drives for a shorter workweek or early retirement may simply reflect a wish to reduce unemployment, rather than a preference for leisure over goods, though the same result could be achieved by expansionary government monetary and fiscal policy. If free choice could be exercised, there would probably be some variation in the selected options, both in terms of the amount of work performed and in the pattern of its distribution through the work year and the work life.

Productivity gains have accrued to mankind in the forms of *both* higher standards of living and greater free time; current questions turn on the preferred proportions of goods and leisure. But the problem of unemployment has obscured the true nature of the choice, with the result that increasing leisure may come to be regarded primarily as a means of reducing the size of the labor force — supposedly preserving jobs for the rest — despite the evidence that such attempts will do little to solve the problem. Viewed in this manner, free time may continue to increase even if its utility (as compared with the utility of additional goods) is low. Retirement leisure, particularly, following a lifetime of work, is likely to be a dubious reward. Given the low incomes available to most retirees, work for pay would probably be preferable to a condition of idle poverty. To conclude, leisure is not always desirable to those who have it, and enforced leisure for the elderly is not a rational means of assuring "full employment."

Work and Old Age

Of the 20 million persons aged 65 and over — a figure which increases by about a third of a million a year — about 57 percent are women, of whom less than 10 percent are in the work force. Most older men, too, are retired; only about 25 percent are labor force participants, and many of these are part-time workers. Work among older men is concentrated largely in the 65-69 age group, with males aged 70 and over having very low work rates. In the past decade, substantial numbers of men have begun their retirement at age 62, when they become eligible for a reduced level of Social Security benefits.

It is clear that in the future age 65 will mark the labor force withdrawal of most males who have not already quit work voluntarily. Women have tended to retire at earlier ages, but their pattern will probably shift toward that of males. Curiously, the pattern of retirement at or before age 65 emerges concurrently with significant improvements in the health and work capacities of older persons; therefore, increases in the proportions of persons in their sixties who are retired cannot be attributed to any increase in health problems among this age group. Rather, the trend reveals the pressure of economic forces — forces which seemingly make retirement not only possible but necessary.

The unemployment problem of part of the 1960's underscored the need for policies that would stimulate the aggregate demand for goods, and hence for labor. But the fiscal policies that were pursued brought full employment by the end of the decade only at the expense of serious inflation, which deterred further governmental action to maintain full employment. Partly as a result of this seeming employment dilemma, industry, labor, and the government have attempted to reduce the size of the labor force by lowering the retirement age.

Business firms, in attempting to find acceptable methods of restricting the number of employees, have increasingly resorted to the practice of mandatory retirement. Labor unions, which have also sought solutions to the problem of unemployment, have recommended spreading the work in various ways: through a shorter work-week, longer vacations (as in the steel, can, and aluminum industries), or arrangements for retirement at age 60 or earlier (as in the case of the automobile industry). The federal government's action in 1961 lowering the male's age of eligibility for Social Security benefits reflected a growing awareness of the shrinking of job opportunities for older workers.

These policies through which industry, labor unions, and the government have attempted to balance the quantity of labor offered with the quantity demanded have often tended to restrict the job opportunities of older men, either by making retirement at age 65 mandatory or by encouraging early retirement. But the implications of these policies have not been fully explored. Nor has adequate attention been given to the problem of income maintenance for older workers, if early retirement is in fact to become the usual practice. Moreover, beyond income, broader issues involved in an extension of the retirement period need to be carefully examined.

Income Levels and Income Adequacy. The low income levels of today's aged point up the double paradox which these economic forces have produced: the individual worker must accept compulsory retirement from work, despite his frequent need for earnings; and the society suffers a reduced labor force size, although manpower is actually scarce relative to the numbers of workers who would be needed to produce the volume of goods and services required to meet our national goals. But since many of the jobs that go undone depend on public spending, the utilization of idle manpower (whether it be the unemployed or involuntarily retired), can occur only when taxation and government spending policies are increased to expand the public sector, with a resulting loss of after-tax income to the "middle" generation in the private sector.

In the meantime, the incomes of older people relegate them to the lowest economic position of any age group in society. Their proportion of the poor is twice that of their percentage of the population; they make up 10 percent of the population, but 20 percent of the poverty group. This proportion has been growing, moreover, while that of younger persons has declined. Within the aged group, one person in four lives in poverty. Two-thirds of the aged poor are women, most often very old widows. The poverty levels used in making these 1969 estimates averaged less than $1,800 per year for an older single person living alone and $2,200 for an elderly couple.

The stark picture, which in 1969 found almost 5 million older people living in poverty, is not relieved by examination of the income figures for aged persons in general. A hypothetical "modest but adequate" budget for retired couples (based on assumptions of existing inventories of clothing, furniture, appliances, and so forth) was priced at a national average of about $2,700 in 1967. Yet even this modest standard of living was beyond the reach of more than a third of all elderly couples. A second budget level of $3,900 was above the income level of more than half, and a third "comfort" budget of $6,000 excluded three-fourths of the older couples.

For that fourth of the aged population living in poverty, or the one-third of the couples unable to achieve a "modest but adequate" living standard, the golden years are likely to appear quite tarnished. The question of what can be done to raise these levels leads in turn to a look at the sources of income in old age and to a reexamination of how well our institutional arrangements are serving the aged.

Sources of Income of the Elderly. The sources of the elderly's income have shifted markedly during the past 20 years, with earnings coming to be a smaller, and income maintenance programs a much larger, proportion of the total. Almost half the aggregate income of the aged comes from social insurance (what we call Social Security), veterans', and public assistance programs. Earnings account for about one-third, with about half the aggregate earnings going to the "younger aged" — those aged 65 to 72 — who do not receive Social Security benefits, in most cases because of their earnings; and income from assets such as rental property, stocks, and bonds account for another 15 percent of the total. Cash contributions by friends or relatives not living in the same household amount to 1 percent of the total income.

The growing significance of income maintenance as a means of support for the aged underscores the need for frequent scrutiny of the role of public transfer payments: their adequacy (however defined), the tax source, possible rates of growth in benefits, and so forth. Currently, public officials are reexamining the question of income supplements for all low-income groups. If a guaranteed income plan is adopted, aggregate transfers will of course be much larger and there may be some departure from the present scheme, described below, in which payroll taxes provide the funds for most of the aged's claims. Payroll-tax financing may give way to a partial general revenue scheme in any case, because of repeated criticisms of the payroll tax's regressivity meaning that the low-income worker bears a larger burden, proportionately, than the high-income worker.

Under the present Social Security arrangement, financed by payroll taxes on the incomes of persons at work and their employers, income claims against the nation's total output are transferred from persons at work and consumers in general (assuming that the employer's share of the tax is shifted to the consumer in the form of a higher price) to retirees. Obviously, the transfer is from workers in 1970 to retirees in 1970, and not from a man who works in 1970 to the same man when he retires in 1990. The retiree of 1990 will have an income claim against the 1990 output, and his claim will be financed by a tax on the workers of that year, even though he is encouraged to believe that *his* Social Security tax payments are a form of saving for *his own* retirement. Transfers thus reallocate the annual output between workers and nonworkers (including the young, the unemployed, and the disabled, as well as the old), the measure of this redistribution being dictated by congressional decision.

1. *Social Security Retirement Benefits.* Monthly cash benefits are available at age 62 for women and at age 65 for men (or at a reduced level, at 62 for men) who have worked in covered occupations and who, with their employers, have contributed to the Old Age and Survivors Insurance trust fund during their work life. The federal trust fund, established in 1940 as a separate account in the U.S. Treasury, holds the funds collected in payroll taxes and handles the financial operations involved in the payment of benefits.

The maximum amount of earnings subject to the tax (the tax was 5.2 percent in 1972 and will be 5.85 percent from 1973 through 1977) was $9,000 in 1972, and is to be $10,800 in 1973, $12,000 in 1974. After that, this "wage base" will gradually rise, automatically, with the general level of wages in the economy as a whole, as part of a major change in the Social Security system intended to provide automatic "escalation" of both benefits and revenues. The original wage base was $3,000, established in 1937; this has been increased by legislation periodically since that time to keep up with the rise in general earnings and to make possible improvement in benefit levels. From now on, the wage base increase will be automatic. Benefits are related to "covered" earnings, and thus only with a higher covered wage, or wage base, is the worker entitled to higher benefits upon retirement in the present system. Any person who has worked a minimum of 10 years in a covered job — the coverage is virtually complete now, having been extended to domestic servants, farmers, and other groups initially exempt — is fully covered for life.

The amount of retirement benefit is related to the worker's taxable earnings, but there is a substantial element of leveling-out of benefits in favor of the lower-income worker, who gets a minimum benefit that is higher than what he would be strictly entitled to on the basis of his earnings while working. As earnings rise, the wage earner's chances of having the maximum benefit improve. Moreover, a wife's supplement to her husband's primary benefit increases the monthly income by half, and additional payments are made for dependents, although most retired couples cannot claim dependents. In addition to benefits paid to retirees and their dependents, OASDI, or Old Age, Survivors and Disability Insurance, cash payments go to disabled workers and their families.

Approximately 26.3 million persons received OASDI benefits, amounting to a total of about $26 billion, during the year 1970. Of that number of beneficiaries, about two-thirds were age 65 and over. As of 1972, under the new law, the average monthly benefit for the retired worker was $134; the average for a retired worker and his wife (aged 62 or over) was $224; and that of widows with two children was $322. To supplement the incomes of the very low-income elderly, funds are also available in each state through the Old Age Assistance Program. OAA, also provided under the Social Security Act of 1935, is supposed to prevent financial deprivation; it serves those aged who do not receive OASDI benefits or whose benefits are quite small. At the time of the act's passage, OAA payments were expected to decline gradually, as Social Security benefits grew large enough to meet the minimum income needs of older people. Unfortunately, the need for welfare payments for this group has not disappeared, though it has diminished. Financed by matching state-federal funds, OAA requires a demonstration of need, defined as the family's inability to meet some minimum standard set by the state. Some states place liens or legal claims on property (such as a home) owned by the recipient, thereby discouraging needy old people from taking welfare payments. In 1970, over 2 million elderly persons received a total of $1.9 billion through OAA. The average monthly payment was $77.60 and was financed from general tax revenues rather than from Social Security payroll taxes. It is simply part of the "welfare" system.

Special attention should be focused on the plight of the aged widow. If elderly persons constitute the poorest sector of our population, it follows that the elderly widow is the poorest of the poor. Surveys of Social Security beneficiaries have shown that women receiving widows' benefits not only have lower benefits, but also less income from other sources. Social Security benefits were first provided for widows in 1939; at that time, the benefits were set at 75 percent of that of the deceased worker. Later amendments raised the widow's benefit to 82.5 percent, and in 1972 Congress increased benefits for widows and dependent widowers to 100 percent of the primary amount.

2. *Social Security's Role in Maintaining Retirement Income*. Reliance on Social Security benefits alone to provide an adequate income in old age is clearly unrealistic,
even despite the benefit increases in 1970 and 1972, given present payroll tax rates
and the assumption that benefits are limited by payroll tax receipts. It is important to
raise anew the question of the role of OASDI benefits in the total retirement income
plan. For if these benefits are intended to meet an individual's income needs for as
much as 20 years of his life, they are clearly inadequate; and if, instead, private pensions and savings are expected to provide substantial supplements to public
benefits, why are they not doing so? There is the further question of equity of treatment of the individual who is taxed at one stage of his life and paid a benefit at
another: how close a relationship should be observed between the tax and the
benefit? Should benefits be wage-related, or should payroll tax revenues from those
presently working be used to guarantee a minimum income for each retiree regardless of his past contribution? Would the problem be eased by the elimination of
payroll taxes in favor of paying benefits from general revenues?

The payroll tax, being a flat percentage of the first $9,000 ($12,000 starting in 1974)
of earnings, is regressive, costing relatively more for those with lower incomes.
Millions of workers now pay more in Social Security tax than in income tax, which is
progressive and has been sharply cut in recent years for those with lower incomes.
Insofar as benefits are weighted in favor of low-wage retirees, it can be argued that
some of this regressive effect is later reversed. But because of the regressivity of the
tax, and for other reasons, many economists have argued for general revenue financing. The major function of the Social Security benefit is also a matter of continuing
debate: should the Social Security revenues be used to provide a minimum income
to the aged, or should this responsibility be left to the welfare system or a family assistance plan? Although there is no unanimity of view, there appears to be a growing
endorsement for the idea of a guaranteed minimum family income for all, which
would allow Social Security benefits to build a second, wage-related tier of income
for the retired on top of that base. This would greatly reduce poverty among the
aged, but would impose large tax costs upon the working population.

Congress regularly conducts discussions of these aspects of the Social Security
system. During the past decade each two-year session has witnessed some revisions
in the legislation. But progress in raising real incomes — that is, after allowing for
inflation — of older people has been slow. The latest Social Security bill was passed
by Congress and signed into law by the President on June 30, 1972. An across-the-
board 20 percent increase was provided by this legislation for all beneficiaries except those over 72. The husband receives the full 20 percent while the wife receives
only half that much. For example:

	1972	
Husband's monthly benefits	$48.30	$58.00
Couple's monthly benefits	72.50	87.00

There were other changes as well. A social security beneficiary can now earn up to
$2,100 a year without losing any benefits, though the earnings limitation was not

abolished altogether. Table 4.1 lists the average monthly OASDI benefits under the new legislation as compared with benefits under the legislation in force before June 30, 1972:

Table 4.1   Average Monthly OASDI Benefits

Beneficiary family group	Current 1972	1973
Retired Worker	$134	$162
Retired Couple	224	271
Widowed Mother and 2 Children	322	386
Disabled Worker with Wife and 1 or More Children	295	354

The additional funds needed to finance this new system are to be provided by an increase in both the tax rate (to 11.7 percent on covered payroll) and the wage base (to $12,000 by 1974 and rising thereafter on a formula basis). The legislation contained a major change, in that benefits will rise hereafter automatically with the consumer price index, and the wage base will rise correspondingly to provide the financing. The 1972 legislation, in setting only a slightly higher level of tax rates to pay for a very large increase in benefits, also recognized for the first time that the former tax schedule had been too conservative — too high — because it had not taken into account the fact that average wages rise every year. This meant that the social security trust fund kept adding to its surplus each year as the tax on wages exceeded the amount of benefits. Congress decided in 1972 to stop that practice and to make total benefit payments reflect fully the reasonably expected annual income of the trust fund from social security taxes.

Regardless of how the benefits are financed and whether the Social Security system or some other public mechanism guarantees a basic income for retirees, it is clear that public benefits will continue to be the aged's major source of income. Private pensions, although growing, are still available to only about one-fourth to one-third of the new retirees. Among those persons already retired, the proportion with private pensions is very low. Equities and other assets are also negligible for most retirees, with the exception of home ownership. The amount of money income provided at retirement through the public sector is thus critical to the welfare of those already retired and to those who will retire in the future. But the size of the benefit at retirement is only half the battle; what happens to the benefit during the retirement years is equally important.

Erosion of Retirement Income Through Time.   The fate of fixed-income recipients in a period of inflation is well known. Those aged whose pensions were pegged in dollar amounts have been caught in the spiraling cost of living, unable to maintain even the standards of living they had at the beginning of their retirement period. A person who retired 10 years ago, for example, has seen the value of his initial pension drop by about one-fourth.

Congressional action has raised Social Security benefits in general to accord with rising living costs, but only after costs have gone up. Price levels have been rising so rapidly since the mid-1960's that increases in benefits were sometimes eroded within a short time, making it necessary for each Congress to enact a new increase in benefits. As a result, there was strong support for tying the OASDI benefit automatically to the cost of living, which Congress finally did in 1972.

But tying benefits to the price index will not obviate the fact that retirement incomes will gradually worsen relative to earnings of the employed, when only the latter reflect the growth in output of the economy and of productivity. For even if the price level remained stable, workers' incomes would rise with increases in productivity; given a retirement period of any length, the older person would then suffer a relative deterioration in income. If real income for the working population is rising at a rate of 3 percent per year, a person who began his retirement on an income that was one-half that of the average worker would have only about one-fourth the worker's income after two decades. The higher the rate of growth, the faster the retired person loses ground relative to the income of the wage earner.

Technological advance and capital accumulation, which produce rising incomes per capita and per employee over time, are in a sense ambivalent in their consequences. They enable workers to produce greater and greater volumes of goods, meanwhile giving them more free time to enjoy the fruits of growth. In the process of this long-run advance, however, industrial dislocations occur, jobs are lost, and the physical environment undergoes an ugly transformation, much of it irreparable. The ambivalence is even more apparent when we consider certain groups in society. Aged persons in advanced industrial societies can now spend one to two decades — perhaps as much as a quarter of their life span — in retirement because output is so high that no one need work till death. Yet the same competitive drive for greater productivity depreciates the skills of earlier eras and pushes the elderly potential worker aside, meanwhile eroding his real income relative to that of the worker.

Lifetime Allocation of Work and Income

The explanation for lowered incomes in old age is simple — deceptively so. Old people do not work and income in our society is based on work or, much less frequently, on the ownership of capital. Significant differences between income during working years and income during retirement years are acceptable in an economy where great stress is placed on the output of the individual worker. Job performance is supposed to be rewarded by a wage roughly commensurate with marginal productivity; in fact, the promise of higher income provides the incentive for greater worker effort. Given a wage structure that is explained largely in terms of output per man-hour, it is easy to develop a rationale for the variations in wages for different jobs (or individual performance on a particular job), for a gradual decline in earnings if productivity declines with age, and for a still lower income during nonworking years.

It is readily apparent that workers' incomes will be higher than those of retirees in a society in which work is central and earnings are related to the worker's productivity *at that time*. A basic question turns on the allocation of that portion of income attributable to the forces of economic growth. For if the fruits of growth accrue entirely to the current worker, the man who preceded him on the job will always be disadvantaged, relatively, as growth elevates living levels for all save him.

The problem of economic support during nonworking periods is bound up with questions concerning the length of these periods and their timing (that is, whether they come at the beginning or at the end of work life). In the United States, whose technology is the most advanced in the world, the years devoted to both the educational and the retirement stages of life have grown markedly during this century. The pressure for lengthening the retirement period has increased during the past two decades; occasional high unemployment has led to attempts to spread the available jobs and to eliminate as many job seekers as possible.

Further growth in the number of years spent in retirement will reveal even more clearly the need to view earnings on a lifetime, rather than an annual, basis and to smooth lifetime income and consumption more evenly over the life span. Individually, each worker now has the option of saving in such a way as to spread his earnings more heavily into the retirement years; yet private savings at retirement continue to be low for most workers. Furthermore, a large amount of saving is required to produce a modest income. At an interest rate of 5 percent, $50,000 of savings yields an income of only $2,500 per year. For the low-income worker, current consumption needs make saving for old age difficult, and private pensions are frequently not available to him, though they are increasingly available to the labor force generally. Despite private savings and company pension plans, a very large proportion of today's workers will reach retirement with only one source of income: a Social Security benefit.

These benefits provide a floor of income during retirement, but they have not been used to smooth out the uneven distribution of income over the long haul. The problem of inadequate *lifetime* earnings persists, and is accentuated by the rise in productivity and real earnings of workers. For the time being, a shortening of the individual's work life relative to his total life span only aggravates the problem still further. We shall live with and debate this economic problem for some time to come.

SUGGESTIONS FOR FURTHER READING

Clark, F. Legros. *Work, Age and Leisure.* London: Michael Joseph, Limited, 1966.

Kreps, Juanita M. *Lifetime Allocation of Work and Income.* Durham, N.C.: Duke University Press, 1971.

Pechman, Joseph A.; Aaron, Henry J.; and Taussig, Michael K. *Social Security: Perspectives for Reform.* Washington, D.C.: The Brookings Institution, 1968.

Riley, Matilda W. and others. *Aging and Society,* Volumes I and II. New York: Russell Sage, 1969.

U.S. Senate Special Committee on Aging. *Economics of Aging: Toward a Full Share in Abundance.* 91st Congress, 1st Session, March 1969.

5 *Rural America*

To some people the notion of "rural America" immediately brings to mind a Christmas card image of a pastoral world where the traditional virtues continue to hold sway, where honesty and hard work still guarantee economic success. Others think immediately of seedy squalor along some red clay tobacco road or up some Appalachian hollow. Most of us probably have a somewhat mixed conception composed of images lying somewhere between these extremes. In any case, it can be commonly accepted that rural America is that part of the country which lies outside the cities. Although there is a rural-urban continuum ranging from the isolated Montana farm to New York City (some students regard the upper boundary as the whole urbanized area — termed "megalopolis" — stretching from New England down to Virginia), most discussions of rural phenomena work within the somewhat arbitrary definitions set by the Bureau of the Census. According to this approach, the rural population includes persons living in the open country or in towns with fewer than 2,500 inhabitants. It is subdivided into the farm population, comprised of all rural residents living on farms, and the remaining rural nonfarm population, which accounts for 82 percent of the rural total. Clearly, "rural" is not synonymous with "farm."

The Evolution of Rural America

The image of the Statue of Liberty welcoming millions of immigrants from Europe is part of the education of all Americans. Less familiar, however, is the massive *internal* migration that has taken place in the past half century. Indeed, the most striking change in the population pattern of the United States since World War I has been the rapid urbanization of the country as a whole and the concomitant decline of the farm population. In absolute terms, the rural population has remained about the same throughout this century. In 1900 there were about 46 million Americans who were classified as rural. By 1930 this number had risen to 54 million, a figure that has remained stable down to the present. Meanwhile, however, the urban population has increased from 30 million in 1900 to about 150 million in 1970. The *farm* population maintained itself at somewhat above 30 million persons from 1920 to 1940, but since then has declined steadily not only in relation to the total population but absolutely. In 1940 the farm population accounted for 23 percent of the national population; in 1970 it was down to 9.7 million persons, or only 4.8 percent of the national population. Except for the years 1945 to 1950, the average annual rate of net outmigration of the farm population during the past three decades has been above 5 percent. During the 1950's the number of off-farm migrants was about one million persons per year; because of the greatly reduced farm population base the comparable rate during the 1960's was about 600,000 persons per year.[1]

About 1,350 counties — well over one-third of all counties in the nation — had such heavy outmigration during the 1960's that they experienced absolute population declines. (About 500 counties had fewer births than deaths in 1970 because so many young adults had left; in 1960 there were only 38 such counties and in 1950 only two!) These counties are overwhelmingly rural in nature and are heavily concentrated in the Great Plains and Corn Belt, central Appalachia, and portions of the southern Coastal Plains.

From the farm point of view the propensity to migrate has been as high as ever in recent years, but because there are fewer people on the farms the impact of this movement on receiving centers has been less. The potential impact of future migration from the farms to the cities is limited by the fact that there are only one-third as many people living on farms today as there were in the 1930's.

Causes of the Shift from Agriculture.   What are the reasons for this phenomenal shift in population out of agriculture in recent decades? First is the rapid rate of technological advance; more and more farm tasks are being performed more and more efficiently by machines rather than by men. The substitution of capital for labor has affected nearly every sector of agriculture, and even the last major exception — tobacco — is on the threshold of mechanization. Relatively high birth rates among the farm population also contribute to the existence of a "surplus" farm population. While productivity has increased rapidly on the supply side, the demand for agricultural products has been limited by the relatively slow growth of total population and by the low income elasticity of demand for most farm products. For instance, a family whose income doubles from $10,000 to $20,000 will usually not double the value of its grocery purchases. The net result is that farm prices and the value of the marginal product of farm labor tend to fall and the wages of farm labor tend to be depressed relative to those of nonfarm labor. Some agricultural workers may even become unemployed in the process. Thus there is an incentive to seek better economic opportunities outside of agriculture, frequently in the cities. This shift reduces the gap between wages in agricultural and nonagricultural employment, but it will not eliminate it so long as technological advance is rapid and there continue to be barriers to outmigration, such as the expense of moving, the social and psychological hardship of leaving relatives, friends, and familiar surroundings, and lack of preparation for better-paying manufacturing or service jobs.

---

[1]Most of the data in this section are taken from U.S. Senate, Committee on Government Operations, *The Economic and Social Condition of Rural America in the 1970's*, Vol. 1. 92nd Congress, 1st Session (Washington, D.C.: U.S. Government Printing Office, 1971).

Underemployment and Low Earnings. The redundancy of the farm labor force is reflected more in underemployment and low earnings than in a total absence of work. For example, in 1966 the average number of hired farm workers in any one month was about 1.4 million, but about 2.8 million persons did some farm work for wages during the year. A high proportion of these workers did only a few days of work, mostly during the planting and harvesting seasons. Over half worked in the South and most worked on large farms. While 1966 wage rates in manufacturing averaged $2.71 an hour, workers on farms earned an average of only $1.23 an hour. Seasonality of employment increases the farm worker's disadvantage. Male adult farm workers averaged $1,452 in income in 1965, compared with $2,988 for farm operators, $3,343 for nonfarm laborers, $4,068 for service workers, and $5,317 for operators of industrial and other equipment. In 1968, per capita personal income in metropolitan counties of the United States was $3,811; in nonmetropolitan counties it was only $2,614. The corresponding value for the farm population was $2,426. It is noteworthy that in 1960 the farm population's income from nonfarm sources was only 38 percent of its total income, but by 1970 the proportion was 48 percent.

It has been estimated that if the rural labor force in 1965 had been utilized as efficiently as that of the nation as a whole, the money income of the country would have been increased by about $10 billion.[2] Though the magnitude of the excess supply of labor in agriculture is difficult to estimate, a number of attempts have been made. One study, working with man-hour requirements based on estimates of optimum resource combinations in agriculture, found that labor was in excess supply for the period from 1952 to 1961 by two-fifths.[3] Another study, using a model of income-efficient agriculture in 13 north central states in 1959, estimated that only 34 percent of the labor actually used in that year was really required.[4] It is apparent that while good opportunities may still exist in agriculture when there is a high capital to labor ratio, the number of farms will continue to decline. Between 1964 and 1969 the number of commercial farms fell from 1.82 million to 1.63 million, while during the 1960's employment in agriculture (including the self-employed and unpaid family workers) dropped from 4.6 million to 3.3 million.

Rural Poverty

While it is clear that millions of farm people need or will need training and preparation for nonfarm work and nonfarm modes of life, this adaptation is often strained by poverty and all its unfortunate attributes. Poverty levels have been defined on the basis of a modified Social Security definition by a federal agency committee so that such factors as family size, sex of family head, number of children under 18 years, and farm-nonfarm residence can be taken into account. The weighted average poverty level threshold in 1970 for a nonfarm family of four was $3,968, whereas that for a comparable farm family was $3,385. In that year the total

---

[2]*Manpower Report of the President, 1968* (Washington, D.C.: U.S. Government Printing Office, 1968), p. 136.
[3]Fred H. Tyner and Luther G. Tweeten, "Optimum Resource Allocation in U.S. Agriculture," *Journal of Farm Economics*, Vol. *48*, No. 3, Part I (August 1966), p. 629.
[4]Donald R. Kaldor and William E. Saupe, "Estimates and Projections of an Income-Efficient Commercial-Farm Industry in the North Central States," *Journal of Farm Economics*, Vol. *48*, No. 3, Part I (August 1966), pp. 578–96.

number of persons in farm families below the $3,385 poverty level was 436,000. This represented 18.6 percent of the farm population, or a figure about twice as high as the 9.6 percent of the nonfarm population who were below the $3,968 level.

Table 5.1   Persons of Poverty Status, by Type of Residence, 1969

(Number of persons in thousands)

Residence Type	All races below poverty level			Whites below poverty level			Blacks below poverty level		
	Total	Number	Percent of Total	Total	Number	Percent of Total	Total	Number	Percent of Total
United States	199,849	24,289	12.2	175,231	16,668	9.5	22,349	7,214	32.3
Metropolitan	130,017	12,320	9.5	112,440	8,200	7.3	15,824	3,855	24.4
Central city	57,781	7,760	13.4	44,392	4,527	10.2	12,439	3,068	24.7
Metro ring	72,236	4,560	6.3	68,049	3,674	5.4	3,384	786	23.2
Nonmetropolitan	69,831	11,969	17.1	62,791	8,468	13.5	6,525	3,359	51.5

Source: U.S. Department of Commerce, Bureau of the Census, *Current Population Reports,* "Consumer Income," *Series P-60,* No. 76, Table 3.

The data in Table 5.1 show the number and proportion of people living in poverty in 1969 by type of residence. The number of persons below the poverty level was about the same in metropolitan and nonmetropolitan areas, but the proportion in nonmetropolitan areas was about twice as high. The poverty of the black population, particularly those in nonmetropolitan areas, is striking. Whereas about one-fourth of the metropolitan blacks were below the poverty level (in contrast to whites, there is little difference between the central city and suburbs), in nonmetropolitan areas over half were in poverty. Rural blacks remain among the poorest of the poor.

It should be pointed out that although the pool of potential rural to urban migrants is less than it was formerly, the problems of urban slums cannot be divorced from the problems of rural poverty. Data for 1967 indicate that rural migrants to central cities were more likely to live in poverty areas than were non-migrants or persons who had migrated from other urban areas. This was especially true for blacks; fully two-thirds of the black rural to urban migrants in central cities lived in poverty areas.

The Varied Faces of Rural America

Several years ago an editorial note in a magazine concerned with employment opportunities for young people pointed out that while the biggest wave of rural out-migration is over, the flow that continues will be overwhelmingly composed of young people, many of whom "are like young adults throughout history who leave small towns for the excitement and opportunities of big city life. But many others . . . leave only because they have no choice; they can't eke out a living where they are. Among these can be found four major categories of desperately poor people:

Southern blacks, Appalachian whites, Mexican-Americans and American Indians.''[5]
This section considers some of the special problems confronted by each of these
groups.

The South and the Black. The proportion of the total U.S. population accounted
for by blacks has remained very stable over the years. In 1890 blacks made up 12
percent of the total and in 1969, 11 percent. The real change in the black population
has been in its location. In 1940, 77 percent of the black population lived in the
South, 22 percent in the North, and only 1 percent in the West. In 1969 these figures
were, respectively, 52 percent, 41 percent, and 7 percent. There was a net outflow of
approximately 3.7 million blacks from the South between 1940 and 1966, though by
1970 the average annual migration rate from the South was 8 percent lower than it
had been in the 1940's. Moreover, despite massive outmigration, natural increase
and increasing longevity resulted in a *growth* of about 2 million in the South's black
population, which now numbers 12 million. Today the overwhelming majority of
northern blacks live in the central cities of metropolitan areas, but even in the South
three out of every five live in an urban area. This still leaves 40 percent of the South's
blacks in rural areas with limited economic and social opportunities.

In 1969 half of all white American families had incomes over $10,000, but this was
the case for only one-fourth of all blacks. In the South only 14 percent of black families were above this level (compared to 41 percent of white southern families). Even
adjusting for cost of living differences, the contrast is striking. It is not surprising
therefore that over a third of all black households in the South live in housing units
that are either dilapidated or lacking in basic plumbing facilities, compared with
about one-tenth in other regions. Moreover, in all regions, housing is far worse in
small towns and rural areas than it is in metropolitan areas. A 1968 survey of 16
counties in the Black Belt of Alabama revealed that 95 percent of black housing was
in a dilapidated condition.

Poor health facilities are a major problem in the South, particularly as they affect
the black population. In 1967 every southern state except Oklahoma had a higher
mortality rate for children under five than the national average. For the 1965–67
period black maternal mortality rates were over five times as high as those for whites
in Arkansas, and over four times as high in Virginia, North Carolina, South Carolina,
Tennessee, Alabama, and Mississippi. In 1968 per capita medical care under
federally aided programs and under general assistance programs financed from state
and local funds averaged $20.20. Oklahoma averaged $30.20, but the range for the
other southern states went from $13.20 in Kentucky to $1.85 in Mississippi.

On the average, rural southerners of both races receive less education than do
their counterparts in the rest of the country. In 1960, for example, 93 percent of
black farm males in the South had less than a high school education, 82 percent had
less than eight years of schooling, and over half had less than five years. For whites
the figures were 71 percent, 46 percent and 19 percent, respectively. Moreover,
there is considerable evidence that the quality of the rural blacks' education is inferior. On the basis of 1960 data it has been estimated that over 80 percent of the
black males who left southern agriculture had less than an effective seventh-grade
education and that well over half had less than four years. The failure to prepare
black (and many white) human resources for transfer from agriculture to growing

---

[5]"Editorial Note," *New Generation*, Vol. *50*, No. 3 (Summer 1968), p. 1.

nonagricultural sectors of the economy lies at the heart not only of rural poverty in the South but of many problems of the North's central cities; for even though the blacks leaving the South tend to be better educated than are those who remain, they are less educated than their northern competitors for jobs.

A recent study of human resource development in the South concludes that:[6]

> Southern political leaders have kept welfare payments low because of resources insufficient to finance adequate programs, but the influence of racial prejudice is too obvious to be questioned. Many apparently hoped that low welfare payments would induce welfare recipients to move to other states. Policy built on that notion was not only morally indefensible, but very shortsighted, since outmigration merely resulted in draining away many of the region's most productive Negroes, leaving the South with both a heavy welfare burden and a residual population which is not attractive to industry. Between 1955 and 1960, for example, the South lost 20 percent of its nonwhite men 25 – 29 years of age who had some college training, but only 6 percent of those with only elementary school training.

Many southern leaders are facing up to the issue of how the South's black population can be fit into an industrializing and urbanizing society. The choice that often has to be made is between tradition and progress because southern tradition contains many elements that cannot be reconciled with the region's economic progress. William Nicholls has effectively argued that these negative elements may be classified into five principal categories: (1) the persistence of agrarian values; (2) the rigidity of the region's social structure; (3) the undemocratic nature of its political structure; (4) the weakness of social responsibility on the part of much of the traditional socioeconomic leadership; and (5) conformity of thought and behavior.[7] Despite the persistence of these barriers to progress, there are at work in the South and in the South's interrelations with the rest of the nation a number of positive forces. These include the relatively rapid industrialization and urbanization of the region, the increasing integration of southern social and economic life with that of the rest of the nation, the emergence of younger political leaders with the courage to deal constructively with racial problems, and a growing realization in the North that southern problems are in many respects national in scope and should be dealt with from that perspective. Indeed, there are those who believe that in the long run the South will reconcile the races in a more profound way than the North. Whether or not this will be the case, it is a worthy goal both from an economic as well as a humanitarian viewpoint.

Appalachia. In 1965 Congress passed the Appalachian Regional Development Act and created the Appalachian Regional Commission (ARC) to coordinate a unique federal-state program aimed at providing substantial investments for the explicit purpose of dealing comprehensively with the economic development

---

[6]Ray Marshall and Virgil Christian, "Human Resource Development in the South," in Brandt Ayers and Thomas Naylor, *You Can't Eat Magnolias* (New York: McGraw-Hill, 1972), p. 257.
[7]William H. Nicholls, *Southern Tradition and Regional Progress* (Chapel Hill, N. C.: University of North Carolina Press, 1960).

problems of a large, lagging region. The Appalachian program was the outgrowth both of preliminary multistate cooperation and of John F. Kennedy's 1960 presidential campaign, during which Appalachia was made the dramatic symbol of an island of poverty within a sea of affluence.

As defined by the ARC, Appalachia embraces West Virginia and parts of 12 other states stretching from the Mohawk Valley in New York to the northern Mississippi hills. The conditions which led to the creation of the ARC were pointed out in a report issued by a special presidential commission. This noted that per capita income in the nation in 1960 was $1,901, but only $1,405 in Appalachia. The unemployment rate was 7.1 percent in Appalachia in contrast to 5 percent for the rest of the country. Unemployment would have been still higher had it not been for substantial migration from the region; between 1950 and 1960 total population in the region grew by 1 percent, but in the 18 – 64-year-old age group it declined by 5.1 percent. These and similar indices of social and economic well-being clearly reflected the character of an area whose population was, in the presidential commission's words,[8] "over 50 percent rural but less than 10 percent farm; deeply unemployed; all too frequently deprived of the facilities and services of modern society; dependent on local jurisdictions with an inadequate tax base and too often reliant upon the marginal comforts of a welfare economy."

Many of the problems of the people of Appalachia are related to their isolation. The early settlers who were bypassed by the mainstream of American life were followed by an influx of workers, many from central and eastern Europe, into the region's coal and steel towns. The miners, like their farmer predecessors, were tied to the land by the nature of their work. Consequently, even though much of Appalachia has a population density greater than that of the nation as a whole, there are relatively few urban centers to provide badly needed hospitals, schools, service activities, and employment opportunities. In central Appalachia only 250,000 of the 1.5 million residents live in towns with more than 2,500 inhabitants.

The Appalachian program has been criticized on a number of counts. For example, some critics maintain that too much emphasis has been put on road building relative to the development of the region's human resources. The ARC, however, maintains that if adequate health, education, and other services are to be delivered to people in need, then there must be a transportation matrix to overcome the isolation of the target population. Critics have also argued that too much emphasis has been placed on the development of places that are essentially unattractive to economic enterprises and that insufficient attention has been devoted to helping low-income families in Appalachia take advantage of the employment opportunities that exist in urban "growth centers" on the fringes of the region. In response, the ARC points out that in addition to regional development, its other main goal is to provide every person in Appalachia with the health and skills needed to compete for opportunities wherever the person may choose to live. Another objection to the Appalachia experience is that the boundary of the region was drawn so broadly that an estimated $7 billion in aid has amounted to only $390 for every man, woman, and child over the last 10 years. The counterargument is that there is a need for regional "scale" if planning is to be effective, though it is often admitted that some areas were included to obtain broader support in Congress for the Appalachian program.

---

[8]President's Appalachian Regional Commission, *Appalachia* (Washington, D.C.: U.S. Government Printing Office, 1964), p. 16.

At present, it is still too early to assess adequately the impact of the Appalachian experiment. Many rural counties in New York and Georgia, for example, have made a solid start at economic recovery, and per capita income in the region has risen from 77 percent to about 80 percent of the national average. However, with the exception of New York, Pennsylvania, Maryland, and South Carolina, per capita income in the Appalachian portions of the other states is still below 75 percent of the national level. In central Appalachia it is only half that in the nation. On the other hand, if the efficacy of the Appalachia program with respect to the most distressed areas is still questionable, it *has* proven to be a valuable experiment in federal, state, and local planning coordination. More will be said about this later in this chapter.

The Mexican-Americans. The Chicanos — "Chicano" being an increasingly favored term among Mexican-Americans indicating something between Mexican and American culture — are the nation's second largest minority group. In 1960, 87 percent of the Chicano population lived in five southwestern states and over four-fifths lived in Texas and California. In Texas, Colorado, and New Mexico they are concentrated in the states' most underdeveloped areas. Officially, about four-fifths of all southwestern Chicanos live in urban areas, but this figure is somewhat deceptive. Whereas much of the rural labor force in the country works in nonagricultural jobs, this is not the case for the Chicanos. Agriculture is the dominant source of employment for most. Moreover, 1960 data indicate that 7 percent of the Chicanos residing in urban areas were actually employed as farm laborers. In Texas less than one-fifth of the migratory farm workers come from counties officially classed as rural. These figures, of course, exclude the many Mexican nationals who are employed in this country. It is estimated that at present there are about a million illegal entrants from Mexico residing on this side of the border.

The 1960 census revealed that 52 percent of Chicano families living in rural areas had an income below $3,000 a year. One-seventh were below $1,000. Even in 1971, in the lower Rio Grande valley of Texas, where 25 percent of the labor force is employed in agriculture, the incidence of poverty was estimated to be 44 percent of all families.

One of the principal barriers to economic progress for Chicanos is their low educational attainment. In 1960, Chicanos 25 years of age and older had a median of 7.1 years of schooling, compared with 9.0 for blacks and 12.1 for Anglos. In Texas the median was 4.8 years, just slightly above the cutoff functional illiteracy level. The relatively poor showing of Texas — a consequence of historical factors, migrant work patterns, and unenforced school attendance laws — is illustrated by the fact that in this state the median number of school years completed by persons 14 years and older was 6.1 for Chicanos, as against 8.7 for blacks and 10.4 for all categories. Rural areas show much less progress than urban areas in educational attainment from generation to generation. This is caused in large part by the disproportionate number of foreign-born Mexicans. In 1969, among families of Mexican origin, half generally spoke Spanish at home. Discrimination has also been a problem, particularly in Texas. Despite the bleak picture that emerges from data for one point in time, it is undeniable that progress is being made in improving educational and training opportunities for Chicanos and in lessening discrimination. There is also sound evidence that education does pay off for the Chicano. However, many face a problem that has not confronted other Americans, namely, the depressing effect on wages and working conditions caused by competition with illegal entrants from a foreign country.

The implementation of any program to upgrade the economic status of Chicanos along the border, and particularly in South Texas, requires that some restrictions be placed on illegal migration and on commuting from Mexican border towns. The Chicano population has for too long borne the brunt of our indirect efforts at foreign aid with respect to these questions. Of course, reducing pressures from the other side of the border will not make an area such as South Texas any more attractive to industry, nor will it improve employment opportunities in the face of the increasing mechanization of agriculture. What is called for first are good basic educational programs that will respect and take into account minority ethnic culture and values, but that will nevertheless not evade teaching the complexities of the urban-industrial society to which Chicanos must inevitably adjust. Adequate job training is also a necessity, but this implies that comprehensive voluntary relocation assistance be made available to persons who choose to leave the border area for opportunities elsewhere.

The Indians. The present size of the U.S. Indian population is not known with accuracy, but estimates vary between 600,000 and 800,000. Most live in 27 states, with Indian populations ranging from 2,500 in Florida to 83,000 in Arizona. About two-fifths of all Indians live in Arizona, Oklahoma, New Mexico, and California.

Most Indians are rural residents and most are poor. To be sure, despite the disadvantages they have faced, a few Indian families have achieved relatively high incomes, educated their children, and found employment in good jobs in cities or in towns near reservations. Others have made a good living from farming or ranching. The majority, however, depend mostly on seasonal work and welfare. About half of all Indian families have annual incomes of less than $2,000 and about three-fourths have less than $3,000. Approximately half the working-age population is chronically unemployed. Some reservations have unemployment rates in excess of 70 percent of the tribal labor force. Among the Navajos, the largest of the tribes, the unemployment rate recently stood at 45 percent. In addition, there is a great deal of underemployment on the reservations. The housing conditions of the Indians are likewise worse than those of any minority group in the nation. At least three-quarters of the 76,000 houses on Indian reservations and trust lands are below minimum standards; most are overcrowded and over half are too dilapidated to repair. Until 1961 little effort was made to alleviate the Indians' housing problems, and even today the total of all federal programs for Indian housing does not keep pace with continuing deterioration. Poor living conditions are in large part responsible for the high incidence of preventable diseases among Indians. Whereas the average life expectancy at birth for the entire population of the United States is 70.2 years, that for Indians is only 63.8 years.

In 1960, 14 percent of rural Indians 14 years of age and older had received no schooling whatsoever, compared with only 2 percent of the total rural population. Only about one-third of the rural Indians had gone to high school and only 3 percent to college. During the 1960's, the Indian high school dropout rate fell from 60 percent to 42 percent, but this was still well above the national rate of 26 percent.

Much has been made of the Indian's attachment to his tribe and to his land; there is a widespread assumption that Indians are unsuited to life off the reservations.

This view was reinforced by the failure of efforts made during the 1950's to "termi-nate" federal responsibility for reservations, from which Indians were encouraged to move. More recently, a rising tide of sentiment in favor of helping Indians attain a higher level of economic well-being while respecting their culture has tended to take the form of efforts to attract industry to the reservations. Despite some progress in this regard, reservations generally have few, if any, attributes that would make them attractive to industry. Moreover, Indians often are not as reluctant to leave the reservations or as unable to adapt to city life as many believe. However, they do need comprehensive job training programs and help in getting established in urban areas.

All concerned parties agree that what the reservations most need is expanded in-vestment in health, education, and other human resource development, including programs to bring the social and psychological outlook of many Indians more into line with what is necessary to hold down a steady job. It is also agreed that Indian culture must be respected and that any relocation program must be established on a voluntary basis. But sentiment about reservation life — which is more often encoun-tered among older Indian leaders and well-meaning whites than it is among the younger, and especially better-educated, Indians — should not obscure the fact that the matching of Indian workers and decent jobs requires a broader perspective than is available from concentrating exclusively on the reservations themselves.

Migrant Farm Workers. Migrant farm workers are among the poorest and perhaps the least served of any minority group in the nation. In 1967 they numbered around 276,000 persons, or 9 percent of the agricultural labor force. It is estimated that about one-fourth of all migrants are Chicanos and that about 40 percent of the Chicanos working in agriculture are migrants.

Migration in search of agricultural employment often intensifies problems of unemployment, underemployment, and low income, and it creates a host of social problems for the workers and their families. Originating in Texas and Florida, two major, distinctive groups of seasonal migratory workers fan out, respectively, through the central and western states, and along the Atlantic Coast and into other eastern states. Smaller groups flow from Arizona and New Mexico into the Pacific Coast states. However, these long-distance movers are a minority; in 1964 two-thirds of all migrant farm workers crossed county lines but remained in their own states. Most traveled less than 75 miles. In 1965 the average migrant laborer worked only 82 days at farm work, though about half did some nonfarm work during the year. The average farm wage paid migrants in 1965 was only $9.70 a day. About half the workers lived in families with an annual income below $3,000 a year. Moreover, the migrant worker's plight is made even more difficult because none of his slack periods are cushioned by health and accident insurance or by workmen's compensa-tion. It is not surprising that a study of 1,700 migrants found that only one worker in five would prefer migratory farm work if given a free choice of occupations. It would surely seem that an affluent society could do more for these deprived workers and their children, who otherwise will reap the bitter harvest of the nation's neglect.

Rural Prosperity. While this chapter is primarily concerned with problem situa-tions, it would be misleading to give the impression that rural areas and small towns generally are no longer viable. Indeed, during the 1960's there were approximately 200 nonmetropolitan-area towns with populations of between 10,000 and 50,000 which grew by 15 percent or more while the corresponding rate for the county as a whole was 13 percent. About half these towns were located in the South. The reasons for their relatively rapid growth were, of course, quite varied, but two of their most common characteristics were location on the Interstate Highway System and the presence of a college or university.

Similarly, there were nearly 500 counties which had lost population during the 1950's but which gained during the 1960's. This phenomenon was most prevalent in upland areas of the South, particularly in northern and western Arkansas and in eastern Oklahoma. Another noteworthy area in this regard was the lower Tennessee valley.

On the other hand, there were approximately 300 counties which had gained population during the 1950's but which lost population during the 1960's. In the Great Plains there was heavy outmigration from the Dakotas down into Texas. There were seven contiguous states from Idaho through the northern plains to Minnesota and Iowa in which *most* counties experienced net outmigration and frequently absolute decline. There are those who view population decline with alarm; in fact, numerous bills currently before Congress would provide special assistance to these "distressed" areas. However, it is difficult to compare the situation in the Plains, the Upper Great Lakes, northern New England — all relatively prosperous areas with relatively heavy outmigration — to the situation in areas such as central Appalachia, South Texas, the southern Atlantic Coastal Plains, and the Mississippi Delta. In the Plains, for example, outmigrants are generally well prepared to take advantage of the economic opportunities in other areas. Of course, in the population left behind there is a relatively high proportion of older people, and it is often difficult to maintain essential services for a widely dispersed population. On the other hand, agriculture is viable and there is little poverty. In addition to savings and farm income, there is considerable income from the federal government in the form of farm subsidies and Social Security benefits. There are also viable small towns, though they probably should be developed as service centers for rural hinterlands rather than as "growth centers" capable of halting or even reversing outmigration. Economic theory maintains that outmigration should raise the marginal product of the remaining labor force, other things being equal. The evidence suggests that in the Plains area both outmigrants and the people left behind have successfully adapted to the population changes that have occurred. The greatest acceleration of nonmetropolitan income in the country has taken place in the Plains, rising from a rate of growth of 2.9 percent in the 1950's to 6.2 percent in the 1960's.

Policies for Rural Areas

Federal Agency Programs.   There are so many agencies and programs devoted to improving economic conditions in rural areas that it would be beyond the scope of this chapter to even begin to describe their nature and functioning. However, some of the more important may be noted. The Agricultural Stabilization and Conservation Service administers agricultural price supports and establishes acreage and crop quotas. The Cooperative Extension Service helps farmers to increase their productivity by providing advice on management and technical problems. The Farmers' Home Administration is supposed to provide aid to small independent farm units and especially to poor farm families. Its loans can be used to buy land, livestock, machinery, and equipment or to pay normal operating expenses for a variety of small enterprises. It also provides farm ownership loans, rural housing loans, and long-term, low-interest loans for watershed development, development of recreation areas, water and waste disposal systems, and rural renewal. The latter loans are made in connection with programs of the Economic Development Administration, an agency in the U.S. Department of Commerce which focuses on projects designed to help develop depressed rural areas. The Farm Credit Administration and the Rural Electrification Administration make low-interest loans to farmers' cooperatives and, in the case of rural electrification, to local community cooperatives or small businesses which provide electric and telephone services. Many states have industrial development programs which, in cooperation with local communities, attempt to attract firms by offering tax advantages, land for industrial development, power, and, quite often, a reservoir of cheap, nonunionized labor.

Among more recent legislation, the Housing and Urban Development Act of 1970 called for promotion of the economic strength of small communities and rural areas and for a reversal of migration trends which reinforce the disparities among states and regions. The Agricultural Act of 1970 outlined the initial steps of a plan to achieve increased development of rural areas. Title IX of this act committed Congress to a policy of rural-urban balance in the provision of public services and called for a series of reports on rural development programs. Moreover, federal agencies are to set up procedures for locating new facilities in areas of relatively low population density. The Department of Housing and Urban Development and the Department of Agriculture are jointly to prepare a report to Congress on their annual planning efforts for multicounty rural areas outside of depressed regions. Moreover, the Commission on Population Growth and the American Future, established by Congress, has investigated the impact of rural to urban migration on the people and communities left behind as well as the advantages and disadvantages experienced by the migrants and the urban areas to which they have gone.

Opportunity Costs. The many public policy measures — farm programs, rural housing, cheap electricity — that have been implemented on behalf of rural areas have undoubtedly resulted in widespread benefits to the populations of the regions concerned. However, economic analysis focuses not simply on the benefits of undertakings but also on the costs. Here the notion of opportunity, or alternative, cost is especially important. To the economist the cost of using scarce resources in a particular way is the best foregone use of these resources. One has to choose and something must be given up. So in examining the policies and programs affecting rural areas it is necessary to consider what opportunities have been lost as well as what benefits have been attained. Here some hard questions must be posed.

Neglect of Human Resources. The emphasis placed on developing rural *places* has tended to result in the neglect of rural *people*. Federal outlays on human resource development programs, such as education, health, vocational rehabilitation, and manpower training and development, disproportionately favor metropolitan over nonmetropolitan areas. In metropolitan counties, per capita federal expenditures for health services are four times greater, for welfare payments four times greater, and for manpower training three times greater than they are in rural counties with pronounced population declines. Nonmetropolitan counties account for 66 percent of all substandard housing units but receive only 16 percent of all federal housing assistance. They also contain half of the children in the country between the ages of 6 and 17 in poverty-level families, yet receive only 20 percent of all federal child welfare service funds, 24 percent of aid to families with dependent children, 26 percent of Head Start and follow-through funds, and 41 percent of federal outlays for elementary and secondary educational programs aimed at the specific needs of disadvantaged children in low-income areas.[9]

Local Development Efforts and Migration. Moreover, even if efforts to force-feed economic development in lagging rural areas were based on social equity rather than on economic efficiency, there is a great deal of evidence to show that they are not effective. In many cases, an inadequate investment in human resources has been made not only because local funds were lacking but also because available funds have been squandered on attempts to attract industry. It is estimated that as many as 14,000 state and local industrial development organizations compete annually for some 500 to 700 new plant locations. Moreover, the types of firms most often attracted by subsidies tend to be in labor-intensive (frequently employing mostly women), slow-growing industries that pay low wages. On the other hand, there is a limited but generally consistent body of evidence which suggests that many persons in lagging rural areas would not mind moving — or might even prefer to move — to intermediate-size cities not too distant from home.[10] In other words, the argument that migration to big-city ghettos is bad does not necessarily justify "rural development" to keep people home, at least not when their aspirations could be satisfied by comprehensive relocation assistance programs that linked them with good opportunities in intermediate urban centers. Of course, a fifty-year-old Appalachian miner or Mississippi Delta farmer might not take much solace from such efforts. But it would perhaps be better to admit frankly that such cases are welfare problems and not confuse them with questions of economic development.

Commercial Banking. Finally, there may be problems with the nature of the local financial community. If banks are not successful in transferring surplus community funds into actual investment projects, "the costs are measured in jobs not available and income not earned."[11] In this regard, efficiency is better measured by loan-to-deposit ratios than by earnings on capital. Loan-to-deposit ratios of rural banks tend to be lower than those of urban banks, primarily because of risk aversion and institutional factors. The loan portfolios of rural banks are usually tied to agriculture; lack of diversification encourages them to keep a smaller proportion of their total assets in loans than is the case with urban banks, with the rest of their funds invested in such things as U.S. government securities. However, a branch bank (or holding company affiliate) would not have to face this problem. A particular branch office does not have to diversify so long as the system of which it is a part diversifies. There is considerable evidence that branch offices in fact have higher loan-to-deposit

---

[9]U.S. Senate, Committee on Government Operations, *The Economic and Social Condition of Rural America in the 1970's*, Vol. 3, p. v. 92nd Congress, 1st session. (Washington, D.C.: U.S. Government Printing Office, 1971).

[10]Niles M. Hansen, *Location Preferences, Migration and Regional Development* (New York: Frederick A. Praeger, 1972).

[11]Mathew Shane, "The Branch Banking Question," University of Minnesota, Department of Agricultural Economics, Staff Paper No. P70-6 (April 1970), p. 2.

ratios both when they are the only bank in town and when they are competing with other branch offices or unit banks.[12] It should also be emphasized that the attitudes of many rural and small town bankers are a barrier to the provision of adequate development financing. Low wages and salaries make it difficult to retain competent personnel, and many of the bankers simply are not growth-minded. Conservative, personal intermediation often confirms and reinforces the local power structure and economic stagnation. The introduction of statewide branch banking in all states would create pressure for reform, but the more efficient use of local resources for local job creation may require other means for replacing entrenched mediocrity with progressive financial leadership.

Toward More Comprehensive Planning

While there are many programs available (or under discussion) to benefit rural places and people, it is important that the means be found for realizing concrete projects that will have genuine relevance to the highest priority needs. In most cases, individual small towns and counties are unable to cope with the task of planning effectively and implementing projects. For this reason there has been increasing pressure from the federal government for counties to join together for their mutual benefit, though in some states the impetus has also come from local groups. Unfortunately, the multicounty district programs set up by the various federal and state agencies tend to use differing boundaries, partly because the various federal laws encouraging, financially assisting, or requiring multicounty organizations were adopted at different times, with little attention paid to overlapping and inconsistencies.

There are, at present, more multicounty districts (state planning areas and federal agency districts) in the nation than there are counties. Nevertheless some states have made considerable progress; Georgia, Texas, Oregon, and Minnesota are among the better examples. If one may generalize about large regions of the country, the states working within the framework of the Appalachian Regional Commission have made the greatest strides in state planning, though even here the picture varies.

In any case, the important point is that disadvantaged rural residents, many of whom are geographically concentrated in various parts of the country, be given a better break than they have heretofore. This means that in addition to regional development programs, which often primarily benefit the local establishment, there should be vastly increased investment in the human resources of disadvantaged rural areas. It also means that programs oriented toward rural people should take full account of the fact that America is essentially an urban society and that the process of urbanization is not yet completed.

Conclusions

Rural America obviously is quite diverse, and problems and opportunities vary greatly among regions. While some areas continue to prosper, others exemplify some of the worst poverty conditions in the nation. Blacks — and many whites — in

---

[12] *Ibid.*, pp. 15–19.

the South, Indians on reservations, Mexican-Americans in the Southwest, Appalachian mountaineers, and migrant farm workers account for much of the geographically concentrated poverty in rural areas, but many other rural Americans suffer from unemployment and, even more prevalently, from low incomes and underemployment. Moreover, population decline in some areas with relatively high incomes, especially the Plains, has left relatively old populations without adequate medical care, retail trade, or other services.

The objective of more "balanced growth" for the nation is frequently cited in the current debates over what policies should be pursued in rural areas. Unfortunately, this term does not in itself provide much in the way of concrete objectives, and it would be unfortunate if it were to become an excuse for simply spending more money in rural areas per se. There may be good reasons for subsidizing agrobusiness industrialists and plantation owners, but presumably the nation's major concern is with helping disadvantaged people.

Critics have pointed to the deprivation of workers employed in agriculture and in small businesses in rural areas. They too, it is argued, deserve the minimum protection afforded by such social legislation as unemployment compensation, workmen's compensation, union organization if desired, welfare safeguards, and minimum wage and overtime guarantees comparable to those enjoyed by workers elsewhere. It has been pointed out that:[13]

> Regardless of race, anyone who is employed in the agricultural sector is a second-class citizen. For although large farm owners are the most privileged group in American corporate society (with import quota protection; anti-trust exemptions; price supports; soil bank purchases; subsidized research, irrigation, land reclamation, and erosion projects; and special property tax rates), farm-workers survive only by the law of the jungle. In no sector is Michael Harrington's famous thesis that the welfare state has brought the benefits of socialism to the rich and the horrors of laissez-faire to the poor more vividly exemplified.

Neither should the "balanced growth" approach be taken as an excuse to develop all rural areas, no matter how meager their potential for growth. On the other hand, all Americans deserve quality medical care and equal educational opportunity, and it is precisely in the area of human resource investment that rural areas are most in need but receiving relatively little. Another gap in public policy is comprehensive relocation assistance to help link persons who choose to leave rural areas with opportunities in uncrowded urban growth centers, preferably ones not too distant from the migrants' homes.

Ironically, one of the major obstacles to the development of rural areas with nonagricultural growth potential is the opposition of the major farmers' organizations. Although most rural Americans are not farmers and although many children of farmers will need nonagricultural employment if they are to remain in or near their home communities, the farm groups oppose the development of rural transportation systems, factory sites, and similar development projects because they fear that it will be at the expense of direct assistance to farmers. Equally deplorable is the lack of

---

[13]Vernon M. Briggs, Jr., "Chicanos and Rural Poverty: A Continuing Issue for the 1970's," *Poverty and Human Resources Abstracts*, Vol. 7, No. 1 (March 1972), pp. 15–16.

creative initiative on the part of so many rural bankers, who often are the key to the success of local development schemes.

Where rural development is feasible, every effort should be made to attract firms other than those in the slow-growing, labor-intensive, low-wage sectors. There are two other kinds of firms that seem more desirable and that could locate efficiently in rural areas. First are those responding to the high-income elasticity of demand for leisure-oriented activities and increased mobility. In this regard rural areas might be used for recreation and related activities or as retirement communities, conference centers, second homes, and so forth. Second, many business activities that are not mere marginal spin-offs from large cities now find it advantageous to locate in rural areas. Examples include agrobusiness, space-extensive manufacturing, research and communications, mail order houses, jet airports, and warehouses. For many, if not all, rural areas, the potential opportunities are there, but private and public financial structures must be adapted to them if they are to be realized.

The multicounty planning efforts now being implemented throughout the country should be instrumental in improving employment opportunities and in securing adequate services for rural people. It is essential, however, that multicounty planning units carefully integrate the various public and private activities within their areas so that they can compete effectively against the economies of agglomeration found in larger urban areas. Moreover, rural development objectives should be formulated and implemented within a national context. It is no longer possible to divorce rural from urban America;[14] the welfare of rural society is too bound up with that of society as a whole.

SUGGESTIONS FOR FURTHER READING

Clawson, Marion. *Policy Directions for U.S. Agriculture.* Baltimore: The Johns Hopkins Press, 1968. A comprehensive description and analysis of the major issues and alternatives confronting public policy for agriculture.

Hathaway, Dale E.; Beegle, J. Allan; and Bryant, W. Keith. *People of Rural America.* Washington, D.C.: U.S. Government Printing Office, 1968. A Bureau of the Census monograph describing the rural population as reported in the 1960 Census of Population.

Marshall, Ray and Christian, Virgil. "Human Resource Development in the South." In Brandt Ayers and Thomas Naylor, *You Can't Eat Magnolias.* New York: McGraw-Hill, 1972. A thorough investigation of the problems of human resource development in the South, with proposals for remedial programs.

President's National Advisory Commission on Rural Poverty. *Rural Poverty in the United States.* Washington, D.C.: U.S. Government Printing Office, 1968. Contains over 30 papers prepared for the commission on the problems of rural people and their communities, mobility and migration, health and family planning, agriculture and natural resources, and the economics of poverty.

Sundquist, James L. with the collaboration of David W. Davis. *Making Federalism Work.* Washington, D.C.: Brookings Institution, 1969. A fine study of how the federal system, through improved program coordination at the community level and within the federal system as a whole, can be made to work for the betterment of social and economic conditions in rural areas.

U.S. Senate, Committee on Government Operations. *The Economic and Social Condition of Rural America in the 1970's.* 92nd Congress, 1st Session. Washington, D.C.: U.S. Government Printing Office, 1971. The most complete set of data on population, income and employment, health and education, housing, government services, and multicounty planning in rural America.

---

[14]See Brian J. L. Berry, "Labor Market Participation and Regional Potential," *Growth and Change*, Vol. 1, No. 4 (October 1970), pp. 3–10.

Part 2

When
Society
Suffers

6 *Pollution: Problems*

Now that the environment has become a national concern, it might be well to clean up some of the economic rubbish associated with the subject. There are, alas, a few "iron laws" that cannot be escaped in the effort to reduce the pollution of the air and water, in disposing of solid wastes and the like. The laws do not preclude a reasonably clean environment, but they do tell us something about the dimensions of the problem and, if they are understood, may prevent people from chasing illusory solutions.

We have all become vaguely aware that there will be a cost — perhaps higher monthly electric bills, higher taxes, or a few cents or a few dollars more on anything made from steel — if there is to be a successful and massive effort to create a better environment. But that is only the beginning. There are other problems.

This chapter will describe the three iron laws that matter. There is no point in hiding that all three are very depressing. The only purpose in adding more depressing information to a world already surfeited with it is a small one: to avoid useless effort based on false premises. A classic example has already arisen in wistful congressional inquiries into whether we might think of a future with somewhat less electric power, or at least much less growth in electric power.

In shorthand, the three laws are:

1. the law of economic growth.
2. the law of compound interest.
3. the law of the mix between public and private spending.

These laws help to explain why pollution has "exploded" upon us and why some of the more simplistic solutions are not practicable. They do not imply that a polluted environment is inevitable. If the three laws are depressing, the discovery of techniques to reduce polluting effluents is heartening. So is the relatively small cost to society — that is, to consumers and taxpayers — of applying those techniques, as measured, for example, in the first serious government discussion of the question, the 1971 report of the President's Council on Environmental Quality. We can clearly afford to control pollution.

Chapter 7 will discuss the economist's approach to the best and most efficient way of solving a problem that is not insoluble. This chapter will describe the connection — dispiriting at first glance — between pollution and the achievement of the economic goals that society has had for a long time.

The Law of Economic Growth

Whether we like it or not, and assuming no unusual increase in mass murders or epidemics, the American labor force for the next 20 years is already born and intends to work. It is hard for any of us to imagine a deliberate policy to keep a large portion of it unemployed. But that simple fact has enormous consequences.

For more than a century, the average output per worker for each hour worked has risen between 2 and 3 percent a year, thanks mainly to new machines, but also to better managerial methods and a more skilled labor force. This increase in *productivity* is by far the most important cause of our gradually rising standard of living, which, pollution aside, nearly everyone has wanted. In simplest terms, each worker can be paid more because he produces more, and he consumes more because he earns more. Inflation only increases the numbers and does not change the facts. Machines increase the productivity of an auto worker more than a barber, but both rightly share, through the general rise in real income, in the expansion of productivity in the economy as a whole.

It is difficult to conceive of this society, or of any other, wanting to halt the rise in productivity, or efficiency, which has made real incomes higher for all of us. But even if "we" wanted to, in our kind of society and economy "we" couldn't. The profit motive will almost always propel individual, daily decisions in the direction of higher productivity. A business will always buy a new machine if it can thereby cut costs and increase efficiency — and thank goodness! That is what has made our standard of living — and we do enjoy it — rise.

It is not a matter of enjoying it, however. By any fair test, the nation is not really affluent; half the households in the country earn less than $9,500 a year. Apart from redistributing income, which has very real limits, the only way the society can continue to improve the well-being of those who are not affluent — really the majority — is through a continued increase in productivity. Anyone who wants to go back to the ax, the wooden plow, the horse carriage, and the water wheel is not only living a wholly impossible dream, he is asking for a return to a society in which nearly everybody was poor. We are not talking here about philosophical ideas of happiness, but of what people have proved they want in the way of material things. This society is not about to give up its growth in productivity. But every increase in productivity adds to output. Now consider the next step.

We can assume that the output of the average worker will continue to rise in the years ahead, as it has in the past. Nearly all current forecasts put this rise in productivity much closer to 3 than to 2 percent and 3 percent has been the average in the years since World War II. So without any change in the labor force at all, our national output will go on rising by some 3 percent a year.

What does output mean? It means electric power produced — and smoke produced. It means cans and bottles produced. It means steel produced — and, unless something is done about it, water and air polluted. It means paper produced — with the same result as for steel. And so on and on. It is true, as we shall see, that the output of *services*, which is growing rapidly, probably produces less pollution than does the output of physical *goods*, but the basic point is unchanged.

But that is not the end, for the labor force will not remain static. As previously noted, the work force for the next 20 years is already born and the number of employable workers will increase year by year (with a caveat, to be described below).

Obviously, we want to offer these people employment opportunity. So, in addition to a 3 percent productivity growth, there will be an added growth of at least 1 percent a year in the available labor force. The result is that we are almost "condemned" to a rise in total output of 4 percent a year. The only escape, it seems, would be a national decision either to have high unemployment or to try to be less efficient. Both are absurd on their face.

The law of economic growth, then, tells us that the national output in 1980 will be, and almost must be, some 50 percent higher than it is today. President Nixon has said so publicly, and he is right. That is the result of an annual rate of real growth of about 4 percent, compounded. It is terrifying. If an economy of $1 trillion in 1971 produces the pollution and clutter we are all familiar with, what will an economy half again as large produce?

Is there no escape from this law? The answer, essentially, is no. But there is one possible way to mitigate the awesome results. We might reduce the labor input (but, we hope, not the productivity input) without creating mass unemployment.

Each working person has a workday, workweek, work year, and work life. Any one of them could be reduced by law or otherwise. We could reduce the legal workweek from the present 40 hours. We could add more holidays or lengthen vacations to reduce the work year. We are already shortening the average person's work life, without planning it that way: increased participation in higher education has meant later entry into the labor force for many, while retirement plans, including Social Security, have brought about earlier retirements for others.

If, by chance or by law, the annual man-hours of employment are reduced in the years ahead from what pure population figures indicate they will be, our output will grow a little less rapidly. That is the only way to cut economic growth, short of deliberate unemployment or deliberate inefficiency.

There is a cost. It is most easily seen in the union-bargained settlement providing for longer vacations without any cut in annual wages, or in a legal reduction of the workweek from 40 to 35 hours, with compulsory overtime payments after that. In each case, more workers must be hired to produce the same output, and if the employer — because of market demand — goes on producing at the same level, wage costs for each unit of output will be higher than they otherwise would have been. Prices will therefore go up. This is widely recognized. Maybe we would be willing to pay them.

But we cannot guarantee less output. Only if employers produce less — because of the extra cost and therefore diminished demand — would that happen. And in the larger sense, the cost of reducing annual labor input is simply less production per capita because the labor force is idle more of the time. But, of course, less production per capita means less consumption per capita; India is poor quite simply because its production per capita is about one-fiftieth of that in the United States. In that case the reason is a complex of factors, including underemployed labor, low efficiency, and many other things. But the point remains that the less we produce, the less we can consume — and most of us are not really affluent.

But lower production was the objective of the exercise — the antipollution exercise. If we start with the proposition that the growth of production is the underlying cause of pollution, which has merit as a starting point, the only way we can get less growth in production, if we want it, is to have more of the labor force idle more of the time. In that case, there will be more leisure without mass unemployment, as we usually think of the term. Our national output, and our standard of living, will rise less rapidly.

That last idea we may learn to accept, if we can cope with the leisure. But under any foreseeable circumstances, our output will still go on rising. With the most optimistic assumptions about a gradual reduction of the workday, workweek, work year, and work life, we shall undoubtedly have a much higher output in 1980 than we have in 1970. To a man concerned about the environment, it might seem a blessing if our economic growth over the next 10 years could be held at 2 percent a year rather than at 4 percent; he cannot hope for zero growth.

The law of economic growth, then, tells us a simple truth: "we" cannot choose to reduce production simply because we have found it to be a major cause of the fouled environment. If we want to reduce the rate of growth of production, we must direct our attention to the number of man-hours spent at work.

The Law of Compound Interest

It is a fair question to ask: Why weren't we bothered about pollution 15 or 20 years ago? In October 1957, to pick a date, the Soviet Union sent the first earth satellite into orbit. The American economy had just begun a recession that was to send unemployment to 7 percent of the labor force. The late George Magoffin Humphrey, who had just resigned as Secretary of the Treasury, was warning that vast government spending (at that time only $77 billion, compared to $250 billion in 1972!) would bring on "a depression that would curl your hair." There were plenty of things to think about.

But hardly anybody was worried about pollution. Conservation groups were properly concerned about saving parts of the wilderness (the Hell's Canyon Dam in Idaho, for example), but that was an entirely different matter. That was an issue of esthetics, not of health. Nobody was talking about air pollution or about the solid waste that might overwhelm the space in which to put it. In a peculiarly sad irony, the late Adlai E. Stevenson had fought and lost an election against Dwight D. Eisenhower in 1956 partially on a "pollution" issue — radiation in the atmosphere caused by the test explosion of atomic weapons. That issue has largely gone away — weapons tests are now underground — but the real matter of pollution has come to the fore.

To repeat, why didn't we worry about pollution then? The answer is that, relatively speaking, there *was* no pollution. Yes, there were electric power plants then, too. Yes, there were paper mills polluting streams. Yes, there were tin cans and paper and bottles. Some snowflakes, though we didn't know it, were already a bit black, and Pittsburgh got national attention because it tried to do some cleaning up.

But here we come to the law of compound interest. Let us take the years 1957 and 1969. In 1957 — only half a generation ago — our gross national product was $453 billion. In 1969, in constant dollars, it was $728 billion. That is an increase of nearly

$300 billion, much of it in tin cans, electric power, automobiles, paper, chemicals, and all the rest. It is an increase of 60 percent.

So what? That was not the result of an unnaturally rapid growth rate, though it was a bit more rapid than it had been in some periods of the past. The *so what* is this: in the preceding 13 years, growth had amounted to *only $100 billion*. We were the same nation, with the same national "drive," in those preceding 13 years. We invested and there was a rise both in productivity and in the size of the labor force, and growth was nearly 60 percent. But in the first 13 years of this example, output rose $100 billion, while in the second 13 it rose $300 billion. With the same growth rate, output in the next 13 years will rise more than $500 billion.

That is the law of compound interest. These are not merely numbers; they are tin cans and smoke and auto exhaust. There is no visible escape from this law, though, as noted, there can with effort and cost be an escape from its pollution consequences. Applying the same percentage growth to a larger base every year, we have reached the point where our growth in one year is half the total output of Canada, fully adjusting for inflation. Another dizzying and rather horrifying way of putting it is that the real output of goods and services in the United States has grown as much since 1950 as it grew in the entire period from the landing of the Pilgrims in 1620 up to 1950.

Most investors know the law of compound interest. There is a magic rule, for example, known as the Rule of 72. It says, with mathematical certainty, that money invested at a 7.2 percent rate of interest, compounded each year, will double in 10 years. Our GNP, happily, does not compound at 7.2 percent. But it compounds at between 4 and 5 percent, and it has been compounding. The result is that the same, routine, full-employment, desirable, nationally wanted, almost unavoidable percentage increase in our national output in 1972 means precisely twice as many extra tin cans, twice as much additional electric power, and so on, as the same rate of growth in 1952. And that is only 20 years ago! We are not doing anything different, or anything awful. We are the same people. Granting approximately the same amount of human carelessness and selfishness, we are the victims solely of the law of compound interest.

The Law of the Mix between Public and Private Spending

Robert S. McNamara, former Secretary of Defense and now President of the World Bank, gave a speech in early 1970 about the plight of poor countries that will be cited here to illustrate a point. In the speech, he understandably criticized the United States for reducing its foreign aid effort. But in supporting his thesis he adopted, almost inadvertently, a piece of partly fallacious conventional wisdom. He asked: "Which is ultimately more in the nation's interest: to funnel national resources into an endlessly spiraling consumer economy — in effect, a pursuit of consumer gadgetry with all its senseless by-products of waste and pollution — or to dedicate a more reasonable share of those same resources to improving the fundamental quality of life both at home and abroad?"

Fair enough. It means tax increases, of course, though Mr. McNamara did not say so. That is what the "mix" between public and private spending is all about. But for our purposes the point is different. Let us look more closely at the phrase: "a pursuit of consumer gadgetry with all its senseless by-products of waste and pollution."

As it stands, it is true. Private consumption does create side effects like waste and pollution. But now, assume a Brave New World in which we are all happy to pay higher taxes and to reduce our private consumption so that the government may have more money with which to solve our problems — ranging from poor education to poverty, from crime to inadequate health services. We shall not examine here the issue of whether more government money solves problems. It is obviously more effective in some areas than in others. But anyway, in our assumption, we are all willing to give the government more money to solve the country's problems, including pollution.

Now let us see what happens.

The government spends the money to reduce pollution. Sewage plants are built. They need steel. They need electric power. They need paper work. They need workers. The workers get paid, and they consume.

The government spends the money on education. New schools are built, which need steel, lumber, and electric power. Teachers are hired. They get paid, and they consume. They throw away tin cans.

The government spends the money on a better welfare system that treats all poor people alike, whether they work or not. Incomes among the poor rise by some amount between $4 billion and $20 billion, and these people consume. Electric power production rises and appliance and steel production rises, and so on and on.

The point is obvious by now. A shift in our national income or production between "public goods" and "private goods" hardly changes the environment problem at all because it does not reduce total spending, or output, in the economy.

A slightly technical point must be conceded here. Government spending is done in three categories: (1) purchase of goods (for example, tanks, typewriters, sanitation trucks, school buildings); (2) transfer payments to people outside government (such as Social Security, veterans' benefits, welfare); and (3) purchase of services, meaning the services of people it employs (for example, teachers, policemen, park rangers, tax collectors).

To the extent that a shift to more public spending, through higher taxes and a resulting reduction of private consumption, involves the first two of these categories, the point stands as made: there will be just as much production of steel, tin cans, electric power, and road vehicles as before. To the extent that the higher public spending goes to the third category, employment of more teachers, policemen, and the like, there will be slightly less production of goods, even though these people spend their paychecks like everyone else. Essentially, what happens in this case is that the society has chosen, through higher taxes, to have more services and fewer goods. If we assume that the production of goods brings pollution, a society with fewer auto workers or steelworkers and more cops and teachers will crank out less pollution.

But this remains a relatively minor matter. Hardly anyone who proposes a solution to our problems thinks in terms of vast armies of government workers. Reforming welfare through the various income maintenance plans, such as the "Family Assistance Plan" proposed by President Nixon or a "negative income tax," would add to public spending but would not reduce private consumption by a penny; on the assumption that the poor spend more of their disposable income than the rich, these proposals to reduce or abolish poverty would in fact add to consumption. They are the classic form of government transfer payment, and whatever their merits, they would not reduce pollution. And for that matter, even the building of sewage plants amounts to a government purchase of goods, the production of which by definition involves the creation of some pollution. The overriding fact is that we can spend 32 percent of our GNP for public purposes, as we do now, or 50 percent, and the GNP will still be there. The laws of growth and compound interest will apply, forcing the GNP upward. To the extent that the environment problem is caused by ever-expanding output, the third law says that it will not be essentially changed by altering the mix between private and public spending.

Conclusion

Three nice, depressing laws. They provide a starting point for any rational discussion of the environment problem. Our output is going to go on growing under any conceivable set of choices we make. But the starting point does not mean despair. It simply means that trying to solve the problem by reducing output, or the growth of output, is a waste of time and energy.

A very good illustration of this proposition is occurring as these words are written, in mid-1971. The nation has excess unemployment, about 6 percent of the labor force. Government monetary and fiscal policy, prompted by practically the entire army of politicians, is directed at spurring output to create more jobs. The debate is almost entirely over how, or by how much, to expand output, not over whether to expand it at all. And it is not a foolish debate. As noted above, spurring total output is the only way to assure full employment in our present system. An "environmentalist" who thinks he can change the system is, in the view of this author, living in a dream world. Put another way, he can stop the growth of production only at the deep human cost of involuntary idleness.

How then is the problem to be solved? The purpose here is not to solve any problems. It has been to try to head off useless solutions. But a few things can be said.

First, there is technology itself. The very energy and inventiveness that gave us this rising output — and got Americans to the moon — can do things about pollution. A fascinating case involves the sulphur dioxide put into the air by coal-burning electric power plants. A very strong argument can be made that under any foreseeable circumstances we will have to burn more and more coal to produce the needed growth of electric power. And the earth does not yield much low-sulphur coal. Thus, somebody is going to have to have an incentive to develop a way to get the sulphur out before it leaves the smokestack; and if this costs the utilities money, the regulatory commissions are going to have to allow that cost to be passed along to the consumer via higher electric bills.

Next, there is the related idea, one that is being increasingly explored by economists, regulators, and some legislators, of making antipollution part of the price-profit-incentive system. In simplest terms, this would involve charging a fee for every unit of pollutant discharged, with meters used to determine the amount. There would be an economic incentive to stop or to reduce pollution, possibly backed up by the threat of closing down plants if their meter readings went above a specified level. The company, say a paper company, would thus be faced with both a carrot and a stick.

There is also the simple use of the police power, as over poisonous drugs or DDT. It is the "thou shalt not" power: automobiles can emit no more than such-and-such an amount of this or that chemical through the exhaust pipe. Once again, if the engineers cannot find a way out, the car simply will not be permitted to be sold legally.

There will be, and should be, all sorts of debate "at the margin" — over whether the higher cost of the different or improved engine is worth the extra reduction of pollution. The argument exists now over DDT; there are clearly costs, as well as benefits, to stopping its use. But the "thou shalt not" power exists.

Finally, there are many possibilities for directing a part of our public spending to environmental purposes. Sewage plants and better local solid waste disposal systems are obvious examples. Admitting that its estimates were necessarily inexact, the President's Council on Environmental Quality calculated in 1971 that a reasonably good job of cleaning up air, water, and solid waste pollution could be accomplished with a combined annual public and private expenditure that would rise to a peak of $18.3 billion in 1975, of which less than half would be in government funds. This is a remarkably small total in the light of a prospective gross national product of almost $1.5 trillion and a probable total government budget — federal, state, and local — of some $450 billion in that year. Later estimates are somewhat higher, but the basic point remains unchanged.

Regardless of the accuracy of the estimates, it is clear that a greater effort on the part of government to abate pollution through more spending — as distinct from "thou shalt not" orders — must be at the expense of some other government program, unless we pay higher taxes. It is proper to point out here the subtle dimensions of the issue. There are all sorts of possible gimmicks, like tax rebates for antipollution devices for industry and federally guaranteed state and local bonds for antipollution purposes. But one way or another, spending more for pollution abatement will mean spending that much less for something else, and that something else could be housing or medical services. Every local sewage plant bond sold could mean, for example, that much less investment money available for home mortgages.

A final reflection is perhaps in order, though it is almost banal. Our rising GNP gives us the "resources" to do the antipollution job. These resources include rising government receipts. Our technology, which has helped give us the rising GNP, might find the way out of one pollution problem after another — and they are all different.

But, in the end, we cannot be sure that the job will be done. Growth of total output and output per capita will continue. Some would say that the best long-run solution is fewer *capita*, a stabilization or even reduction of the population. But that in any event could not begin to reduce the growth of total output until well after the turn of the next century, given the number of persons already born. In the meanwhile, we shall have to live with growth and — remembering that even in the United States affluence is hardly universal — like it.

SUGGESTIONS FOR FURTHER READING

Barrett, Harold J. and Morse, Chandler. *Scarcity and Growth — The Economics of Natural Resource Availability.* Resources for the Future. Baltimore: The Johns Hopkins Press, 1967.

Council on Environmental Quality. *Evironmental Quality.* The Second Annual Report. Washington, D.C.: 1971.

Crenson, Matthew A. *The Un-Politics of Air Pollution.* Baltimore: The Johns Hopkins Press, 1971.

Culbertson, John M. *Economic Development: An Ecological Approach.* New York: Alfred A. Knopf, 1971.

Dorfman, Robert. *Economics of the Environment.* New York: W.W. Norton & Company, 1972.

Forrester, Jay W. "Deep Knowledge of Social Systems." *Technology Review, MIT.* April 1969, pp. 21 – 31.

Goldman, Marshall I. *Ecology and Economics.* Englewood Cliffs, N.J.: Prentice-Hall, 1972.

Jarrett, Henry. *Environmental Quality in a Growing Economy.* Resources for the Future. Baltimore: The Johns Hopkins Press, 1966.

Johnson, Warren A. and Hardesty, John. *Economic Growth vs. The Environment.* Belmont, Calif.: Wadsworth Publishing Company, 1971.

Keynes, John Maynard. "Economic Possibilities for Our Grandchildren." pp. 359 – 373 in *Essays in Persuasion.* New York: W.W. Norton & Company, 1963.

Kneesee, Alyne V. et al. *Economics and the Environment.* Resources for the Future. Baltimore: The Johns Hopkins Press, 1971.

Meadows, Donella; Dennis, Jorgyn Randers; and Behrens, William. *Limits on Growth.* Boston: Universal Press, 1972.

Phelps, Edmund S. *The Goals of Economic Growth.* New York: W.W. Norton & Company, 1962.

Ridker, Ronald G. *Economic Costs of Air Pollution.* New York: Frederick A. Praeger, 1967.

Van Sickle, Drick. *The Ecological Citizen.* New York: Harper & Row, Publishers, 1971.

7 *Pollution: Policy*

Pollution is with us. For many it is *the* crisis of the decade and, as we have seen in Chapter 6, we are likely to be bothered by it for a long time to come. Given our past record of economic growth and the workings of compound interest, there is little likelihood that pollution will take care of itself and disappear. In fact, unless the attitudes and practices that prevailed among the public, government, and industry in the 1960's are significantly altered, pollution will increase quite a bit.

Having seen what the future is likely to hold for us, it is important to know what we can do to transform some of the forces which have been generating pollution into forces which will hold it down. To do this it is first necessary to understand a little about the process of pollution itself and about how economic forces presently work to intensify the problem. Maybe then we can better understand why individuals commit such antisocial acts with such evident ease. Once we understand their motivations, then perhaps we can come up with some suggestions for at least partial remedies.

Environmental Disruption

Almost all of us think we know what we are referring to when we use the word pollution. Technically, however, it is not an accurate description of what concerns us. In a sense, the very presence of a human in a forest is a form of pollution, but we do not normally worry about it too much. Most natural ecological systems provide for the processing and reuse of what at first glance appears to be waste. Thus, when we exhale carbon dioxide, plant life is usually able to convert this into oxygen. Similarly, the food that we eat in this little ecological system of ours is transformed by us into energy for our bodies and into human waste. Our excrement in turn contains phosphates which in some societies, such as China, even now serve as plant fertilizers. Similarly, the plants provide food for both animals and humans. Moreover, what is pollution to one user may be perfectly fine for another. For example, carp may thrive in water that would be unhealthy for humans. At the same time, drinking water that is safe for a human may be harmful for a steam boiler. Boilers are very sensitive to some minerals that humans can take in their stride.

Of course, there are many wastes, especially those made out of synthetic compounds, which do not break down naturally and work their way back into the ecological cycle. At one time, it was assumed that such wastes "were just thrown away." Now we are coming to realize that there is no such thing as "throwing something away." Whether it be released in the air, flushed into the water, or shoveled into a pile, the waste remains with us. If we are lucky, the substance will break down into its component parts and recirculate within the ecological system. If not, it will remain as a lump — but it will not just fade away. Kenneth Boulding refers to this phenomenon we face by using a "spaceship" simile. Everything on our planet must be recycled or stored somewhere. There is no such thing as throwing an object away, as the astronauts learned.

The concept of recycling and the spaceship should help us to be more precise. Human, animal, or factory waste or effluent in and of itself is not necessarily pollution. It will be considered pollution, however, when it is released in such large quantities that it cannot be reabsorbed effortlessly into the system. We can say then that it disrupts the natural processes. For that reason, the expression "environmental disruption" seems to be a more useful way of describing what concerns us. Thus, the chopping down of a tree is usually nothing to worry about since, in time, another tree can grow to replace it. Similarly, there may be no need to worry about dumping human waste into a river because most rivers have the ability to renew and to cleanse themselves. There is cause for alarm, however, when so many trees are cut down that the soil washes or blows away. It is also time to worry when so much human waste is discharged that the river is overtaxed to the point where it loses its ability to break down the effluent. Then we have environmental disruption.

It's Always the Other Guy

At first glance, it is hard to comprehend why anyone would knowingly cause environmental disruption. It often happens, of course, that environmental disruption is unintentional or the result of lack of information. Many plant managers, for example, are so concerned with insuring the quantity and quality of their production that they never take time out to see what is being discharged from their chimneys and sewer pipes. They simply have never bothered. Lest ignorance be written off as a not so subtle case of special pleading, the readers are invited to ask themselves if they know what happens when they empty their shampoo or cooking fat or shaving cream or electric razor cleaner down the drain?

Poor as our knowledge is, more information in itself will not mean an end to environmental disruption. Many people are aware of the consequences of their actions but they pollute nonetheless. Again, how can anyone do this knowingly? How can a factory manager sleep at night when he knows that he is spewing acids into the water and sulfur into the air? Most of us would agree that if we were in charge, things would be different. But would they?

No one knows for sure what he or she would do until actually faced with the necessity of having to make a decision. But lest we get carried away with our own sense of personal integrity, let us switch from speculating about what we would do to asking what we have done. How many have burnt trash in the backyard or corner lot? How many have sprinkled salt on an ice patch? How many have set fire to a leaf pile in the fall? How many of us leave our engines idling while we dash from our cars on a quick errand? How many of us think nothing of having a roaring fire in our fireplaces on romantic winter nights?

For the most part, these are minor forms of pollution, and normally our actions are not enough to cause serious environmental disruption. Essentially, we are correct when we say to ourselves that burning my little leaf or trash pile isn't enough to cause any trouble. But that is no justification for doing what we do, especially if everyone else comes to the same conclusion. Nor is it any excuse to say that if we did otherwise, it would probably cost us more money. For example, if someone could haul our trash and leaves away to a well-regulated incinerator or mulch pile, it is no defense to say that we would have to spend more than if we simply light a match.

Many economists reason that it is the "added cost" aspect of these various acts which explains as much as anything man's readiness to pollute. We are not "evil," but we act upon normal economic motives. It is not just private citizens or private industrialists who respond this way, but government officials at the municipal, state, and federal levels. Moreover, it is something which affects authorities in communist as well as noncommunist countries. Environmental disruption in the U.S.S.R. is as serious as it is in the U.S.A., if not more so.[1] Despite the relatively recent passage of sophisticated and elegant laws banning pollution, environmental disruption remains a serious concern in all countries of the world.

The Social Cost of Pollution

The reason why it is cheaper for us to dump our wastes into the air and water is that air and water are generally treated as if they were free goods. Some of us (though by no means all) pay something for the water we use. In many cities (not New York City), a man comes around to read the water meter and we have to pay according to how much we consume. Even where meters are in use, however, the water rate usually does not cover costs. It is usually heavily subsidized. But even those who pay for the water they use usually do not have to pay anything for the air they use or the air *and* water they discharge. Either the quantities discharged are too hard to measure or the quantity consumed is not what matters most. What happens to the air and water in the course of consumption — their transformation — may be more important than how much is used.

Air and water are also social goods in the sense that when we are finished using them, we can almost always dispose of them in someone else's backyard. If we have any common sense, our pile of leaves is located so that most of the smoke blows into our neighbor's yard. It was more than luck which led the town of Wellesley, Massachusetts, to erect its incinerator on the town line upwind from neighboring Needham. Similarly, campers as well as municipalities withdraw their drinking water upstream and discharge their wastes downstream. Unfortunately, what is downstream or downwind to me is usually upstream or upwind to someone else. Nonetheless, by pushing off our air and water effluent on to others, we force them to share the costs of dirty air and water that rightfully should be charged against us.

---

[1]Marshall I. Goldman, *The Spoils of Progress: Environmental Pollution in the Soviet Union* (Cambridge, Mass.: The M.I.T. Press, 1972).

As opposed to private costs, which must be paid for by the person who benefits from the purchase and use of the commodity in question, costs that are pushed onto others or the community as a whole are called social costs or external diseconomies. Another term is "externality."

Since air and water are only social costs, not economic costs, environmental disruption is almost inevitable under existing circumstances. When a manufacturer has to decide what inputs to use in making his product, he almost always seeks to *minimize the costs* he has to pay. Thus, if either $10,000 worth of machinery or $15,000 worth of labor will enable him to increase his output by 500 chairs a year, he almost certainly will opt for the machinery and not have any more laborers. Even if the extra batch of labor costs only $11,000, he would still settle for the machinery. In other words, the manager tries to "economize" on his expenses as he attempts to produce a certain output. Municipalities and homeowners will normally react the same way. They will both do what they can to hold down their own costs.

Unfortunately, while everyone is concerned with holding down the inefficient use of labor or machinery, there is no need for most of us to make similar calculations with respect to air and water. Since they are virtually free goods, it is only natural that resources like air and water are taken for granted. For example, in trying to decide which type of fuel to use, home owners will usually choose fuel oil instead of natural gas because fuel oil is cheaper in most places. The fact that most fuel oil causes the release of sulfur dioxide, and natural gas is virtually emission-free, doesn't enter into our calculations since the release of sulfur dioxide causes social, not private, costs. Thus we end up polluting the air and consuming fuel oil, which we wouldn't do if we were willing to pay more for natural gas. But this is a consequence of treating air and water as if they were free goods. Economists have found that when anything is free there is a tendency to consume it to excess. Like free love, however, there is a limit to how much air and water can be consumed. After a time, we run the risk of exhaustion, not to mention disruption or degradation.

Internalizing the Costs

Having discovered the economic nature of the problem, most economists are quick to prescribe a cure. If polluters are able to avoid their responsibilities because the costs created are external, the solution is to internalize them. In other words, something must be done to prevent the polluter from pushing the damage he creates onto society as a whole. He must be made to bear the full burden, or cost, himself.

The decision to internalize is easier said than done. To be effective, presumably the polluter would have to be assessed for all the costs he created. The first problem is that most pollution costs are hard to evaluate. In the simplest case — the cost of cleaning up the water a factory has polluted — it is the money needed to treat the water. But if more than one factory is responsible for the pollution, and more than one kind of pollutant is involved, who should bear what proportion for what pollutant? Yet if it is hard to measure and evaluate the quality and quantity of water a factory takes in and then discharges, it is even harder to make such a calculation for the intake and exhaust of air. Air basins and quality are so much harder to define. Measuring air intake and discharge is usually beyond the competence even of skilled engineers.

Assuming that a determination can be made of who is responsible for what percentage of the damage, there is still no certainty that an accurate assessment of the magnitude of the damage can be made. At any given time, we can never be sure that we know how much damage is being caused. For example, it took about 20 years to realize that DDT could be as much a menace to mankind as it was a blessing. Yet to provide for a proper calculation of the total social costs that arise from the use of DDT, we should have been aware that DDT was potentially destructive from the minute production of the chemical began.

Given the enormity of the difficulties involved in drawing up social costs, some authorities are prepared to throw up their hands in surrender. Certainly those who insist on elegance in whatever they do will not be happy. Yet the analysis of external costs is more than just a satisfying exercise in economic theory. Internalization does have some practical use even if the model cannot be worked out in complete detail.

The potential is best illustrated in the Ruhr Valley of Germany. One of the most heavily industrialized areas in the world, the Ruhr Valley accounts for almost half of all German industrial production and for as much as 80 – 90 percent of its iron and steel industry. Moreover, the area is relatively short of water. The water from the Rhine River could be used as a supplement, but its quality is so poor that there is a reluctance to do this. Therefore, the residents must rely almost entirely on the Ruhr and four other small rivers for their water supply and sewage needs. This means that they have only about one-third of the water that is available in a place like Trenton, New Jersey, on the Delaware River.

Given the limited water resources available to them, the cities in the area were forced to work out cooperative solutions starting from early in the twentieth century. Towns downstream had been suffering from typhoid caused by the dumping of wastes by upstreamers. In self-defense they obtained a legal ban on the dumping of sewage into the rivers. The upstreamers then had a crisis. Unless they were willing to swallow it, there was no place for them to put their sewage. Consequently, beginning in 1904, a series of cooperative organizations were formed to provide water and to process wastes in a systematic way throughout the area.

It was decided that each consumer of water should be charged an appropriate fee for its use and for the subsequent discharge of wastes. For the reasons mentioned earlier in this chapter, it was impossible to calculate what the exact social cost of water use and discharge was, but nevertheless an approximation was made. Chemical analyses of the sewage content of each outlet were prepared so as to ascertain how dangerous a particular outlet might be. A charge proportionate to the damage that resulted was then collected. The administrators of the program recognized that any effort to calculate precise costs would probably increase administrative costs and bureaucracy so much that the system would be less efficient than if a somewhat less precise assessment procedure were used. Consequently, everyone was content to settle for an approximate schedule of charges.

As imprecise as the system is, it is nonetheless remarkably successful in promoting the conservation of water. First of all, it accomplishes what we called for earlier; water is no longer a free good to the cities and factories in the Ruhr Valley. Therefore, like employers of labor and machinery, employers of water now know that there are real costs involved. Unlike most of the rest of the world, water users in the Ruhr try to economize on their consumption. Each user must decide whether it is cheaper to take in new water or clean up and recycle old water. That is one saving.

Economies of Scale. Often a plant manager finds that it is more efficient or cheaper for him if he combines with another user to build a water treatment plant. Economists say that building a larger plant usually makes possible *economies of scale.* The more gallons of water a treatment plant is designed to process, the less per gallon it costs. That is a result of the fact that certain kinds of equipment must be purchased in any treatment plant, no matter what its size. Thus, if the capacity of a plant is small, its pump is used only partially. But if the capacity is large, then the pump will be used full-time to handle more gallons per day. For example, assume that a small plant handles 1,000 gallons of water a day and needs a pump costing $1,000. If there were no other expense, the cost of treating that water would be $1 per gallon. If that same $1,000-pump, as is quite common, could process 10,000 gallons a day, then the cost of processing would fall to 10¢ per gallon. That is an economy of scale.

It also happens sometimes that two water users can be found whose wastes tend to neutralize each other. Thus, if one factory discharges acid and another discharges alkaline material, the effluent that results may need little additional treatment. This could also result in substantial savings.

Given all these possibilities, it may still happen that a town or factory in the Ruhr Valley will decide that its waste is so difficult and expensive to treat that it is cheaper to discharge it raw. It is allowed to do so. But in this case, the money the town or factory must pay as a charge goes to the local cooperative organization, which then finances the operation of regional treatment plants. This is yet one more step in reducing the effluent.

No one would claim that the Ruhr system is perfect. Even though the Ruhr itself is used for recreation, an adjacent stream called the Emscher is used as a sewer. The Emscher has been attractively designed to make its neighbors as happy as possible, but a sewer is still a sewer. Yet as much room as there may be for improvement, the fact remains that Ruhr steel mills require only 2.6 cubic yards of water to make a ton of steel while steel mills in most of the rest of the world consume an average of 130 cubic yards. Obviously, such a system has a lot to offer others who are short of water or who want less water pollution. With this in mind, plans have been drawn up to introduce somewhat similar methods in Vermont as well as in several other areas of the United States.

Cease and Desist Power. The Ruhr system with its charges and attempts to internalize externalities will upset many true conservationists. To some of them, this system is nothing but crass materialism. In their minds, paying for the use or discharge of water is equivalent to possessing a license to pollute. With this kind of system, the rich can abuse nature so long as they have the money. Many conservationists feel that it is sacrilegious to place any monetary value on fresh water or air. In some cases, the continued or new discharge of effluent may endanger entire species. How can this be tolerated? Instead of issuing licenses to pollute, they feel, the state should strongly ban all pollution. The polluter must simply cease and desist.

Economists tend to take a completely different view. (This only proves what these conservationists have always thought about economists anyway.) They reason that it is not necessarily the rich who will pay more for the right to pollute, but those who are able to bring forth the highest value from the region. Just because a manufacturer or a city is rich does not mean that it will find it worthwhile to conduct operations there regardless of cost. If the cost of using water in the area is larger than the return the use of such water will bring, the likelihood is that no one, rich or poor, will use the water. Any community can make its water (or even its air) so costly that the value added to production from the use of the water will not exceed the water's cost. Essentially, the "value" is set by the national or local price level for the goods concerned, and manufacturers will invariably use a sharp pencil in figuring their costs and possible profits. The community or region that sets a very high cost for water, of course, would be sacrificing jobs. Each community can weigh its preferences as between more jobs or cleaner water, and set its water costs accordingly. In effect, a simple ban on pollution would deprive the whole nation of this choice.

But there is an even more important point to be made. The conservationists who protest the placing of a value on air, water, or even land are just as guilty as the economists they criticize. What are they doing when they say there should be a ban on all activity in an area? Implicitly, they too are attaching a value. In effect, they are saying that the natural resource they are worried about has an *infinite* value. In other words, each drop of water or air is not worth just $100 million — it is priceless! It happens that there are some places about which we would probably all agree that this was true: the water in Lake Baikal, for example, the air or view in the Swiss Alps, or the geysers in Yellowstone Park. But we should recognize that when such statements are made, the speaker — whether he knows it or not — is attaching a value to the object in question. Then it merely becomes a question of how high that value will be. As the economists say, everyone and everything has a price and what we are trying to do is to ascertain a realistic, not an idealistic, level for the value of air and water.

Recycling

By suggesting that a price be placed on air and water, the economist then is saying that these raw materials are not free. In doing this, the economist tries to encourage greater economy in their use. For the most part, this leads to recycling, which, as we saw earlier, is the most hopeful solution if we are to continue to make do with our environment. In some cases, of course, when the price system is working in our favor, recycling does not have to be forced on us. In fact, the best type of recycling is that which we are not even aware of. For example, most of us take it for granted that after our new car is three or four years old, we will not drive it into the river but to a used car lot where it will fetch us at least a few hundred dollars. That sum is attractive enough to make it worth our while. At an earlier time, we did much the same thing with cars that no longer had a useful life. In this case, we drove them directly to the junk man for whom the car had value as scrap. Regrettably, the price of labor rose as the price of scrap fell. Together, this caused the value of junked cars to fall, so that the junk man was no longer willing to pay much for these cars. This in turn reduced the incentive of the owner to bring it in to collect his bounty. To increasing numbers of auto owners, the solution was simple: When the car gives out, abandon it on the street. In 1970, over 70,000 autos were abandoned on New York City streets in this fashion. The normal recycling system had broken down. To start it going again, several officials have suggested that an extra charge be imposed on every new car sold. When the owner delivers the car to the junk man, this deposit would be refunded. By use of such devices, economists hope to revitalize the recycling process not only for automobiles, but also for such things as cans and bottles and used crankcase oil from autos. At one time, all these products were recycled. This not only eased the drain on nature since it meant that fewer virgin materials had to be used, but it also reduced the amount of waste that had to be treated, burned, or dumped into the air, water, and land.

Who Will Pay

Assuming that effective steps are taken to limit environmental disruption, who will have to pay for this? Generally, it is fair to say that everyone will have to pay, at least something. However, it looks as if a disproportionate burden will fall on the lower-income groups.

The reasoning behind such an assertion is that if what we have said above has any validity, the proper solution for environmental disruption would be to require each consumer of air and water to bear the social costs that the use of this air and water gives rise to. Consequently, production costs for all goods requiring pollution control would increase. Where the demand for a product was inelastic, that is, where there was little alternative to choose from, almost the full cost would be passed on to the consumer. For example, an electric utility should without difficulty be able to pass on the full cost of its "cleaner" fuel to its customers and still sell almost as much

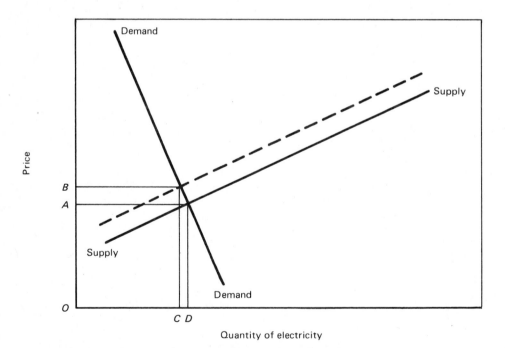

FIGURE 7.1 Supply schedule after pollution control for an *inelastic* product such as electricity. The consumer has little choice in shifting to another product; therefore, an electric company can pass the full cost of pollution control equipment onto the consumer and experience at most only a small loss in revenue.

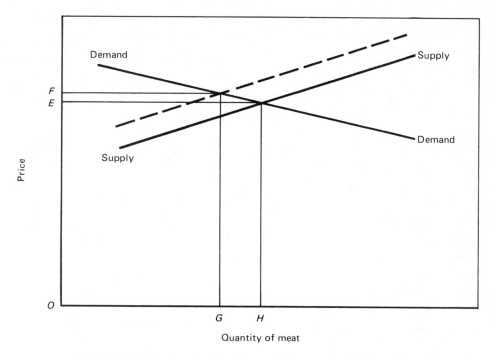

FIGURE 7.2 Supply schedule after pollution control for an *elastic* product such as meat. An individual meat packer could suffer considerable loss in revenue were he to include the cost of pollution control equipment in the price of meat. The consumer has the option to buy meat elsewhere or to change to fish.

power. Thus, in Figure 7.1, the price of electric power would rise from *OA* to *OB* and the quantity sold would fall only from *OD* to *OC*. Where the demand was elastic, that is, where an increase in price was more likely to cause the consumer to buy another product instead, the producer would be less likely to pass on his higher costs in the form of higher prices. Thus, a meat packer would be reluctant to pass on the costs of his new sewage equipment because enough of his customers might switch to fish if meat prices rose so that his total revenue would fall even though price per unit sold was higher.

In Figure 7.2, the price would normally rise from *OE* to *OF*, which is not much. To avoid the sharp falloff in sales volume, that is, from *OH* to *OG*, the meat packer might try to absorb some of the cost by offering his product at a price somewhere between *OE* and *OF*. However, even though it might appear at first that the consumer in this case would not have to pay for the entire cost of environmental control, the victory might only be a temporary one. If the meat packer could not raise his price to cover his higher costs, several meat packers might find themselves going broke. This would tend to reduce the supply of meat being offered in the market. At a given price, therefore, suppliers would offer less for sale. This would cause the industry supply curve to move to the left, and so meat prices might rise after all. Again, meat consumers would be forced to pay more because of the cost of minimizing pollution. Supply and demand work in the case of pollution too.

The introduction of pollution charges would have much the same effect as the introduction of a sales tax. Those who consumed the most would find a larger portion of their income going to fight environmental disruption, through the higher prices they paid, than those who spent a smaller proportion of their income on consumption and saved a larger portion. In other words, like most sales taxes, the environmental tax would probably be regressive; that is, it would fall disproportionately on the lower-income groups, though this effect might not be great. If, for some unforeseen reason, the goods the poor buy cause significantly less environmental disruption than the goods the rich consume, this regressive impact would be diminished. At present, however, there seems to be little evidence to indicate that there is any such correlation. Consequently, it must be assumed that one way or another the poor will bear a relatively high percentage of the burden.

To provide for more equity, some have suggested that greater use be made of the income tax to finance environmental control. Indeed, the federal government plans to spend about $2 billion a year toward the $10 billion in municipal sewage treatment plants that it is estimated will be needed by 1974. Since the bulk of federal funds are collected by means of the income tax, which is more progressive than a sales tax, it is inevitable that corporations and upper-income groups will have to bear a larger burden than would be the case if the whole cost were in the price of goods. Surprisingly, this does not make most economists as happy as it might appear they should be. First, a good portion of any increase in corporate income tax will also be passed on to the consumer by the corporation. Economists disagree among themselves as to how much of the tax is passed on, but almost all agree that some of it is. Second, economists worry that if the costs of cleaning up the environment are not directly charged to the party that causes the damage, then nothing will have been done to root out the basic cause of environmental disruption. The whole point of the exercise is to attach a price to air and water and to discourage the consumption and production of those products which devour inordinate amounts of air and water. If the penalty is not made to fit the crime, the crime will continue to be perpetuated, and the innocent "downstreamers" will be made to bear too much of the burden. To the economist, this is a sign of a misallocation of resources.

This conflict — making pollution costly for polluters versus cleaning it up through government money and hence taxation — is real, but it should be kept in perspective. Human waste and the runoff from storms, for example, are simply unavoidable and have to be cleaned up by some form of government treatment, normally financed by taxation. Essentially, the issue concerns industrial pollution. Economists tend to favor making pollution costly rather than cleaning it up with tax money, even though the added cost of goods from this solution might fall, like sales taxes, a little more heavily on the poor.

International Aspects of the Problem

As serious as environmental disruption is in our country, it often seems just as bad, if not worse, elsewhere. The Japanese seem to have the most severe case of environmental disruption in the world. Gather up one-half of the American population and squeeze it into the state of Maryland and you can imagine what the Japanese have to deal with. Moreover, a rampant rate of growth that has been averaging 12-15 percent a year generates such rapid change that no one is prepared for the emergencies that stem from such growth. But as we saw, environmental disruption is not limited to capitalist countries. The Russians have their difficulties, as do the countries of the Third World.

In almost all instances in the United States, as well as overseas, a good portion of the trouble arises from the inability to include the social costs of production along with the private costs. An additional factor for many developing countries is that even where environmental costs can be identified, there is a reluctance to charge for them. This was particularly evident in Japan in the 1950's and 1960's. In order to break into foreign markets, the Japanese decided that they would sell their products as cheaply as they could. This meant that costs would have to be held down as much as possible. One way to do this was to push off the costs of environmental disruption onto the public as a whole. Since this is what normally happens with environmental disruption, it was not hard to do. With time, however, the environmental disruption in Japan has become so serious that it is now no longer possible to avoid the burdens. As health conditions have deteriorated, demands for action have mounted dramatically. To avoid the costs that some manufacturers fear will fall due, many Japanese companies are now seeking to locate elsewhere, mainly in Southeast Asia. For the time being, countries like Indonesia, Taiwan, and Korea continue to be lenient about environmental quality since they too want more production.

Americans who criticize such easygoing attitudes toward environmental disruption risk being called hypocrites because we have been tolerant so long of similar conditions in our own country. Yet some international standards probably must be set if we are to maintain any kind of environmental quality anywhere. To the extent that environmental standards are lower in Japan than they are in the United States, the Japanese have an unfair competitive advantage. Similarly, to the extent that American steel producers have lower standards than German producers, we have an unfair advantage. In the second instance, the Germans are likely to resist any further efforts to clean up their environment until the Americans do and, in the first instance, the Americans are likely to resist until the Japanese do. There is a sort of Gresham's law at work here whereby the poor quality standards drive out the higher standards. The developing countries may view efforts at international standard-setting as a device to make them noncompetitive and to hold back their efforts at industrialization. But whether the developing countries like it or not, environmental disruption is a matter of international concern. As long as the Russians, French, and English are permitted to fly their SST's, the pressure for American manufacturers to resume their production will increase. There may have to be an international agreement to bring to a halt all manufacture of the SST, unless it can be shown that it will have no adverse effect on the environment. If need be, such questions may require the subordination of material gains and national sovereignty to international standards of environmental quality.

Conclusion

Economic theory has a major contribution to make toward improving the quality of the environment. Much of the trouble in the past has stemmed from an inadequate understanding of the economic forces at work. At the same time, some economists go to the other extreme and insist that economics alone is the answer. Sometimes it is hard for a believing economist to understand that man does not live by economic theory alone. Education, moral pressure, and legislation are needed as supplements. Hopefully, a proper balance of all such measures will move us closer to the environmental quality we all seek.

SUGGESTIONS FOR FURTHER READING

Commoner, Barry. *The Closing Circle*. New York: Alfred A. Knopf, 1971. An excellent statement of the effect of technological growth on the environment.

Council on Environmental Quality. *Annual Reports*. Washington, D.C.: U.S. Government Printing Office, 1970, 1971, 1972. A comprehensive survey of pollution and the progress or lack of it in dealing with pollution control.

Dolan, Edwin G. *Tanstaafl*: The Economic Strategy for Environmental Crisis*. New York: Holt, Rinehart and Winston, 1971. An analysis of pollution by someone who favors a minimum of government interference in coping with the problem. If designed properly, Dolan argues, private enterprise alone can eliminate pollution.

Goldman, Marshall I. *Ecology and Economics: Controlling Pollution in the '70's*. Englewood Cliffs, N.J.: Prentice-Hall, 1972. An economic analysis with selected case studies of how the problem of pollution arises and how it can be solved. There is also a discussion of the costs of environmental control. *The Spoils of Progress: Environmental Pollution in the Soviet Union*. Cambridge, Mass.: The M.I.T. Press, 1972. Although socialist theory preaches that pollution can't happen there, the Soviet Union is afflicted in the same way that other developed noncommunist countries are. This study analyzes the reasons for this and what can be done about it.

Kneese, Allen and Bower, Blair. *Managing Water Quality: Economics, Technology, Institutions*. Baltimore: The Johns Hopkins Press, 1968. A revised version of the classical study of the interrelationship between economic theory and pollution.

Mishan, Ezra J. *The Costs of Economic Growth*. New York: Frederick A. Praeger, 1967. One of the first formal calls for zero economic growth.

Tsuru, Shigeto. *Proceedings of the International Symposium on Environmental Disruption: A Challenge to Social Scientists*. Tokyo: Asahi Evening News, 1970. One of the first gatherings of social scientists concerned with pollution around the world. This is a report on their papers and discussions.

Ward, Barbara and Dubos, Rene. *Only One Earth: The Care and Maintenance of a Small Planet*. New York: W.W. Norton and Company, 1972. A social scientist combines with a biologist to examine how the pursuit of economic development has come to endanger the life of the planet and whether or not the world can find happiness with a lower rate of growth and a more rational relationship with the environment.

8 Housing and Renewal

A peculiar kind of "crisis" hovers over the U.S. housing market in the 1970's. Especially after back-to-back record years of new housing production in 1971 and 1972, there is not, strictly speaking, a housing shortage. What is more, the 1970 census showed that Americans on the average were better housed than ever before. The crisis is that a significant, though minority, segment of the population is having an extremely difficult time finding decent housing at a price it can afford — evidence of a partial failure of the market system, in this special area, to meet a social need. We would probably all agree that a family with a low income should not expect to own two cars or a color television set; but we all suffer when we see pictures of broken-down rural shacks that lack even rudimentary plumbing or of New York slum apartments with broken windows and broken furnaces to boot. We feel that way because from the beginning of time shelter has been a basic human need.

Government efforts to do something about the problem have met with only indifferent success and have been surrounded by a good deal of scandal besides as get-rich-quick operators and a few corrupt government officials take advantage of well-meant federal programs. The private market, with no guidance from the government, has also done something about it, in the form of an amazing boom in relatively cheap mobile homes, which are the only homes many families can afford. But, varying with the locality, the problem remains: a gap between the price of a decent house or apartment and the ability of those with low incomes to "buy" it.

Unlike other consumer goods, a house is an investment. It is not consumed directly like food, or even in a few years, like clothing. This makes the market for housing very different — involving such things as mortgage financing for both houses and apartments — even though housing is just as basic a need as food and clothing.

Demand for Housing

Individual demand for houses responds both to the price of housing and to what personal income and assets are available for such major purchases. For instance, a head of household might want to buy a $100,000 mansion, but if he has only $2,000 in assets and his annual income is only $10,000, he obviously will not be able to buy it on these resources. The market demand for houses, that is, the total number of housing units demanded at any one time, is determined mainly by the size and the age distribution of the population. It makes a great deal of difference whether or not there is an increase in the number of persons in the 20 – 35-year-old age bracket. For this is the age group in which most people are marrying and forming new families, and this in turn can create an increased demand for housing. Sometimes it is simply a matter of replacement. Each year a certain number of houses become vacant when their occupants die or move. However, such vacancies do not necessarily occur in areas where the newly formed families work or care to live. Thousands of farmhouses in rural America are abandoned annually; yet young people continue to flock to the cities and suburbs. Because of a 35-percent rise in the number of marriages over the 1960's the pressure on housing has increased considerably in the 1970's. If changes in family unit formation do not match changes in housing construction, shortages will continue. Marriages declined by 9 percent between 1950 and 1960 but increased by 35 percent between 1960 and 1968. On the other hand, between 1960 and 1965 housing starts (that is, beginning of new construction) increased by 18 percent, while between 1965 and 1970 they decreased by about 25 percent.[1]

Besides the number of marriages taking place, family size and family living patterns also determine demand. The greater the size of the average household in relation to the total population, the fewer the number of dwelling units that will be needed. In other words, larger, multigenerational families can and do tend to live under more crowded conditions. In Italy, for example, the housing problem has always been relatively less acute than it is in the United States because there three or four generations often live in the same unit, so that the formation of a new family does not always require extra housing units.

Migration and Occupational Patterns. The United States is known for the mobility of its population. Partly as a result of this, the "extended family," or family of more than two generations, is quite rare. In the United States, the "nuclear family," consisting of a father, mother, and children in one household, is the norm. Only occasionally are members of other generations included in the family unit. In addition, over the past century even the size of the nuclear family has decreased.[2] This still does not fully explain why, on the average, the United States family fares well in terms of the number of people per room, with 1.6 rooms per person, while Italy fares poorly, with 1.0 rooms per person.[3]

In the short run, migration plays an important role in the U.S. housing market. Internal migration is characteristic of our technological society. Given that techniques

[1] *Wall Street Journal,* February 18, 1970; *United States Statistical Abstract* 1969 and 1970.
[2] In 1970, the median size of the American household was 5.43, in 1890, 4.48, and in 1968, 3.23. See *Historical Statistics of the United States,* 1960, and *United States Statistical Abstract* 1969.
[3] The *United States Statistical Abstract* 1969 shows a median of 4.9 rooms per housing unit and a median of 3.0 persons per housing unit. For Italy, see *Compendio Statistico Italiano,* 1969.

of production are constantly changing, jobs, too, are continually being created and destroyed, thus forcing people to move about in search of new employment. An area where jobs are on the increase is likely to face a housing shortage; eventually new housing is added. In areas losing jobs, a reduction of housing occurs partly because few new homes are built but also because old housing is allowed to deteriorate. In recent years, many urbanites have migrated to the suburbs because most new industries have located there. But the jobs and income have also created a huge demand for more housing in the suburbs.

Elasticities. In general, the relationship between demand for housing and price or income alterations is fairly high. Richard Muth claims that "the elasticities of new construction with respect to price and income are about 5.5. . . ."[4] By "elasticities" he means the degree by which a percentage change in one variable (in this case, prices or income) induces a percentage change in another variable (that is, housing construction). Elasticities measure the weight or strength of relationships among variables. According to Muth, a change in either the price of housing or in income will greatly affect the rate of new housing construction.

Demand elasticity depends on the availability of substitutes. The fewer alternatives there are available to the purchaser — in other words, the narrower the purchaser's choice — the more inelastic his demand for a good will be. Demand for housing is more elastic with respect to income and price at high and/or price levels than it is at low levels. This is so because the demand for housing is connected with demands for other goods or services. An example is the demand for transportation. A wealthy person has the option of either living close to the urban core in a very expensive house or living in the suburbs, whereas someone of modest income may find himself forced to live in a certain type of housing in a particular location. Employment opportunities play a similar role. Employment and unemployment exert an influence on housing above and beyond the obvious fact that employment is necessary for income. People who are employed in industries which are subject to wide fluctuations of employment cannot help but be affected in their demand for housing. Greater security in employment generates a stronger demand and renders the price less important. Someone who is fairly certain of receiving an income for the foreseeable future, regardless of his present income or the price of a particular house, is more likely to buy than is someone whose job is in jeopardy.

Single-Unit and Multiunit Housing. Variation in income also determines *what kind* of housing someone has, for example, rental housing as opposed to owner-occupied housing. But cultural differences can also affect the type of housing desired. Most people in the United States live in single-family homes, while in Europe most people live in multidwelling housing. Immigrants to this country had a wealth of land at their disposal, and the vast expenses affected not only the pattern of mobility that developed in America but each individual's feelings about privacy and private possessions as well. In 1890, 36.9 percent of all families in the United States lived in owner-occupied dwellings, and by 1960, this figure had risen to 61 percent. In Europe, cities are much older; centuries ago the inhabitants walled themselves in for

---

[4]Richard D. Muth, "The Demand for Non-Farm Housing," in Alfred N. Page and Warren R. Seyfried, *Urban Analysis* (Glenview, Ill.: Scott, Foresman & Company, 1970), pp. 104-105.

safety and thereafter grew accustomed to living in crowded quarters. Only the very rich could afford to build single-unit urban dwellings. Thus, in Europe, multiunit structures became the standard. In the United States, most housing typically consists of only one to four units.

Ordinarily, multiunit housing in this country is not owned by those who occupy it. To be sure, over the last decade condominiums have made big inroads in the United States. (A condominium is that type of housing ownership in which a multidwelling building is occupied by several owners; absentee ownership is the exception rather than the rule.) Though of long standing in Europe, in the United States the condominium is still an exception, while the rule for multidwelling buildings is the absentee landlord.[5] This is one reason why slums develop more rapidly here. The self-interest of an owner-tenant differs markedly from that of the absentee owner.

The difference between U.S. and European patterns is partly due to variations in income or employment. Moreover, the urbanization of Europe started earlier and took longer. There, the eventual switch within the urban area was from rental in a multidwelling building to ownership in a condominium. Early emigrants to the United States wanted to farm their own land, which they had not been able to do at home. Later, they wanted to buy their "own homes," reflecting still a peasant mentality in which security is associated with land ownership.

Financing and Income. The type of housing an individual enjoys is determined not only by his present income but also by what his income is expected to be over a lifetime. Variation in income over a short period is less important than the trend of income over a long period of time. Among other things, it is much more difficult for a person with a variable income to obtain financing than it is for a person with a more predictable income. We see evidence of this in the ghettos. The ghetto dweller frequently has periods of unemployment. This is anticipated by the banks, which to some degree discriminate against this type of borrower because of his short-term (monthly) variation in income, regardless of his average long-term (yearly) income.

Tax laws in this country have created peculiarities in the demand for housing. Income from owner-occupied homes that could be imputed in the form of rent paid to the owner is not taxed. That is, if a man owns a $30,000 home and occupies it, he doesn't pay himself rent, yet he receives (imputed) income that is untaxed. For example, Mr. X owns a home which he does not occupy and for which he receives $3,000 a year in rent from a tenant. Mr. Y owns a home similar to Mr. X's, but he occupies it. With equal expenses on upkeep, Mr. X has to report his "explicit" $3,000 income and pay, let us say, $1,000 in income tax. Mr. Y does not pay this tax; this way he is ahead by the amount of the tax.

A home owner generally fares better than a tenant because (1) the net cost of his housing is usually smaller and (2) there is an accumulation of net assets. Table 8.1 compares the costs of (A) renting an apartment in a multidwelling building of old vintage and (B) owning and occupying one unit of a two-family home of about the same size and vintage in an average-sized city in the United States. Data in both columns pertain to white-collar professionals with similar incomes and expenditure patterns.

---

[5]Yet, by 1971, 40 percent of all new construction in Boston was of the condominium type. Perhaps a new trend is developing.

TABLE 8.1   **Housing Budget for Rented (A) and Owner-Occupied (B) Homes, 1972.**

	Monthly Costs	
	B	A
Rent paid	-	$225.00
Mortgage and Interest	$210.00	-
Heating	48.00	-
Water	3.00	-
Gas and Electricity	22.00	22.00
Rental from Second Home	175.00 CR	-
Insurance	20.00	-
Credit Tax	80.00 CR	-
Income Foregone on Money Down	120.00	-
Net Monthly Cost	$168.00	$247.00

From the breakdown it would appear that the owner-landlord pays about one-third less for housing than does his apartment-dwelling counterpart. It is obvious that there are strong incentives for home ownership. In addition to lower rent, the owner of a dwelling has net assets accumulating; that is, he accumulates net equity in the property. Whereas the tenant cannot, the owner of a house can deduct local property taxes and several other kinds of expenses from his income. Even the portion of property tax attributable to the income earned from a second unit of an owner-occupied two-family house is deductible. No wonder that in the United States three-fourths of the population live in their own houses.

From a social point of view, land would perhaps be more efficiently utilized if more housing were built in multiple units for the upper- and middle-income groups as well as for the lower-income groups.

Optimal Allocation of Housing

There is a dichotomy between what constitutes the optimal allocation of housing resources from the social point of view and what optimal allocation seems to be from the private point of view. As in any other industry, higher profits for the real estate industry should insure a larger supply of housing. Producers will put on the market (construct) the number of houses at the price that will maximize their profits. Supply is an increasing function of price in a "perfectly competitive market." One would suppose that at high prices, more new housing would be put on the market. In the long run, a "perfect market" adds enough new units so that the discrepancy between the cost and price of housing should be minimal. But a perfectly competitive market is an "ideal" type of situation. In such a market, there are many sellers and many buyers for a homogeneous product. Entry into the specific field is easy, and both sellers and buyers have full knowledge of the characteristics of the product, its price and what can be expected of it. But it is not always true that we have perfect markets; quite to the contrary, they are the exception.

First, in the housing market there are few sellers and many buyers. In general, the limited number of sellers creates a noncompetitive market. Second, housing is not a "fungible" (interchangeable) good; no two sites of land are exactly alike in terms of their particular characteristics, price, or location, and they are completely immobile; two housing situations are not like two sets of dishes or pairs of shoes or cars. Third, land available in the core city is limited. Typically, the urban core has been demanded increasingly for other uses (highways, for instance), with the result that housing units have been destroyed and not replaced. Low-income individuals displaced in this process are driven away from the core to areas less accessible to jobs. Not only do they have to search for alternate housing, but they may have to pay more for it as well.

Such a move does not often benefit the urban poor, even indirectly. When they are displaced, it is not the tenants who reap the capital gains resulting from the growing alternative use for land. It is the landowners who get that. This occurs because of market imperfections, such as control by a few of most of the multi-dwelling buildings. In general, the housing market is characterized by an oligopoly (that is, few sellers) and landlords who operate in collusion with each other to fix rents. The number of "service units" (housing units) is large, but the number of sell-ers (landlords) is small.

It is thus more economical for those who can afford it either to buy or to build a single (or two-family) house. However, this costs society more. This paradox is simi-lar to the paradox presented by the individual's need for private cars versus society's urgent need for mass transportation.[6] More land has to be used, thus adding to urban sprawl; more services of all kinds (sewer and water pipes, electric wires) are required and it becomes increasingly difficult to get to and from work. From a social point of view, it would be far more reasonable to have more multidwelling buildings than single-unit houses.

Home Financing

But there is a special problem connected with the financing of housing that relates mainly to government laws and regulations going back many years and to the fluc-tuations in current government policy on interest rates and the general availability of credit. Because of tax and other provisions of the legislation that created them, savings banks and savings and loan associations find it advantageous to invest mainly in mortgages. But they can invest only so much as their savings inflow permits. At times when market interest rates are much higher than the thrift institutions can safely pay to savers, many people take their money out of these institutions and in-stead buy government or other securities that yield a higher rate of interest. The result is that the savings institutions have far less to lend, and, as occurred in 1966 and 1969, new housing construction falls steeply. The drop is not because of any lack of underlying demand for housing or even a lack of income on the part of home buyers, but simply because of a lack of available mortgage financing. One possible solution to the problem is the "variable rate" mortgage, used by some other coun-tries and just starting to be used in the United States. The borrower's interest rate would rise and fall according to some acceptable index of market rates, meaning that the interest income of the savings institutions would rise when market rates rose. This would enable them to pay more to savers and thus to keep the flow of new mortgage loans going.

Other solutions involve ending the distinction between ordinary banks and the

[6]See Chapter 9, "Mass Transportation."

savings institutions. All these ideas are aimed at doing away with the "feast or famine" nature of the housing construction industry, which is based on the sudden plenitude or scarcity of mortgage funds. But no solution can, or is intended to, insulate the ordinary mortgage borrower from higher interest rates when the condition of the economy as a whole produces an upward swing of rates in the market for bonds and other debt instruments.

Government's Role in Financing Houses. Over the years the federal government has entered the housing business in a big way. Government aid takes four principal forms:

1. *Mortgage insurance.* The Federal Housing Administration (beginning in the 1930's) and the Veterans Administration (beginning after World War II) have offered government insurance to lenders of qualified loans, which were made almost entirely to middle- and upper-income borrowers until recently. This has produced a slightly lower interest rate for the qualified borrowers and, in general, has undoubtedly helped foster the huge expansion of housing construction which started in the late 1940's and which has continued, with interruptions, ever since. However, these programs now cover only about one-fifth of the new housing, and it is undisputed that their main effect has been to encourage the boom in suburban housing. To say that is not to disparage the programs; after all, millions of Americans find suburban living satisfactory.
2. *Secondary markets for mortgages.* The Federal National Mortgage Association — now privately owned but still a creation of the government — has increasingly been able to ease the severe pinches in mortgage loan availability in times of credit "crunch." It sells its own notes and bonds in the money market, with what amounts to a government guarantee, and then uses the money to buy older mortgages from mortgage lenders so that they will have funds to make new mortgage loans. Fannie Mae, as it is called, greatly helped in preventing an outright collapse of housing construction during the money squeeze of 1969 – 70.
3. *The Federal Home Loan Bank System.* The Federal Home Loan Banks provide a reserve "line of credit" to savings and loan associations, the most important source of mortgage credit. Again, their loans have helped moderate the effects of a general shortage of credit on mortgage money. Similar devices, which we need not elaborate here in detail, include the Government National Mortgage Association (Ginnie Mae) and the Federal Home Loan Mortgage Corporation, a part of the Home Loan Bank System. All are intended to alleviate the special squeeze on housing that occurs when money is "tight" and interest rates high.
4. *Outright subsidy.* The first three items are aimed essentially at keeping housing construction going, and their main direct help has been to families who could afford housing anyway. The most serious problems involve subsidies.

"Public housing" started in the late 1930's and continues to this day. Local governments build and own the projects, but the projects are subsidized in various ways by Washington to permit a charge of below-market rents to low-income tenants, who take what is in effect a "means test" to qualify. The tragedy and paradox of these projects is that there remains a long waiting list for public housing in many cities, while at the same time many of the projects have turned into miniature slums of their own. Some have become almost totally racially segregated — all black. The story is by no means one of total failure; public housing has provided accommodation for many families in desperate circumstances. But hardly anyone would now argue that public housing has met the goal of a "decent living environment" for all Americans. It has turned out that housing alone is far from the whole social problem of the nation's poor, and that better housing does not, in itself, change attitudes toward a range of matters from marriage to cleanliness. The values of the poor are not here at issue; but the serious deterioration of many urban public housing projects has created great skepticism concerning the value of this approach, and the number of new units started has remained small for many years.

Given the quasi-failure of public housing combined with the "mismatch" between housing demand and housing supply (causing serious difficulties for those with low incomes), the government, since the early 1960's, has tried a variety of other approaches. One involves home ownership for the poor, with a subsidized mortgage interest rate. Another involves rental apartments, with the rent kept low by a subsidized mortgage for the builder or owner of the apartment building. Another involves various subsidized means of "rehabilitating" run-down dwellings (mainly in cities) that landlords were ready to abandon. A special program of subsidies for housing for the elderly and another for rural housing also exist.

Each one of these means has had some success. Whatever else government aid has done, it has increased the overall level of housing construction and hence the nation's total supply of housing. By 1971, nearly one-fourth of all new starts, counting single-family homes and apartments together, were subsidized under one or another of these programs. Many families undoubtedly occupy better housing today as a result of these programs than they would be able to afford otherwise.

But the problems have been mounting. In the 1970's, more and more of the subsidized mortgages were in default. The problem began, ironically, when the suburban-oriented Federal Housing Administration was ordered to move into the central cities with its regular mortgage insurance program (containing no other subsidy). Clever real estate men, landlords, and speculators spotted a get-rich-quick scheme — in effect cheating both the government and the poor — and thousands of mortgages went into default. The eventual mortgage default rate on the subsidized projects will not be known for years, but the early results were not heartening.

Plaguing the entire issue, apart from finance, is the problem of the *location* of government-aided housing. In brief, many suburbs have resisted new government-aided projects because they would bring lower-income people, including black people, into the community. The resistance is not just racial or social, though that too is an important element; each new housing project also means that more schools and sewers and other locally financed services will be needed, and this in turn requires higher local property taxes.

Nonetheless, despite many failures, there remains a strong desire in much of the society and in the national government to use government money and power to make housing conditions better for the poor and near-poor. The *financing* part of the problem is now, perhaps, the least important in the sense that the government has shown itself willing to spend large sums. Subsidies already contracted for involve expenditures of more than $20 billion for the period up to 1980. The social and cultural problem remains, and is much harder to solve.

Labor Input in the Construction Industry

In addition to financing, labor is a major factor on the supply side. In general, the demand for a factor of production — in this case, labor — is a function of the demand for that good or service requiring it — in this case, housing. But as we have noted, the demand for middle-income housing is quite inelastic, or unresponsive to small variations in prices (rents). Therefore, the demand for housing doesn't affect the demand for labor directly.

The supply of housing is mainly a function of the elasticity of funds for construction; therefore, the demand for construction labor is principally a function of the availability of funds for construction. Another constraint is that the labor supply for the construction industry is artificially restricted by labor union requirements and not significantly expanded when construction activity peaks. The shift of construction workers into nonresidential construction rather than housing construction at cycle peaks further limits the supply of housing construction workers. Furthermore, unions use various gimmicks to create scarcity. For example, they demand long apprenticeship periods and/or fix an exorbitant initiation fee. Also, it seems that many of these unions have been successful in keeping minorities out of the trade. This makes housing construction more expensive, and since this sector is labor-intensive, the labor share of the total cost is large.

The Role of Advanced Technology

The cost of construction can be also affected by technological change. For instance, in U.S. agriculture, cost per bushel of wheat has decreased over the last century even though the cost of both land and labor have increased. The cost of land and labor for urban housing has similarly increased. Through land grants and other kinds of subsidies, technology was both developed and applied on the farm. Modern methods of building urban housing have also been developed but they have not yet been widely applied. But in housing today, as in agriculture in the last century, technological change can shift the supply schedule. In Figure 8.1, before the introduction of new technology, the supply curve is S_1; with technological change, it increases (that is, it shifts to the right) to S_2. Depending on demand, the following can happen at any point on S_2: (a) prices remain unchanged at P_1 with increased quantity, Q_2; (b) quantity remains at Q_1; thus we have a lower price, P_2; or (c) prices shift to an intermediate level, P_3, where in a competitive market both prices decrease and quantity increases. This actually happened in agriculture in the United States.

The same thing could happen in the housing market with the introduction of new technology and more competition. But for this to happen, the government would have to subsidize and encourage experimentation. At present, there is little incentive for the individual private contractor to spend the funds necessary to achieve major breakthroughs when these will primarily benefit the industry or society rather than his own firm. Theoretically, it can be expected that once the profit potential of the new technology is proven, accelerated output at lower prices will follow. In practice, one may expect other difficulties. Housing is different from cars, soup, or most other consumer goods in that it must be consumed on the spot, where it is built.

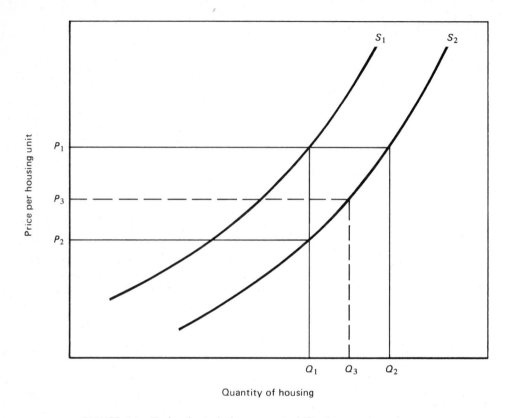

FIGURE 8.1 Technological change as it shifts the supply and cost of housing: S_1, relationship between change in price per unit and change in the number of housing units supplied; S_2, new quantities of housing available at the same prices.

Mobile Homes. One development is the "mobile home," or house trailer. It is mobile only in the sense that it is put on wheels to be shipped out to wherever it is going to go in the country. Then the wheels are taken off, the unit is attached to sewer and water mains, and there is a new "home." These mobile home units are becoming more and more luxurious and their prices cover a broad range. Although the trailer home may solve the problem of shelter, it is not an ideal substitute for a stationary home because aesthetically it is an eyesore. The trailer camp is not a village, not a city, not suburbia. The atmosphere is temporary; people may live in mobile homes for many years, but most of them also live in the hope of changing location. Generally, trailer homes do not solve the housing problem. This is only a stopgap, and a fragile, desolate-appearing one at that.

Module Units. A more exciting innovation in the housing industry is the mass production of prefabricated module units. Whole rooms are preconstructed and shipped out. These units can be applied to permanent structures as well as to temporary ones. The big publicity breakthrough for prefab construction was achieved at the Canadian World's Fair, "EXPO," in 1967. The now famous "Habitat" is innovative because it lowers construction costs. Moreover, the units do not have to be "matchbox-type" houses; these units would not be as drab as the mass-produced houses of the past. The knowledge of this technology has existed for decades, but it has been only sparingly applied. We still build houses by a one-brick-at-a-time method. (The building codes do not allow for innovation. Some laws specify structural requirements for housing that are no longer valid. For example, in Cambridge, Massachusetts, the risers in every stairway must be precisely 18 inches apart. This may have been fine for wooden frame houses in the eighteenth or nineteenth century, but it is hardly necessary with new construction materials and methods.)

Institutional Constraints on the Housing Market

Legislation regulating construction has been designed for existing methods and building materials. But laws have not kept up with innovations in construction technology. There are incentives for the construction industry to maintain high housing costs in order to keep high earnings. For example, construction workers are afraid to be displaced by automated prefabricated techniques. Therefore, they attempt to preserve the status quo.

The interests of the construction industry do not necessarily correspond with the interests of society as a whole. Responsible government officials, businessmen, and union leaders have repeatedly insisted that the housing shortage problem can easily be solved by applying twentieth-century technology. Unfortunately, for decades their leadership has been ineffective. Instead, the government has interfered only to correct some inequities in the allocation of the existing housing stock rather than for the purpose of rapidly incrementing the stock. This was accomplished through rent-control legislation and subsidies.

Price Controls and Rationing of Scarce Goods. The history of rent control legislation is connected with general attempts to prevent runaway inflation during World War II. Rent controls were designed as price ceilings. But usually when price ceilings are introduced, some system of rationing accompanies them. This has not been the case with housing and accounts for the difficulties in administrating rent control.

During World War II, the Office of Price Administration (OPA) set price ceilings and ordered the rationing of certain consumer goods such as meat, butter, and sugar. In Figure 8.2 we can see that during wartime the supply of consumer goods decreased at *all* prices because (a) an increased fraction of resources was directed toward the war effort and (b) some of the existing supply was effectively legislated out of the consumer sector by the army's needs. For example, the supply of clothing diminished (shifted leftward) because many of the nation's textile firms had large war contracts that took priority. They were unable to supply the civilian market, no matter how profitable it might have been, because they had a priority commitment to the government. Consumer use of such materials as gasoline, copper, and rubber was strictly limited by the government. In the case of a price-controlled consumer good, the government often set a price ceiling based on the reduced quantity supplied (that is, at P_1 in Figure 8.2). This resulted in some people being able to obtain consumer goods, others not, on a "first come, first served" basis. Under this kind of system, everyone is ready to pay the (ceiling) price set by the government, but there is not enough for everyone to buy.

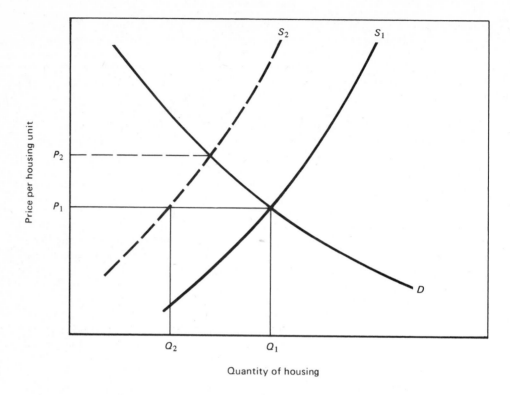

FIGURE 8.2   Price controls.

Indeed, the demand exceeds the supply by $Q_1 - Q_2$. For example, before price ceilings were introduced, there were on the U.S. market a million pounds of sugar. This was selling at 5¢ per pound. Consumers were buying this million pounds every week. When the war started, the government used sugar from this market; therefore only 500,000 pounds of sugar per week were available for consumers. That is, the same number of people were competing for only half the amount of sugar. Without an imposed ceiling, the price might have doubled. Price ceilings by themselves avoid discrimination against the poor, but they still discriminate against the people who cannot stand in queues — usually older, incapacitated, or slower people. It also encourages the development of black markets; that is, some people buy larger quantities than they need and then resell them under the counter at above-ceiling prices. Without ceilings, because of the shrinkage of supply (shift of supply curve from S_1 to S_2), prices would increase to P_2. With ceilings, prices remain the same (P_1), but the quantity diminishes to Q_2.

Black markets are prevented by the enforcement of rationing. During wartime, when the market supply cannot meet all the existing demand at ceiling prices, rationing is introduced to avoid inequities. When the price ceiling (P_1) is equated to the preceiling price (P_1), and the quantities received by each individual are restricted (Q_2), everyone receives an equal quantity of sugar but less than he is willing to buy. In other words, the comfort of everyone is diminished to a certain extent.

Rent Control and Rationing of Houses. On the other hand, rent control has provided only price ceilings *without any direct rationing* of the housing supply. "First come, first served" has been the war means of rationing the stock of housing. This worked pretty well during the war when families were forming at a very reduced rate (total demand declined) and not much new housing was started. In some places, however, such as New York, rent controls have been retained to this day. Recently, some metropolitan areas have been considering the reintroduction of rent controls. In Massachusetts, some townships enacted such a law in 1970. These laws have been introduced because of acute housing shortages in metropolitan areas, not because rent control worked so well in New York.

Rent control discriminates against the tenants who live in nonrent-controlled apartments in favor of those living in rent-controlled buildings. This discrimination occurs because only some apartment houses are under rent control while others are not. This can happen when ceilings are imposed only on a limited number of houses within a city or on a restricted number of cities within the same area. Without rationing, there is an excess demand for rent-controlled housing. In New York, rent control is applied to old housing (houses built before World War II). Rental prices are fixed; increases are allowed only under certain specified circumstances related to improvements in the property and not to rising prices generally. An exception is made when people move out: a 15 percent rise is then permitted.[7]

Partial rent control causes reduced mobility between cities because the person renting a controlled unit will not be able to obtain a new uncontrolled rental unit at a comparable price if he moves elsewhere. If people are going to move to another neighborhood, they will have to pay a higher price. Therefore, they are not likely to do so. People may willingly forego economic opportunities for the sake of inexpensive housing. An extreme case happened a few years back in southern France. In one provincial town, most of the people were employed in mining. When the mines closed down, almost everybody was out of work. The French government encouraged those people to move to some other towns not far away where many job openings were available. But nobody moved! This was probably due in part to cultural inertia. But economic incentives were minimized too. Most of the people were living in rent-controlled multiple-apartment buildings for rents that amounted merely to token payments, because ceilings for rents had not changed in 150 years. Therefore, a transfer to a place with a job would have entailed much higher rent payments.

While ceilings are not that unreasonable in New York, there is still a strong incentive to stay put. For people with fixed incomes and insecure jobs, having a roof over their heads is the predominant consideration. But often rent controls induce the landlord to cut down on services, which he can do and still remain competitive. When a price ceiling is imposed, the suppliers tend to change the quality of output (services plus space).

---

[7]There are other exceptions: if the new tenant has paid rent for two successive months at the old rate, a rise is not allowed. This induces outgoing tenants to find new tenants and collude with them to fulfill the "two-month" rule. The new tenants can then occupy the apartment at the old rate, while the old tenants are compensated by the new tenants for this favorable arrangement. In June 1971, the New York State legislature modified rent control for New York City. Any apartment becoming vacant is now decontrolled. This, however, may induce landlords to harass tenants to move out.

The Housing Market as a "Natural" Monopoly

Although rent control has some ill effects on the housing market, at least it protects some families who are unable to afford noncontrolled buildings. As long as there is a large gap between supply and demand in housing, we are faced with a seller's market. We have already noted the monopolistic characteristics of this market. To combat these monopolistic practices, rent-control laws were implemented. But they are neither effective nor equitable. Rent control is more a palliative than a solution.

In the United States, whenever monopolistic practices in any sector are encouraged, attempts have also been made to mitigate or even to prevent monopolistic profits. The best examples are public utilities. These are "natural" monopolies in that it would be wasteful to have two gas, electric, or water companies serving the same location. Housing is also specialized as to locations and because of the shortage of land is, in a sense, a "natural" scarcity which can be exploited for monopolistic gain. Landlords are often in a position to charge "what the market will bear." In this case, rather than having rent control and thus discouraging the building of new houses, it would be advisable to treat the housing sector as a "public utility." This type of control can be more effective and equitable than rent ceilings are. "Equity" for landlords is assured by a nearly certain return on their investment. Here is a hy-

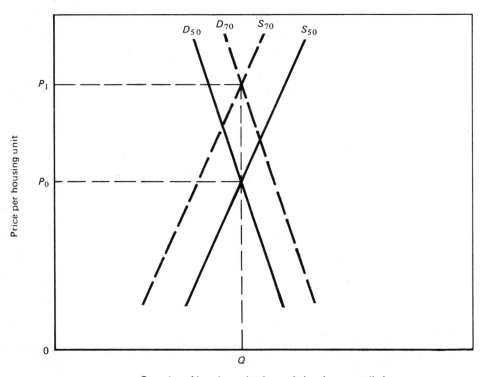

Quantity of housing units demanded and, or, supplied

FIGURE 8.3   Shift in demand for and supply of housing.

pothetical example. Suppose that supply and demand for middle-income housing in cities is quite inelastic, that is, that the response to price change is not significant. As illustrated in Figure 8.3, demand and supply in 1950 meet at a price of "P" and quantity Q of housing units. In most large cities, even without rent control, more units would have been abandoned than built by 1970, with supply moving to S_{70}. At the same time, suppose many people wanted to shift from ghetto or slum dwellings to superior housing because of an improvement in economic circumstances which moved demand to D_{70}. The result would have been that the quantity of housing units rented remained about the same but that the market clearing price rose to P_1.

Rate ceilings can be replaced with controls of the type that are applied to gas, electricity, and transportation, where prices are adjusted according to the return on capital. In most cases, prices are adjusted in such a way so as to render a maximum return of 6 percent on the firm's net capital. To apply this to the housing market, we would need to know the minimum return necessary to avoid discouraging investment in new housing; the provisions of a proper rent control law would naturally have to be relative to other investments. If other investments earned more than 6 percent, then so should housing.

The result would be that rents would not reflect monopolistic profits but only the competitive level of profit. Monopolistic profits are profits in excess of a "fair return" on investment — quantitatively, let us say, the return on a government bond. In other words, a monopolistic return is higher than that which would be earned in a competitive market, higher than that which is necessary to induce capital into an area. For example, if I am the only supplier of water to a town, then everyone has to buy water from me. I may well find that I can charge a price sufficient to give me a return higher than the minimum necessary to induce me to stay in this business. In fact, I could charge *any* price I wished! This is why we regulate public utilities such as water.

To regulate the housing market would require a cumbersome and large-scale administrative effort because of the variety in quality, location, and size of dwellings. Housing is very different from public utilities, where the product is fairly homogeneous. Because of this, until such time as we succeed in devising an efficient administrative mechanism, the public utility concept would be difficult to implement. In the short run, palliatives such as rent subsidies can be used.

Subsidies could be doled out from the public purse to families below a certain income level; this would make up for the gap between their ability to pay and the administered price set by the rent control law.

Public Housing.   The ultimate solution still lies in having the supply of housing increase sufficiently to match the rise in demand. In the United States, the government has interfered *directly* to meet the challenges in the housing sector for at least a quarter of a century. Housing additions brought about this way affect the price and quantity of housing units. This could be part of the solution, because it could shift the supply curve to the right. When aggregate supply shifts to the right, it intersects the demand curve at a lower price regardless of whether the market is monopolistic or not. The problem is that the public authorities involved in building this kind of housing have not always come up with a beautifully designed utopia.

The large public housing unit is often built according to a file cabinet design and of poor quality so that these housing units become large-scale high-rise slums in just a few years. The problem is not really one of costs, but primarily one of design and city planning. A house that is built as a potential slum (say, due to the repetitive use of battleship grey and paper-thin walls) may decrease in value quite rapidly. This may be why the public housing solution has thus far not enjoyed the success that we had hoped for it at one time.

Public housing differs in many ways from private housing. For one thing, financing is different. Public housing can take advantage of the credit offered by the governmental agency involved and avoid financing problems. Since slum dwellers cannot get credit, how else is anyone going to finance housing for them? The second difference, of course, is that public housing is typically built in large project-type units. Whether or not this mode of housing ought to be favored is another matter.

The scale on which public housing is built is doubtless too large; and units tend to be clustered. Projects more often than not consist of many drab apartment buildings without either individuality or charm. Clustering of public housing in effect establishes a new ghetto plagued by the same old problems. This is why it really should be scattered. A mix of high-, middle-, and low-income units on one block may be the solution. At least, this type of planning has proved quite successful in New York City urban renewal areas along Amsterdam Avenue. In short, the government can interfere in the total housing market.

There are precedents for the government assuming such a role. For many years the government has adjusted the prices of agricultural produce by buying and selling produce, by restricting the acreage cultivated, and by direct subsidies. When necessary, as during World War II, it built and operated factories. More recently, it has built the plants for the defense aircraft industries and then leased them. Considering the extreme shortage of housing units, government interference would hardly replace private efforts; it would merely supplement them. An unrealistic assumption still prevails in some government quarters. This is that entrepreneurs build all modes of housing — high-, middle-, and low-income types. In reality, the supply of low-income housing (in the urban centers) is brought about mainly through a filtering process involving depreciated middle-income housing. Government-built, low-income housing thus replaces no *private* low-income housing, because the source of the private low-income housing is former middle-income housing, now old and deteriorated.

Indeed, public housing has a direct connection with the private market. But the need for housing is so great that, in the short run, there is room for both private and public housing at low- and especially at middle-income levels. If eventually the public sector did displace the private sector, the government could step out of the market. But for the housing market of the 1970's the argument against "too much government" is irrelevant. Unfortunately, the tendency is for government to operate in a disconnected fashion. Low-income public housing is planned in a vacuum; private housing is not considered, nor are middle-income or high-income housing ever considered.[8]

Row after row of multistory, drab, brown-brick matchbox buildings create little incentive on the part of tenants to retard deterioration. It seems therefore that a major question is not whether we should build more housing but whether we should build

[8]See, for instance a statement in 1970 by the Housing Secretary, who praised the President when HUD's budget was cut to the bone. He implied that the cut in public housing expenditures would encourage private entrepreneurs to build more private low- and moderate-income housing. (John Herbers, "Budget for Housing Is Slashed 'to Bone' and He Is Glad of It," *New York Times*, February 3, 1970.)

different types of housing. Perhaps one problem is that we are afraid to provide the poor with more attractive housing because if they lived comfortably, how then would the poor know they were poor? But this kind of naiveté, or selfishness, ignores the cost to the whole society of constructing unattractive housing. When we create another public eyesore, we inflict it on everyone.

How can we make public housing an integral part of the community, and how could this solve some of the socioeconomic problems of the American city in the 1970's? For one thing, "housing integration" (that is, a mix of housing for various income levels) would induce social and racial integration more rapidly, more cheaply, and less disruptively than, for example, interurban school integration. Private enterprise by itself cannot accomplish this because it is in the market for profits, not to achieve social goals. The role of business enterprise is to optimize efficiency and maximize profits.

Social goals can and must be pursued by public agencies which are more concerned with optimizing social efficiency than they are with augmenting profits. That is, a mural on a public building, color, some fringes which beautify, combined with some differentiation as to types of housing, would increase the short-run cost but optimize the quality of life in that society. Public agencies should have a broader view! Unfortunately, public agencies, in the United States and elsewhere, act on short-run considerations, not unlike private enterprise, while cities are fast becoming unlivable monstrosities. As Ada Louise Huxtable puts it: "It is the rare developer who has a sense of style. . . . The barbarians are invading, bringing their squalid square footage with them."[9]

Slums and Urban Renewal.   Every state and some cities have housing development agencies whose purpose is to finance urban renewal. After World War II, an entire array of new housing laws was passed by Congress. Also a new Department of Housing and Urban Development (HUD) was created. But public policy concerning housing has failed dismally, and blight and slums are still very much with us. Some observers say that it mitigated poverty by adding new housing units through public projects. But in Detroit there are 3,000 abandoned buildings; and in Boston, the number of vacant buildings has nearly doubled in the last two years. The *New York Times* reports that in Philadelphia there are 24,000 vacant buildings, in Houston, 7,500, and, in New York, an estimated 114,000 apartments have been lost since 1965 because of abandonment.[10] True, more apartments have been built than have been abandoned over the same period. But again, very few private entrepreneurs have built low-income housing. The abandoned housing units have all been slum, low-income units which were once middle-income or even high-income apartments. Slums created by depreciation are often marginally profitable, low-income housing units. These units become slums from whatever they were before because of underinvestment, that is, through the owner's neglect. This happens because for tax reasons housing units are more profitable in their first years of life than they are later on. The owner may deduct a larger fraction of total depreciation for tax purposes when houses are new.

Suppose a housing unit costs $1 million and that the owner is allowed to consider the house "consumed" (this is what depreciation really means: an annual consump-

[9]"Tales of a Few Cities — Everywhere," *New York Times*, March 9, 1970.
[10]*New York Times*, February 9, 1970.

tion of capital) for tax purposes at a rate of 1/20 of cost every year. If the house lasts for more than 20 years, then an unduly large "consumption" allowance is given to owners of new houses. This procedure has been changed by the 1969 depreciation tax reform. Depreciation will be decelerated so that owners will be encouraged in future years to maintain their buildings. This might solve some of the abandonment problem for houses that are built *now*, but it will hardly affect houses that have already been completely depreciated.

A possible solution would be for public agencies to take over slum dwellings or abandoned buildings with the intention of renovating them and giving them adequate maintenance. This solution has been proposed repeatedly by housing specialists, but the funds are not available. In fact, even more public housing is now in danger of becoming (if it is not already) slums. For example, in Massachusetts, "nearly 5,000 public housing families . . . may be doomed to living in tax-supported slums because of a financial crisis which has put state-aided projects for the poor in four cities on the verge of bankruptcy."[11] And in New York the situation is so far out of hand that more than two years ago the state Senate asked the President to recognize New York City's slums as a disaster area. They claimed that over the next five years, 75,000 families would become homeless annually.[12]

Conclusions

There is not just "one crisis" in housing. As is true of other areas in modern urban society, all social problems are to a large extent interdependent. To achieve a solution, the public sector would have to allocate more funds and select an encompassing and well-coordinated plan for metropolitan areas. Planning has to be directed beyond mere "zoning laws" and further allocations for "urban renewal." It must encompass both additions to public housing and the rehabilitation of old structures, which to date has been very haphazard. It is generally accepted that such planning must take into consideration long-term demand (let us say, for more than a decade), which means forecasting and evaluating patterns of net family formation, net migration, and income distribution.

Planning for housing is like a balance sheet forecast where, at a particular moment, demand is a given constant to which supply must be adjusted. Therefore, the public sector's role is to change the shape of the supply curve. The public sector could bring about a change in the quantity, quality, and location of housing units supplied at given prices. It must first assess the potential supply from the private sector. The government could tell the private sector how, when, and where a house should be built. This is now done in a very frustrating manner through zoning laws, public housing regulations, rehabilitation schemes, and the financing power of the federal and local governments (FHA, VA). By concerted coordination of these public activities, the housing problem could be substantially reduced.

An all-out effort is needed to rehabilitate old structures and to replace the current practice of simply abandoning them or demolishing them or partially replacing them with even less sturdy and uglier project housing. Public housing programs should make a serious attempt to effect an income mix at all locations. Encouragement of

---

[11]*Boston Sunday Globe*, March 1, 1970.
[12]*New York Times*, February 18, 1970.

the condominium would work in the same direction. Especially for the core city, the condominium will allow a more rational use of land and do away with the evils of absentee landlord ownership. Slums would hardly develop under these conditions. Perhaps subsidization of condominiums could be attempted. If one looks abroad (at Italy, for example) one can see that some condominium structures have been standing for hundreds of years without ever becoming slums. The tender care of owner-occupants is evident.

A slum, a decaying neighborhood, is like a decaying human being; life can be pumped into it at high cost, but not restored completely. Accelerated death is inevitable. To prevent this, the housing sector has no alternative but to turn to the "preventive medicine" of preventive maintenance. Social costs will be incurred for these social goals; the public sector must play the "monitoring" role.

SUGGESTIONS FOR FURTHER READING

Bloomberg, L. N. "Rent Control and the Housing Shortage." *Land Economics,* Vol. *24* (May 1949), pp. 214 – 218.

Carr, J. L. "Rent Control and Housing Policy." *Economic Journal,* Vol. *64* (March 1954), pp. 25 – 38.

Downs, Anthony. *Urban Problems and Prospects,* pp. 115 – 165, 192 – 228. Chicago: Markham Publishing Company, 1970.

————"Housing the Urban Poor American." *American Economic Review,* September 1969, pp. 646 – 651.

Federal Reserve Bank of Chicago. "The Twelfth Year of Rent Control." *Business Conditions,* April 1953, pp. 3 – 5.

Netzer, Dick. *Economics and Urban Problems,* pp. 72 – 108. New York: Basic Books, 1970.

Olsen, Edgar. "A Competitive Theory of the Housing Market." *American Economic Review,* September 1969, pp. 612 – 622.

Rodwin, Lloyd. *Nations and Cities,* pp. 217 – 267. Boston: Houghton Mifflin Company, 1970.

Schreiber, Arthur F., Paul Gaton, and Richard Clemmer. *Economics of Urban Problems,* pp. 63 – 80. Boston: Houghton Mifflin Company, 1971.

Thompson, Wilbur R. *A Preface to Urban Economics,* pp. 293 – 333. Baltimore: The Johns Hopkins Press, 1968.

Wilson, J. K. *The Metropolitan Enigma,* pp. 170 – 225. Garden City, N.Y.: Anchor Books, Doubleday & Company, 1970.

Wilson, James. *Urban Renewal,* pp. 24 – 29, 293 – 352. Cambridge, Mass.: The M.I.T. Press, 1966.

9 *Metropolitan Transportation*

The economist has long been faced with a dilemma. Ideally, the free exercise of consumer choice in the marketplace, with sellers responding to consumer choice through better products at competitive prices, in the end produces the greatest well-being for the greatest number, including the laborers who make the products. But sometimes there arises a clear clash between the benefits of this market principle and the general "social good." The most spectacular example of this clash, all over the advanced industrial world, is the automobile.

The automobile has opened vast new horizons of mobility and pleasure for millions upon millions of people here and abroad. If there were a Gallup poll in the United States on whether the car ought to be abolished, it is doubtful that 5 percent of the people would answer "yes." This is important. The "problem" of the auto itself, and the subtle additional problems it has created, exist because we, as consumers, like cars and are able to afford them.

As with other social problems, the economist tries to identify, or narrow, this one in a practical sense. No matter what esthetes may say about the "ribbons of concrete" that make up the nation's 43,000 miles of connecting superhighways, constructed since 1956 and nearing completion in the early 1970's, they now exist and will not go away. Apart from that hard fact, the interstate highway system has contributed somewhat to the efficiency of nonrail transportation, occupies a small fraction of the nation's land space, and is highly welcome to most motorists. The practical problem lies elsewhere: inside the nation's metropolitan areas, in which nearly three-quarters of the population live.

The Urban Setting

The traditional metropolitan area, spawned before the advent of the automobile, consisted of an urban core together with its outlying fringes and those surrounding communities which were associated with it by way of employment or cultural dependence. Examples of surrounding communities (urban rings) would be Long Island's Suffolk and Nassau counties outside New York City, Arlington and Alexandria south of Washington, D.C., Wellesley west of Boston, and Evanston north of Chicago. The core city plus its suburban fringe is called a "standard metropolitan area." In the later twentieth century, this urban ring type is gradually being replaced as the "model" of a city by a sprawling conglomerate such as Los Angeles, which consists of an amalgam of suburban areas minus any real core. The emergence of the automobile was a *key casual factor* in this transformation, whose pace varies by city. Most of the cities in the United States are still more like Boston, New York, and Chicago — concentrated metropolitan areas — than they are like Los Angeles; but they are changing fast. For instance, in the last 25 years, Boston has assumed a number of characteristics of Los Angeles. The Boston inner city is very small; the city of Boston itself has less than one million people, but the total metropolitan area numbers over two million, with a low density in many places. Metropolitan areas generally have low densities in much of their outlying territory, and this is a major reason why transportation difficulties arise, as we shall later see.

One hundred years ago, use of the horse and buggy was still common in most American cities. Seventy-five years ago saw a tremendous expansion of streetcars, followed by the development of rapid transit elevated or underground railways. Today, urban transportation consists mostly of cars, plus buses, and, occasionally, subway trains. The results are often unsatisfactory, as any rush hour commuter can testify — even if he is driving his own car.

Private Wants and Public Needs

In a society where "consumer sovereignty" reigns, one would expect that vast improvements would be demanded. According to the consumer sovereignty doctrine, the consumer gets what he wants, and thus the producer is obliged to cater to the consumer's wishes. However, as is often the case, there are large discrepancies between theory and actuality. Advertising may browbeat the consumer into wanting certain things: *want* can be equated with a *belief in a need*. Yet people may want things which they really do not need at all. For instance, when the pace-setting Jones family purchases goldplated silverware, they obviously *want* it, but they do not necessarily *need* it. An individual's demand may not match society's demand. There may, as we noted be a dichotomy between private wants and public needs. Yet this could cost the lives of other people (which is not demanded in the least). An analysis of metropolitan mobility (or transportation patterns) must consider both the costs and benefits to the individual and the costs and benefits to society at large.

Here is an example. Suppose that one is riding along the highway at rush hour and one more car enters the road. Now, the difference between private and social costs is just this: for those who are already on the road, the cost of having one more person join the procession is the time they lose by the entry of another into the crowd; but for the driver just entering, the cost is simply the time it takes to get to work. In other words, one more automobile on the road adds to the time it takes everybody else to get to work, and so this is a social *cost*. This inter-relationship between the action of one person and the consequences for everybody else is of legitimate concern to all.

Demand for Transportation

People purchase transportation services because for whatever reasons they want to move around. The demand for transportation can be defined as the willingness and the ability to purchase it. Transportation is an economic service for which price is an important factor. But of at least equal importance to the person making a choice among different types of transportation is the time lost or gained, the degree of comfort, the safety of the specific means of transport, its convenience in terms of commuting, and the distance from the place of departure, or destination, to the transport vehicle. Among these factors, some are more important than others; the degree of importance depends greatly on substitution possibilities. To use the economist's jargon, we are faced with elasticities — price elasticities, service elasticities, and so on, which determine what the change in demand for a certain type of transportation will be when price or service or any determinant changes.

Charles River Associates, Inc., of Cambridge, Massachusetts, have carried out a study of the Boston metropolitan transportation situation. Their findings show that "... the demand for transit trips is very inelastic with respect to changes in fares."[1] That is, the price of transportation is not an all-important determinant in the use of public transit. Most persons who take the subway, bus, or streetcar would take it at almost any price within reason. Results of this study are interpreted graphically in Figure 9.1.

Figure 9.1 shows that the cost per trip would have to jump from 5¢ to 30¢ before an individual passenger would curtail his use of public transit by so much as one trip per week. Or, vice versa, if the price per trip were cut from 30¢ to 5¢, an individual would take only one more trip each week. On the other hand, if the transit service were poor or deteriorating, a smaller price rise might induce a person to take another means of transportation. Furthermore, there is an "outer limit" on price; if the price of transit should rise from 30¢ to 45¢ without an accompanying improvement in service, more commuters would drive their cars downtown, and some would have to buy cars in order to do so. This has happened in some places.

Moreover, the Charles River report shows that the "haul time," as opposed to total trip time and convenience and comfort, is not important. A passenger generally will not fuss over a time loss of 10 or 15 minutes in his total trip from a failure of the bus to be on time, even though it constitutes a 50 percent increase in the haul time. The report indicates that "proposals for rapid transit or express bus services, which chiefly reduce line-haul time, may be less attractive to users than improvements in the collection and disbursement services."[2] This refers to the convenience of the boarding stations to the departure and arrival points, to how long one must wait, and to how far one must walk in order to take the train or bus. The degree of convenience is one of the most crucial factors determining the consumer's choice of urban transportation.

To the poor, who do not have even the choice of using their own cars as an alternative to public transit, these factors are not so important. To them, it is public transit or nothing; and for them there arises a genuine price elasticity of demand. If the price of public transit goes too high, some of the poor simply cannot travel at all,

---

[1] *An Evaluation of Free Transit Service*, prepared for the U.S. Department of Transportation by Charles River Associates, Inc., Cambridge, Mass. (August 1968), p. 46.
[2] Charles River, *An Evaluation of Free Transit Service*, p. 50.

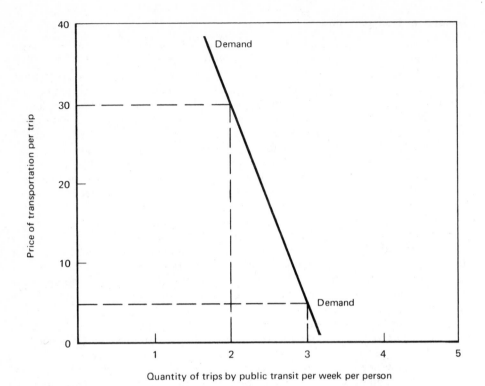

FIGURE 9.1 Demand response to change in price for transportation. To measure elasticity, we compare the percent change in price per unit to the quantity of trips taken by an individual at each price. At 5¢ a trip, the consumer takes 3 trips, at 30¢, only 2. Thus, a 500 percent change in price brings about a change of only 33 percent in the quantity demanded.

or not nearly as much. To summarize, the price of public transit is not a key factor in its use for the great majority with adequate incomes, though they too raise their voices in protest when the price goes up. But higher transit prices can make a big difference to the relatively poor, and at times can even foreclose opportunities to work.

The Economics of the Automobile

Can we safely generalize and say that this pattern of demand elasticities characterizes all modes of transportation, not just mass transportation alone? Price elasticities, it turns out, play a minor role in the demand for automobile travel, too. An increased cost per auto trip would not greatly affect the number of trips made. This is partly because of a consumer illusion: the consumer considers only his out-of-pocket, or variable, costs — the costs actually encountered on each trip.

Costs for a private automobile can be divided between fixed (capital) costs and variable costs. Fixed costs are the outlay for the car itself plus insurance, licensing fee, and so on. Variable costs include gasoline, oil, tolls, and parking fees. Fixed costs are unchanging regardless of the number of miles or trips, while variable costs rise for each trip undertaken; more miles mean more gas, oil, tolls, and so forth. To assess his total per mile cost, the consumer should allocate some of his fixed costs to each mile.

On the average, the American car owner travels 10,000 miles per year, and the life expectancy of a car is about five years. Therefore, the car should be considered fully depreciated at 50,000 miles — depreciation meaning consumption of a durable good over time. To figure his cost per mile, the owner would have to include the cost of the car, annual repairs and maintenance, annual insurance, and license fees. The computation of fixed costs could be broken down as follows:

Cost of car		$2,700
Repairs (within 5 years)		1,000
Insurance (within 5 years)		1,200
License fees		100
	TOTAL COST	$5,000

Therefore, fixed cost per mile is equal to $5,000 divided by 50,000 miles, or 10¢ per mile. To this one must add the variable costs.

To be sure, the consumer rarely considers his fixed costs. His demand for automobile transportation is actually based on only part of his total costs. Due to this illusion, he is barely responsive to minor changes in costs. His costs may change by a few pennies per gallon of gasoline, per toll fare, or per parking fee, but he will only begin to reckon the cost per mile when large changes in tolls and parking fees occur, and even then he may decide to continue using his car. Since the consumer does not convert his fixed cost in private car travel, his demand is biased. Demand is inelastic because of a distorted substitution. On one hand, the individual trip cost for mass transit is all inclusive, while for cars it is only partly so. Moreover, when it comes to comfort, mass transit is usually at a disadvantage.

No wonder the "captive" patrons of mass transit are its main customers. The captives are the people who have no choice, such as the young, the very old, the poor, the sick, or people without a driving license. A survey in Pittsburgh showed that 85 percent of the transit riders did not have a driving license or did not drive.[3] For Chicago, another survey determined that 65 percent of mass transit users were nondrivers.[4]

The Private Automobile and Specialization

Suppose we were to forget for a moment personal wishes and what many commuters regard as their "convenience" in commuting by car. How would an economist design a transit system within the metropolitan area? He would immediately look for efficiency, productivity, and specialization. And he would quickly conclude that the auto fails on all counts. The private car for commuting purposes is

[3]Louis E. Keefer, "Choice Transit Trips," *Pittsburgh Area Transportation Study Research Letter*, Vol. 3, No. 1 (January-February 1961), pp. 4-5.
[4]Illinois State Mass Transportation Commission, *The Mass Transportation Problem in Illinois* (Chicago: 1959), pp. 38-40.

a denial of the specialization of labor that has been at the very heart of the industrial revolution and of the economic growth and affluence that have flowed from it.

Railroad, truck, and air transportation involve specialization; that is, few workers are needed to transport many persons or tons of freight. Transportation by private car can be regarded as a movement backwards because of the tremendous need for labor to move automobiles about. At most, one person can move five or six people in an automobile, whereas a train or a plane can move 10 or 100 times as many. In other words, productivity (output per unit of labor) is relatively very low for the private car.

The Automobile's Encroachment on the City

In the early 1960's there existed the equivalent of 270,000 miles of registered motor vehicles in the United States but only 380,000 miles of city streets. Since the number of cars has been increasing far faster than street capacity, the age of complete immobility could be near, though this remains a largely theoretical horror so far. In Boston, on December 23, 1963, traffic came to a complete standstill. "For five solid hours, thousands of Bostonians fumed, fretted, and sat. Nothing moved."[5] A headline in the *New York Times* on October 12, 1969, tells a similar story: "Traffic Outlook for '75: Get Horse." The same issue of the *Times* quotes the Washington traffic chief as saying, "By 1975, every single center-city area of every big city will be absolutely choked with automobiles." Whether these episodes and prophecies of doom foretell the future or not, the problem is real.

Many specialists suggest that with more off-street parking and better roads, this situation could be ameliorated. However, the cost of such "ameliorations" could be prohibitive. According to Edgar N. Hoover, "Each additional automobile entering the downtown area in the rush hour requires an additional investment in street and parking space of about $25,000."[6] Also it is increasingly claimed that the continuing demand on urban land by the automobile is a menace to urban living. Parking is part and parcel of the automobile's encroachment on the city. In most cities, there are fewer legal off-street parking spaces than there are cars entering the city daily. In desperation, motorists park illegally, thus further preventing traffic from moving. Perhaps Los Angeles presents a futuristic image. One-third of the downtown area is taken up by streets and roads, another third by parking facilities.

The Auto Industry. Before social planners, economists or anyone else can begin to think of limiting, somehow, the use of the automobile — at least *within* the metropolitan area — the role of the auto industry in the economy as a whole must be considered.

First, the industry is not nearly so all-important as most Americans believe. To be sure, it uses much steel, glass, rubber, and textiles, apart from its own employment of some 600,000 workers. But the Department of Commerce has long calculated

[5]*Washington Post,* June 26, 1966.
[6]Edgar N. Hoover, "Motor Metropolis, Some Observations on Urban Transportation in America," *Journal of Industrial Economics,* Vol. *13* (June 1965), p. 187. Data implied from *Transportation Plan for the National Capital Region,* p. 456. Hearing before the Joint Committee on Washington Metropolitan Problems. Congress of the United States, 86th Congress, 1st Session, November 9-14, 1959.

what is called "gross auto product" as part of the overall gross national product. Each measures output the same way, and there is no double counting. In 1972 (a boom auto year, incidentally), the automobile industry accounted for only slightly less than 4 percent of the GNP.

However, this figure does not account for such things as gasoline sales or road-building, which some people include in the auto's "share" in the economy. If we account for all inputs going into the manufacturing of cars and sectors resulting from car use, such as coil products, road construction and maintenance, auto and related insurance, and the auto repair industry, the car industry would account for nearly 10 percent of the nation's output.

Second, the automobile industry may take on strong monopolistic characteristics, despite its proportionately low sustenance of the gross national product. In the auto industry, one firm, General Motors, controls about half the output of cars and thus dominates the domestic new car market. The consumer's choice may be either severely limited or even nonexistent, depending upon his financial resources. So it remains that if General Motors, as the largest of the auto firms, can undercut any potential competitor, it can — in some areas where foreign imports are not available — control the new car market and decide by itself the level, price, and quality of new automobiles available to the consumer. Given the current state of mass transportation in the United States in which the car cannot be replaced, one might indeed treat the automobile industry as a "natural" monopoly, whereby, as with the natural monopolies of the housing situation — the public utilities: the telephone, electric, gas, and water companies — the public would regulate the quality, price, and flow of the automobile.

Third, auto sales themselves would by no means cease, or even necessarily decline, if the use of the car in cities was reduced. The growth of the industry now projected might be less, but there would be no mass layoffs, or even necessarily any layoffs at all. Probably fewer families in the future would have three cars instead of two, while other families would decide to have one car instead of two. But replacement demand alone would assure a large, and probably thriving, auto industry.

None of this, by itself, proves the case for limiting auto travel in cities. But we can safely conclude that the national economy would not be harmed if such a decision were taken. The auto industry would in all probability continue to be profitable and would surely be a major employer of labor.

Regulating City Auto Transport. One suggested alternative is to ration the use of cars in metropolitan areas by charging high fees for cars entering the city area. For example, commuter drivers could be charged a fee depending upon the number of passengers in the car; a relatively empty car with only one passenger would be charged much more than one carrying five passengers. The fee would also depend on the time of day and the direction of travel. In other words, social costs would be charged directly to the auto user in order to induce a more optimal usage of vehicles. Such a price system would be an attempt to regulate demand, with no coercive rules on any driver. This idea is suggested because, among other reasons, it is very difficult to regulate supply. The stock of cars is abundant enough to choke any city in the United States at any time. This kind of plan might induce people either to use mass transportation or to use the existing stock of cars more efficiently.

In addition, there are many proposals to shift working hours so that traffic loads can be more evenly spread out. Studies show that the major problem confronting urban transportation is traffic peaks, or "rush hours." There are more than twice as many people on the road during the morning and evening rush hours than during the midday slack period. The number of cars coming into the city at peak hours could be decreased by increasing tolls at that time, which would be an inducement to business firms to stagger their working hours. But of course such a plan would involve an elaborate system of toll gates at all entrances to the city. Another, possibly more workable, idea is to have local government establish very high parking fees for all-day parking.

There is some additional flexibility so far as industry is concerned. For example, in the inner city all deliveries could be made at night. This is not done now partly because labor costs would be prohibitive, reflecting the fact that night rates are usually twice as high as day rates. This is so because most people in our society prefer to work in the daytime and because the labor market generally provides jobs for most persons who want to work. The employer could not get labor unless he paid more for night work, though occasionally union contracts reinforce the day/night wage differential. But this situation need not, by itself, deter a ban on daytime deliveries made by trucks in the city. If it costs more to deliver at night, then a ban on daytime deliveries would be reflected in a somewhat higher price for goods so delivered, and thus in a higher price for the consumer. But this same consumer is often the auto driver, who would thereby find himself able to move much more freely on the city streets. It is what economists call a "trade-off," though the nondriving, relatively poor city resident would find little gain and some loss.

The High Price of Public Transport

A barber can set himself up in business with relatively little capital outlay, his principal needs being a barber chair and a pair of scissors; after that, his costs vary essentially only with the cost of labor and hair tonic. His chief costs are *variable*, not fixed. He does not have to float a huge bond issue to set up shop, and pay interest on it every year as a fixed cost, though he may need a modest bank loan.

A metropolitan transit system is different. It has to make an enormous capital outlay to build a subway, and quite a large outlay even to purchase a fleet of buses. This outlay — expressed each year as interest and gradual repayment of the principal of bond issues, and depreciation of the equipment — must be covered by the fares charged. That would be easy enough if every bus and every subway car were full on every ride. Then even a low fare could cover the fixed costs as well as the variable costs, mainly the cost of labor. But consider the case of the relatively thinly populated suburb.

The city could build a subway line to the suburb at great cost or increase the number of buses serving the suburb at somewhat less cost. But at best the subway cars and buses would not be full. Some car owners might take mass transit, with the result that fewer cars would enter the city; but the mass transit lines would lose money on every ride because their vehicles would not be full and their fixed costs, therefore, would not be covered. A full bus is a profitable bus; a half-empty bus, whatever other purpose it serves, is likely to be a losing proposition. This problem is not unique to transportation, but it is more serious in transportation than in other industries.

The problem can be described another way. Whether it is full or empty, a bus needs only one driver and a subway only a few motormen. Suppose the transit company calculates that its total cost for each bus trip is $12 — $3 for the driver and gasoline, and $9 in fixed costs to cover paying off the debt incurred to purchase the buses and depreciation. The bus holds 60 riders and the fare is 25 cents. If the bus is full, the trip yields $15, and the transit company makes a profit. But if only 30 riders use the bus, the collection is only $7.50, and the trip has been run at a loss.

We have seen that, within limits, a rise in fare will not deter much transit. But it does deter some. Suppose, after long experience with buses averaging 30 travelers a ride, the bus company increased the fare to 40 cents. Then the trip would at least break even, yielding $12, *provided the number of riders did not decline.* But this large fare increase, amounting to 60 percent, would undoubtedly price some poor people out of transportation altogether and would induce some "marginal" middle-income people to start driving to and from work. If the number of riders dropped back to an average of 20, yielding only $8 at the new rate, the company would be right back in a loss position again. Unlike a manufacturing company, it cannot simply cut production, and hence labor and material costs, when demand falls off.

A distinction must be made between transport for suburban communities and "pure" urban transportation. Demand for transportation is largely based on the fact that people do not live in the same location where they work. They come from inside the urban core and from suburbia. Thus, there are two types of transportation tasks: transporting the suburban worker into the urban core, and providing some means of transportation for the urban worker within the city. These call for different transportation modes depending on what the urban density is. But because of high fixed costs, a fairly high density is needed to justify *any* mass transportation.

There may be some gain to be expected simply from using what we now have in a more efficient manner. It is true that it is exciting to conjure up new modes of transportation such as monorails and moving sidewalks, but whether or not these means of transport could handle the high density has yet to be established. There is even the constructive idea of using partly abandoned railroad lines to create a form of rapid transit. But most of the newer ideas run up against many of the same obstacles that would be involved in the expansion of what we already have. To the extent that local government subsidy or capital outlay is involved — a point we shall examine later — there is the inevitable problem of strained budgets and taxpayer resistance. To the extent that the project involves more than one political jurisdiction, as is usually the case with a city-suburb transit system, there is, at the very least, prolonged delay in getting the various government units to reach agreement on such matters as sharing cost. Finally, there is the relatively new problem posed by the awakening of more and more publicly conscious Americans to the use of the courts. It is hardly an exaggeration to say that a single group of storekeepers or home owners or tenants or environmentalists which, for some reason, is opposed to a given transit project can often use the courts to delay it for years. Economists cannot solve problems like this; they can simply point out, mournfully, that delay means higher costs in the end.

A word is in order about foreign countries, particularly those of Western Europe. At this time, mass transit in Europe is by far superior to that in the United States. Intercity passenger travel by both bus and train is far more pleasant and convenient, and there have been more innovations inside European metropolitan areas than in the United States. But almost without exception, the problem of city streets clogged with autos is at least as bad in European cities as it is in the United States, and very often it is worse because of the original narrowness of the streets. Europe has by no means solved the problems posed by the automobile. In fact, Rome was the first city in the world to approach total traffic paralysis on a regular basis (though Paris and London often come close); in 1972, Rome began experimenting with totally free public bus transit in an attempt to keep cars out of the city. It did this even though the city government had a vast budget deficit and had to subsidize the buses with money it did not have. It seems that there public service prevails over short-run budgetary considerations. Moreover, Milan is in the process of completing a new network of underground rapid transit which it started from scratch. Paris has not only been extending its metro lines into the suburbs but has also introduced noiseless rubber tires for the subway train. In contrast, New York City has toyed for some 25 years with the idea of building a Second Avenue subway line, a project which thus far has not gone beyond the drawing-board stage. In the meantime, an entire generation of straphangers has had to make do with truly incredible conditions on lines which needed modification and amplification half a century ago.

Capital Costs and Efficiency.   Non-auto transit, especially rail transit, requires a large outlay of capital for each unit of demand. If the demand is small, the amount of fixed capital for each unit of output — passenger or ton of freight carried — is very large. This applies not only to the "occupancy" of each train but also to the number of trains that use a given section of track. For example, if a track is used by only 10 trains a day, the cost of fixed capital per train will be 10 times higher than for a track used by 100 trains a day, assuming the same "occupancy" of all trains in terms of passengers and freight.

Where the public transit of passengers is concerned, there is the issue of efficiency versus the public's idea of its comfort or convenience. Apart from commuting, which we have examined, a study for the RAND Corporation concludes that "public mass transit is less than a fully popular travel mode for social, recreational, and shopping activities."[7]

However, there is plenty of evidence of the advantage, in terms of efficiency, of mass transit over highway travel. For instance, the *Boston Globe* reported on June 26, 1966, that "studies based on occupancy of up to 1.7 passengers per car indicate that the maximum capacity of multi-lane highway is 4800 persons per lane per hour. A double track rail system can move 40,000 to 50,000 per hour." Furthermore, one set of tracks moving trains at 40 miles per hour (the U.S. average) can replace 20 highway lanes. Even technologically, rails are superior to highways. For example, the same load needs about 15 percent less power to be moved on a steel-wheeled rail than over a rubber-concrete highway because of friction.[8] Yet, this being so, how can one explain the fact — in view of how public monies are spent — that both the individual and society as a whole (by power of the public purse) would appear to prefer highways to railways?

---

[7]J. R. Meyer, J. F. Kain, and W. Wohl, *The Urban Transportation Problem* (Cambridge, Mass.: Harvard University Press, 1965), pp. 310–311.
[8]Clairborne Pell, *Megalopolis Unbound* (New York: Frederick A. Praeger, 1961), pp. 8, 9, 132.

Externalities and Diseconomies Created by Urban Transportation

If we are to examine all aspects of the costs of urban transportation, we must also consider "externalities" and "diseconomies" resulting from the various modes of transportation. Externalities and diseconomies transcend the direct relationship between an output and an input. They appear outside the activity of the vehicle itself. And they can bear some heavy costs to society as a whole if they are not reckoned with.

Pollution.   One immense diseconomy is the pollution arising from the various transportation vehicles. The automobile accounts for about 50 percent of total pollution. Mass transportation could significantly reduce the total pollutant output. But buses produce pollutants, too. An experiment now being carried out in New York City shows that electrically powered buses produce far fewer pollutants. Yet we create pollution in generating the electricity needed to run the system, using either coal or atomic power, both of which are high in pollutants. Still, the pollutants emitted by the 100 million motor vehicles in the United States exceed by far those from all other sources, including production of electric power. Few, however, want to give up the main pollutant, the car, with its internal combustion motor, nor are people ready to pay the extra cost of building cleaner sources of energy. Still fewer are willing to pay higher taxes to endow the government with the funds necessary for cleaning up the air we breathe. Most citizens do not believe that they, as individuals, are affected. It is always someone else who should give up his car, who should pay higher taxes, or who will eventually get emphysema.

Uglification of Cities.   Another diseconomy is the uglification of cities caused by the building of superhighways within them. Every city in Europe is now doing this, emulating the patterns long since established in the United States. In Chicago, Boston, and New York, the elevated railways built at the beginning of the century adequately served city transportation needs, but they were extremely unattractive. Still, they took up little space and created little dislocation in comparison with what urban expressways have done more recently. It may well be that many engineers and highway construction companies, as well as mass transit construction companies, do not view esthetics as an important factor. Often one hears that at 60 miles an hour, a passenger cannot distinguish colors or forms. Perhaps it does not occur to the individuals who design the ugliness that the people who live near, or walk by, these intrusions come to a standstill at the very sight of the expressway, the elevated train, or the dingy station. These areas often become slums as, for instance, did those areas around 125th Street where the Harlem Division of the New York Central line surfaces.

The Suburbs.   Herodotus observed that Egypt was the gift of the Nile; in the United States, suburbia is the gift of the automobile. Yet in a number of ways suburbia is a very inefficient form of living, that is, the individual resident is getting less in terms of the quality of life for every additional dollar he spends than he could get elsewhere. There is also a great deal of "lost time," in the economic sense.

Consider, for example, the time the suburban dweller has to spend going to and from work, shopping, and entertainment. Most shopping is done relatively locally in those huge parking lots called "shopping centers," which give a universal form of uglification to America — that certain sameness everywhere. The time lost by individuals getting to these places could be used to enjoy themselves or to improve themselves and society. According to an educated guess, a suburbanite uses up about a fifth of his lifetime just driving. From a social point of view, suburbia is costly both to the cities and to the nation as a whole. This is a psychological as well as an economic cost. It means that as the countryside retreats ever farther from the city, the city dweller must go farther and farther afield to find the green spots. In consequence, he asks for more and more highways in order to get there, even though when the highways are built, more "development areas" open, more green disappears, with the certain result that he will then have to go still farther at still greater expense.

Urban Land Use. Even quantitatively, the spread of highways diminishes the space available in cities themselves. Both in the city and in suburbia, each mile of a four-lane highway takes away 26 acres of land.[9] There is a destructive cycle brought to the cities by highways. The additional cars coming into the cities require more off-street parking (garages). They, in turn, attract more cars, which only puts pressure on public officials to build still more highways and garages for the ever-increasing numbers of cars traveling the new highways. Less land on which to build houses is then available, and thus the city ends up with a diminished tax base.

Urban Transportation and the Poor Minorities. A special problem of urban transportation is the way it offsets to the poor minorities, who tend increasingly to occupy the urban cores. First of all, the inadequacies of public transportation are hardest on the urban poor because the poor have no alternative transportation and little job mobility. The movement of industries to the suburbs, in the existing state of public transit, works further hardship on ghetto dwellers. As Buel points out:[10]

> It may cost a resident of central Harlem some $40 a month to commute by public transportation to an aircraft factory in Farmingdale, Long Island. But the current day resident of one of California's ghettos, Watts, Hunter's Point or West Oakland, for example, more often finds it impossible to get to the suburban factory just as the doors seem to be beginning to open for him.

Second, the building of highways inside the cities creates other kinds of hardship. The cliché "white roads through black bedrooms" turns out to be true, for ghetto property is cheap and absentee-owned and well located for highways. Thus, it becomes the first choice of planners as a highway route that can be easily obtained by eminent domain. As a result, the transportation demand of ghetto dwellers is ultimately displaced, not just a few hundred yards but perhaps 10 or 20 miles outside the urban core. As already noted, these people can ill afford the resulting rise in the cost of home-to-job transportation. Further, highways devastate neighborhoods, dividing the city irrevocably and sealing the isolation of the ghetto. A final negative effect is the dwindling of the value of center-city real estate, which leaves an inadequate tax base for dealing with city problems, including, of course, public transit.

---

[9]Ronald Buel, "Rapid Transit, Plan Politicians," *Interplay,* November 1968, p. 40.
[10]Buel, "Rapid Transit," p. 39.

The Politics of Urban Transportation

Highways are much criticized for the variety of diseconomies they produce. Yet cars do have more flexibility than rail transport. The private car provides access to those places which are not located on or near mass transportation. In addition, the use of the automobile involves no waiting time (as in the subway station), though the time wasted on the highway can be and, at rush hour, is usually greater.

The first step toward eliminating the adverse effects of the car in metropolitan areas would seem to be the improvement of mass transit. Though public officials generally take this view of the situation, neither the executive branch nor Congress (nor the individual states) have done much of anything to promote change. In Washington, D. C., planners worked eagerly on a transit system to Arlington and Alexandria for a decade. But recently they were forced to concede priority to the building of new highway bridges and highway extensions, which will bring even more cars into the capital. In New York, public policies have been highly detrimental to mass transportation. When the George Washington Bridge was built over 40 years ago, the lower level was reserved for rapid transit, but in the 1960's, the New York Port Authority simply converted this level into another multilane highway.

Urban transportation constitutes a problem of national dimensions. Yet, unfortunately, it does not seem to be recognized as such. As the *New York Times* noted on February 3, 1970, " . . . despite some modest evidence of 'new priorities' in aviation, transit, and the Merchant Marine, the new budget makes it clear that highway construction remains the heart of the Government's transportation program." While *billion*-dollar highways continue to proliferate, the transportation bill of 1970 allocated a mere *$80 million* for fiscal 1970/71 in loans and grants for urban transit for the entire United States.

It is claimed that highways are self-supporting through the gasoline tax and that taxes cannot be diverted for other uses.[11] But most other taxes are not earmarked for a specific outlay. When we pay a tax to the government, we are really supporting those programs that cannot be carried out by a small number of individuals. These activities should be carried out by our elected representatives in such a way as to benefit all or at least some of the larger groups within the society. This is in line with the old classical economic theory that the government should do what single individuals cannot do by themselves. The government must also arbitrate among the various competing factions.

Taxation plays a role in redistributing public funds to where they are most needed. Everybody pays school taxes, for example, whether or not they have children to send to school. Therefore, should the motorist whose gasoline tax is directed to modes of transportation other than highways be any more upset than the millions of childless people who regularly pay school taxes? Yet if everyone agrees that a fresh look is needed in metropolitan transportation, why is so little actually done?

In part, the reason can be attributed to power politics. In the United States, we have usually been lucky in that most powerful interest groups, such as big business, have been offset by competitive interests, such as powerful labor unions. But it seems that the users of metropolitan transportation are not, nor cannot be, as well

---

[11]Legislation enacted in 1956 called for an extensive interstate highway program to be financed mainly through a tax on gasoline, that is, on highway users. By 1973, over $57 billion will have been spent on this highway system.

organized as the various groups which stand to gain from the further spread of asphalt. In urban transportation, individual benefits and social benefits do not coincide. In short, in many states the highway lobby is just too strong.

Technology

Public policies for adequate metropolitan transportation need consider all kinds of technological alternatives. For instance, the monorail system offers the advantage of being able to move large numbers of people without requiring the excavation of tunnels. It may be cheaper within an existing city to build the superstructures needed for a monorail than to build subways.

As in the past, most labor unions would be opposed to the introduction of new technology. Unions are organized and administered for short-run aims. Samuel Gompers, first president of the American Federation of Labor, said back in the 1890's that what labor unions stood for was "more *now*." And this psychology is still evident today. For example, train conductors' unions view the new technology as a threat to their jobs. They do not realize that new kinds of jobs can also be created by technological change. It is true that in the short run some displacement and hardship usually occur, but these hardships can be minimized by social action. In the early 1800's, frightened homespun textiles workers in England destroyed the new mechanical weaving machinery for the same reasons. But in the long run, millions of people found employment because those machines were introduced. What is more, the displacement and hardship at that time were much greater than they would be today.

Somehow we tend to become entrenched in old ways of doing things. Around 1800, shortly after achieving independence, we were a major shipbuilding country, famous for our clippers. But at about the same time, the iron steamboat was developed, in which Europeans took the lead, and we never again gained the advantage. We were as enamored of our clipper then as we are with the gasoline-propelled automobile today. On the other hand, during World War II we produced and delivered one Victory- or Liberty-type ship every week. This goes to show that we do have the capacity, though not necessarily the will or foresight, to innovate. Both business and labor are wary of changing the status quo. What it boils down to is that in a free market individual freedom often entails the protection of specific group interests.

It is hard to explain why we have nothing similar to the Tokaido in Japan — a rail line capable of moving many hundreds of people at 120 miles per hour. This service is still based on the old railroad technology; it is just an improvement on it. Today we speak about completely new systems. The only problem is that neither enough funds nor enough energy are devoted to testing and implementing such schemes. For years New York has entertained a proposal for a system of moving sidewalks that would connect Grand Central Station and Times Square and carry a tremendous volume of traffic each day. Yet nothing has happened, principally because of union reluctance. Also in New York, about 10 years ago, the Transit Authority introduced automatic shuttle trains which dispensed with conductors. They functioned very well, but because of union pressure they had to be abandoned. The unions insisted on two conductors for every train. Yet considering the crime rate in New York, especially on subways, the introduction of automatic trains would not necessarily constitute progress. Shuttle service between Grand Central & Times Sq. would be an exception simply because of the volume of traffic. On the other hand, Philadelphia has a new transit line that is completely automatic; it stops and speeds without help or hindrance from any conductor.

In short, all the technological know-how is present; it just remains to use it. But, for the moment, it would appear that while modern technology allows us to fly at supersonic speeds to and even reach the moon, we still cannot get to the city.

SUGGESTIONS FOR FURTHER READING

Charles River Associates. *An Evaluation of Free Transit Service.* Prepared for the U.S. Department of Transportation. Cambridge, Mass.: August, 1968.

Dickman, Joe. "Transportation in Cities." *Scientific American,* September 1965, pp. 163 – 174.

Lang, A. Scheffer and Soberman, Richard M. *Urban Mass Transit: Its Economics and Technology.* Cambridge, Mass.: The M.I.T. Press, 1964.

Leavitt, Helen. *Superhighway-Superhoax.* Garden City, N.Y.: Doubleday & Company, 1970.

Luna, Charles. *The UTU Handbook of Transportation in America,* Chapters 2 and 3. New York: Popular Library, 1971.

Nader, Ralph. *Unsafe at Any Speed.* New York: Grossman Publishers, 1965.

Netser, Dick. *Economics and Urban Problems,* pp. 137-163. New York: Basic Books, 1970.

Pell, Claiborne. *Megalopolis Unbound.* New York: Frederick A. Praeger, 1961.

Perloff, Harvey S. *The Quality of the Urban Environment, Essays on New Resources for the Future,* pp. 205 – 227. Baltimore, Md.: The Johns Hopkins Press, 1969.

Schreiber, Arthur F., Paul Gaton, and Richard Clemmer. *Economics of Urban Problems,* pp. 81 – 100. Boston: Houghton Mifflin Co., 1971.

Stone, Tabor R. *Beyond the Automobile.* Englewood Cliffs, N.J.: Prentice-Hall, 1971.

Vickrey, William S. "Pricing in Urban and Suburban Transport." *American Economic Review,* Vol. 53, No. 2 (May 1963), pp. 452 – 465.

Williams, Ernst W., Jr., ed. *The Future of American Transportation.* Englewood Cliffs, N.J.: Prentice-Hall, 1971.

10 *Crime*

There has been much public protest in recent years against what are thought to be the rising trends in the number of crimes committed, especially "crime in the streets," and against the tendency for crimes to become more violent.

The Amount and Cost of Crime

One would expect that the number of crimes committed would rise simply as a consequence of the increased population both in the world at large and in the United States; more people will produce more behavioral phenomena, of both a fortunate and an unfortunate kind.

One would also expect that the number of crimes committed in relationship to the population, for example, the number of crimes per 1,000 people, would increase as a result of increased urbanization in the world. It is easier in large cities than in small towns to conceal one's actions, and the cheapened cost of escaping detection in large cities can be expected to produce more criminal behavior as the population of a country becomes more urbanized.

However, very little is known about the quantity of crime that occurs. The Federal Bureau of Investigation publishes an annual volume of "uniform crime reports," but this contains, at most, only information on crimes reported to the police. A large number of crimes are not reported to the police at all and the magnitude of the unreported fractions varies among crimes. In addition, many crimes reported to the police are not recorded by them. Thus, the changes that occur over time in the amount of reported and recorded crime may reflect no substantive changes, but simply changes in police recording standards.

The question is further complicated by the fact that it is not the amount of crime per se that is most interesting but, rather, the amount of socially offensive and harmful behavior. Behavior is "criminal" only if the legislature has defined it as such. Street gambling may be illegal one year and legal the next; the amount of crime committed will have diminished, but social behavior may not have changed at all.

And the complication is compounded by the fact that one of the costs society incurs as the result of crime is the cost of escaping victimization. A Presidential Crime Commission organized a survey a few years ago of "high crime areas" in two large cities. That survey found that because they feared crime, almost half the respondents stayed off the streets at night, more than one-third did not speak to strangers, one-fifth used cars and taxis rather than walking, while another fifth expressed an intention to move to another neighborhood. Precautions such as these are costly and the amount of care taken to avoid victimization may reflect less the total quantity of crime than its distribution in space and time. Thus, the same amount of crime could be made less socially costly, or more, if it were more or less equally distributed among neighborhoods and if it were more or less concentrated in a temporal sense—say, at night or on weekdays.

Even though the data are not trustworthy and, if trustworthy, are not completely meaningful, the uniform crime reports of the FBI do give some sense of the magnitude of the crime situation.

They distinguish seven "index crimes" from all others. These are murder and non-negligent manslaughter, forcible rape, robbery, aggravated assault, burglary, larceny over $50, and auto theft. In a recent year, there were, in the United States, three and a quarter million such offenses reported and recorded by the police, or about 1,600 per 100,000 people in the country. The total number has been increasing, as has the number in relationship to the population. These crimes are unequally distributed spatially; in relationship to population, there are about three times as many of them, taken together, in metropolitan centers as there are in rural areas.

In addition to the index crimes, there are literally thousands of other acts or forms of behavior that are criminal. The number of such offenses known to the police is not reported in aggregated form, but it is reported that for every arrest for an index crime offense, there are some five other arrests for other offenses.

The Optimal Amount of Crime

Whatever the quantity of crime that occurs in a community, one cannot know a priori that it is too much, and it might be that the amount of crime experienced in successive time periods is, in each, the appropriate quantity. Every community would be better off, of course, the smaller the quantity of harmful criminal behavior it experienced, if avoidance of criminal harm were costless. But such avoidance, unfortunately, is not costless. Crime is prevented by the expenditure of resources, both private and public. Householders may install alarms or build fences; the public sector employs police, prosecutors, judges, and prison wardens. All these resources have alternative uses; they could be employed in the production of other useful commodities rather than in crime prevention. Resources used to prevent crimes, therefore, are foregone from other valuable uses. There is, thus, some optimal size for the crime prevention industry. On familiar principles of economic calculus, the optimal size of that industry is such that the value of the last unit of resources employed — say, the salary of the last policeman hired — should be equal to the value of the harm that would have been done had the crime not been forestalled by the use of that resource unit in the crime prevention industry rather than in some other industry.

It is not possible for the optimal size of the crime prevention industry to be one that reduces crime rates to zero so long as the cost of preventing crimes is greater than zero. The welfare of the community would not be maximized if too many crimes were prevented from occurring because then some resources would be put to less productive uses. In that case, some resources would be employed in preventing crime that would have a higher social value if they were employed elsewhere. A society made up entirely of policemen, prosecutors, and judges would obviously be ridiculous.

Once the optimal size of the crime prevention industry has been defined in principle, the socially optimal quantity of crime is also defined. It is the difference between the quantity of crime that would occur if there were no preventive precautions taken at all and the quantity of crime that is prevented by an optimally sized crime prevention industry.

We do not assert that the amount of crime in the United States is an optimal amount, but only that zero crime rates would be suboptimal so long as prevention is costly.

The quantity of crime that is optimal will vary among societies because the values of the relevant parameters will vary among them. The cost of crime prevention, for example, will be partially determined by the distribution of population over a country's landscape. The rate of crime, in the absence of a crime prevention industry, will be affected by the incidence of opportunities for gainful criminal behavior, the distribution of income, the magnitude of remuneration in legal occupations, and the psychic costs sensed by transgressors. All these, too, will vary among societies. The quantity of crime that it pays a society to forestall by the erection of an apparatus for preventing crime will, therefore, be larger in some than in other societies, and the unforestalled residual of crime that societies will optimally tolerate will be different among different societies.

Thus, in the early 1960's, the residual homicide rate per 100,000 of population ranged from 36.5 in Colombia, 31.9 in Mexico, and 21.8 in South Africa to 0.7 in England and Wales and 0.4 in Ireland. In the United States, it was 4.8.

The quantity of crime experienced in different countries will also be greatly affected by the laws and traditions in each of them that distinguish legal from illegal acts. Acts that are criminal in some places are not criminal in others; they may be defined by the law in these "other places" as not offensive or, if defined as offensive, they may generate only civil suits brought by private parties against other private parties instead of triggering the laying of charges by state authorities that characterizes the criminal process. The larger the fraction of all possible behavior that the law defines as criminal, other things being equal, the larger will be the quantity of crime that a society will optimally not forestall.

The Allocation of Crime Prevention Sources

The number of crimes committed will be affected by the quantity of resources employed to prevent crime. The distribution of crime among types of crime, and among neighborhoods, and the distribution of victimization among social classes will be affected by the allocation of crime prevention resources.

Some types of crime are more harmful than others. Subject to expenditure constraints, the community's welfare is maximized if the quantity of criminal harm done is minimized. If the quantity of crime is taken as a datum, the community will want to experience that "crime mix" which will contain a large component of less harmful crimes and a small component of more harmful crimes. The crime mix will be affected by the allocation of crime prevention resources among crime types. By moving police from squads dealing with theft to squads dealing with assault, the community will achieve gains with respect to the incidence of assault at the expense of losses with respect to the incidence of theft. Given the scale of all policing resources, some police are assigned to the prevention of assault and to the discovery of those who have committed this offense while others are assigned to the achievement of the same object in cases involving theft. Therefore, since assaults are "traded off" for thefts, police commissioners now, at least implicitly, determine the relative "values" of the two crimes. That is to say, the commissioners make judgments as to how much additional theft is worth some negative increment of assault. Rational allocation would, of course, require the fulfillment of the condition of equimarginality. That is, the last police officers moved from the theft prevention squad to the assault prevention squad should cause the number of assaults experienced by the community to be reduced by a number the social value of which is equal to the social value of the number of additional thefts experienced as a result of that officer's transfer among squads.

It might be thought that values cannot be put upon such commodities as assaults and thefts, but there are at least two methods of establishing their relative values.

One method would calculate costs explicitly. As a first approximation, a marginal assault's cost might be the sum of the cost of medical care resources employed in the repair of the assaulted person, the value of the loss of output resulting from his absence from work, and the extra cost of the cautionary strategies employed by the whole community to avoid victimization from that marginal assault. The cost suffered by the assaulted person is inferentially included when the amount spent to avoid victimization is incorporated in the calculus. The cost of a marginal theft would be approximately the sum of the value of the time spent in the enterprise by the thief (for which the wages he could earn, in that time, in legal employment would be a proxy) and the extra cost of the defenses taken by the whole community to avoid victimization by a marginal theft.

Another method of establishing the relative values of harm done by different crimes would be the polling of the community. People might be asked a question taking something like the following form: "Suppose the chances that you will be the victim of an assault during the coming year are 8 in 1,000 and that the chances that you will be a victim of theft are 63 in 1,000. By how much more would you be prepared to increase the chances of victimization by theft, if it were necessary to pay the price of such an increase in order to reduce the chances of victimization by assault to 7 in 1,000?" Such a poll would permit the calculation of the marginal value of assaults in terms of thefts, because the responses of members of the community, and hence their own social valuations, could be computed.

Once the relative marginal values of different offenses were established, by one method of reckoning or another, the way would be open to calculating a socially optimal mix of offenses; crime prevention resources could then be allocated among types of crime so that this mix would tend to be achieved.

The execution of such a calculation would require, in addition, estimates of the costs of preventing different crimes. The prevention of some crimes is more costly than the prevention of others. It is cheaper for criminals to conceal their identities when they commit some crimes than when they commit others; opportunity for stealth is unequally distributed among crimes. It is easier to doctor the company's accounts to cover embezzlement than it is to hide a body and conceal the fact of death by homicide. And, assuming that some police are better than others at identifying criminals and that some criminals are better than others at concealing their identities, the cost of preventing marginal crimes can be expected to rise as the quantity of crime rises.

In much the same way that the allocation of police among types of crime optimizes their use in the sense that a mix of crime can be achieved which will minimize the cost that given quantities of crime impose upon the community, the allocation of police among neighborhoods will also tend to achieve an optimal spatial distribution of crime among neighborhoods.

The form that optimization takes — that is, the goal to be achieved — cannot be defined by economics. For example, the goal might be the equalization of crime rates among neighborhoods or it might be the minimization of crime rates for the city as a whole. These are not the same thing and only in rare and exceptional circumstances would the two goals imply the same allocation of police among neighborhoods. The reason for this is that the marginal cost of preventing crimes is commonly different in different neighborhoods. If one wanted to minimize aggregate city crime rates, one would want to allocate police among neighborhoods in such a way that the last policeman in every neighborhood forestalled the same quantity of crime; but the application of such an allocational rule would probably leave higher crime rates in some neighborhoods and lower crime rates in others. The achievement of equal crime rates in all neighborhoods would mean having some police in some neighborhoods who would actually be more efficient (that is, they would forestall more crimes), if they were removed to some other neighborhood. The equal distribution of crime rates would not be consistent with the minimization of aggregate crime rates.

Factor combination in law enforcement. Mention has already been made of the police allocational problem. Police efficiency is also affected by the solution of the problem of combining factors of crime prevention "production."

Resources employed in policing are available in a wide variety of forms. Human labor itself has diverse properties; some are skilled at reading fingerprints and others at repairing communications equipment. The optimal organization of a police force requires the combination of human labor of different kinds in the right proportions. But, additionally, labor is combined with tangible capital of different kinds in the production of policing services. Patrolmen may walk beats or they may ride patrol cars. If they ride in cars, they may ride two paired to a car or one in a car. With a given police budget, there may be a larger number of patrolmen having slower access to centrally filed information or a smaller number of patrolmen with quicker access to information; that is, funds saved on the employment of police officers may be spent for the installation of improved communication equipment. A crime-prone area in a crime-prone period may be observed directly by a policeman stationed in the vicinity or it may be scanned by hidden television cameras. The opportunities for factor substitution are immense and, in principle, factors should be combined in proportions that permit the fulfillment of cost-minimizing rules.

Rational Calculation by Criminals

Much of the foregoing discussion has contained the implicit postulate that criminals engage in rational, maximizing, calculated decision-making. For example, it was suggested that the amount of crime of a given type that is committed and the distribution of crime among neighborhoods would be affected by the allocation of police among crime types and among neighborhoods. But the allocation of police will have such effects only if criminals seek to avoid costs, including the costs which they incur if they are found out by the police, taken into custody, and charged with the commission of a criminal offense.

It might be said, on the other hand, that criminals behave irrationally, on the "spur of the moment," or in moments of passion when they have lost the capacity to be sensible.

One way to discover which of these postulates is properly descriptive of the real world would be to examine the criminal psyche in depth. But this would be an unproductive venture and the reason why it would be unproductive is that the discovery of the forces that influence criminal behavior is irrelevant to the framing of a crime prevention policy.

The public sector designs and executes such a policy when it determines the scale of its law enforcement effort, the distribution of that effort in space, and the kinds of resources it will combine in this enterprise. The private sector designs and executes such a policy when private households and firms take precautions to reduce the probability that they will be victimized by criminals.

Both sectors want to know something about the consequences of their policies. They are indifferent to the causes of crime. If criminals are in fact moved irrationally by passion, but if, nonetheless, the assumption that they are rational calculators leads to predictive statements about the consequences of crime prevention policy that are valid, that suffices. Valid predictive statements are those that are found to be consistent with observed experience in the world.

The few studies that have been made seem to indicate that criminals do behave as if they were rational calculators. For example, the research shows that criminals seek to avoid costs.

The costs of criminal behavior which are borne by the criminal are resource and time costs, just as in legal behavior, plus the punishment inflicted upon the criminal if he is discovered. Only a small fraction of all criminal behavior results in punishment. Except for a few crimes like homicide, most criminals go undetected. The *ex ante* cost of criminal behavior is, therefore, the value of the punishment, if detection, charging and conviction occur, multiplied by the probability that such conviction *will* occur. This calculation produces what is called the "expected value" of the punishment.

It can be seen that the magnitude of the expected value of a punishment will be greater the more severe the punishment, if inflicted, and the larger the probability of conviction. Suppose the punishment consists of a prison term. Since freedom to move about at will has value and since imprisonment denies the prisoner the capacity to engage in income-earning employment, the value of a prison term can be calculated, in principle.

When someone contemplates whether he will engage in a criminal act or not, the "as-if-he-were-rational" postulate assumes that he takes account of these costs. The cost of imprisonment falls upon an imprisoned person over time. The tenth year of a

10-year sentence is felt only 10 years hence. Since events occurring nearer in time have greater value than events occurring more distantly in time, events that will occur in the future must be discounted in computing their values in the present. Using usual rates of discount, an event taking place 10 years hence will have a much smaller value in the present than its nominal value, when it actually occurs. The difference in the present value of a 10-year prison term and a nine-year prison term will likely be very small. If, therefore, it is sought to diminish the quantity of crime done by increasing the *ex ante* costs taken into account by persons who are engaged in deciding whether or not to commit criminal acts, it would be more efficient to increase costs via an increase in the probability of conviction than to do so via an increase in the magnitude or duration of punishment.

Constraints on the Police

The most important task performed by the police in law enforcement and crime prevention is the discovery of information. With resources devoted to this activity given, the quantity of output — that is, the quantity of relevant information discovered — will be determined by the level of police efficiency. Police efficiency can be expected to be negatively correlated with the constraints put upon the process of discovery. Police work is fashioned by a network of rules, some of which facilitate, rather than constrain. For example, a rule prohibiting the use of torture to extract confessions will diminish the number of false confessions by eliminating those given to avoid the pain of torture; thus, such a rule will probably increase the net output of information by the police, net output being true information adjusted for false information. However, a rule requiring that suspected persons be informed by the police that they have the right to remain silent when questioned, or one limiting the police in eavesdropping or searching, might have adverse effects on police efficiency and output.

This is not to say, of course, that constraint on police behavior is a social discommodity. There are socially useful objects other than crime prevention and some of them may be competitive with crime prevention. In such cases, the social optimum is a complex quantity, and society trades off one commodity for another. Privacy, including freedom from police intrusion, has a utility of its own. A Rand Corporation paper reports that it is now technically possible to trace the flow of printed money and checks by printing a coded pattern on them (as is presently done with cigarette coupons), to record all long-distance telephone conversations, to record the place and movement of all automobiles, and to identify the drivers of all automobiles. By continuously feeding this information into a network of interconnected computers, some central authority could have at fingertip recall a very substantial record of the movements, associations, behavior, and conversations of the whole citizenry. Such a system would deter crime greatly but it would also so grotesquely reduce the limits of individual privacy that the net social outcome of such an arrangement would surely be negative.

There is still another reason for constraining police behavior, even at the cost of efficiency. The police monopolize the legal power to coerce. Yet not all of them are completely to be trusted. Their decisions are also governed by criteria other than the desire to discover criminal behavior; they serve personal wealth and utility interests as well. The information they come to command is capable of misuse. The larger the flow of information coming into their possession, with given propensities to put it to improper use, the larger will be the quantum of misued information. Some checks on the police, therefore, have social utility, and society is well served by them, even at the cost of some increment in crime.

Selective Law Enforcement

There is an optimizing allocational problem that is produced by the very large difference between the resources available for law enforcement and the quantity of law-breaking that occurs. Offenses against the traffic laws can be taken as prototypical of this more general case. It would require an enormous quantity of resources to enforce maximum-speed laws completely and the case for less than full enforcement has already been discussed. If the law is to be incompletely enforced, upon which infractors should it be made to fall and which should be left free of its effects?

Speeding is a criminal offense presumably because it can cause harm through collision with property or persons in a probability sense. The probability that harm will be done differs in different places. It is high where children frequently cross highways; it is low on limited-access expressways. Differences in the probability of harm imply not only that different speed limits are appropriate to different places but also that there are appropriate differences among different places in the allocation of resources to enforce the speed laws.

This is an example of optimal law-enforcement behavior in general. It suggests that, other things being equal, law enforcement should be more vigorously pressed against thieves who take assets of large value than against those engaged in trivial theft. It suggests, in general, that the law should be *selectively enforced*. Enforcing laws is an activity that is socially costly; it is also a socially gainful activity in the sense that it alters behavior and diminishes the quantum of harmful behavior that society experiences. The costs associated with law-enforcement ventures will vary among ventures and the gains will also vary among ventures. Every person charged with a criminal offense is objectively guilty of that offense only in a "probability" sense. Conviction requires judgment "beyond reasonable doubt" and this, in turn, requires the collection of evidence admissible in court. Some evidence is more difficult to come by than other evidence and it is for this reason that the resource cost of law enforcement differs from one case to another.

The social gain of successful law enforcement is, mainly, that it deters offensive behavior; it raises the *ex ante* probability that harmful, criminal behavior will be punished, diminishes the mathematically expected value of criminal ventures, and, therefore, alters behavior in a way that causes society to suffer less criminal harm done.

The police are confronted with a vast array of known offenses by identified offenders; they should optimally choose among them in laying charges. The prosecutor is also confronted with a vast array of charged offenders; he too should optimally choose among them in preparing cases for prosecution. The principles of choice are those that take account of the costs of pursuing successful prosecutions and of the gains expected to be derived from such pursuit.

It is clear that prosecutors do make choices among charged offenders. Almost nine out of every 10 criminal charges are disposed of, in the United States, without trial. This is because trial is usually preceded by a process of "plea bargaining," usually ending in a pretrial settlement. The settlement can take the form of a plea of guilty by the charged person to an offense less serious, and implying less severe punishment, than that with which he was initially charged; or the charges may be dismissed.

If all charged persons and all prosecutors were to insist that every charge be brought to trial, the courts would be swamped with cases and the criminal justice system would break down completely. Since court resources are scarce commodities, they ought to be allocated among cases on some principle of choice that takes account of opportunity costs; court time and personnel employed in the execution of judgment in one case are lost to the execution of judgment in other cases.

One author has constructed a model in which the decision whether to go to trial or to settle short of a trial is determined by the probability of conviction if the case is brought to trial, the seriousness of the crime, the quantity and efficiency of resources commanded by prosecutors and defendants, the relative costs of trial and settlement, and attitudes toward risk.[1]

The probability of conviction if a case is taken to trial is, of course, a subjective estimate made in conditions of uncertainty. Separate estimates are made by both prosecutor and defendant. If both are sure of winning — the prosecutor of securing a conviction and the defendant of securing acquittal — the likelihood of reaching a settlement can be expected to be smaller than if both are sure of losing. Or, put in other words, the terms of the settlement — for example, the charge to which a guilty plea will be entered — will be affected by the paired probabilities assigned to possible trial outcomes.

The magnitudes of these probabilities will be affected by the resources employed by prosecution and defense in the preparation of evidence. Each side may devote many investigative man-hours to the case, or few. The prosecutor's willingness to settle will be affected by the appropriation of funds to his office. The willingness of the defendant to settle will be affected by whether the defendant is detained or released pending trial. Pretrial detention, as distinguished from release on bail, can foreclose opportunities to assemble defensive evidence.

The Magnitude of Punishment

On utilitarian principles, the magnitude of the punishment of convicted offenders should be only so severe that marginal costs and gains will be equated. It should not be larger than that.

We can suppose that punishment for *all* crimes is imprisonment for a period of some length or, alternatively, that we refer here only to that set of crimes for which imprisonment is thought to be the appropriate punishment.

The cost of imprisonment to the prisoner is the sum of a number of values. He foregoes income while in prison. His lifetime income stream, after release, is diminished as a result of the stigmatization of imprisonment and the assimilation by the community of information that he has offended; once convicted of embezzlement, a bank teller is not likely again to be employed by a bank or any place where he will have access to the mobile and valuable assets of others. His choices

[1]William M. Landes, "An Economic Analysis of the Courts," *Journal of Law and Economics*, Vol. *14*, No. 1 (April 1971), pp. 61 – 107.

will be constrained while in prison; others, wardens and guards, will exercise power over him.

To calculate the value of imprisonment, values must be assigned to all these variables and then summed. From this sum must be netted out the value of room and board provided the prisoner by the community.

To the cost to the prisoner must be added the cost to the community in putting him in prison (the cost of identifying him, taking him into custody, and prosecuting him) and keeping him in prison. This aggregated sum is the social cost of imprisonment. Since the values of some of these components, such as the prisoner's foregone income, rise with the length of sentence and since none decline with sentence length, the summed social cost of imprisonment must also rise with sentence lengths.

How long should prison sentences be? Only so long that the value of the last increment of the sentence — say, the sixtieth day in a 60-day sentence — should be equal in value to the value of the harm forestalled by a sixtieth day of imprisonment.

A calculus of this kind requires estimation of the probability that an offender will be punished. This probability is invariably less than one because in the case of *no* crime are all offenders punished; indeed, for most crimes, the vast majority of offenders escape detection. The calculus also requires the estimation of the social harm that would have been done by forestalled crime.

One econometric study has concluded that, when optimal sentence lengths are calculated this way, prison sentences imposed in the United States are, for the offenses studied, suboptimally too long, not too short.

An assumption embedded in the foregoing discussion is that, for given crimes, sentences will be of uniform length. However, they need not be uniform. Uncertainty is costly, and an additional component of the cost to criminals could be introduced by permitting sentence lengths to be uncertain. With given mean sentence lengths, for example, variance around the mean could be inserted into the sentencing model by having sentences less — or more — than the mean chosen by some random process.

Prisoner Choice of the Place of Imprisonment

A serious consequence of imprisonment as a punishment is that it puts some, such as prison guards, in a position to exercise power over others. This is obnoxious and should be avoided, if possible. Presently, particular prisoners are assigned to particular prisons. If they are mistreated, there is no escape for them. It should be possible to modify the system so that prisoners could exercise choice with respect to the institution in which they were held, and rewards to the administrators of prisons could be made proportional to the number of prisoners who chose to be held by them.

One such possible arrangement might be a system of privately operated prisons whose owners would be able to redeem vouchers delivered to them by prisoners. The redemption value would, of course, have to be sufficient to yield them a normal return on their investment; in this way, competition among them for the favor of prisoners would come about. Prisoners, of course, would have the right to recontract — in short, the right to move from one prison to another where they believed their treatment might be better. In such an arrangement, prisoners could locate close to their homes, where it would be convenient for family and friends to visit them, and incentives would come into play for humane treatment by guards, for providing simple conveniences in cells, and for the enforcement of improved feeding standards. The government payment of the vouchers could be reduced or canceled if the prison failed to perform its primary function — that of holding the convicted offenders in confinement.

Crime is a social phenomenon, as is the enforcement of the criminal law. The application of even unsophisticated principles of microeconomic analysis to such phenomena produces some suggestive, surprising, and, hopefully, fruitful outcomes.

SUGGESTIONS FOR FURTHER READING

Beccaria-Bonesana, Cesare, Marchese di. *On Crimes and Punishments.* Translated with an introduction by Henry Paolucci. Indianapolis: The Bobbs-Merrill Co., 1963. Bentham, Jeremy. *Theory of Legislation.* New York: Harcourt, Brace Co., 1931. These two classic works expound the utilitarian grounds for defining criminal behavior and for punishing crime.

Becker, Gary S. "Crime and Punishment: An Economic Approach." *Journal of Political Economy*, Vol. 76, No. 2 (March/April 1968), pp. 169–217. One of the most important recent papers on the economics of crime and crime prevention. Uses economic analysis to develop optimal public and private policies to diminish illegal behavior.

Ehrlich, Isaac. *"The Supply of Illegitimate Activities."* Ph.D. dissertation, Columbia University, 1967. A distinguished doctoral thesis that discusses the determinants of criminal behavior.

President's Commission on Law Enforcement and the Administration of Justice. *The Challenge of Crime in a Free Society.* Washington, D.C.: U.S. Government Printing Office, 1967. This report contains a great deal of factual material on the incidence of crime in the United States and on the methods of operation of law enforcement agencies.

Rottenberg, Simon. "The Clandestine Distribution of Heroin, Its Discovery and Suppression." *Journal of Political Economy*, Vol. 76, No. 1 (January/February 1968), pp. 78–90. Treats various economic aspects of the trade in opiates, including the management of heroin distribution, the meaning of price differentials, the consequences of the enforcement of drug laws, the market for corrupt police behavior, and the allocation of police resources in drug law enforcement.

————"The Social Cost of Crime and Crime Prevention." In Barbara N. McLennan, ed. *Crime in Urban Society.* New York: The Dunnellan Co., 1970, pp. 43 – 65. This article distinguishes between crimes that produce harm and those that do not and suggests that resources are wasted if they are employed in the enforcement of laws that inhibit harmless crimes. It also discusses the distribution of the costs of crime and shows that costs may fall upon others than the immediate victims and that, sometimes, the market arranges compensation to victims.

Schelling, Thomas C. "Economics and Criminal Enterprise." *The Public Interest* (Spring 1967), pp. 61–78. A discussion of the economic aspects of "organized crime."

Stigler, George J. "The Optimum Enforcement of Laws." *Journal of Political Economy*, Vol. 78, No. 3 (May/June 1970), pp. 526–536. A paper that offers proof of the proposition that full enforcement of the criminal law would be suboptimal.

Tullock, Gordon. *The Logic of the Law.* New York: Basic Books, 1971. Part III of this book deals with the criminal law and suggests some nonobvious outcomes that are produced by the application of conventional economic analysis to criminal legal questions.

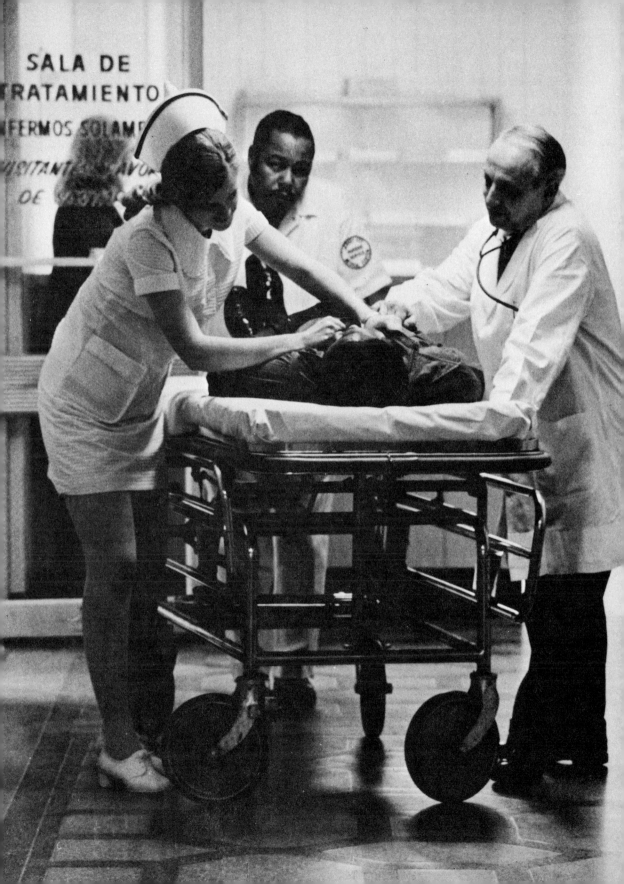

11 *Health and Medical Care*

The economics of health care is an old, old problem on which social scientists have only recently focused their attention. Many studies have criticized the quality, quantity, and economic impact of medical care in the United States. Such studies have examined the alleged shortage of physicians and of associated (paramedical) professional help, the inferior quality and rising cost of medical care, and the overall poor regional distribution of professional health care. Unfortunately, the organized medical establishment has not rushed to publicize the results of these studies or to implement changes based on their findings. Outside the medical fraternity, social scientists have begun to examine the socioeconomic nature of health care delivery systems — a term that means getting medical help to the person who needs it, when and where he needs it.

Demand and Supply of Health Care

From an individual point of view, the purchase of health care would not seem to be different from purchasing any other good or service. In a market economy, such as prevails in the United States, demand — the willingness and ability to purchase goods and services — depends directly on price and income and the availability of substitutes. But it just so happens that there is no substitute for health care, regardless of one's ability to purchase health services; inability to acquire them does not alleviate one's medical ailments. This type of demand is inelastic; that is, demand for health services is affected only slightly by price. Health care is not a commodity like coffee, where an increased price will reduce demand because of the existence of close substitutes such as Sanka or tea. Thus, because demand is inelastic, health services — apart from all social implications — are different from most goods and services in a market.

In general, physician and medical care services face a relatively inelastic demand curve. Ordinarily, a demand curve is sloped downward from left to right, as in Figure 11.1.

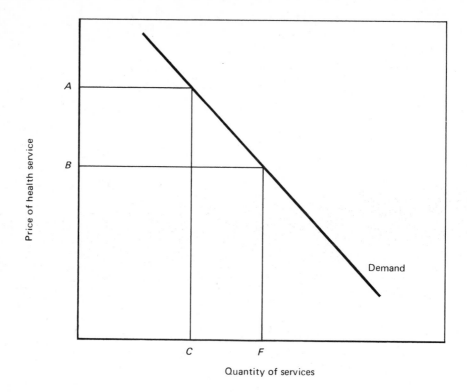

FIGURE 11.1   A relatively elastic demand curve.

The higher the price, the less the consumer will normally purchase. If the price rises from *B* to *A*, the quantity sold will fall from *F* to *C*.

However, medical care services do not follow this economic form. When a child contracts polio or breaks a leg, the average American parent, regardless of income, will attempt to acquire fast, high-quality medical care, without considering the cost. The normal reaction is to consider the health, safety, and life of the individual first — and to postpone thoughts of the cost. Therefore, when medical costs rise, the consumer, for the most part, is unresponsive to the increase. He will continue to purchase as much or almost as much as before. The demand curve for medical care will therefore be relatively inelastic and look like it does in Figure 11.2. As the price rises from *B* to *A*, there is little change in the quantity demanded, as seen by the difference between *F* and *C*.

The second major characteristic of health care is not inherent in the service performed as such but is affected by the operation of the specific market. In the United States, the economic system is supposedly based on the votes of consumers (demand) and on the willingness and ability of sellers to deliver their goods and services (supply). In such a market, the price mechanism regulates the allocation of goods and services. Depending on elasticity, when prices go up, demand declines and supply increases. The reverse happens when prices go down. In reality, the U.S.

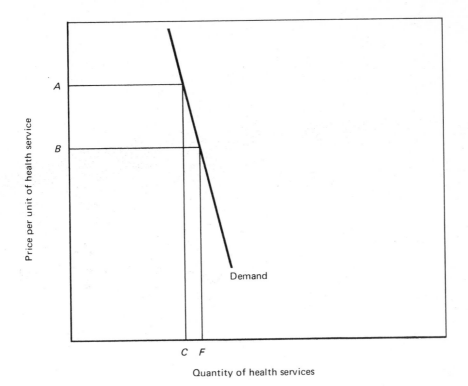

FIGURE 11.2   A relatively inelastic demand curve.

market by no means always operates in this fashion. Imperfections occur when supply, especially for goods or services — like health care — with inelastic demand, is controlled by the sellers and when income is distributed in such a way that not everybody has the ability (albeit the willingness) to purchase the good or service involved.

Organized medical groups — chiefly the American Medical Association (AMA) — have deliberately limited the supply of medical services in order to keep physicians' incomes high. One of their public explanations is that the number of physicians must be limited in order to maintain quality medical care. The result has been that, in general, people with high incomes can afford the prices charged, while low-income groups are often deprived of basic medical care. Many other countries have expanded their medical schools and increased health care coverage to protect everyone, including the poor. In this respect, the United States still has not caught up with the civilized world. This also helps to explain why about half the countries in Europe have higher life expectancy and lower infant mortality rates than the U.S. has. In 1971, a Swedish male could expect to live four years longer than his American counterpart. Not only in Sweden but also in Japan, infant mortality (deaths of infants one year or less) is one-third less than it is in the United States.

Health Expenditures in the United States

In 1969, total health care expenditures amounted to $67 billion, which was approximately 7 percent of the gross national product, a larger fraction than ever before, and the projected trend is for further percentage increases over the next decade. However, if prices increase, even though the amount of goods and services actually sold remains constant, the dollar value of GNP increases, which is deceiving; it is a money illusion. For example, it is projected that almost three times as many dollars will be spent on health care in 1980 as in 1969. But this, of course, does not necessarily mean a 300 percent increase in the delivery of health care; it is, rather, a reflection of both rising medical prices (inflation) and, to some extent,

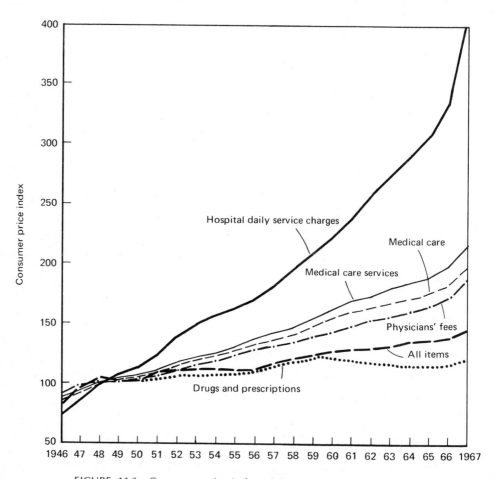

FIGURE 11.3 Consumer price index of the average cost of all medical items and selected medical subgroups in U.S. cities, from 1946 to 1967, compared to the average cost of all other goods and services. (1947 – 49 = 100.) (Source: U.S. Department of Labor, Bureau of Labor Statistics, *Monthly Labor Review*, November 1968, p. 4.)

increased services. At times, inflation can account for a large portion of the increase in value of GNP and of any of its components.

At unadjusted prices, the quantity of health care delivered increased by about 120 percent between 1950 and 1970, but it turns out that this is merely the increase in the money cost of health care. On the average, prices increased by 35 percent between 1958 and 1970 for all goods and services, but prices paid for health care far outstripped those for most other consumer goods and services. Figure 11.3 shows the price changes for medical care compared with the price changes for all other items between 1946 and 1967. Not all this increase can be explained easily.

Causes of Medical Care Price Increases. Some of the reasons for the runaway rise in health care costs are more obvious than others. Wage increases, the expansion of medical insurance programs, the relative shortage of physicians, the implementation of new and more expensive medical techniques, and the high profits of drug concerns have all played a part in the spectacular price increase for medical services.

Although some categories of paramedical personnel still receive low wages, in general, their earnings have improved substantially, and this has caused significant increases in hospital costs. Especially in hospitals and clinics, skilled and semiskilled professionals such as nurses, nurses aides, and technicians (paramedical personnel) are the bulk of labor input and constitute the largest portion of the total cost. Medical care is a very labor-intensive industry; that is, the lion's share of inputs and costs are services performed by labor — including janitors and cooks as well as paramedical personnel — rather than capital. Therefore, when the cost of unskilled, paramedical, or medical personnel increases, prices will rise commensurately. Paramedical and unskilled costs, especially, have increased over the last decade because of the rapid unionization of these groups. Physicians' costs have increased even more rapidly, as mentioned above, in part because of the AMA's policies. This type of inflationary pressure is generally known as cost-push inflation, which is different from demand-pull inflation, when consumers' willingness to purchase services is greater than the market can offer. Actually, inflation in medical care has elements of both cost-push and demand-pull.

Demand-pull inflation for medical care originates with various medical insurance plans. An increasing number of Americans over the last 20 years have been covered by medical plans (third-party payers), thereby increasing the demand for medical services, especially the services of physicians. More people can now afford medical treatment — it is that simple. Over this period there has been no increase in the number of physicians relative to the population; therefore, prices were pulled up.

Another source of rising health care costs is the increased use of new technology and equipment. Sophisticated medical techniques and hardware have been developed over the last few decades. Moreover, there has been considerable duplication by medical facilities, chiefly hospitals, in providing these new services. Most authorities believe that a 70 percent utilization rate is required to justify the purchase of sophisticated medical equipment and the creation of, say, a cardiac medical team. Yet many of these facilities operate at only 20 percent capacity. This condition obviously leads to substantial price increases for the consumer.

The rather large profits earned by pharmaceutical firms (20 percent on investment) give some indication of one important area which has caused higher medical costs.

Indeed, about 5 percent of all health care expenditures are for drugs. No wonder that the common stocks of drug companies have been held in such high esteem on the stock market.

Relative Low Standing of U. S. Health Statistics. High and ever-increasing costs for medical care deprive a large segment of the American population of decent care. Perhaps this explains why "health" in the United States is in a more precarious condition than it is in many other countries. This worsening of the nation's health is obvious from an examination of death and infant mortality rates and of statistics on the availability of hospital and health personnel.

In the United States for the last 15 years, the crude death rate has been stationary at about 9.5 per 1,000. In 1968, of the 70 countries listing crude death rates, 44 countries had lower rates than the United States. A similar situation exists with respect to infant death rates: 10 countries had lower rates than the United States.

Within the United States it also appears that the mortality rate for blacks and other nonwhites is more than double that for whites. Also, infant death rates vary considerably as between the white population and others (principally blacks). Both in 1960 and 1967, infant death rates per 1,000 live birth rates were twice as large for blacks as for whites. The highest infant death rates have been consistently found in the low-income southern states.

The United States is also far behind other countries in terms of per capita hospital facilities and health personnel. In 1967, 45 countries had more hospital beds per capita than the United States and nine countries had more physicians per capita. Indeed the physician-population ratio for the United States has barely changed over the last two decades.

Between 1960 and 1968, the civilian labor force increased by 13.1 percent, while the number of persons employed in the health field grew by 43.1 percent. Yet apparently the shortages of paramedical personnel continue in spite of the health field's increased share of the total labor force.

Regional Variation in Health Care Facilities

This shortage is closely related to the geographical distribution of physicians, registered nurses (R.N.), and licensed practical nurses (L.P.N.). In 1967, while the United States as a whole averaged 158 active physicians per 100,000 population, Mississippi had a low of 28 and New York had a high of 228 physicians per 100,000 population.

One encounters similar variations in the number of registered nurses. Connecticut, a high per capita income state, employs 536 R.N.'s per 100,000 population, while Mississippi, one of the lowest per capita income states, employs only 157 R.N.'s. The average for the nation is 313. Some states maintain a high rank in the number of R.N.'s and show a considerably lower rank in the number of L.P.N.'s. As a result of state restrictions on the performance of various functions by such personnel as L.P.N.'s and R.N.'s, the ratio of one occupation to the other will vary significantly among the states.

L.P.N.'s and R.N.'s must be considered together since the ratio between them depends largely on each state's licensing board. In some states the functions of an R.N. are performed by an L.P.N., with lower costs and less required training. Moreover, the states with more realistic training requirements employ a larger percentage of L.P.N.'s. Some observers maintain that if R.N.'s could be substituted for physicians in the performance of various minor and marginal tasks, some of the domestic shortage of physicians would also be alleviated. Naturally, organized medicine is opposed to such a scheme because, as shown in Figure 11.4, their pricing power would thereby be diminished. The consumer would receive more service (Q_1 to Q_2) at a lower price (P_1 to P_2). This is possible because, given demand D, supply of medical services (because of substitution) would increase from S_1 to S_2.

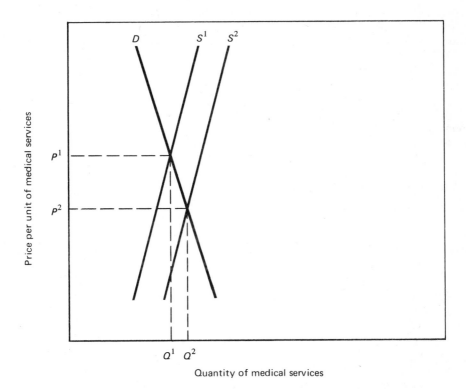

FIGURE 11.4   By substituting R.N.'s for M.D.'s the supply of health services can be increased and the cost of medical care decreased: D, demand for medical services; S_1, supply of M.D.'s; S_2, supply of services rendered by M.D.'s and R.N.'s.

The substitution of R.N.'s for M.D.'s increases the supply of health services and decreases the cost of care. But variation among the states in professional standards and entry requirements is not the only factor that determines regional distribution of the quantity and quality of health care. The general fiscal capacity of each region, state, or country also determines the kind of medical service rendered.

Fiscal Capacity of the States to Bear Medical Care Costs.   "Fiscal capacity," as used here, refers to the financial ability of each area to bear the costs of medical care. This depends greatly on the income of the population and on how much of this income can be taxed. The United States has the highest per capita income in the world, and even most of the industrialized nations have per capita incomes that are at least half that of the United States.

But the variation in per capita income within the United States is also substantial. In 1969, overall per capita income was $3,680, ranging from a high of $4,537 in Connecticut to a low of $2,192 in Mississippi. However, even the low per capita income in Mississippi was surpassed by only eight countries. Also, in the United States, equally significant is the variation in income between whites and blacks. In 1968, 1.5 percent of all white families had incomes under $1,000, while 3.9 percent of Negro families were in this category, and the same unevenness shows up in the $3,000 and $5,000 categories as well. The variance was greater in the South than it was in the North and West. Therefore, more people in this area, and more blacks among them, are unable to acquire medical services. Moreover, because a disproportionate share of the poor are located in those states with low per capita incomes, there is in such places both a greater demand for public assistance for health and less fiscal capacity to meet this need. Because these states can tax less, they cannot provide the services that wealthier states can afford.

Health Care and Income Distribution

We continue to spend an increasing proportion of our GNP on health care, more, in fact, than any other country spends, yet our death rates and infant mortality rates are significantly above those of many countries. Since health care in the United States is still essentially on a fee-for-service basis, those with relatively low incomes receive only marginal or inferior medical services.[1] For example, there is a strong correlation between income level, as represented by job classification, and typical mortality rates. In general, those with the highest income level, such as "professionals," have lower mortality rates due to tuberculosis than do lower-income groups, such as "unskilled labor." In the 1930's, the mortality rate from pulmonary tuberculosis per 100,000 people between the ages of 25 and 44 years in 10 states was:

Professionals	28.6
Clerks	67.6
Skilled Workers	69.0
Unskilled Workers	193.5

The percentage of deaths per 100,000 people due to pneumonia was:

Professionals	5.8
Clerks	6.5
Skilled Workers	7.2
Unskilled Workers	9.4

During the same period the annual number of deaths per 1,000 population averaged 8.7 for all who were gainfully employed; it was:

---

[1]*Public Health Reports, 1934*, Vol. 49 (Washington, D.C.: U.S. Government Printing Office, 1934), pp. 1101–1111.

Professionals	7.0
Clerks	7.4
Skilled Workers	8.1
Unskilled Workers	13.1

Although we continue to spend more and more on health care, lower-income groups fail to participate in the benefits which might accrue from these services. While health facilities and health manpower continue to increase, their distribution is geographically inequitable. Even in locations where adequate medical facilities and health manpower are available, health services are not distributed evenly, as indicated by infant mortality rates. The question then remains what can or should be done to alleviate regional and family income problems surrounding the delivery of quality medical care.

Anarchy in the Health Care Delivery System

In addition to the differentiation in health care that results from variations in state legislation, individual income differences, and geographical preferences, there is the larger problem that there is no cohesive approach to medical care within any one state or, for that matter, within any single municipality. In the United States, in general, each hospital has gone its own way in developing facilities and services to suit the needs of pressure groups within the hospital administration. Few states or municipalities have established regional systems to oversee the development of medical facilities that fall within their geographical jurisdictions.

This chaotic health delivery system is sometimes referred to as the market economy. Allegedly, in such a market there are many sellers and buyers who compete with each other for services through independent decisions. However, this is not characteristic of the medical market because of the previously mentioned monopolistic elements (partly controlled by the AMA) which can make services artificially scarce. One way to counterbalance these deficiencies (since the AMA is here to stay) is to consolidate, at the metropolitan or state level, health facilities such as clinics, hospitals, and personnel. This might contribute to a higher quality of health services for a larger number of people.

True, physicians might be reluctant to reduce their options, an unavoidable result of full-scale regionalization. Treatment location, availability of sophisticated medical equipment, and the population to be served would no longer be under the sole option of the physician. Also, the consumer might be reluctant to embrace regionalization of the health-care system. In some instances, the consumer would be forced to travel greater distances to receive specialized care. Also, the consumer might fear that regionalization would increase the depersonalization of health care — by reducing his choice of physician, for example.

The Supply and Training of Physicians

Certainly, regional problems would be alleviated if the total supply of medical facilities and personnel were increased. One way would be to raise the number of trained physicians.

For the most part, the educational system through which the student physician must travel has remained substantially unchanged for centuries. The most constructive criticism leveled at any profession is often made by those practicing within the profession. One such criticism pinpoints the refusal by medical schools to utilize the new technology or to organize change in the medical curriculum:[2]

Few of the recent important innovations in medical care — for example, multiple varieties of group practice, experimental comprehensive neighborhood health centers, the increasing use of paramedical personnel and subprofessionals, the application of computer and engineering technologies — are reflected as yet in the undergraduate curriculum.

Therefore, students graduating from medical schools are ill prepared to use modern techniques which are both cost-saving and quality-improving.

A second criticism concerns the long years required for the training of physicians. For each year of training, society is burdened not only with the direct cost of that training but also with the loss of productive services that could otherwise have been rendered. The opportunity cost to society for a resource is measured by the services that could have been generated in its next best use. Currently, medical training consists of four years of undergraduate work, four years of medical school, and a lengthy residency. In 1970, the Carnegie Commission on Higher Education recommended that the number of years required for a physician's training be shortened. The specialists on the commission did not feel that the compression of this period or a new emphasis on technology would in any way diminish the physician's skills. The commission furthermore stated that:[3]

A surplus of qualified candidates for medical schools exists . . . because medical schools have been accepting just half of their applicants in recent years. Women, members of minority groups and those who go abroad to learn medicine could fill the proposed new places in medical schools . . .

Yet the AMA since its inception in 1847 has successfully pursued its goal of limiting the number of entrants into the profession. Thus indirectly, it supports the recent unreasonable increases in physicians' fees. It can easily be seen in Figure 11.5 why the AMA abuses its power to increase physician revenue.

With the actual number of physicians today, total revenue, that is, quantity of service times price per unit (quadrant P_1, E_1, Q_1, O), is much larger than it would be if there were an additional number of physicians (quadrant P_2, E_2, Q_2, O), because when the supply curve moves to the right with more service rendered, total revenue declines sharply. This is particularly the case when the response to price changes is relatively small in the quantity demanded, or, in the economist's language, when demand is price inelastic. With a more elastic demand for and/or supply of medical

[2]Fremont J. Lyden, Jack H. Geiger, and Osler L. Peterson, *The Training of Good Physicians* (Cambridge, Mass.: Harvard University Press, 1968), pp. 237 – 238.
[3]Lawrence K. Altman, "Medical Schools Urge to Expand and Alter Goals," *New York Times*, October 30, 1970, p. 16.

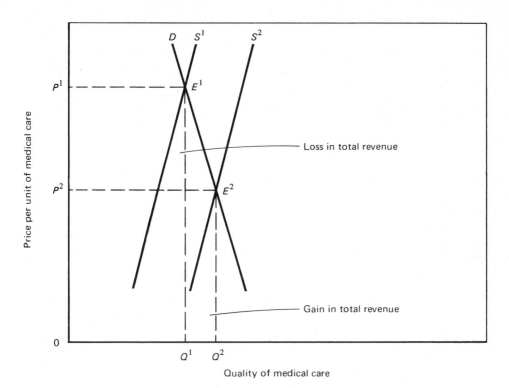

FIGURE 11.5 AMA restrictive policies as they increase physicians' income: D, demand for physician services; S_1, actual supply of physicians; S_2, potential supply of physicians; E_1, loss in total revenue; E_2, gain in total revenue.

services, the quantity demanded would increase more with a lower price and total revenue would not change as sharply, as shown in Figure 11.6. In such a case, there would be less incentive to use monopolistic powers.

As mentioned at the beginning of this chapter, the demand for medical services is inelastic with respect to price (as shown in Figure 11.5A). Under these conditions, the powers of organized medicine are brought to bear to keep medical services scarce — in much the same way that other monopolistic economic sectors (discussed in Chapter 14) act to protect their interests.

The Nation's Need for Family Physicians. In order to improve even slightly the current physician-patient ratio in the United States, it has been estimated that a 53.1 percent increase in the number of physicians will be required during the period 1968 through 1980.[4] Many doubt that this substantial increase can be achieved by

[4]Michael Pilot, "Health Manpower 1980," *Occupational Outlook Quarterly* (Washington, D.C: U.S. Department of Labor, Government Printing Office, Winter 1970), p. 3.

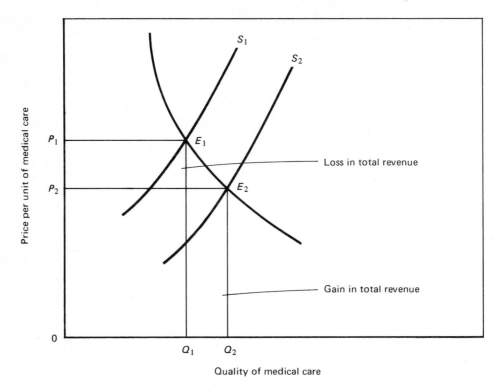

FIGURE 11.6 A more elastic demand for supply of medical services.

the medical schools as they are presently constituted. Others suggest that even if the number of physicians doubled over the next decade, unless there were a change in the system of medical education, the delivery of quality medical care would continue to be inequitable with respect both to socioeconomic status and geographical location.

There are approximately 325,000 physicians in this country, but only 195,000 are actually practicing medicine. Of these 195,000 physicians, 55,000 (28 percent) are generalists, whose average age is nearly 55; the remaining 140,000 physicians are specialists, whose average age is about 38. This is a reflection of the present trend in medicine, and there is no reason to believe that any significant change will be forthcoming. In addition, the physicians who are practicing are not evenly distributed throughout the nation. For example, in 1969, approximately 1,000 new pediatricians came into the marketplace. Of these, approximately one-half stayed in teaching hospitals, while the remainder went into private practice, principally in the states of California, New York, and Massachusetts.

It is generally accepted among many physicians that one physician (including in that term general practitioners, internists, and pediatricians) can provide quality medical care to 500 families (approximately 2,000 persons). Assuming that the population of the United States is 200 million, this means that we require the services of only 100,000 such physicians, geographically distributed according to need, to provide a point of entry for the primary health care requirements of the nation. If we total the 55,000 generalists, the 15,000 practicing pediatricians, and the 35,000 practicing internists, we are already well over this 100,000 mark. However, we are still left with two major problems: (1) the 105,000 generalists, pediatricians, and internists are not equitably distributed over the nation according to need; and (2) the number of generalists is decreasing each year.

The entering medical student has recently gained a reputation for being a starry-eyed idealist who is eager to maximize his social usefulness by becoming a "family physician." This is questionable. Of the medical students entering Harvard Medical School in 1967, only 4 percent indicated a preference for becoming family physicians; in 1969, this percentage rose to 25 percent. However, what their final decisions will be with respect to medical specialty is sheer conjecture. In the past, by the time the medical student had completed his traditional medical training and been exposed to and influenced by the many factions within the medical establishment, he had been convinced of the importance of being a specialist. Should this trend continue, the number of per capita practicing family physicians will not increase sufficiently to improve medical services in the United States.

Quality of Medical Care.   Aside from the quantity of physicians available, one must also raise the issue of the quality of medical care. Over the last 20 years many studies have evaluated the quality of medical care in the United States, and by and large these studies present a rather dismal picture of the quality of medical care received by Americans, rich and poor alike.

An examination of the records of the Kansas Blue Cross Association in 1969 showed that the level of effective operations for the removal of (1) tonsils, (2) hemorrhoids, (3) varicose veins, and (4) hernia repair in all hospitals in 11 regions of the state supported a medical variation of Parkinson's law: patient admissions for surgery expand to fill the available beds, operating suites, and surgeon's time.[5]

In another study, the records of 246 hysterectomies performed in three states at 10 hospitals were examined. The findings revealed that about 33 percent of all patients operated upon either had no disease of the organs removed or else another disease was found which indicated that the hysterectomy operation was useless or even harmful.[6] Dr. John H. Knowles, a leading medical authority and now President of the Rockefeller Foundation, faced censure by his fellow physicians when he pointed out[7] that "30 to 40 percent [of American physicians] are making a killing in their practice of medicine through incredible amounts of unnecessary surgery."

The quality of medical services performed by physicians can also be deduced from a study of 159 physicians and approximately 1,000 of their 100,000 prescriptions. According to Dr. Robert McCleery,[8] "Despite the author's lenient criteria for therapeutic acceptability, 37 percent of the prescriptions examined were found to be nonacceptable." The study also revealed that 44 percent of all prescriptions written by private practitioners in their offices were nonacceptable, while only 16 percent of the prescriptions written by physicians in hospitals were nonacceptable.

---

[5]C. E. Lewis, "Variations in Incidence of Surgery," *New England Journal of Medicine,* October 16, 1969, pp. 880 – 884.

[6]N. F. Miller, "Hysterectomy: Therapeutic Necessity or Surgical Racket?" *American Journal of Obstetrics and Gynecology,* Vol. *51* (1946), pp. 804 – 810.

[7]*New York Times,* June 5, 1972.

[8]Robert S. McCleery, *One Life — One Physician* (Washington, D.C.: Public Affairs Press, 1971), pp. 21 – 22.

But the quality of medical care rendered is deficient not only because of overservicing (unnecessary operations and drugs) but also because of the lack of continuous training of physicians. Studies have shown that at least half of all general practitioners seldom, if ever, participate in medical updating programs.[9] Considering the rapid growth in medical knowledge, a physician can easily become outdated after his first few years of practice.[10]

One must conclude that there are many persons in the United States who receive only marginal medical care. Moreover, not all those who *are* serviced by physicians and the medical establishment are fortunate enough to receive acceptable medical care. Apparently, the rich can receive unacceptable medical care almost as easily as the poor. What seems to be indicated is the establishment of a system of quality control that would range from the teaching hospital to the office of the physician practicing in private. Where quality control by peer groups has been established, the quality of medicine has improved significantly.

The Way Out of the Medical Mess

Assuming that adequate health care is a right, not a privilege, how should this country pay for the necessary services? In general, in the United States, "ability to pay" determines who receives health care. Some of those with limited financial resources purchase health care at a discount through various governmental programs such as Medicare and Medicaid. The Medicare program which affects 18 million persons, 65 years and over, comes under the jurisdiction of the Social Security programs and consists of two parts: (1) hospital and extended care benefits financed by payroll deductions from employees and employers through Social Security and (2) supplemental medical insurance (for physicians' services) financed through premiums paid voluntarily by each beneficiary. This amount is matched by the federal government. Medicaid offers federal assistance to three special groups: persons under 21 years of age for whom there is a proven inability to pay, persons permanently and totally disabled without income, and parents receiving Aid to Families with Dependent Children (AFDC). Others, through the purchase of hospitalization insurance, use private third-party payers such as Blue Cross and Blue Shield. Also, there are national health insurance plans in proposal form and experiments with group practice.

Existing Health Care Insurance Plans. In many hospitals in the United States, well over three-quarters of the fees are paid by third-party payers. But a large group of citizens without the financial ability to purchase sufficient health care insurance must go without such services because they do not qualify for the current government programs. Under the present system, the government pays approximately 36 percent of the nation's health care bill. Yet Blue Cross-Blue Shield fees have soared over the last two decades — some say because of waste and failure to regulate physicians' fees. In fact, according to a *New York Times* article appearing September 13, 1971, "Congressional investigators found some local plans were paying the country club dues of Blue Cross executives, while others were paying for executives'

---

[9]C. E. Lewis and R. S. Hassonein, "Continuing Medical Education — An Epidemiologic Evaluation," *New England Journal of Medicine,* January 29, 1970, pp. 254 – 259.
[10]McCleery, *op, cit.,* pp. 60 – 61.

vacations in Hawaii." Health care costs have also spiraled because neither private nor nonprofit insurance companies maintain effective control over the fees of physicians and hospitals. The fees charged to the government under Medicaid are habitually met without question or the imposition of controls of any kind.

Some Recent Proposals. An increasing number of countries have adopted national health insurance plans through which every citizen, regardless of income, can receive health care. This type of plan, besides being capable of fulfilling the needs of all income groups for adequate health care, also indirectly redistributes income. Since the lower-income groups pay less taxes but receive proportionately the same health benefits as other income groups, there is a shift of buying power away from the higher-income group. In the United States, for the last decade, such plans have only been debated. Some of the proposals currently before Congress include the following:

1. The Kennedy-Griffiths bill would provide a universal form of comprehensive national health insurance, with funding being supplied by employers, employees, and general tax revenues. It is the only proposal that offers totally comprehensive benefits, while placing a minimum cost directly on the individual.
2. The Rockefeller proposal is essentially a state plan that would retain Medicare and provide basic, but not comprehensive, coverage, with optional benefits available through private insurance. It too would be compulsory.
3. The Feldstein plan would be a universal major risk insurance that would provide comprehensive coverage, with deductibles existing as a percentage of income. Cash grants would be made below the deductible level.
4. The AETNA Life plan would offer voluntary health insurance for low-income persons, with a percentage of premiums to be paid by the family, and voluntary major medical expense coverage for all. Deductions before payment for major medical expenses would be determined by family income and size.
5. The Javits plan is very similar to the Kennedy-Griffiths plan. The difference lies mainly in deductibles and substantial co-payments — the payments shared by the health agency and subscriber.
6. The Medicredit plan is a proposal of the American Medical Association. It would offer a voluntary program of tax credit inducement for those having private health insurance. It would also have deductibles and co-payments.

Group Practice. There is only hope that a national insurance plan will soon be adopted in the United States. Therefore, besides the idea of financing health care through third-party payers, other palliatives have been sought. One of these is "group practice," or the sharing of facilities and paramedical personnel by a consortium of physicians. Those in favor of group practice claim: (1) that financial and organizational advantages accrue to member physicians; (2) that group practice has a favorable effect on the quality of care provided; and (3) that there are social benefits resulting from the more efficient allocation of scarce resources.

The sharing of facilities and of paramedical personnel may lower fixed and variable costs and increase patient-physician contact for lower-income families. Fixed costs include office space and equipment which physicians use regardless of the number of patients they have. Variable costs could include the utilization of medical personnel, which will vary with the number of patients. The economies derived could keep the cost of health care from increasing as fast as it has in the past.

The number of group physicians has tripled from 15,009 in 1959 to 40,093 in 1969, while the total number of groups has more than doubled. However, group practice in many states is still discouraged by restrictive legislation that is organized either directly or indirectly by the AMA. The AMA may threaten group physicians with damaging actions; for instance, it can refuse appointments to hospitals or discourage referrals of patients by individual practitioners. This could explain why group practice has not had a more significant increase since 1950.[11]

Better Utilization of Medical Manpower. The restructuring of paramedical personnel and other problems in the health field are related in great measure to a single issue — the physician shortage. A basic question is whether tasks now being performed by physicians could be done as well, or even better, by others and what impact this restructuring would have on the total supply of health care personnel.

The substantial increase in the use of paramedical personnel could improve the quality and quantity of health care to groups previously denied the services of physicians due to high cost and limited supply. The primary justification for the increased use of paramedical personnel is based on the following premises: (1) the supply of physicians has not increased in proportion to the demand for medical services; (2) the geographical distribution of physicians is inequitable; (3) the traditional structure of the medical establishment has been unresponsive to the pressing needs of contemporary society.

The main intent behind better utilization of paramedical personnel is not to lower medical costs but to improve and increase medical services. Yet studies on the more effective utilization of paramedical personnel show that despite manpower shortages in many of the paramedical occupations, various barriers exist which prevent a solution to this shortage. Arbitrary licensing of personnel in certain occupations is sometimes required. At times, an unnecessarily high level of education and training is set as a prerequisite for entering an occupation. Paramedical personnel frequently are not utilized efficiently, and there is often a considerable overlap of functions between occupations which have significantly different hiring-in standards. Training programs with unduly high entrance requirements have lengthened training time beyond the reasonable need of the occupation. Finally, paramedical jobs are so structured that there are few opportunities for upgrading and promotion.

Conclusions

It is obvious that a great deal of improvement is required if the nation's medical system is to provide even adequate care. The main avenues to reform of the health care system lie in: (1) the modification and improvement of the training of physicians, including quality control and peer review; (2) regionalization of the health care system; (3) new federal health care plans for payment of services; (4) the encouragement of group practice; and (5) improved utilization of paramedical personnel.

---

[11]John M. Glasgow, "Issues in Medical Economics: The Health Care Costs and Organization" (Paper presented before the Association of Evolution Economics, Detroit, Michigan, December 1970), pp. 27 – 29, passim.

SUGGESTIONS FOR FURTHER READING

Abse, Dannie. *Medicine on Trial.* New York: Crown Publishers, 1967.

Anderson, Ronald and Anderson, Odin W. *A Decade of Health Services.* Chicago: University of Chicago Press, 1967.

Cronkhite, Leonard W. "Allied Health Personnel — The Shortage and the Solution." *The Massachusetts Physician,* Vol. 26 (December 1967), pp. 1052 – 1056.

Fein, Rashi. *The Doctor Shortage: An Economic Diagnosis.* Washington, D.C.: The Brookings Institution, 1967.

Goldstein, Harold M. "More on Profits and Hospitals." *Journal of Economic Issues,* Vol. 5, No. 4 (December 1971), pp. 113 – 123.

————and Horowitz, Morris A. "Paramedical Manpower: A Restructuring of Occupations." Paper presented before the American Public Health Association's 99th Annual Meeting, Minneapolis, Minnesota, October 12, 1971.

————. *Restructuring Paramedical Occupations,* Final Report to the Manpower Administration. Washington, D.C.: U.S. Department of Labor, Government Printing Office, January 1972.

Lasagna, Louis. "Why Are Doctors Out of Step?" *The New Republic,* January 2, 1965, pp. 13 – 15.

Lyden, Fremont J., Geiger, Jack H., and Peterson, Osler L. *The Training of Good Physicians.* Cambridge, Mass.: Harvard University Press, 1968.

Pratt, Lois. "The Relationship of Socio-Economic Status to Health." *The American Journal of Public Health,* Vol. 61, No. 2 (February 1971), pp. 281 – 292.

Somers, Herman M. and Somers, Ann R. *Medicine and the Hospitals: Issues and Prospects.* Washington, D.C.: The Brookings Institution, 1967.

12 *Education*

Education in the United States today is a giant, complex undertaking in which all parts of the society play an important role. It is primarily financed by the government through public institutions, but the efforts of individuals, families, and private institutions are also very important. Through education, democracy's need for an informed electorate combines with the goal of every individual for a higher income and better life, and with the desire of every company for better qualified workers who can be more productive. Yet though educational aims are often very personal ones, the only instruments by which they can be achieved is government — whether national, state, or local.

Economists who specialize in the study of public or government spending often view education as part of the whole package of social welfare expenditures. These include government cash grants or services which benefit persons or families directly. Social welfare expenditures for students in schools (or patients in hospitals) provide direct benefits to recipients, as compared with spending on defense or fire protection which benefits society as a whole but which may help the individual only indirectly.

The decision, then, as to how much to spend on education is a very complex one. The purpose of this chapter is to discuss a number of views of education, and some of the ways education must compete for resources with other uses, in order to have some basis for deciding how much we should spend on education.

Education must compete with other programs, such as health spending, for a share of the government's total social welfare expenditures. Similarly, the whole set of social welfare expenditures must compete with the other functions of government that benefit society as a whole. The President, the governors, the mayors, and other elected officials who have responsibility for government spending decisions must give their attention to all the programs competing for support. At the same time, they must concern themselves with the total spending undertaken by their unit of government. Even when resources and people are fully employed, the income of the total economy is limited, and the more government spends and taxes, the less there is left to be spent in the markets.

Educational Spending as Related to Income and Other Spending

For these reasons, the amount of spending on education should be related to the income of the nation as a whole, to the total expenditures of the government, and, in particular, to·the total spending on programs that make up the social welfare expenditures. Table 12.1 provides a basis for making these comparisons. Over the past 20 years, from 1950 to 1970, total spending on education rose from less than $11 billion to $60.5 billion. Some of this increase was the result of price and salary increases, but not all of it was. In 1950, total spending on education was 4.1 percent of the gross national product, a measure of the total spending available to the country for everything. By 1970, spending on education had risen to 6.3 percent of the gross national product, almost as much as spending on defense, though in 1950 defense had a far higher share than education.

These increases, in total spending on education and in education's share of the gross national product, reflect a trend toward greater government spending on social welfare generally. The increases in spending on income maintenance (including Social Security and public assistance cash payments) were even greater than those for education. Total expenditures for health also went up dramatically. The increases in health spending were partly in the private expenditures of patients' families and insurance companies, but the government's share rose sharply after 1967 with the introduction of Medicare and other programs.

The increased spending on social welfare expenditures in general, and on education in particular, reflects more than price increases. The increases indicate that, as a nation, we are now willing to spend a larger *share* of our increasing income on these social welfare expenditures. The increases also indicate that, over the past 20 years we have been willing to do this as individuals, by paying these out of our own family incomes for tuition bills and other expenses, and as taxpayers by meeting the needs of government budgets. The government's *share* of social welfare expenditures rose little in the latter 1960's, but it has varied very widely from 1950 to 1970.

Government Share of Spending for Education. The government *share* of education spending has also been fairly constant over the past two decades. Some 82.4 percent of the $60.5 billion spent on education in 1970 were government dollars. Of these $49.9 billion, the federal government paid more than $5.6 billion, the highest amount ever, reflecting the new programs of the late 1960's. But the lion's share was the 88.5 percent spent by the states and local governments.

The importance of education in government budgets can also be demonstrated by the share of total tax dollars spent on education. In 1970, one of every six government tax dollars (16.5 percent) was spent for education. The federal government's share represented less than 3 percent of total federal spending. But on spending education constituted nearly 40 percent of the 1970 budgets of the state and local governments combined.

Many of the decisions that have led to increased spending on education have therefore been made in or near our homes. There have been personal and family decisions to meet higher tuition costs. Taxpayers in cities and towns have decided to

Table 12.1   Public and Private Expenditures for Social Welfare, 1949 – 50 and 1969 – 70

Type of Expenditure	1949 – 50	1969 – 70 [a]
Total, net [b]	$35,439	$206,091
Public	23,508	143,046
Private	12,262	65,633
Income Maintenance	10,723	72,235
Public [c]	9,758	61,510
Private	965	10,725
Health	12,129	67,240
Public	3,065	24,982
Private	9,064	42,258
Education	10,914	60,519
Public	9,366	49,869
Private	1,548	10,650
Welfare and Other Services	2,004	8,685
Public [d]	1,319	6,685
Private	685	2,000
Public expenditures as percent of total expenditures for specified programs		
Total [e]	65.7	68.5
Income Maintenance	91.0	85.2
Health	25.3	37.2
Education	85.8	82.4
Welfare and Other Services	65.8	77.0
All expenditures as percent of gross national product		
Total, net [b]	13.5	21.6
Income Maintenance	4.1	7.6
Health	4.6	7.0
Education	4.1	6.3
Welfare and Other Services	.8	.9

Source: Alfred M. Skolnik and Sophie R. Dales, "Social Welfare Expenditures in Fiscal Year 1970," *Research and Statistics Note No. 22 — 1970* (Washington, D.C.: U.S. Social Security Administration, November 30, 1970), pp. 1 – 4.

[a] Preliminary data.
[b] Total expenditures adjusted to eliminate duplication resulting from use of cash payments received under public and private social welfare programs to purchase medical care and educational services.
[c] Includes cash benefits and administrative costs under social insurance, public assistance, and veterans' programs. Excludes cost of medical services provided in conjunction with these programs and other welfare programs. These medical services are included under "Health."
[d] Work relief, food stamps, surplus food for the needy and for institutions, child nutrition, institutional care, child welfare, special OEO programs, veterans' welfare services, vocational rehabilitation, and housing.
[e] Before adjustment for elimination of duplication.

provide increasing support for the schools of their communities, though in many places this attitude now appears to be changing. And state governments have increased spending on local schools and on state colleges and universities.

Why have we as a nation continued and even increased our spending on education? One reason is that we are rich and are getting richer; we can afford it. But that is not an adequate answer because we have seen that national spending on education has gone up even faster than national income has risen, and there have been very few taxpayer revolts against higher school budgets as compared with the number of big budgets accepted willingly every year.

Another reason is that over the past two decades we have had more people to educate. The birthrate went up dramatically when veterans returned to their homes and started new families after World War II. The results of this "baby boom" were more pupils in the schools in the 1950's and 1960's; many more people had to be educated. But that is not an adequate answer either because education spending *per pupil* also rose. There are other reasons for the willingness to spend more.

Education as an Investment.   One view of education that would help to justify these increases is that education is like an investment. As an industrial country, we have seen investments in machines and factories pay off. Those who make the investments usually get their money back with interest or profits. A major reason for the continued increases in national income is found in the extra production we get from these investments in machinery, factories, and other types of capital that make industry more productive.

But no machine is productive by itself; ultimately, the machines and processes must be operated and managed by people. Therefore, as we invest in even more complex machines to achieve greater productivity in industry, we must find better educated people to operate and manage them. And we must find yet more sophisticated people to generate the new ideas and knowledge that will make it possible to invent the new machines and perfect the processes in the first place.

Education is therefore viewed by some economists as a kind of investment in human capital that is much like the investment in machines and other physical forms of capital. Employers find that a worker with better training, one with more education, can produce more. They are willing to pay higher wages to someone who is better qualified, because the worker's production will justify the higher rewards and still leave a profit for the employer.

Education and Economic Growth.   For society as a whole, then, investment in human capital through spending on education is likely to lead to a higher national income by providing higher wages for workers who are educated and higher profits for their employers. Some studies have dealt with the reasons behind the historical trend toward an increasing national income. For example, in one study[1] the figures on national income from 1929 to 1957 were adjusted to determine the change in real national income, after increases in the level of prices had been accounted for. Then the change in real national income was related to the number of employed persons to determine the average increase in real national income per employed person. Finally, when the different sources of the growth were explored, it was estimated that greater education of the labor force accounted for 21 percent of the increase in real national income per employed person, while another 36 percent of the growth was related to the expansion of knowledge.

One good reason for a nation to continue increased spending on education, therefore, is this historical growth in our nation's income that appears as the reward

---

[1]Edward F. Denison, *The Sources of Economic Growth in the United States and the Alternatives before Us* (New York: Committee for Economic Development, January 1962).

for or return on the investment in human capital. Such economic growth motivates individuals, as workers and employers, to make the investment through taxes or through their own spending because they can see *how* they share in the fruits of the growth.

Individual Rewards for Education. The individual as a worker, for example, can see that the average wage for a high school dropout is substantially lower than the pay for a high school graduate. He can also see that having some college education brings the pay level higher than that of the high school graduate, that the college or university degree brings still higher rewards, and that the highest salaries often go to those with advanced or professional education. Table 12.2 shows how family income rises with increases in the head of the family's level of education, regardless of race. While studies of the U.S. Department of Labor periodically demonstrate this trend that more education brings greater personal income, those who check the want ads, agencies, and employers also have this pointed out to them time and again, even in good times. When there is unemployment, unless it occurs in industries where there are many workers with advanced training, the unemployed see that the jobs available tend to go to those who have better qualifications and that unemployment is greatest for the high school dropout.

While the individuals already in or entering the labor market can see this for themselves, they are also continually reminded by their parents (and by evidence like that in Table 12.2) that the differential is increasing. Over the years, the educational requirements for many jobs have gone up as both the jobs and the educational level of the population changed. To become a policeman some years ago, for example, it was not necessary to show a high school diploma; but in some cities

Table 12.2   Median Money Income of Families by Years of School Completed and by Race of Family Head, 1961 and 1969

Race and Education	1961	1969
White Families	6,100	10,089
Elementary School	4,419	6,769
High School		
1-3 years	6,036	9,342
4 years	6,548	10,563
College	8,560	13,426
1-3 years	7,586	11,949
4 years or more	9,503	14,685
Other Families	3,340	6,340
Elementary School	2,593	4,754
High School		
1-3 years	3,711	6,217
4 years	4,773	7,875
College	6,593	10,555
1-3 years	n.a.	9,194
4 years or more	n.a.	13,682

Source: *Statistical Abstract of the U.S., 1971* (Washington, D.C.: U.S. Government Printing Office, 1971), p. 319.

today, a college degree is required. And for the new jobs being developed in new industries, such as electronic data processing, the educational requirements start out at a high level.

As a result, for strictly financial reasons the individual and his family often see that the investment in more education will bring a high rate of return. The "interest" rate on this investment seems to be a good one, over the work lifetime of a student, even if he includes in the costs of education the money that he would have earned if he had spent his class and study time at a full-time job.

There are, of course, exceptions to these wage averages at each level of education. A great deal depends on how much a person has learned, and some may learn more with fewer years of education than others who stay in school longer. Some jobs require high skill levels or high risks and pay very well regardless of educational attainment — professional sports, for example. Other individuals of superior intelligence or ability, perhaps helped by daring and luck, may do very well as compared with their more educated friends. But these are the exceptions to the rule and to the averages. And one of the rewards for greater education is the ability to avoid the very risky jobs and to get more comfortable working conditions. On the average, these better conditions are accompanied by the higher lifetime earnings and more comfortable life style of the better educated person.

Employers' Views.   Similarly, employers find that their own investments in education bring profitable returns. Many employers do much more than seek the most qualified employees; many run their own training programs or pay tuition for their employees in educational institutions. This may appear to be a risky investment. After all, the employer who invests in training a worker may find the worker leaving for another firm that will pay him more for his new skills and knowledge — something that will not happen to his investment in the plant and equipment he owns. Yet employers continue such programs because they find that enough of their workers will stay with them to use their training. Despite the loss of some trained workers and despite the costs of their education, these employers find that they get sufficiently high production from the workers who remain. This increased production yields enough profit to justify paying the trained workers higher wages and to justify continuing the educational programs because, for the owners of the firm, there is still a return on the investment.

These are good reasons why individuals — as workers, employers, and owners of firms — invest their own money in training and education. Beyond these investment reasons, however, there are social motives that help to explain why our nation has been willing to invest tax dollars in free education, available and even compulsory for all who qualify.

Education and Social Goals

One of the basic goals of American society has always been the preservation of democracy as we practice it and the prevention of an authoritarian type of government, whether a dictatorship of the right or the left. Many believe that an informed electorate, an educated group of citizens voting in this democratic process, is the only way to maintain the quality of democracy itself. Therefore, a foreigner who applies for citizenship must be able to read, write, and show an understanding of our Constitution. For the same reason, we stress in the most elementary grades the history of the United States and an understanding of the foundations of democracy. As a society, we look upon a minimum level of education for all as a keystone in the structure of our system and as a prerequisite to its preservation.

Another basic goal of our society is to provide for greater equality among people than would result if the rewards of the market, in wages, prices, and profits, were the sole determinants of who got what share of the national total of income or production. There are many policies designed to meet this goal. For example, we tend to tax the rich, who have higher incomes and more property, at a higher rate for the support of our public services. We also have public assistance and other forms of income maintenance for those who would have little or no income from the sale of their services or property, and minimum wage laws which dictate the least a worker can be paid for his hire. By such policies and laws, we provide for a more equal distribution of the individual shares of the national income.

Even with such policies, however, there are a large number of families living in poverty or on substantially lower incomes than the average for all American families. Studies have shown that the children of these low-income families also tend to have low incomes, that, in a sense, poverty may be hereditary. Similarly, studies have shown that the children of richer families tend to be richer than their parents, partly because they inherit property and partly because they tend to reach the higher levels of education that permit them to earn more.

Free public education is seen as one way of breaking this hereditary cycle. By providing easy access to education, we permit the children of poorer families to get the qualifications that their families may not have had. When we include the value of educational services as part of each family's income, income differentials are, to some degree at least, ironed out. Even more importantly, by providing the education for the children of poor families, we tend to improve their chances of obtaining the jobs that will pay higher wages. In this way, increased government investment in public education tends to establish greater equality of opportunity for the children of all families. But this does not come wholly at the expense of the rich. To some degree, all share in paying the costs of education. Though the poor may benefit more from primary and secondary schools, research has indicated that the rich tend to be subsidized in higher education. In California and Wisconsin, for example, the cost of college education per student exceeds the cost of tuition by a substantial amount. Children of richer families tend to go to the higher-cost state universities, while enrollments in the lower-cost state colleges or junior colleges derive largely from families with lower incomes. Even after allowing for the fact that richer families pay more taxes in these states, the richer families get more of a subsidy for their children's university education than do the poorer families whose children attend lower-cost or no institutions.[2] In higher education, then, the richer families get some extra benefits, though the opportunity to attend may be important to all.

There are, then, three important reasons for the continued increase in the investment in public education: (1) it will help maintain and improve our system of democracy; (2) it will bring returns in the growth of national income and in the increases in wages and profits that are part of the total national income; and (3) it will promote social goals of greater equality of income and opportunity.

---

[2]W. Lee Hansen, "Income Distribution Effects of Higher Education," *The American Economic Review*, Vol. 9, No. 2 (May 1970), pp. 335 – 340.

Educational Spending: Past, Present, and Future

Yet the role of education in achieving these goals does not guarantee that educational spending can, or should, continue to increase at a particular rate or that increases at any rate can be justified and paid without difficulty. As we have already indicated, educational spending is paid for both out of the private incomes of families, firms, and institutions and out of the tax dollars collected at all levels of government. This means that education has to compete with other kinds of family spending and with other government programs for the dollars needed to serve students both in public and in independent, nonpublic institutions.

Enrollment Trends. Enrollment, by level of institution and by whether the institution is under public or nonpublic control, is shown in Table 12.3. The vast majority of students in primary and secondary schools are in public institutions; the nonpublic schools are largely those sponsored by church affiliations or are for the richer families of the nation. It is interesting to compare the growth of enrollment over the last decade for all levels of education with the projected fall in enrollments in elementary schools by the end of the current decade. The projected decline in the number of students in the lower grades reflects the expected continuation of a lower birthrate.

Table 12.3   Enrollment in U.S. Educational Institutions (in thousands), by Level and Control, 1959, 1969, and Projected to 1979

Year (Fall)	Elementary (Grades K-8)		Secondary (Grades 9-12)		Higher Education (Degree and Nondegree Credit)	
	Public	Nonpublic	Public	Nonpublic	Public	Nonpublic
1959	26,911	4,600	8,271	1,000	2,134	1,438
1969	32,597	4,300	13,022	1,400	5,840	2,078
1979	30,600	4,000	15,000	1,400	9,806	2,451

Source: *Projections of Educational Statistics to 1979 – 1980* (Washington, D.C.: National Center for Educational Statistics, 1970), p. 18.

For secondary and higher education, on the other hand, continued increases in the number of students are expected for the 1970's. This reflects the age of the population, with the advancement of the additional grade school graduates. It also reflects the continuing goal of more education for each student — and the expectation that more of the students who enter grade school will finish and go on to graduate from high school and that more of the high school graduates will continue their educations and eventually graduate from a technical school, junior college, or university.

But while public secondary school enrollment is expected to rise in this decade, the number of nonpublic school students is expected to remain about the same. In the institutions of higher education, growth is expected for both public and private enrollments, but the number of students in the public institutions is expected to rise by nearly 70 percent, that in private institutions by less than 20 percent. In other words, nearly all of the increase in the number of secondary school students is expected to be in the public schools, while more than 90 percent of the increased enrollment in higher education is expected to occur in the public institutions.

Expenditure Trends. These enrollment trends are reflected in the expenditures shown in Table 12.4. In this table, the spending figures have been adjusted to remove the effects of general inflation, or changes in prices that have brought about a devaluation of the dollar, so that all reflect the value of 1969 – 70 dollars. This adjustment permits us to compare the 1959, 1969, and projected 1979 spending data without having to estimate a rate of inflation for this decade.

Table 12.4   Expenditures (1969 – 70 dollars) of Educational Institutions, by Level and Control, 1959, 1969, and Projected to 1979 (in billions of 1969 – 70 dollars) [a]

Year (Fall)	Elementary and Secondary Schools, Grades K-12		Institutions of Higher Education (Degree and Nondegree Credit)	
	Public	Nonpublic	Public	Nonpublic
1959	21.1	2.8	5.0	8.9
1969	37.7	4.4	15.1	8.4
1979	49.7	5.5	28.7	13.5

Source: *Projections of Educational Statistics to 1979 – 1980* (Washington, D.C.: National Center for Educational Statistics, 1970), pp. 88 – 90.

[a] Adjusted for price index changes for 1969.

It is clear from this table that both public and private expenditures for education have risen in the 1960's and that they are expected to continue to rise in the 1970's. However, the increase in expenditures for the public elementary and secondary school grades has occurred at a much greater rate and is expected to be several times the amount of increase for private education at that level. Similarly, in higher education, where private institutions have traditionally tended to account for a more substantial share of the total costs, the share of the private institutions has been declining and is expected to go on declining. In the last 10 years, public expenditures for higher education tripled, and they are expected to come close to doubling again in the 1970's. Nonpublic expenditures for higher education are expected to expand at a much slower rate in the next decade.

But spending for higher education, and for education generally, reflects more than just the changes in enrollment. These trends show that the cost of education per student has been rising and will continue to rise, even after inflation is accounted for by using constant dollars, as in Tables 12.3 and 12.4.

The High Cost of Education

One reason for this is the relationship between a teacher and his students, as compared to that between a factory worker and his production. As stated earlier, a factory worker's pay is expected to increase as his production increases with the use of new machines and techniques. For a teacher, on the other hand, we know that less learning will occur if class size increases beyond a certain point, yet, at the same time, we tend to measure the production of a teacher on the basis of how many students there are in a class rather than on the basis of the level of knowledge that is imparted. Therefore, if teachers get salary increases that are related to the raises of factory workers, and if class size does not increase, the cost of educating each student is bound to rise. This tendency is not unique to education; it relates generally to all service industries and occupations, where salaries rise but productivity or output is constant or simply does not rise as fast. The result is an increase in costs.

Another reason is that higher levels of education do tend to be more expensive. As more students continue through high school and take science courses, for example, more students will need the expensive laboratory facilities required by such a program. Each extra year of study tends to be more expensive, and increased enrollments at higher grade levels therefore tend to increase total spending for education and the cost per student.

The nature of the "production" costs of providing education, added to the expectation that each person will get more education, leads to projections of increased costs. But these do not explain why public costs and spending must rise so much more than private expenditures for education.

There are several reasons for the disproportionate increase in the government share of educational spending. One reason is the willingness of taxpayers to pay for new programs and institutions, especially those offering higher education. Many cities and counties have, in recent years, established new community colleges; states have established new two-year institutions, new state colleges, and new branches of existing state university systems, as well as increasing the size of their state universities; and the federal government has started student loan programs and grants as well as special educational programs for the unemployed and disadvantaged. These steps have increased the educational opportunities available and have tended to attract people who previously could only have had an education at the expense of substantial travel and the price of living away from home.

Public and Private Costs Compared. Another reason is the increased cost of private education. Although average family income has risen, the cost of education has risen even faster in the private institutions. In some of these, the difference between tuition rates and the cost to the school of a student's education has been made up by contributions, mainly from alumni, and by endowment income. Nevertheless, these institutions have found that endowment income has declined as a proportion of the total cost of education, and they have increased tuition rates dramatically in order to meet their budgets. These increases have had an equally dramatic impact on the budgets of families considering whether to send their children to private institutions.

Comparisons of these costs are shown in Table 12.5. Again, the figures are adjusted to the 1969 – 70 value of the dollar. The figures compare the average costs of a full-time student living away from home in a private college with the costs borne by his counterpart in a public institution. The bulk of the difference between the charges for a private institution and those for a public one lies in the tuition fee charged. State university tuitions are usually considerably lower because these institutions receive the bulk of their funds from the state legislature, with a much smaller portion coming from the student or his family. In 1959, the private education

Table 12.5   Estimated Average Charges (1969 – 70 dollars) per Student [a] in Higher Education, 1959, 1969, and Projected to 1979 (1969 – 70 dollars) [b]

	Total Tuition, Board and Room	
Year	*Public*	*Nonpublic*
1959	1,057	1,965
1969	1,198	2,520
1979	1,367	3,162

Source: *Projections of Educational Statistics to 1979 – 1980* (Washington, D.C.: National Center for Educational Statistics, 1970), pp. 106 – 108.

[a] Full time, undergraduate, resident.
[b] Adjusted for price index changes for 1959.

charges for the resident student were nearly twice those for the resident at a public institution. In the 1960's, the costs of attending public institutions rose by less than 15 percent, while the costs of a private higher education rose by more than 25 percent. This same trend is projected for the 1970's.

As a result, the family of the college-age student today and in the future is far more likely to decide that the sacrifice involved in obtaining a private higher education is too great. The high quality of education offered by many public institutions makes the difference in cost in many cases appear to be a poor investment, one that is unlikely to bring in any extra returns. Only the most outstanding private institutions are likely to continue to justify the additional investment for the student and his family. Furthermore, families as taxpayers may well feel that they have already paid for a large part of the cost of education in the public institutions and should, therefore, get the benefits that result. This is another source of substantial enrollment pressure and therefore of increased government spending for education.

Future Trends and Conflicts

The increased spending will not come easily, as we noted earlier. While until recently there have been few taxpayer revolts against the increased costs for operating expenses, teachers' salaries, and school supplies, there has been a rising trend in the number of rejected bond issues intended to finance new buildings and facilities. Further, as teachers have organized into unions, they have found a need to strike more frequently, and one result is resistance to their demands for pay increases. In addition, declining elementary school enrollment may be expected to lead to a less generous attitude on the part of local taxpayers, since it will be more difficult to justify rising costs to serve fewer students.

Moreover there has been increasing dissatisfaction with the quality of education that poorer communities can afford with their property tax payments. Increases in property taxes are often viewed as similar to the rental increases that affect families in rented apartments or homes and to the increased business costs borne by local firms, and they are therefore resisted. Greater state participation in financing elementary and secondary education, which would relieve the property tax burden, will nevertheless be countered by demands for more state-supported higher education, and will conflict with the obligations for income maintenance and health spending that are included in the states' social welfare expenditures.

Recent court decisions suggest that the differences in the quality of public education as between poor and rich communities may not be justified. If these court decisions have any impact, it will be upon the states to spend still more for elementary and secondary education in order to improve the systems in the poorer communities. Yet it is likely that the citizens of the rich communities will thereafter be less generous with their tax dollars if these are to be used to support the education of children in other communities. This will occur despite the general social motivation to provide greater equality of opportunity by having a high quality of public education for children in every community.

Inevitably, these attitudes will lead to an increased emphasis on reforming the educational process, to provide greater efficiency and to reduce costs. Some of the proposals involve the use of "teaching machines" and programmed texts, instruments that will assist in more self-teaching or independent work, so that a teacher can deal with more students. Other proposals involve the use of the more highly paid, professional teacher exclusively for those tasks for which that level of competence is required, the use of television as a supplementary teaching device, and the use of teaching assistants who could grade papers and supervise work while the senior teacher was occupied with other students. Such calls for the reorganization of the teaching process and the use of new technology in education will increase in number and volume as the tax pressures resulting from higher levels of spending become more severe. This is partly because the rate of return on educational spending may decrease with substantial rises in the amount of investment required to maintain a given educational system. The analogy with a machine is useful. No matter how good it may be in increasing production, a machine costing $1 million may not provide sufficient return to a factory owner to be worth buying, while if it cost $500,000 it would be worth buying.

Another source of resistance to increased public spending for education is likely to be the private institutions and the families that support them. Even more than others, these will resent the increased tax burden to finance public spending. They will feel the threat to the lives of their institutions. They will regret bitterly the loss of choice between public and private education because of the prohibitively higher costs of private tuition charges. There will, for these reasons, be attempts to rescue those institutions which are unable to compete with the public systems. One such attempt is the proposal to provide vouchers which taxpayers might use in partial payment for private education, with the institutions entitled to collect cash from the cities or states in exchange for these vouchers. The result of this system would be to subsidize — supposedly in recognition of the taxpayer's contribution — the private education of those who might otherwise attend public schools. But the constitutionality of such voucher systems is doubtful. Another type of subsidy, one proposed by President Nixon, would be for parochial institutions, but here there is conflict concerning the propriety of using public funds to support church-related activities. Further, it is contended that the use of vouchers or other subsidies might encourage the maintenance of racially segregated private institutions at the expense of integrated public schools.

Unless such a system is established, however, it is likely that some private institutions will close, that others will seek to join and become part of the public system of education, and that the remainder will be able to serve only the children of the rich families plus the few to whom they can offer scholarships.

Although spending for education has been demonstrated to be a profitable investment in human capital, both for society as a whole and for individual members, increased spending on education following the enormous rise that has already taken place, is likely to occur in an atmosphere of conflict. In the process of expanding expenditures, therefore, there is likely to be a substantial change in the methods and structure of the public educational systems, as well as in the relationship between such systems and the private institutions.

SUGGESTIONS FOR FURTHER READING

Cartter, Allan M. "The Economics of Higher Education." In Neil W. Chamberlain, ed., *Contemporary Economic Issues*. Homewood, Ill.: Richard D. Irwin, Inc., 1969. A clear discussion of social investment in human capital, including international comparisons, and an analysis of the problems of higher education.

Innovation in Education: New Directions for the American School. New York: Committee for Economic Development, July 1968. A concise discussion of educational goals and some recommendations for change.

Peterson, Willis L., *Principles of Economics; Micro*, Chapter 11, "The Economics of Education." Homewood, Ill.: Richard D. Irwin, Inc., 1971. A clear discussion of the returns on private investment in human capital with an illustration of the elements in the computation.

Projections of Educational Statistics to 1979 – 1980. Washington, D.C.: National Center for Educational Statistics, 1970. An annual publication which presents and interprets data on major topics in education.

Part 3

The Perennial Problems: A Look at Today

13 *Technology and Obsolescence*

Technology has been defined by Jacob Schmookler, one of its leading students, as the "social pool of knowledge of the industrial arts." Notice that this is a definition of *knowledge* rather than of machinery or of capital goods in general. There can, of course, be no economic development without the human and natural resources needed to produce capital and consumer goods. But while the availability of resources is an essential condition for economic growth, resources and people alone are not enough to guarantee a prosperous economy, as many of the world's underdeveloped countries illustrate. Men must know how to use their resources to produce goods if they are to prosper, and it is the total pool of knowledge of the industrial arts that makes up a society's technology. Having skilled carpenters, farmers, or computer operators is more important to a nation's well-being than having, for example, coal or oil in the ground. It follows that *technological change* is the *advance* in knowledge of the industrial arts.

It is important to distinguish between a method of production that is currently being used — this is called a *technique* — and the advancement of knowledge that has been defined as technological change. Technological change results in new products, and this includes both goods and services, or it may result in new processes or methods for providing the same goods and services.

Technological Change: What It Is, What It Does

How does technological change come about? Because technological change is based on new knowledge, it is related to discovery and invention. A technical discovery or an invention results in a *new* product or a *new* process. As Edwin Mansfield, another leading student of technology, has noted, the new product or process must be *useful* as well as novel to eliminate the results of tinkering or the invention of Rube Goldberg devices that have no economic relevance. When a technical discovery or an invention is put to use for the first time, the result is called an *innovation.* The person who applies the discovery or invention is called an *innovator.*

The inventor and the innovator need not be the same person; in fact, it is unusual for the two to be the same today. In an earlier day, some inventors marketed their own discoveries, though some proved to be poor businessmen. The inventor who is also an innovator is a rare exception today; Edwin Land, inventor of the Polaroid camera, is such an exception. Generally, the inventor is motivated by scientific curiosity while the innovator is motivated by the search for profit. It should not be surprising, therefore, to find that the two types of persons have significantly different characteristics.

Until fairly recent times, most economists excluded technological change and its effects from their analyses. One exception was Karl Marx, who related technological change to the process of economic development. Another was Joseph Schumpeter, a staunch defender of capitalism, who believed that the innovator or *entrepreneur* was the central figure in the process of economic development. But most other economists concerned with the problems of economic growth and development assumed that capital accumulation — savings and the resulting investment — was the prime mover of economic change. This view was challenged by the leading student of invention and economic growth:[1]

> ... since technological change has to be introduced into the traditional analysis *ad hoc,* like war or an earthquake, it was easy and natural to assume that capital accumulation was the prime factor in development. But it was, unfortunately, also wrong ... the accumulation of *intellectual* capital — reflected in the production of better products and the use of better methods — has been much more important than the accumulation of physical capital in explaining the rise of output per worker in advanced countries when the period studied covers several decades.

Today, few economists would question Edwin Mansfield's statement that "Without question, technological change is one of the most important determinants of the shape and evolution of the American economy." Indeed, the study of technological change has now become — again in Mansfield's words — "one of the most fashionable areas of economics" because of the growing awareness of the close connection between economic growth and technological change.

Technological change is now generally regarded as the prime mover of economic growth in modern industrial societies. Inventions and innovations have led to steadily rising standards of living, and every aspect of life in a modern society is touched in some way by technology. Electronic and mechanical devices have removed much of the drudgery from both household and factory. There have been phenomenal advances in transportation and communication. Recreational habits also have been affected by technology, not only as a result of inventions such as television, but also as the result of shorter hours, longer vacations, and higher income. Finally, no discussion of technological change would be complete without at least a passing reference

---

[1]Jacob Schmookler, *Invention and Economic Growth* (Cambridge, Mass.: Harvard University Press, 1966), pp. 4 – 5.

to the accomplishments of the scientists and engineers, the astronauts and cosmonauts, and all of the supporting personnel who have contributed to the exploration of space in the post-Sputnik era.

It is easy to compile an impressive list of man's technical accomplishments, but technological change has its negative as well as its positive consequences. The age of abundance in which we live in the United States is also an age of increasing congestion and pollution. Agriculture is a perfect case in point. Technological change — all of it improving farm productivity — has reduced the demand for farm labor to less than 5 percent of the labor force, and this has resulted in a highly urbanized society. Cities have their advantages, but they tend to be noisy, congested, and dirty. The negative aspects of technological change have been widely recognized only in recent years; for example, there is now a general awareness of the problems of environmental deterioration (discussed in Chapters 6 and 7 of this book). But the national dedication to technological change has not diminished. President Nixon's 1972 budget provided for new programs designed to spur innovation. And the government is making a major effort to increase productivity, a major by-product of technological change. Technology is also being counted on to provide new methods for dealing with environmental problems, such as eliminating the pollution from auto exhaust. Up to now, at least, society has continued to regard technology as good rather than as evil.

Technological change has negative effects other than its environmental impact. For one thing, it produces *obsolescence*. When a new product or process is discovered, the old product or process becomes obsolete. This, of course, is what technological change is all about. Either an existing product is made with less mechanical and human effort, or a new and better product is made. Thus technological change, while benefiting society as a whole, renders the services of some workers obsolete, and it may create pockets of persistent unemployment.

An outstanding example of labor displacement due to technological change is the massive reduction in employment in coal mining that took place in the United States during the 1950's. Because of competition from other fuels, prices and employment in the highly competitive bituminous coal industry were declining in the late 1940's. John L. Lewis, then President of the United Mine Workers, took the initiative to increase mechanization of the mines. This was a unique experience in American industrial history. Ordinarily, it is management which proposes technological change, not union leaders. Although the production of coal continued to decline during the 1950's, employment fell about twice as fast. One of the consequences of the substitution of capital for labor in the nation's bituminous coal mines was massive unemployment throughout large areas of Appalachia. Technological change is by no means the only cause of the displacement of labor, but it is one of a number of causes of persistent unemployment in specific industries or geographic areas.

There are other kinds of obsolescence that may be economically wasteful. Some economists, particularly those of a radical bent, have been critical of "planned" obsolescence — or what Herbert Gintis has called "enforced obsolescence of commodities, style changes, and the culturally enforced norms of conspicuous consumption. . . ." As obvious examples, most economists have questioned the necessity of annual style changes in automobiles and clothing. If such changes are accompanied by improvements in quality, consumers may realize an economic gain. If not, the consumer is a victim of the "culturally enforced norms" referred to by Gintis.

The Diffusion of Technological Change

New inventions lead to improved methods of production, but they are not always adopted as soon as they become available. Even after some firms in an industry have adopted an invention or an innovation, others may not do so. Thus, at any given time, the technology of an industry will consist of a mixture of the old and the new. The rate at which an invention or innovation is adopted by an industry is referred to as the rate of *diffusion*. Mansfield has estimated that "... for major innovations ... the average lag between invention and innovation is about 10 – 15 years." He has also indicated that the lag is shorter for mechanical than for electronic inventions, and that it is shorter for consumer goods than for industrial products. Innovations resulting from research supported by government funds have a shorter lag than those developed by private funds.

Even after an innovation has been adopted by one or more firms, the rate of diffusion tends to be slow. One interesting study of the diffusion of a technological change was made by the Harvard economist Zvi Griliches, who studied the rate at which hybrid corn was adopted by various parts of the agricultural economy. The rate of diffusion of this technological change was most rapid in Iowa, which went from zero to 100 percent use of hybrid corn between 1933 and 1943. Wisconsin corn farmers planted no hybrid corn in 1934, but 90 percent of all their corn was of this variety by 1946. At the other end of the spectrum, producers of corn in Texas and Alabama produced no hybrid corn as late as 1941, and hybrid corn accounted for only 80 percent of their total output as late as 1958.

In the industrial sector, Mansfield has studied the rate at which 12 innovations were diffused throughout four industries. The industries were bituminous coal, iron and steel, brewing, and the railroads, and the innovations included such major inventions as the continuous mining machine in bituminous coal, the continuous wide-strip mill in iron and steel, the high-speed bottle filler in brewing, and the diesel locomotive on the railroads. The details of this study cannot be given here, but the general conclusions may be summarized. As might be expected, he found that the rate of diffusion tended to be faster for innovations that rather quickly demonstrated their profitability or that required relatively small investments. Since his study dealt with only four industries, Mansfield was cautious about comparing rates of diffusion among industries. He thought that there was a tendency, at least, for the process of diffusion to be somewhat faster in the more competitive industries, such as coal mining, than in those such as steel, where price competition is not very common. Mansfield also found that large firms "tend to be quicker" than small firms to adopt innovations. But he does not conclude that this by itself means that the large firms are the most progressive. He believes that "... technical leadership ... has not been very highly concentrated in most of the industries for which we have data."

Technological Change and Productivity

There is no satisfactory way to measure the rate of technological change directly; thus, Mansfield has noted, "economists often measure it by its effects." One of these effects is an increase in *productivity*, which is generally measured in terms of *output per man-hour*.

The measurement of productivity is a complex statistical process that cannot be discussed here. It is important to stress, however, that although productivity is expressed in terms of output per man-hours, one should not conclude that increases in productivity are entirely, or even primarily, attributable to increases in labor efficiency. One man working with a bulldozer can move more earth in a day than 10 men working with shovels can move in a week, and the man driving the bulldozer will exert less effort than any one of the men wielding a shovel. The difference in productivity in these two cases is the result of different amounts and kinds of *capital equipment*. A shovel, too, is a "capital good," because it is used to do work rather than for direct consumption, but a bulldozer is a far more efficient piece of equipment than a shovel. Bulldozers are also much more expensive than shovels and this is reflected in the relative returns to labor and capital. Since shovels are inexpensive, when earth is being moved by hand, most of the returns to primary inputs will go to labor. The owner of the shovels will expect to receive less than the workers.

In the case where one man and one bulldozer are employed, we would find a larger share going to the owner of capital. Although the worker driving the bulldozer is skilled, and thus is paid more than the man using a shovel, the owner of the bulldozer will expect a return at least equal to the going rate of interest on the amount he has invested in this piece of equipment. This will be substantially larger than the return to the owner of the shovels. The point of this discussion is that technological change affects the proportions of capital and labor used in given production processes, and it also influences the distribution of output or payments to the factors of production, of which labor is only one.

What has happened to productivity in the economy as a whole, and how can the observed changes be explained? There is widespread agreement that technological change has proceeded more rapidly since the end of World War II than it did before the war. Output per man-hour in the private sector of the American economy increased at an average annual rate of 3.2 percent between 1947 and 1969. This compares with an annual rate of increase of about 2 percent for the period 1910 through 1945. Can this increase in productivity be explained entirely in terms of more and better capital equipment? Not entirely. Some of the improvements in productivity are due to the introduction and diffusion of improved managerial and engineering techniques.

Some types of technological changes are *embodied* while others are *disembodied*. An embodied technological change is one that requires new investment in plant, equipment, or both. An illustration of an embodied technological change is the use of a continuous mining machine in place of hand labor. Disembodied technological change is that which follows from the adoption of improved managerial and engineering techniques which improve the efficiency of all inputs, including old and new capital. An example of disembodied technological change is the improvement of a plant layout which speeds the flow of materials along an assembly line, eliminates bottlenecks, and thus leads to a substantial increase in output without the use of any new machines at all. The application of advanced mathematical techniques to various managerial problems — a new activity which is called *operations research* or *management science* — has resulted in a considerable amount of disembodied technological change.

There is another way to view technological change, and this is in terms of its effects on factor proportion and on returns to the factors of production. From this point of view, technological change may be classified as: (1) labor-saving; (2) capital-saving; or (3) neutral. If a technological change results in a greater percentage reduction in capital input than in labor input, it is capital-saving. If it results in a greater percentage reduction in labor input than in capital input, it is labor-saving. But if the technological change results in an equal percentage reduction in both capital and labor inputs, it is neutral. If a technological change is either labor-saving or capital-saving, it can have an influence on the distribution of income between labor and capital, which is, of course, a major social and political issue. Robert Solow, who analyzed technological change in the United States between 1909 and 1949, concluded that during this period technological change was neutral; labor, in effect, benefited as much as "capitalists." He also found that output per man-hour had doubled during this 40-year period, and attributed slightly more than 87 percent of the increase to technological change. The remaining 12 percent he attributed to the increased use of capital.

Automation

Automation is a term that gained currency during the 1950's. It describes a method of production in which high-speed electronic computers are linked to machine tools and materials-handling devices. There are various types of automation, but all have the common objective of substituting electronic controls and mechanical energy for human decisions and direct labor input.

During the early days of automation — after a number of automated assembly lines and small factories had demonstrated its practicality — this new approach to production was hailed as a harbinger of the Second Industrial Revolution. And this revolution was expected by some to have dire consequences. Norbert Wiener, a leading mathematician at MIT who contributed to the development of the modern computer, believed that automation would destroy jobs on a large scale. In his words:[2]

> ... remember that the automatic machine ... is the precise economic equivalent of slave labor. Any labor which competes with slave labor must accept the economic conditions of slave labor. It is perfectly clear that this will produce an unemployment situation, in comparison with which ... the depression of the thirties will seem a pleasant joke.

On the other hand, Walter Buckingham, one of the early experts on the economics of automation, had the following to say:[3]

> Since 1870 productivity in the United States has more than quadrupled. . . . Yet employment increased over six times — from ten to over 65 million — in this period. . . . Case after case can be cited to show that total employment in firms and in our industries *has increased* following the introduction of mechanization or automation.

More recently, Charles Silberman and the editors of *Fortune* magazine published a book about what they consider to be the mythology of automation. In a chapter

---

[2]Norbert Wiener, *The Human Use of Human Beings* (2nd ed., rev.; Garden City, N.Y.: Doubleday and Co., Inc., 1954), p. 162.
[3]Walter Buckingham, *Automation* (New York: Mentor Executive Library Books, 1960), p. 102. Emphasis added.

entitled "The Real News About Automation," the authors discuss increases in the growth rate of output per man-hour. This jumped from 1.3 percent a year between 1850 and 1889 to 3.6 percent a year, on the average, after 1960. But they point out: "An acceleration in the growth rate of productivity is no new phenomenon, as so many enthusiasts of automation seem to think. On the contrary, the rate has been accelerating for a hundred years or more." Silberman and his associates leave the definite impression that there is no need to be concerned about technological unemployment. They conclude that electronic computers and automation are not genuinely revolutionary developments, but simply represent the latest phase of continuing long-run technological change.

It is important to stress that the automation-unemployment debate was conducted in terms of *total* employment, unemployment, and productivity. Even the most ardent defenders of the thesis advanced by Buckingham and Silberman — that automation creates rather than destroys jobs — would not argue that individual workers are not displaced or replaced by machines. As noted at the beginning of this section, that is what automation is about. Studies that deal entirely with totals and averages obscure the problems created for specific groups of workers when major technological changes occur. In some cases, workers are not actually displaced by technological change, but fewer new workers are hired. A major result of such changes is a long-run change in the structure of employment.

Not all technological unemployment is the result of automation. Other kinds of technological change may have similar adverse employment effects for a specific occupation. Changes in cargo technology, for example, have reduced the demand for longshoremen at some of the nation's major seaports on both coasts. Formerly, most cargo was shipped loose to the docks, there to be loaded by men; now, many types of cargo are shipped to seaports by truck or rail in large containers — some up to 40 feet in length — which are then loaded directly by high-speed cranes. Containerized cargo can be loaded in a fraction of the time required for hand-loading, which is a good illustration of direct labor displacement as the result of a technological change. It would be easy to provide others. This is not to say that, *in the aggregate*, technological change has been the cause of mass unemployment. But the individual worker who loses his job when he is replaced by a machine is not impressed by changes in total employment, unemployment, and average productivity. He is concerned about his job and the support of his family. From a purely statistical point of view — and from the point of view of the national economy as a whole — technological unemployment may not be a problem. For the individual worker affected, it may be more than a problem; it may be a personal tragedy.

Technological Change and Economic Growth

Technological change, productivity, and economic growth are interrelated. As an economy grows, its structure changes. A century ago, for example, more than half the working population was engaged in agriculture, while less than one-quarter of all workers were employed in what we broadly call the trades and services. Today, 4.4 percent of all employed workers are in agriculture, while 60 percent are in the trades and services, including government employment. Technological change lies behind this restructuring of the economy. Technological change together with the productivity increases it has engendered have also resulted in major gains in living standards. There have been problems, of course, and these are not always clearly understood.

Technological change has reduced the demand for manpower in rural areas, and this is indeed why there has been a long-run shift from farm to city. Since many of the migrants ended up in slums and ghettos, this shift has contributed to today's urban crisis. But the major gains in productivity have contributed to a rise in the *general* standard of living. In an ideal economic system, workers displaced by technological change would shift to occupations with expanding labor requirements, but in the real world, such shifts are not easy to make. Even if aggregate demand is maintained by government monetary and fiscal policies at a level which would provide jobs for all those employed or seeking work, there is no mechanism to guarantee a perfect match between unemployed workers and job openings. It is a mistake, however, to blame this condition on technological change. It is the result of many impediments to labor mobility that are not themselves caused by technological change.

Historically, one of the causes of economic growth has been an expanding population. Recently, however, the U.S. birthrate has started to decline. This is partly the result of technological advance in fertility control, particularly the contraceptive pill.

There has been concern over the effects of population growth intermittently since Thomas R. Malthus published his famous *Essay on the Principle of Population* in 1798. Throughout most of this period the major concern has been with what troubled Malthus — namely, that population would outrun the means of subsistence. But technology has permitted rapid increases in agricultural productivity. There have been famines, and a substantial proportion of the world's population is chronically underfed and inadequately housed and clothed. But as can be seen in Chapters 19 and 20, this is partly because the lagging countries have been unable to duplicate the agricultural technology of advanced industrial societies.

More recently, the focus has shifted from the Malthusian problem to the ecological problem. There has been growing concern about the effects of an increasing population on the environment. This has led the ecologist Paul Ehrlich and his followers to advocate Zero Population Growth. And there are some demographers who believe that the rate of population growth in the United States will be negligible before the end of the present century.

Does a zero population growth rate mean the end of economic growth? It does not. Economic growth is properly measured not by the total national output but by changes in *real per capita* income, or income per person adjusted for changes in the cost of living. Even without population growth, real per capita income will continue to increase as long as productivity, or output per worker, continues to rise. Further increases in productivity, in turn, would depend upon additional technological change. Thus economic growth can go on as long as man continues to exhibit the ingenuity he has demonstrated in the past.

Public Policy and Technological Change

When Hitler gave the command that started World War II, the American economy was only beginning to emerge from the doldrums of the Great Depression. Periods of depression are typically not associated with bursts of inventive activity or rapid technological change. But when a nation becomes involved in a major war, as did the United States in 1941, the pace of technological change quickens. Societies which depend upon the market system for allocating resources and the distribution of income have not mobilized their resources to attack social problems, such as the problem of poverty. But under wartime conditions they have mobilized their resources to make numerous technical military advances, and the momentum of technological change often continues into the postwar period.

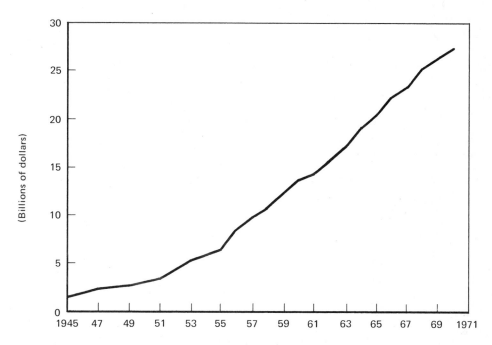

FIGURE 13.1 Research and development expenditures in the United States, 1945 – 1970. [Sources: 1945 – 1951, Edwin Mansfield, *The Economics of Technological Change* (New York: W. W. Norton, 1968), p. 54. 1953 – 1970, National Science Foundation, *National Patterns of R & D Resources*, NSF 69 – 30 (Washington, D.C.: 1970), p. 34.]

Research and development spending has increased steadily in the United States since the end of World War II. In 1945, for example, total R & D expenditures in the United States came to $1.5 billion. The rate of R & D spending had already increased rather substantially before October 4, 1957, when Russian scientists successfully launched Sputnik. This rate was maintained until 1968 and has tapered off only slightly since then. The trend in R & D expenditures from 1945 to 1970 is given in Figure 13.1. Throughout this period, most R & D funds were provided by the federal government. Details for early years are not available, but in 1953 the federal government accounted for 53 percent of total R & D expenditures. The federal government's share rose to a peak of 65 percent in 1964, but had declined to 55 percent by 1970. The relative contributions of the federal government, industry, universities and colleges, and other nonprofit institutions are shown graphically in Figure 13.2.

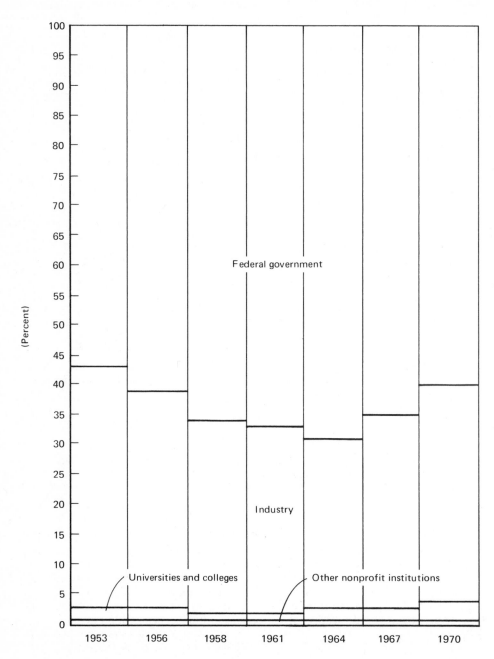

FIGURE 13.2   Percent distribution of sources of funds, by sector, used for research and development, 1953 – 1970. [Source: National Science Foundation, *National Patterns of R & D Resources*, NSF 69 – 30 (Washington, D. C.: 1970), p. 34.]

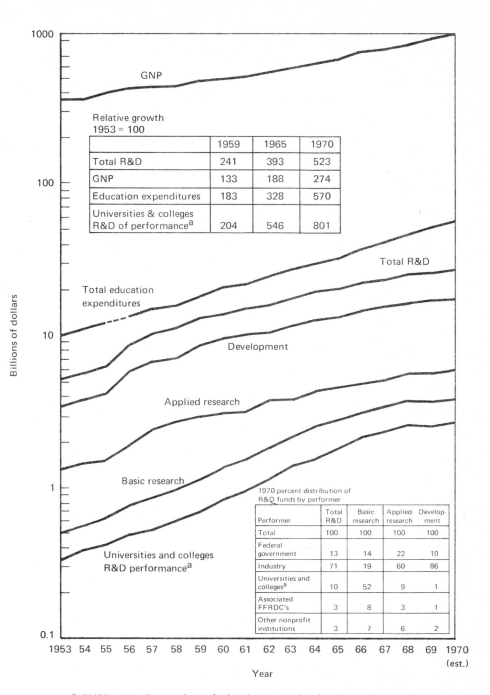

Billions of dollars

GNP

Relative growth
1953 = 100

	1959	1965	1970
Total R&D	241	393	523
GNP	133	188	274
Education expenditures	183	328	570
Universities & colleges R&D of performance[a]	204	546	801

Total R&D

Total education expenditures

Development

Applied research

Basic research

Universities and colleges R&D performance[a]

1970 percent distribution of R&D funds by performer

Performer	Total R&D	Basic research	Applied research	Development
Total	100	100	100	100
Federal government	13	14	22	10
Industry	71	19	60	86
Universities and colleges[a]	10	52	9	1
Associated FFRDC's	3	8	3	1
Other nonprofit institutions	3	7	6	2

Year

FIGURE 13.3 Research and development funds, Gross National Product, and education expenditure, 1953–1970. ([a] Excludes federally funded research and development centers.) (Sources: National Science Foundation and U. S. Departments of Commerce and Health, Education, and Welfare.)

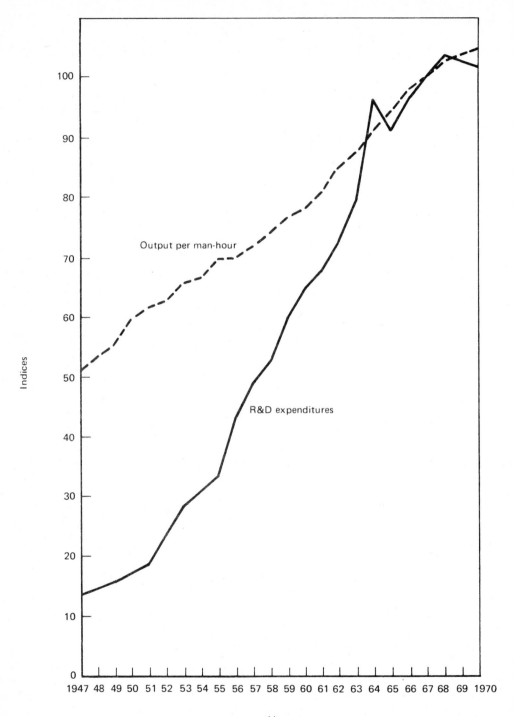

Output per man-hour

R&D expenditures

Indices

Year

How does the trend in R & D spending compare with other economic indicators? In Figure 13.3, R & D spending is compared with total educational expenditures and with the trend in GNP. Notice that this is a semilogarithmic chart. Equal vertical distances on the chart represent equal percentage changes. R & D spending increased at a faster rate than GNP, but increased somewhat more slowly than education expenditures. Notice also that more money was spent for development than for applied research, and that more was spent for applied research than for basic research.

What effect did this upsurge in research and development expenditures have on the long-run trend in productivity? An index showing output per man-hour has been plotted on Figure 13.4, and this is compared with an index of R & D expenditures. Two things stand out from this chart. First, there is no close correlation between R & D expenditures and output per man-hour. Second, in relative terms, R & D expenditures have declined rather substantially since 1968.

How does one explain the divergence between the index of output per man-hour — or productivity — and the index of R & D expenditures? Part of the explanation is purely statistical. R & D expenditures started from a relatively low base in 1947 (about $2.3 billion), and increased to more than $27 billion by 1970. This is more than a tenfold increase. The index of output per man-hour started from a much higher base and it continued to follow a relatively smooth long-term trend.

Not all of the difference between R & D expenditures and output per man-hour can be explained on purely statistical grounds, however. Much of the research and development spending of the postwar period, particularly since 1957, has been earmarked for space exploration and related research. And a substantial part of the remainder was for military research and development. The index of output per man-hour reflects increases in productivity in the private sector of the economy. While there have been some spillover effects from the space and military research programs, there has not been enough spillover to cause any appreciable change in the long-term trend in productivity in the private sector. There has been some diffusion of space and military technology to the private sector, but it seems clear that much space and military technology is not readily transferable to civilian activities and therefore has little impact on productivity.

FIGURE 13.4 Indices of research and development expenditures and output per man-hour, private sector, 1947 – 1970. (1967 = 100) [Sources: Output per man-hour, U.S. Department of Labor, *Economic Report of the President, 1971* (Washington, D. C.: U. S. Government Printing Office, 1971), p. 236. The R & D index is based on data from Edwin Mansfield, *The Economics of Technological Change* (New York: W. W. Norton, 1968), p. 54; National Science Foundation, *National Patterns of R & D Resources*, NSF 69 – 30 (Washington, D. C.: 1970), p. 34; and U. S. Department of Labor, *Economic Report of the President, 1971* (Washington, D. C.: U.S. Government Printing Office, 1971), p. 236.]

SUGGESTIONS FOR FURTHER READING

Buckingham, Walter. *Automation.* New York: Mentor Executive Library Books, 1960.

Carter, Anne P. *Structural Change in the American Economy.* Cambridge, Mass.: Harvard University Press, 1970.

Griliches, Zvi. "Hybrid Corn: An Exploration in the Economics of Technological Change." *Econometrica* (October 1957), pp. 501 – 522.

Mansfield, Edwin. *Microeconomics.* New York: W. W. Norton & Company, 1970.

————. *The Economics of Technological Change.* New York: W.W. Norton Company, 1968.

————. *Industrial Research and Technological Innovation: An Econometric Analysis.* New York: W. W. Norton & Company, 1968.

Mishan, Ezra J. *The Costs of Economic Growth.* New York: Frederick A. Praeger, 1967.

National Science Foundation. *National Patterns of R & D Resources, 1953 – 1970.* NSF 69 – 30. Washington, D.C.: 1970.

Schmookler, Jacob. *Invention and Economic Growth.* Cambridge, Mass.: Harvard University Press, 1966.

Silberman, Charles E. and the editors of Fortune. *The Myths of Automation.* New York: Harper & Row, 1966.

Solow, Robert M. "Technical Change and the Aggregate Production Function." *Review of Economics and Statistics,* Vol. 39 (August 1957), pp. 312 – 320.

Wiener, Norbert. *The Human Use of Human Beings.* 2nd ed., rev. Garden City, N.Y.: Doubleday & Company, Inc., 1954.

14 *Economic Power Centers*

About 20 years ago, John Kenneth Galbraith published *American Capitalism, The Concept of Countervailing Power.*[1] In this, Galbraith showed that while a number of different groups together control the American economy, opposing interests among them limit the economic power of any single group. This is similar to the system of constitutional checks and balances which limits the power of the three main branches of the United States government.

Industry, labor, and government are also three sources of countervailing economic power. The government provides the ground rules for both corporations and labor unions, limiting what they can do. In turn, corporations and labor unions affect each other. The consumer, of course, also has some say in the marketplace. For example, while the corporation may manufacture automobiles, ultimately it is the consumer who must decide whether or not he wants them. In the long run, this checks the power of both the auto workers' union and the auto manufacturing firms. Any firm has to make goods that will succeed in the marketplace; theoretically, the arbiter is the private consumer; but, in practice, the government also plays an important role.

The Visible Hand: Government in the Marketplace

The power of the government serves to check private economic power in the marketplace. One important tool of government is its procurement policy. All governments (federal, state, and local) purchase annually over $350 billion worth of goods and services. This constituted almost one-third of total final demand in the United States in 1972. Final demand consists of all goods and services not used for further production. For instance, oranges bought to be eaten as they are would be included in final demand; oranges that go to a canning plant to be transformed into juices are an intermediate good. The government produces only a few services such as police protection, firefight-

---

[1]Boston: Houghton Mifflin, 1952.

ing, and traffic control, but does not use its procurement for further production. Therefore, most of its procurement is final demand. Since the government's share of total procurement (both public and private) is so large, it bears greatly on both the total and the composition of U.S. production.

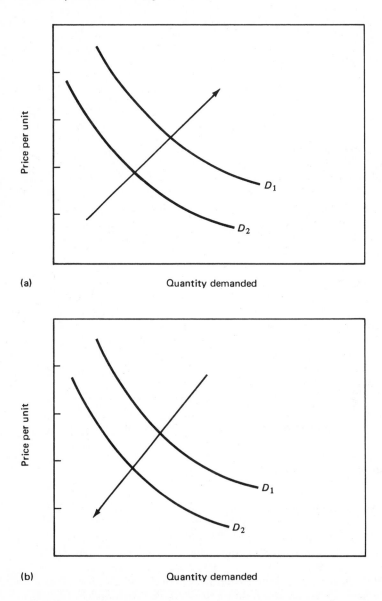

FIGURE 14.1 Consequences of a shift in government spending. (a) Demand moves up and price down when government decides to purchase a product whereas (b) demand moves down and price up when government ceases to purchase the product.

Figure 14.1a shows what happens to market demand for one product, say trucks, if the government decides to purchase that product: D_2 (demand for trucks) moves to the right to D_1 for each price. In Figure 14.1b, the reverse happens when government ceases to purchase a product, call it napalm. At every price, more trucks will be necessary to satisfy total demand — both public and private — in 14.1a, while less napalm will be required in 14.1b. This has wide repercussions because of the sheer volume of government procurement and the interdependence of the economy. In order to produce trucks, steel, rubber, and glass are needed and in order to produce napalm, chemicals are needed. We call this "derived demand"; that is, the demand for final goods (trucks and napalm) creates a demand for raw materials and semifinished goods needed in the production of final goods. Therefore, a shift in government procurement not only changes the total demand for the product bought by the government, but it affects all other sectors to a greater or lesser extent as well.

The Power to Regulate. Another source of power possessed by the government is the power to regulate what can and cannot be produced. The government may decide that some goods, such as thalidomide, should not be produced at all or that other goods, such as heroin, should not be marketed. Automobiles are not permitted to be sold unless they conform to certain standards of safety in design set by the government. No doubt, this is interference in the marketplace. However, few of us would disagree with the government's decision on thalidomide, which produces gross deformities in babies born to women using it. Yet private corporations might produce this drug were they not checked.

Government as a Producer of Social Goods. The government is also, in a sense, a producer because any good or service that cannot be produced privately must be produced, if society needs it, by the government. Toll turnpike and water supply are examples. State governments set the price for the use of turnpikes and even determine the quality of the service available. The cost of traveling between two points on the turnpike is determined by a government authority. This is not a decision made in a free marketplace by thousands of purchasers and thousands of sellers of a good or service. In this case, there are thousands of purchasers — anybody who is traveling on such a turnpike — but there is only one seller of the service, and frequently little competition by way of alternative routings. In the case of a turnpike, or water and sewer service, the government is a monopoly regulated only by its own laws.

Ground Rules. Government can regulate business and industry through "ground rules." But often the spirit of these rules is violated in practice. For example, the government has decided that banks may not own manufacturing corporations. Accordingly, corporate power may not be directly concentrated in the hands of bankers. In countries like Germany and Japan, banks own, or are owned by, many industrial enterprises. Indeed, in these countries, it is difficult to distinguish between the industrial and financial communities. In the United States, this practice is not as pervasive. Banks do not own industrial enterprises or vice-versa, but because banks provide heavy financial backing to industries, they are strongly represented on the corporate boards of industrial firms and are thus in a position to "control" the decision-making power of these firms. For example, in 1970, eight out of 10 members of the Board of Directors of Raytheon Company — a large multiproduct firm — were also directors on at least one bank board.

Concentration of Financial Power

It is generally said that banks have representatives on corporate boards because they make loans to these firms and have an interest in their efficient operation. However, through this representation banks can indirectly control the operations of manufacturing enterprises.

While a bank may get as high a return on a loan to a small customer as on one to a large customer, the banks know that the large customer is more likely to take his business to another bank should he be refused. Therefore, big business receives preferential treatment in borrowing funds vis-à-vis small business. Small businesses have no interlocking representation with the financial fraternity. Accordingly, they are given little consideration, especially in a tight market (where demand for loans runs very high). When credit is not easily available, small businesses are left out. The long-term relationship between banks and large business is the one most valued by the banks. Therefore, they deliberately direct credit to their prime customers in tight money markets.

Even when both small and large businesses are steady customers of the bank, small businesses are viewed by the bank as more risky propositions than large businesses. This results in large firms paying less for funds than do small firms. When the cost of funds is higher, the firm's returns must also be higher to cover costs. In the economist's language, the marginal efficiency of capital must equal or exceed the interest rate (the cost of loanable funds). But in general, large enterprises are more efficient than small enterprises. Therefore, through their loan policies, banks give added competitive power to the large firms, which can often price their smaller rivals out of the market altogether.

A further consideration which reinforces the banks' tendency to charge higher rates to their small loan customers is the difference in bank competition for local versus national firms. The national firm may deal with a large number of banks, spread throughout the country, whereas the local firm is forced to deal only with local banks. In some cases, there may be no alternative source of borrowed (bank) funds for the small firm in a one-bank town. The national corporation does not have to borrow in the community where its headquarters are located. Accordingly, the small firms fare worse on all counts. No wonder that the rate of bankruptcy among small firms is as high as it is. The Dun & Bradstreet *Quarterly Failure Report* shows about 9,000 business failures in 1969 and over 10,000 in 1970.[2]

Furthermore, when giant firms face bankruptcy, even the government seems ready to bail them out. In 1970, the largest railroad firm in the United States, the Penn Central, declared bankruptcy. This company had at the time a net worth (assets minus liabilities) of about $4 – 5 billion but no cash on hand to cover taxes, payroll, or creditors. Congress authorized a loan that allowed the railroad to continue operating though not to pay its debts. In 1971, Lockheed Aircraft Corporation faced similar problems. For many years Lockheed had been assured of government orders for war materiel at high prices and profits. It could not withstand the shift to civilian production and was unable to pay its creditors. Yet Congress voted Lockheed a bonus of $250 million of taxpayers' money for excellent mismanagement. While we have a Small Business Administration (SBA) to aid small firms, the recent rescue operations for failing large businesses suggest that in the United States there is a much more effective "Big Business Administration."

[2]*Fourth Quarter 1970*, February 1971.

The Corporation Defined

A corporation is a business firm authorized by a state government to carry out some economic activity. In this form of business, owners (that is, equity stockholders) have limited liability; at most, they can lose their investment in the corporation if bankruptcy occurs. This differs from individual or partnership proprietorship, where the liability of the owners extends to *all* assets, personal as well as business. Furthermore, a corporation has a greater capability of raising funds because (1) its life goes on in perpetuity (it is a going concern) and (2) it may expand its capital base by issuing more equity stock. While in the past, individually owned firms resulted in large accumulations of capital — by, for example, Rockefeller, Carnegie, and Ford — today this is rare. A J. Paul Getty or a Howard Hughes can still control personally large fortunes, but these will be in the form of equity stock in a range of corporations.

The framers of the United States Constitution were wary of empowering the federal government to charter corporations. Only a few years later, however, in 1791, the federal government chartered the first corporation, the Bank of the United States. The two Banks of the United States (1791 – 1811 and 1816 – 1836) together with the more recent Comsat, for satellite communication, and Amtrak, for passenger rail service, are rare examples of the corporate form as chartered by the federal government. But these corporations have a dual private and public ownership. Typically, private corporations have been chartered only by states, with the exceptions of some banks and savings and loan associations.

The corporate form of business is more prevalent in the United States than it is in European countries, where families often control even giant businesses. The corporation's stockholders usually delegate their powers to a board of directors allegedly elected by them at an annual meeting. Since ownership is sometimes dispersed among hundreds of thousands of stockholders, management groups solicit proxies (voting rights). There is sometimes competition for control among a few groups which often own only a minimal percentage of the total stock but which succeed in accumulating proxies. As long as a corporation performs reasonably well (that is earns profits and pays dividends), there is little likelihood of a challenge to the directors, so that the controlling group may perpetuate itself. This group, including the corporate management, may own relatively little stock.

A corporation has a choice of paying out its earnings to the shareholders (dividends) or retaining them for further growth (capital accumulation). When a corporation retains income, the tax against dividend receivers is postponed (from the point of view of owners of the corporation) until they sell their stock at a presumably higher price to reflect the growth of the company's assets. Moreover, the tax rate on capital gains due to the addition to capital from retained earnings is lower than the tax rate on wage or dividend income. The tax system may produce a bias in favor of large size because it creates an incentive for reinvesting a sizeable share of earnings.

Corporate Size. By no means are all corporations big. But there is no doubt that, in the public mind, the most salient characteristic of the best-known corporations is their enormous size. The assets of General Motors are greater than the entire gross national product of some countries. The revenues of AT&T are larger than the revenues of many governments.

The size problem can be expressed most dramatically — and most troublesomely — by what are called "concentration ratios." By 1968, in the important manufacturing sector of the economy, the largest 100 firms by asset size controlled almost exactly one-half (49.3 percent) of the total assets in manufacturing, according to the Federal Trade Commission. The 200 largest firms controlled 60.9 percent of the assets. Comparatively these figures had increased from 39.3 percent and 47.2 percent in 1947. The increase in concentration was accounted for chiefly, though not entirely, by mergers and acquisitions which enabled the big to grow bigger.

Economists make an important distinction between overall concentration, as expressed above, and concentration by product line. While overall concentration has been increasing, the dominance of specific markets by a handful of large firms has become little if any more pronounced than it was a generation ago. Markets such as tires and breakfast cereals continue to be concentrated, in that more than half of the sales are accounted for by four firms or fewer; but other markets, such as textiles, many of the foodstuffs, and shoes continue to be competitive in the classic sense, with many sellers and none of dominant size.

The paradox can be in part explained by a phenomenon known as the "conglomerate." A conglomerate is a corporation that, by acquisition, has interests in numerous wholly unrelated businesses.[3] If an aerospace firm buys a meatpacker, there is just as much — or as little — competition in meatpacking as before, but the nation's overall concentration ratio has increased.

As we shall note, the nation's antitrust laws have been much more successful in holding at least stable the degree of concentration by product than they have been in blocking conglomerate mergers. But conglomeration, while often achieving enormous size, does not always mean success. A conglomerate merger "wave" in the late 1960's receded as some of the leaders in the movement, such as Ling-Temco-Vought, turned out to be far from profitable.

The problem of market power by corporations, in cases where there are few large sellers, has long been recognized and studied by economists. It is known as "oligopoly" as distinct from pure monopoly.

Monopoly is uncommon in the United States, except in the case of local electric, gas, and telephone utilities where duplication would be wasteful and prices are regulated by public bodies. But the concept of "monopolistic profit" applies in all cases where full and free competition is not the sole determinant of prices. If a corporation is large enough, it can influence the character of its own market. The ultimate case is that of a corporation so big, with per unit costs so low, that it can undercut the price of any other seller and drive all competitors out of business. When a corporation does this, it enjoys monopolistic economic power. But there are other ways of achieving a market monopoly. A patent licenses a firm to produce something for 17 years without competition, while a franchise, which is an exclusive right to operate a particular business, such as an airline route or the distribution of electricity, can be purchased.

Monopolistic Profits. Generally, the monopolistic power acquired by corporations is detrimental to society. It induces them to maximize profits at the expense of the consumer. If a monopoly set its prices so that they covered only production costs, the consumer would pay a minimum price; but a monopoly has no incentive to do this. Profits, in the economist's language, are a return to the entrepreneur for risks undertaken and services rendered. This is different from the accountant's defi-

---

[3]For example, IT&T, which started in the communications business, has interests in hotels, auto rental, insurance, and several manufacturing concerns.

nition of profit as the difference between cost and revenue. The economist includes under cost of production the equivalent salary payment rendered to the entrepreneur, much like the wage cost for labor or interest cost for capital. When returns to the corporation exceed the coverage of all costs, then the corporation receives surplus income, that is, an income not in return for a service rendered but due to a particular situation of the corporation in the market, characteristically monopolistic. This surplus is called monopolistic profit.

A monopoly would not be satisfied to charge a price that covered only its costs; it would consider both the cost of production and how much people would be willing to pay for the product. Thus, the monopoly would not charge the minimum price at which it could produce the goods, but something more. There is actually an economic incentive for a corporation with monopoly power to produce less than it is capable of producing economically and to charge more for the product.

An extreme example: a corporation sells "manna" that drops from heaven on its own plot, costless. This corporation is run by a very good-natured fellow, who likes to give away things at cost. Since the manna costs nothing, he would give it away free. On the other hand, what would the profit-maximizing entrepreneur do? He

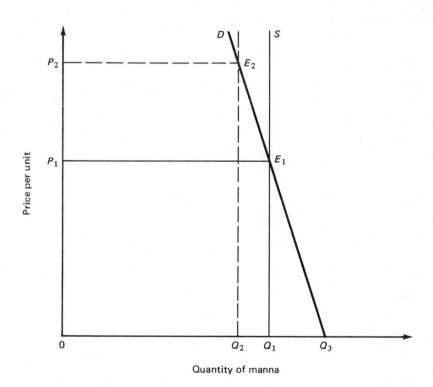

FIGURE 14.2 Monopolistic behavior with "costless" production. Q_1P_1 represents a price at which the market is ready to buy "manna", $P_2E_2Q_10$, an extreme situation in which a profit-minded entrepreneur could produce artificial scarcity by cutting back quantity of manna thus raising the price.

would charge a price higher than nothing and he would keep raising the price until profits reached the maximum.

In Figure 14.2, line D represents the demand for manna while S is the fixed supply of manna per year. At zero price, manna would have to be rationed because too many consumers would want the quantity Q_3, which is not available. At *all* times, only Q_1 is available. The corporation can raise the price of manna up to P_1 without decreasing the quantity. At Q_1P_1, indeed, no rationing occurs because this is the price at which the market is ready to buy Q_1. However, if the supply is reduced artificially to Q_2, prices would rise to P_2 and profits would possibly increase if the revenue rectangle $P_2E_2Q_10$. To achieve this, the profit-minded enterpriser would produce artificial scarcity. He would cut back on sales until profits reached a maximum.

This extreme example suggests why economic power misallocates resources: there is an incentive to restrict the quantity of goods put on the market; the price is higher than the cost of production; and profits accrue to the owner of a resource that he is in a position to make "scarce."

Our example is of the case of only one seller. If there are 100 sellers, this would be impossible. The real-world problem is that of a market in which three or four or five large companies dominate, controlling well over half the sales.

Economists are still debating the effects of this kind of "oligopoly." The issues are not simple. The steel industry, for example, has long been cited as an example of an industry in which "price leadership" by one or two large firms can prevent competitive price-cutting; and yet steel industry profits have been low compared with most other industries in the period from 1965 to 1972. The aluminum industry is among the more concentrated, but when excess capacity appeared in the 1969–1971 period, prices were shaved downward and profits plummeted. On the other hand, price leadership by General Motors in the auto industry is a widely recognized fact, as is the high profitability of this industry leader. Something that can be called "corporate power" undoubtedly exists, and not only the power in some cases to maximize prices by control of markets.

"The Military-Industrial Complex."

A variant on private monopoly power is the defense industry, which presents the unique example of a situation in which there is only one buyer of the final output (monopsony). Monopoly power exists when there is only one seller; more often, there are a few sellers rather than just one, and these are called oligopolies; in contrast, monopsony power exists when there is only one buyer. The United States government is the only purchaser of Nike missiles, tanks, and military airplanes. Typically, there are also only one or two sellers of military output because the government buys highly complicated hardware. "In fiscal year 1968," according to Senator William Proxmire, "the 100 largest defense contractors were awarded 67.4 percent of total defense contracts."[4]

With only one source of contracts — the government — the large defense contractors are really more public than private. Furthermore, the control over defense contracts is exercised in a most peculiar way. There are both on the boards of directors and in the management of defense firms many retired or former employees of the Pentagon. In addition to this, the government owns a large share of the assets used by these corporations; the government leases at nominal fees plants built with public funds to be used by defense contractors.[5] Under these circumstances, it is no

---

[4]"The Pentagon vs. Free Enterprise," *Saturday Review*, January 31, 1970, pp. 14–17.
[5]*Ibid.*, pp. 15–16.

wonder that the late President Eisenhower referred to this institution as a "military-industrial complex." Because of the ramifications of all the products that go into the production of defense goods, the same corporations that control the defense business industry are, for the most part, dominant in the rest of the American economy.

Wealth and Income Inequality

Economic power takes another form largely unrelated to the corporate form of business organization. This stems from the simple fact that some people are richer than others, as we all know, and money can mean power. The disparity is in both *income* and *wealth*. The distribution of income received by individuals is lopsided not only because of the large variation in wages and salaries but because of implicit non-wage income. The president of a large corporation may receive as much as $300,000 in salary, on which he pays taxes plus "expenses" that are often almost as large as his base salary and on which he does not pay taxes. Some of this "expense" money constitutes a form of income to the executive because if it were not provided by his firm, he would be compelled to spend funds of his own: it is hard to deny that a meal at a luxury restaurant constitutes income, although only business-related meals count as non-taxed expenses. A factory worker usually has no expense account and receives on the average about $8,000 a year. However, these differences, large as they are, play a relatively small part in the disparity of purchasing power.

Wealth, inherited or acquired, is also a source of inequality because it is a source of purchasing power. A person who has assets has more purchasing power than a person with no assets, and assets have always been distributed unevenly. A few individuals over the last few generations have been able to accumulate large fortunes for which they receive income in the form of dividends (for equity stock), interest (for loans, bonds, savings accounts), and rents (for real estate). There are a few hundred people in this country who have incomes of a million dollars or more derived from the ownership of assets. Then there are about 40 million people who have almost no assets at all.

Apparently, inheritance is the main source of income inequality because a large fraction of wealth is allowed to be transferred from one generation to the next. Wealth can be self-generating. Wealth begets income when it is properly invested in stocks, bonds, real estate, and physical assets. Thus, in the United States, as in all capitalist systems, accumulation is allowed and occurs even though some of the inheritance is taxed. But some capitalist systems have stronger regulations than others to prevent any exaggerated accumulation. In Sweden, for instance, both inheritance and income taxes are more "progressive" than those prevailing in the United States. There is, therefore, less disparity of income and wealth in Sweden than in the United States — not because of more equality of ability but simply because different social decisions have been made.

Labor Power

One might expect that strong labor unions in the United States would tend to equalize income distribution and diffuse the power base. But it appears that on the first count labor unions have been less successful than on the second. Labor unions are now part of the establishment and, in some ways, they prefer to preserve the status quo.

Once the labor unions became part of the institutional framework of America,

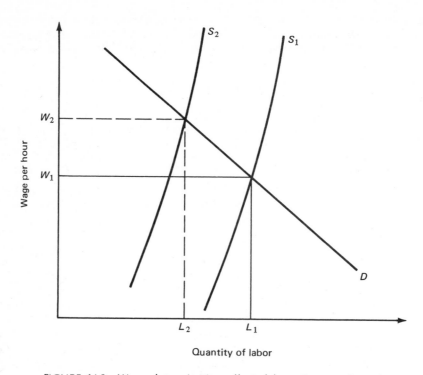

FIGURE 14.3 Wage determination affected by union practices. A union can diminish the supply of a certain labor skill by limiting the quantity of labor (by various discriminatory practices) thereby raising the wages for that labor and inevitably the price of the product.

they began to behave rather like corporations. Their interests also became parochial. Concentrating on the winning of shorter hours and higher wages, unions tended to try to maximize the welfare of their *particular* members only, regardless of the consequences to society at large. If they want the supply of a certain labor skill diminished, some unions charge high fees, demand long apprenticeships, and block minorities from entering their ranks. As shown in Figure 14.3, by these monopolistic practices they are capable of shifting the supply curve from S_1 (potential supply) to S_2 (actual supply). Therefore, the actual supply of workers available is smaller (L_2 rather than L_1) and the wage rate much higher (W_2 rather than W_1) than they need be. Within the present institutional framework and existing legislation, little can be done to avoid this situation even though it is detrimental to society as a whole.

A further restriction that unions sometimes achieve is a limitation of productivity per man-hour by insisting on overly large work crews. This behavior applies to unions which are seeking to maximize their employed membership. In a technologically changing industry, where the required labor per unit of output is constantly falling, the result is "featherbedding." The railroad industry in particular has been subjected to this practice. Firemen specialized in the shoveling of coal into steam locomotives are redundant on a modern diesel or electric locomotive. Nevertheless, unions long insisted that this class of workers be retained in the railroad industry. In the summer of 1971, after 20 years, an agreement was finally reached to eliminate this type of featherbedding.

At times, certain strong unions will act in collusion with management to increase their returns, even though the price of the product is thereby increased greatly. This often results in wages pushing up prices, or, in the economist's phrase, a "cost-push inflation." This is different from the inflation that is caused by an excess demand (relative to supply) for goods, which is called by the economist a "demand-pull inflation." Cost-push inflation can occur if costs increase faster than productivity. One such cost is labor; the other is capital. If the output (and return for each cost of output) does not increase as fast as the cost of the product increases, then the price to the consumer must increase regardless of how competitive the market is.

To be sure, most American workers are not union members and are therefore not protected as part of the establishment. Out of a labor force of approximately 80 million, only about 18 million workers belong to labor unions. Only indirectly does unorganized labor benefit from the wages and hours framework pushed through by organized labor, and even then usually not by as much or as rapidly. Much of organized labor works for large corporations that control market prices anyway. In fact, these firms often use labor's wage hikes to "justify" increasing their prices by several times more than the wage increases — always at the expense of the consumer. For instance, assuming everything else to be equal, labor input for producing steel is about 25–30 percent of total cost. If one ton of steel costs $100, the labor input is about $30. If a union wage settlement increases the wages paid to labor by 10 percent, the cost of labor per ton of steel becomes $33. Thus, 30 + (.10 × 30), and the total cost of a ton of steel is $103. However, steel companies, in an attempt to rationalize a price increase, would reason differently and argue for a 10 percent increase.

Unorganized laborers, usually unskilled blue-collar workers who do not belong to any craft union, are the ones who suffer most from such a cost-push inflation because they then have to pay higher prices for products which directly (for example, cars) or indirectly (steel for cars) originate with monopolistic firms. And as we said the great majority of workers are not union members.

Similarities notwithstanding, there is a major difference between the economic power of labor unions and that of corporations. Unions derive their power from existing legislation. This gives them the monopolistic tools with which to restrict the labor supply; however, they still cannot accumulate wealth. Corporations, on the other hand, have the power to restrict output and, much like individuals, can over a period of time accumulate wealth.

The Social Role of Business

In a market economy it is difficult enough to reach any real degree of working competition, much less pure competition. Under pure competition there are many sellers; no single seller can influence the market, and there is a standardized product. Anybody can start a firm in a particular line of business. In major areas of the economy, however, conditions making for competition simply do not exist. Therefore, we may say that the economy is generally controlled by monopolies or oligopolies. A monopoly occurs when there is only one seller, and an oligopoly when there are only a few sellers. Even an operation such as a gas station is not truly competitive because it depends on the oil corporation that controls the production and distribution of gasoline in an oligopolistic fashion.

Because a small group of people control most of the economic activity in the United

States, some scholars have suggested that public and community representatives ought to sit on the boards of directors of large corporations as public watchdogs. This would mitigate the private power of narrow groups when a conflict arose between profit maximization and the social welfare. However, this concept of the social responsibility of corporations is challenged by Milton Friedman, an economist who for years has fought for maximizing the role of private enterprise and minimizing that of the public sector. "Few trends could so thoroughly undermine the very foundation of our free society as acceptance by corporate officials of a social responsibility other than to make as much money for the shareholders as possible," says Friedman.[6]

It is debatable whether corporations should have a social responsibility or not. If their only purpose is to produce and sell goods in order to satisfy demand, then, of course, the answer is no. But in a sense corporations do have a public role because they are chartered by the states. It is argued that public services can best be performed by a public organization — in short, the government — and that there is no incentive for a private firm to efficiently perform a public role. The private organization appears to be best suited for maximizing profits. Yet if a competitive situation making for maximum output and minimum feasible prices is not insured, it is due more to the failure of existing legislation than to the corporate form of business.

Through the tax system, society can decide on the proportion of private, as opposed to public, output. Collectively, members of a society vote for their representatives, who in turn allocate a proportion of the available resources for those goods and services that individuals alone cannot provide for themselves; in other words, individuals get together and provide goods and services collectively. They pay a tax which pays for collective consumption through any level of government. The government provides social goods such as streets, street lighting, highways, mass transportation, police and fire protection, and parks. Certainly the government is best suited to be the supplier of these public goods.

Control of Monopolistic Practices

Theoretically, private enterprise in the United States operates within certain constraints set by the government. There is a form of public representation in some sectors of the economy. Regulatory agencies are the most formalized means of this representation. In practice, regulatory agencies are typically underfinanced and understaffed, not very effective, and often do not serve the purpose for which they were originally established. These agencies cannot easily check the power of corporations.

The Regulatory Agencies. For instance, the price-setting power of public agencies may not necessarily be used in the best fashion. It is only recently that IATA (International Air Transport Association) was forced by public pressure to lower air fares on the North Atlantic run. Even though most airlines flying the North Atlantic were operating far below capacity, IATA continuously refused to lower fares enough to allow airlines to operate at high capacity. The largest airlines claim that fares are very elastic; that is, a small downward change in fares induces a large upward increase in the number of passengers. Thus, by promoting high prices, this agency has operated against the interests of both the public and the major airlines.

---

[6]*Business Week*, November 2, 1968, p. 17.

Over the years the regulatory agencies have been criticized for being inefficient and for pursuing goals that were inconsistent. For instance, the FCC (Federal Communications Commission) is supposed to issue licenses to television stations that operate in the public interest. Yet no specific guidelines as to what constitutes the public interest are set forth, so that the granting of TV licenses seems to take place more or less haphazardly. There are few clear-cut standards for determining why one particular group of people should have a license rather than another.

Agencies seem to be self-perpetuating. Often personnel in regulatory agencies identify closely with the industry that they are supposed to be regulating. For example, senior officials of the Federal Reserve System think automatically in bankers' terms. Banking regulations often consist of sustaining banks with monopoly props through prohibitions against giving interest on checking accounts and interest ceilings on savings accounts that are drawn up to eliminate forms of price competition. The Federal Reserve Board in approving applications for new banks appears to take the view that profits for existing banks are more important than the benefits of potential competition.

Another example of government control that is intended to serve the public interest but that ultimately serves neither the public nor the corporations is the regulation of railroads. The Interstate Commerce Commission (ICC) was created in 1887 to regulate the service provided by and the prices charged by railroads. Competing means of transportation that came later on — the automobile, the bus, the truck, and the airplane — are not regulated in the same manner. Regulation by obsolete laws has been hampering railroad operations since alternative means of transportation were first introduced.

Moreover, for the last two decades, according to Robert Fellmeth, the ICC "has watched the demise of the passenger train and has done little to halt it."[7] Yet Section 13a of the ICC Act specifically states that no discontinuance of service can occur when a train run is "required by the public convenience and necessity." The ICC chooses to use the "profitability criterion" instead. Since railroads decided in the 1950's to kill passenger service, "it appears that . . . they have purposefully downgraded their facility in an attempt to show that both their profits and the public's interest in railroad travel are declining."[8] Indeed the ICC meekly obliged and between 1958 and 1971 discontinued 1,110 out of 1,448 existing passenger runs.

Such examples of the unsuccessful regulation of business for the public interest by United States government agencies could fill volumes. Perhaps at the time these agencies were first created by Congress, some played a positive role, but as conditions changed, the regulatory agencies definitely did not change with them. Therefore, far from defending the public interest, they have either acquiesced in the profit aims of industry or they have operated at cross purposes with the interests of both the public and business.

Antitrust Legislation. A corporate enterprise is in business to maximize profits. This allows for capital accumulation in a restricted number of firms which aim as a matter of course at eliminating other firms. In 1890 and again in 1914, the American public through its representatives in Congress found this to be intolerable and instituted antitrust legislation as a countervailing power. However, antitrust policies have not worked well.

---

[7]Robert Fellmeth, *The Interstate Commerce Commission* (New York: Grossman Publishers, 1970), p. 285.
[8]*Ibid.*, p. 287.

In 1890, the Sherman Antitrust Act aimed at regulating monopolies or any other form of organization which conspired to restrict trade. The courts and the executive branch continued to be unsympathetic to enforcing this law and up until 1914 only a few antitrust cases were successfully fought by the government. On the other hand, this law was effectively used against labor organizations, which were looked upon as conspiracies to restrain trade. In 1914, the Clayton Act modified the Sherman Act by textually stating that "labor is not a commodity of commerce." Subsequently, labor unions were not covered by antitrust legislation. For a short while in the 1930's a moratorium was called on antitrust legislation in order to allow business to keep prices high to fight deflationary trends in the economy. The courts found this illegal, and eventually more restrictive modifications of antitrust legislation were adopted by Congress. Yet, in the 1970's, monopolies and oligopolies still dominate the market to roughly the same extent that they did in 1890 because of poor implementation of the existing laws.

The Public Enterprise. In the latest institutional arrangement, the capitalist system depends on two sets of bureaucracies: (1) the government, which theoretically operates for the purpose of meeting social needs; and (2) the corporation, which operates for profits. Yet both these vast bureaucracies suffer from the same sluggishness of response, the same internal politics and feuds, and pursue goals which only incidentally correspond to individual or social needs. Some argue that because of their concentration of power and ineffective regulation, basic industries such as steel, railroads, automobiles, oil, and electricity should be nationalized. Most European countries — including the United Kingdom, the cradle of laissez-faire economics — have attempted this, at times quite successfully. The publicly owned industry is not unknown even in the United States.

In fact, the U.S. government created the TVA (Tennessee Valley Authority) project. In the 1930's, the electric companies refused to electrify rural areas in the South and Midwest. In collusion, they charged extremely high rates since they enjoyed a local monopoly. Regulatory agencies could not control the prices charged because the companies showed high balance sheet costs to justify their high prices. Therefore, in the 1930's, Congress created a public corporation called the Tennessee Valley Authority for three purposes: (1) to lower prices; (2) to electrify the rural areas; and (3) to save the land through which the Tennessee River runs. In the beginning, subsidies had to come from the government; but in time the Tennessee Valley Authority became one of the best electricity-producing systems in the United States. Today, TVA is thriving as one of the largest, most efficient business enterprises in the country — and, lo and behold, it is government-owned and operated. The TVA operates as an independent corporation. Its profits, which are substantial, are paid back to the government. In a sense, the government put up the capital and thereafter received a return on it, much as would any private stockholder.

Mixed Public Enterprise. It appears that Americans, unlike their European counterparts, are not yet prepared for the government taking over any large-scale operation of business. On the other hand, the control and regulation of natural monopolies (public utilities such as railroads, electric power, gas, and so forth) first instituted in 1887, have not been effective. The new concept of mixed corporate ownership, half public, half private, may at this point be more appropriate; Comsat and Amtrak seem to be good beginnings in this direction. The First and Second United

States Banks (1791 – 1811; 1816 – 1836) were both of this form and operated quite successfully. This type of corporation is jointly owned by both private and public stockholders, who do not necessarily enjoy proportional representation on the board of directors. In Italy, corporations of this type own most of the basic industries and banks of the country and earn substantial income for the government. In the United States, as in Italy, some firms and investors might become free riders on the coattails of these mixed government enterprises. Still, it could be a distinct improvement over the private oligopolistic corporation; at the very least, this type of corporation would have a sense of social responsibility.

SUGGESTIONS FOR FURTHER READING

Berle, Adolf A., Jr. *Power Without Property: A New Development in American Political Economy.* New York: Harcourt Brace Jovanovich, Inc., 1959.

Friedman, Milton. *Capitalism and Freedom.* Chicago: University of Chicago Press, 1962.

Galbraith, John Kenneth. *The Affluent Society.* Boston: Houghton Mifflin, 1958.

————. *The New Industrial State.* Boston: Houghton Mifflin, 1967.

Kolko, Gabriel. *Wealth and Power in America.* New York: Frederick A. Praeger, 1962.

Lilenthal, David E. *Big Business: A New Era.* New York: Harper and Brothers, 1962.

Means, Gardiner C. "The Problem and Prospects of Collective Capitalism," *Journal of Economic Issues,* Vol. 3, No. 1 (March 1969), pp. 18 – 31.

Mills, C. Wright. *The Power Elite.* New York: Oxford University Press, 1959.

Reagan, Michael D. *The Managed Economy.* New York: Oxford University Press, 1963.

$ ◗ ◖ ◗ ◗ ◗

TOTAL SALE

◖ ◖ ◖ ◗

GALLONS

3 1 8

$ ◗

TOT

G

3

Regul

OR USE AS A
OR FUEL ONLY
ONTAINS
LEAD

15 *Taxation: Social and Private Good*

Taxes are an almost inevitable aspect of a community's life. One reason why people form communities, with some type of government, must be that there are some activities that are better or more desirably performed by and for a group than by and for each individual. To pay for these activities, such as police and fire protection, taxes are levied. In simpler societies, "taxes" may include hours of labor committed to the construction and repair of community facilities such as roads or bridges. In modern economies, taxes involve the compulsory payment of money to the government to implement the transfer of resources from individual or private use to group or public use.

The Main Issues

There is an important truth that we all should know but that we sometimes forget: the provision of public goods and services uses up real resources which are then no longer available for private use. Taxes perform the function of transferring command over resources from the private to the public sector as painlessly as possible. Taxes, however, are not necessary to assure the transferral of economic resources. Alternatively, government could: (1) conscript resources (tons of steel, man-hours of labor, and so forth) on command; (2) borrow from the private sector by selling government bonds; or (3) print money in order to bid away resources from the private sector, with almost certain inflation of the price level. Modern governments have generally avoided the first and third alternatives, although an important exception is the use of the draft to raise manpower for military purposes. Governments have tended to use a combination of taxes and borrowings to finance their undertakings, mostly taxes.

In the United States, every family pays at least some taxes: income taxes, sales taxes, Social Security taxes, property taxes, estate (death) taxes, gasoline taxes, cigarette taxes, liquor and beer taxes. Almost everyone has some complaints about the tax system and the way in which some of the receipts are used. Four major issues are involved.

The first we shall treat only briefly. As readers of this chapter will have learned elsewhere, the level of taxation by the federal government matched against its total spending makes up what is called "fiscal policy," which has a large influence on total demand, production and employment in the economy, and also on the rate of inflation. Deficits in the federal budget, it is now widely agreed, are sometimes desirable and sometimes not. A classic example of an undesirable deficit — and there is almost no argument on this — occurred in 1968 at the height of the war in Vietnam, when the economy was operating at near full employment and inflation was becoming an ever more serious problem.[1] It was a bad time for the government to spend more than its receipts, because it was adding to an already excessive level of total spending in the economy. By contrast, deficits in the early 1970's, at a time when many men and machines were idle, probably helped to keep a mild recession mild and to start the economy expanding again.

For our purposes here, the other three issues of taxation are more relevant. The rest of this chapter will be devoted to them.

One can be called simply: How much? What share of our total resources — really meaning our total incomes — do we want to devote to the public sector?

The second can be called: What is fair? What should each of us contribute? To what extent should the tax system try to equalize incomes in the society? The issue of fairness or "equity" involves not only the way taxes are levied but how the tax money is spent. The progressive federal income tax, with all its loopholes, still takes a larger share of the income of the average man earning $25,000 than of one who earns only $10,000. The Social Security tax, with its maximum "wage base," has the opposite effect — taking a higher portion of the earnings of the $10,000 man than of the man earning $25,000.

The question of how the tax money is spent is also relevant, as noted. At one extreme, we could spend the entirety of our tax revenues on national defense, in which case "fairness" would concern only how the taxes were collected. At the other extreme, we could spend all our tax receipts on welfare or some other system of income improvement for low-income families. In that case, no matter how the taxes were *collected*, the equality of income distribution would almost certainly be improved.

In the real world, of course, we are somewhere in between. But in any debate on the fairness of how the taxes are collected, the question of how the tax money is used or distributed should also be considered. We shall conclude this chapter with an examination of the "negative income tax," an idea which would have the tax system make payments as well as collect revenue.

The third issue involves use of taxation to affect the private sector allocation of resources, or to accomplish social purposes other than reducing income inequality. Why do we tax cigarettes and alcohol as highly as we do? The question answers itself: Because society has decided that these particular items of consumption deserve to be taxed and are a relatively noncontroversial means of raising revenue. A tougher question arises in connection with something like pollution. In 1970, the President decided that a social purpose could be achieved by levying a tax on the sulphur content of various fuels, thus giving an economic incentive to producers to

---

[1]There is, however, debate as to whether a temporary tax increase would have been nearly as effective as a cut in government spending, especially military spending, as the best means of reducing the undesirable deficit.

reduce the emission of sulphur oxides, which, in turn, would help clean up the air. Congress at this writing has not approved the tax, but the point remains. Taxation can be used to try to direct, or to change, economic activity. Another example is the off-again, on-again special federal tax credit for business investment, which allows a business buying a new machine to subtract 7 percent of the cost of the machine from its tax bill. The purpose of this tax provision is to increase total business investment in plant and equipment, on the grounds that the economy needs more such investments to go on growing and to remain competitive with foreign countries. Regardless of the merits of the argument, this is a good example of the use of taxation to alter the allocation of resources.

The Problem of Public Choice

Having recognized that the scarcity of resources creates a trade-off between public and private sector output, we may ask in what manner society determines how resources should be allocated as between public and private uses. One thing is clear: no "invisible hand" exists to guide resources between public and private uses. While the price system does act as an "invisible hand" within the private sector and does a tolerable job of transmitting consumer preferences to producers, it does not work for most of the services which must be provided by government. The main reason why this is so is the group nature of the consumption of such services as police and fire protection, the court system, public health services, city streets, and national defense. That is, one person's consumption of the benefits resulting from these services does not prevent others from benefiting from the *same*, or nearly the same, level of service. While my purchase of a shirt excludes my neighbor from the use of that shirt, many public services provided me can be consumed more or less equally by my neighbors. For example, the benefits of mosquito eradication are available to all persons in the eradication area irrespective of their financial contribution to the program. Thus, the price system does not work well or does not work at all when my consumption of a service does not *exclude* my neighbor from consuming the same service. The problem of who should pay for the good or service arises, and becomes more difficult to solve in a noncoercive fashion, the larger the number of persons simultaneously consuming the same service. As numbers increase, the problem of the "free rider" — one who consumes the service but contributes nothing to finance it — increases, unless some *compulsory* method of financing, such as taxation, is relied upon.

The group consumption nature of many public services complicates the determination of the composition and level of these services. If — alas, very unlikely — all individuals residing within a given political unit (municipality, state, or nation, depending on the geographical extent of the service provided) had the same preferences for public services, the problem of determining the level and composition of public sector services would be greatly simplified. The political process would provide a trial and error method for approximating the point at which the benefits from an extra unit of public service equaled the cost of other (private sector) goods and services foregone — an example of the concept of "opportunity cost." However, individuals and families have different preferences for public services just as they have differing preferences for privately marketed goods and services. For example, it is conceivable that most citizens would be willing to support some provision for space exploration, while differing widely as to how much should be spent to get to Mars by 1980. Since the *same* level of public service is available to all members of the group to which it is provided, and since some financial contribution is demanded from all or most members of the community regardless of their preference for the service, inevitably conflicts arise. In many cases, these conflicts are resolved through political compromise, but the result may be a very imperfect one and many members of the community may be unhappy about the outcome. Consider, for example, local conflicts over building highways, airports, and public housing; conflicts at the state level over the amounts to be expended on higher education and medical facilities; or conflicts at the national level over the SST or ABM. And most of us feel that the *grand total* of public spending is too large and thus tend to resist higher taxes.

The problem can be restated in a somewhat different manner. As long as there are important differences in the tastes and opinions of the citizenry, no decision binding on all members of the community is likely to assure unanimous agreement with, support for, or happiness with the outcome. Here, goods produced by the private sector and subject to the "exclusion" principle (that is, one person's consumption excludes others from consuming the good, as in the case of shirts or apples) differ from the public goods and services under consideration. Almost any mechanism that provides for the market-clearing distribution of goods subject to the exclusion principle allows what Milton Friedman has termed "unanimity without conformity." Individuals may purchase goods and services in accordance with their tastes, though we must note a fundamental assumption that individuals have the wherewithal to purchase goods and services in the first place. Unanimity is reached in the sense that each consumer unit can cast its dollar votes in accordance with its own ranking of preferences. No conformity among consuming units is required. But this is not so in the case of goods that are collectively consumed, that is, consumed by the group. To a certain extent, conformity is required and so long as diversity of taste and opinion exist nothing like unanimity of agreement will be reached. One should not conclude, however, that marketed goods and services are superior to publicly provided goods and services. So long as society prefers at least some of the latter, provision by the government is surely better than no provision at all.

The difficulties in reaching collective agreement are no less severe when the allocation of resources between public and private uses is *not* at issue. Government, as noted above, is also regarded by most of us as responsible for correcting inequalities in the *distribution* of income. While there is probably some sort of consensus that income and wealth should not be distributed "too unequally," there is no consensus as to what minimum level of equality ought to be achieved. Thus, while there is broad support for assistance to the aged, disabled, and other groups not able to support themselves, there is less agreement on the level of assistance to be maintained. Even more difficult is the question of whether or not to supplement the income of a family whose head is capable of working, but incapable of earning enough income to "adequately" support his family. While there is growing support for some form of guaranteed income, there is by no means a consensus on the issue, and even its supporters often disagree over the level to be guaranteed. And to the extent that transfers are made to lower-income groups, how should the required taxes be distributed among the taxpaying population?

One implication of the foregoing is that in societies where the population is relatively homogeneous in background, tradition, outlook, and socioeconomic circumstance, consensus on public matters may be easier to achieve than in societies where heterogeneity of background, tradition, outlook, and socioeconomic circumstance is the rule. The United States, at least at this point in its history, seems to fit the latter category, and Sweden the former. Moreover, in the United States there are demands from all sides that an increasing number of social and economic ills be eliminated or cured. The resources available do not permit us to launch an effective attack on all the problems facing the nation at once even if there were agreement on higher taxes, which there is not. Priorities must be established. But how? Which problems should be tackled first? Who is to decide? These questions are important in a democratic society in that success requires that there be broad support for the action to be taken. If the citizenry is divided and in conflict with itself, it is likely that the various goals sought will be compromised, leaving almost everyone unhappy.

Allocating the Costs of Government?

How should the costs of government be distributed among the citizenry? In accordance with the benefits received from publicly provided goods and services? Or in accordance with some standard of ability to pay — that is, in relation to the taxpayer's financial "capacity" to pay taxes? These are two quite different principles of taxation. In terms of equity or fairness, each carries substantial weight. On the one hand, it is argued that those who benefit from a particular government service — say, national parks or bank deposit insurance — should pay their share of the cost of providing that service. On the other, it is argued that it is hardly equitable to refuse a government service to a person simply because he cannot afford to pay his full share. If the standards of the marketplace were accepted, the former argument — the benefit principle — would appear to carry more weight. He who receives the use of the shirt should pay for it. But why should the standards of the marketplace be adopted when the goods and services to be paid for cannot be supplied through the market mechanism? Most of the goods and services to be paid for through taxation are available to all members of the group in the sense that no one can be *excluded* from the benefits of the service. Presumably, all members of the community benefit equally or nearly equally from a fire department. But since tastes and incomes differ, not all individuals would be willing to pay for the benefits of public services currently received. Does this mean, however, that *all* the costs of government should be financed on an ability-to-pay basis? Not necessarily, since some government services are capable of being financed on the basis of the benefit principle. Let us look at the issues involved in a bit more detail.

If the only goal of taxation were to raise the revenue required to finance a given activity, *and* if it were possible to identify and isolate those individuals who benefited from a given public service, it might be desirable to levy a tax on the public service in the form of a fee or toll to be paid by the individual consumer. For example, part of the cost of some highways is borne by users who must pay tolls at selected points along the highway. Clearly, the car owner who uses the highway — and presumably benefits from its use — pays, while the nonuser does not pay or pays less than the user where tolls do not cover the full costs of providing highway services. However, the construction and maintenance of city streets are usually financed through general revenue taxation. Why? Partly because it would be extremely costly and inconvenient to establish toll booths at each intersection of unlimited access roads, and partly because a system of streets and roads conveys substantial *indirect* benefits to nonusers, even to people who do not drive. The indirect benefits include the lower costs of other goods and services (such as food and clothing) that are made possible by the existence of a transportation system, of which streets and roads form a part. In fact, the indirect benefits from limited-access intercity highways — where the collection of tolls is clearly an alternative to general revenue finance — are evidently considered important enough that the 15-year-old interstate highway system is largely toll-free. Even here, however, the average automobile user (as opposed to the interstate highway user) pays more for the interstate system than does the average nonautomobile user because the major portion of the costs of that system come out of federal gasoline taxes earmarked for the federal highway fund.

In general, it is not feasible to place the burden of government finance on a beneficiary or user basis, quite apart from whether or not it would be desirable to do so. For example, it would obviously be impossible to levy charges on individuals according to the price they were willing to pay for a space exploration program, the local police force, national defense, public health measures designed to reduce contagious and infectious disease, the court system, and many other public services. The reason, of course, again lies in the fact that many services are consumed by the group, in the sense that one individual's consumption of the service does not prevent others from receiving the service. Thus, all or most members must be compelled to pay if the service is to be provided at all. But even where it was *feasible* to charge the chief beneficiary of a service for his use of that service, it might not be *desirable* to do so. For example, public schools could be priced, the user student (or his parents) being asked to pay part or all of the educational costs incurred by him. The same applies to medical care. Yet public education, financed by taxation, is widespread, and an increasing share of the cost of providing medical care is being paid for out of public (tax-raised) funds. Here, society's objective may be to assure some minimum level of education and medical care regardless of whether or not people have the desire or the ability to pay for these services. In this way, some of the costs of education and medical care are distributed on the basis of income or other indices of taxable capacity and not simply on the basis of the use of, or direct benefits received from, educational and medical facilities. Childless couples and single people help pay for the local public school, for example.

The Fairness of the Revenue System

The thrust of the preceding section is that it is neither feasible nor desirable to rely chiefly on user charges to finance government. Nor is any level of government financed chiefly through user charges. But which of many forms of general taxation should be adopted? Table 15.1 shows how the federal, state, and local governments raise their revenues. At the federal level of government, the chief revenue raiser is the income tax, which, in 1969, provided 65 percent of the revenue intake when the personal and corporate components were combined. Two important taxes not used by the federal government are general sales and property taxes. The former is the chief revenue raiser for state governments, the latter the financial stalwart of local governments.

Role of the Graduated Income Tax. The income tax receives broad support as a revenue raiser because of all taxes it is perhaps best fit to accomplish the widely accepted objective of distributing the costs of government in an equitable manner. In

Table 15.1   Federal, State, and Local Revenue and Expenditures by Source and Use (1969 – 1971)

	$Billion			Percentage of Total		
	1969	1970	1971	1969	1970	1971
Federal (Receipts)	200.6	191.5	198.8	100.0	100.0	100.0
Personal tax and nontax receipts	95.9	92.2	89.0	47.8	48.1	44.8
Coporate profits tax accruals	39.2	30.6	33.6	19.5	16.0	16.9
Indirect business tax and nontax accruals	19.1	19.3	20.3	9.5	10.1	10.2
Contributions for social insurance	46.5	49.3	56.0	23.2	25.7	28.2
Federal (Expenditures)	191.3	205.1	221.9	100.0	100.0	100.0
Purchase of goods and services	101.3	97.2	97.6	52.9	47.4	44.0
National defense	78.8	75.4	71.4	41.2	36.8	32.2
Other	22.6	21.9	26.2	11.8	10.7	11.8
Transfer payments	52.1	63.4	75.9	27.2	30.9	34.2
To persons	50.0	61.2	73.4	26.1	29.8	33.1
To foreigners (net)	2.1	2.2	2.5	1.1	1.1	1.1
Grants-in-aid to state and local government enterprises	20.2	24.4	29.6	10.5	11.9	13.3
Net interest paid	13.1	14.6	13.7	6.8	7.1	6.2
Subsidies less current surplus of government enterprises	4.6	5.5	5.1	2.4	2.7	2.3
Less: Wage accruals less disbursements	0	0	0	0	0	0
Surplus or deficit (-), national income and product accounts	9.3	-13.6	R -23.1 E	4.6 4.9	-7.1 -6.6	-11.6 -10.4
State and Local (Receipts)	118.3	133.4	151.7	100.0	100.0	100.0
Personal tax and nontax receipts	21.4	23.6	26.8	18.1	17.7	17.7
Corporate profits tax accruals	3.5	3.5	4.3	2.9	2.6	2.8
Indirect business tax and nontax accruals	66.1	73.6	81.8	55.9	55.2	53.9
Contributions for social insurance	7.1	8.3	9.2	6.0	6.2	6.1
Federal grants-in-aid	20.2	24.4	29.6	17.1	18.3	19.5
State and Local (Expenditures)	118.9	132.9	148.9	100.0	100.0	100.0
Purchases of goods and services	110.8	122.2	135.5	93.2	91.9	91.0
Transfer payments to persons	11.5	14.4	17.1	9.7	10.8	11.5
Net interest paid	.1	.1	.5	0	0	0
Less: Current surplus of government enterprises	3.6	3.8	4.1	3.0	2.8	2.7
Less: Wage accruals less disbursements	0	0	0	0	0	0
Surplus or deficit (-), national income and product accounts	-.6	.5	R 2.8 E	-.01 -.01	.004 .004	1.8 1.9

Source: U.S. Department of Commerce, *Survey of Current Business*, 1971 and 1972.

taxation, there are two mutually compatible aspects of the equity issue: *horizontal equity,* which implies "equal treatment of equals" (all families with $25,000 of income should pay about the same tax); and *vertical equity,* which implies "unequal treatment of unequals" (the family with $25,000 of income should pay more of its income in taxes than a family with $8,000). While "equal treatment of equals" logically implies the corollary "unequal treatment of unequals," it is easier to reach agreement on the former principle than it is on the latter. The reason, of course, is that it is meaningless to simply specify that unequals should be treated differently. The fundamental question is *how differently,* and appeals to fairness provide no final answer to this question. Nevertheless, the important role of the graduated, or progressive, income tax in the United States suggests that some degree of consensus has been reached on both the horizontal and vertical equity issues.

Income is a widely accepted basis for measuring taxable capacity. Horizontal equity implies that all forms of income should be treated similarly for tax purposes. Most, but not all, forms of income are so treated in the federal income tax system. If taxpayers A and B have the same amount of income, as defined in the tax law, they will have similar tax liabilities unless other recognized differences, such as the number of dependents or medical expenses they have, intercede.

One may deduce a modicum of agreement on the vertical equity issue in the fact that progressivity in the federal income tax has survived numerous congressional efforts to alter and reform the income tax in other ways. Apparently, there is a broad agreement that unequal treatment of unequals should be carried at least to the point where taxpayers with higher incomes should pay not only *absolutely* more of their income in the form of taxes to the government than taxpayers with lower incomes, but *relatively* more of their incomes than those in lower-income tax brackets. However, the tax rates specified in the Income Tax Act are a poor guide to the actual degree of progressivity in the U.S. income tax. To look at the tax rates specified in the Income Tax Act one would think that there is broad agreement on "soaking the rich." The rates for married couples run from 14 percent on the first $1,000 of taxable income to 70 percent on taxable income in excess of $200,000. However, these legal rates are more "nominal" than "effective." Some sources of income are excluded from the definition of income for tax purposes, such as half of capital gains, interest on state and local bonds, and government welfare, veterans', and Social Security benefits. In addition, deductions from gross income for such things as charitable contributions, state and local taxes paid, and mortgage interest are allowed. The result is that, on the average, "effective" tax rates rise from close to zero at the bottom of the scale to about 33 percent for incomes in excess of $200,000, above which there is almost no increase at all. While the income tax is not, therefore, as progressive as it seems at higher levels of income, the tax changes enacted in 1969 and 1971 have reduced or eliminated income taxes for nearly all at the level of $8,000 of income or less.

The exclusion of some forms of income from taxation limits the progressivity of the federal income tax and creates wide divergences from the principle of horizontal equity. In practice, agreement on equal treatment of equals is undermined by special pleading and preferential treatment as well as by honest attempts to adjust taxable income for real differences in taxpayer circumstance. The divergence from horizontal equity in the U.S. income tax not only deceives the taxpayer-citizen as to the extent to which the tax system redistributes income but reduces taxpayer morale (and perhaps his willingness to comply with the tax law) when from time to time he is made aware of the fact that others who appear equally or better circumstanced than he are paying far less in taxes. Moreover, it is likely that achieving some sort of agreement as to the division of resources between public and private uses is made more difficult when millions of taxpayers feel that the divergence from equity principles surpasses their limit of tolerance. People will support public services and activities when they feel that they are paying "only their fair share." But when they feel that they are paying considerably more than their fair share, then they are inclined to give less enthusiastic support to such services and activities. Perhaps income tax reform should be considered a priority goal precisely because it may be a prerequisite to reaching broad agreement on other social objectives which require public spending. Broadening the income tax base by including more forms of income and eliminating difficult-to-justify (on social as opposed to individual grounds) deductions could add tens of billions of dollars to the tax base, thereby allowing a substantial reduction in tax rates. For example, elimination of the deductions for mortgage interest and property taxes, which benefit only home owners and not renters, would raise more than $3 billion in revenue.

Does an equitable distribution of the costs of government imply that all or most tax revenues should be raised through income taxation? Clearly, income taxation currently plays only a relatively small role at state and local levels, as Table 15.1 indicates, though its use has been growing; and at the federal level, payroll taxes finance an important fraction of all health and welfare expenditures, and have been growing rapidly.

Regressive Taxes. Much can be said for and against each of the other three major revenue raisers: the retail sales tax, the property tax, and payroll taxes. The incidence of these taxes — that is, their impact on the distribution of personal disposable income — and their other effects are complicated and cannot be discussed in any depth here. It will suffice to say that each of these taxes is more regressive than a proportional, let alone a progressive, income tax. That is, each of these taxes places a relatively greater burden, on lower-income groups than it does on upper-income groups.

The payroll tax is regressive because it is a flat tax levied on the first $10,800 of wage income. The retail sales tax tends to be regressive — unless food and clothing are exempt from the tax — because low-income households, on the average, spend (as opposed to save) a higher proportion of their income than do upper-income households. The incidence of the property tax is much harder to deduce. Home owners can deduct property taxes in calculating their income tax while renters cannot, though the tax adds to their rent. In many areas, lower-income people are more likely to be renters than are high-income people. Moreover, higher-income households are more likely to hold forms of wealth such as stocks and bonds, which are not subject to property taxation. Thus, the property tax is probably no more than proportional and is quite likely regressive.

Despite the apparent regressiveness of the three taxes, they have enjoyed prosperity as revenue raisers. Revenues derived from each of these sources have greatly expanded since World War II, a period in which the personal income tax came into its own as a major peacetime revenue raiser and potential alternative to other forms of taxation. Why have the sales, property, and payroll taxes enjoyed continued public support? The answer is not easily discernible, but three reasons can be tentatively suggested. First, as long as the rates for each of these taxes are low, the taxes are not particularly "visible." That is, low sales, property, and payroll tax rates may not generate taxpayer wrath to the same extent that higher income tax rates required to raise the same amount of revenue would. However, recent political debate suggests that higher tax rates, especially for property and sales taxes, in many locales have made these taxes more visible and onerous. Second, it is perhaps the case that progressivity in the personal income tax is tolerated in part because it is offset by regressivity in other important taxes composing the federal-state-local revenue system. In fact, there is good evidence that when all of the major taxes are taken together, the tax system as a whole is remarkably proportional throughout a wide range of income classes. But while the total tax system is not very progressive, neither is it regressive. Third, state and local governments undoubtedly desire to maintain access to important revenue sources independent of the chief federal source: the income tax. It is doubtful whether state and local governments would give up their chief sources of taxes without a fight that would go to the very roots of the federal system in the United States.

The income tax is not likely to become the sole important revenue raiser — nor perhaps should it — in our lifetime. Equity as reflected in a single tax base and set of tax rates is simply not important enough to most Americans to warrant giving up what appear to many to be the relatively desirable features of other taxes. If anything can be expected, it is that the various major revenue sources will be "reformed" to prevent placing excessive tax burdens on those taxpayers at the bottom end of the income ladder. In addition, federal "revenue sharing" with lower levels of government should reduce the pressure to increase the more regressive state and local taxes in order to finance increasing state and local expenditures.

Some Effects of Taxation

Failure of the income tax system to achieve horizontal equity can do more than produce "unfairness" in taxation. The allocation of resources may also be affected. This can happen when certain forms of income or compensation are taxed at lower rates than other forms of income or when the net income or profits of certain industries are taxed at lower rates than the profits of other industries.

The Effect on Allocation of Resources. When some forms of income are not taxed, or are taxed at preferential (lower) rates, an incentive is created to receive as much of one's income as possible from the tax-advantaged source(s). For example, the highly paid corporate executive is subject to high income tax rates if he receives all of his income in the form of a regularly paid salary. However, if he takes some of his compensation in the form of his company's common stock and if stock prices rise over time, he will pay taxes at lower rates on the capital gain portion of his income. (The capital gain is the amount by which the price of the stock increased between the date on which it was received or purchased and the date on which it is sold.) Under U.S. income tax law, capital gains are taxed at one half of ordinary tax rates. Thus, the highly paid executive has an incentive to take only part of his compensation in the form of a monthly check. In effect, he has an incentive to save part of his income by holding his company's shares, rather than taking all of his income in salaried form, paying taxes, and then saving some of the remainder by placing it in a financial institution such as a bank or savings and loan association or "investing" it in another firm's shares or in government or corporate bonds. While concrete evidence is lacking, one might expect the preferential tax treatment of capital gains to put a premium on investment in, and expansion by, *existing* corporations. Capital needed for the growth of new firms may consequently be that much less available, though new companies do succeed in selling stock issues each year.

Another example of how preferential tax treatment may affect the allocation of resources is presented by the U.S. oil and gas industry. For many years, oil and gas companies have been allowed to deduct for the purpose of computing taxable income a substantial fraction of their gross income — 27½ percent until 1970, when the rate was reduced to 22 percent — in the form of a "depletion allowance." The write-off substantially reduces the oil and gas company income subject to tax. Firms in most other industries may for tax purposes amortize their plant and equipment by annually subtracting from gross income a depreciation allowance which, summed over the years of the life of the asset, is limited to the original cost (price paid when purchased) of the firm's plant and equipment. Oil and gas producers can deduct much more.

The favorable tax treatment of the oil industry has not only resulted in millionaire oil men with no or negligible tax liabilities; it has also probably influenced the allocation of capital resources. That is, substantially more capital may have been induced to flow into the oil and gas industry than would have been the case if that industry did not receive special tax treatment. The other side of the coin, of course, is that fewer capital resources are available for investment in other industries. The preferential tax treatment of the oil and gas industry has continued to receive strong political support, based on industry arguments that there is exceptionally great risk involved in oil and gas exploration and development and that the long-run requirements of national defense make potential self-sufficiency in the supply of oil and gas desirable. However, there are probably better ways of stimulating oil and gas exploration, if, in fact, it needs stimulation, than by grossly compromising the fairness of the tax system.

Effect on Economic Growth. The goal of equity may come into direct conflict with the goal of economic growth. If vertical equity implies substantial progressivity in the income tax system, the behavioral reaction of persons subject to high tax rates cannot be ignored. High tax rates can affect the incentive to work and save. If they do, economic growth may be affected since the determinants of growth are the size of the labor force and the hours of work it will supply, the rate of capital formation, and the increase in the productivity of labor and capital. In the case of work effort, the effect of high taxes is not certain. High tax rates reduce the extra income from working another hour, thus making the substitution of leisure for work less costly. On the other hand, high taxes mean less take-home pay, thereby motivating the taxpayer to increase his hours of work, or his ambition for advancement, in order to raise his disposable (after-tax) income. Studies of the impact of high income tax rates on work behavior have almost unanimously concluded that, on the average, the impact on hours of work is negligible.

The likely impact of high tax rates on savings (and investment) is more clear. High income tax rates can reduce savings in two ways. First, the chief savers are upper-income families and corporations. High personal income taxes which substantially reduce the after-tax incomes of the wealthy will reduce their saving as well as their consumption. The effect on savings will be all the greater if high-income households attempt to maintain high levels of consumption in the face of high tax rates. High corporation income tax rates reduce the net after-tax income of corporations, assuming that the tax is not wholly "shifted" forward onto consumers via higher prices for the goods and services produced by corporations. A reduction in corporate net, after-tax income almost certainly means reduced corporate "savings," out of which a substantial fraction of corporate investment is financed. And this investment is an element in economic growth.

A second way in which high income taxes may reduce the level of savings is by adversely influencing the *incentive* to save. Income recipients may choose between consuming or saving their incomes. One, although not the most important, motivation for saving (or not consuming) is the return that saving brings in the form of interest or profits. Since interest and profits constitute income that is subject to taxation, the effect of income taxes is to reduce the net return to saving, thereby weakening somewhat the incentive to save.

The actual impact of high taxes on the rate of economic growth is unclear, although it appears to be small. True, the rate of economic growth does depend, in part, on the rate of investment, or capital formation, and high taxes which reduce total savings may, under certain conditions, adversely affect the amount of investment. However, it is estimated that it would take a substantial increase in savings and investment to raise the rate of economic growth even one-tenth of a percentage point. Even a substantial reduction in the *effective* progressivity of the tax system — thus enabling the "rich" to save more — is not likely to increase savings enough to have more than a negligible effect on the rate of economic growth. Moreover, tax-induced reductions in the growth rate can be partly or wholly offset if tax revenues are used to finance government expenditures on activities such as education, public health, and research — in short, on activities which contribute to increasing the productivity of labor and capital equipment. Thus, the conflict between the goals of vertical equity and economic growth may not be very severe — at least in already developed nations with a large amount of capital in place relative to their populations. If the conflict is not severe, then compromising the goal of vertical equity in the name of economic growth is difficult to justify. This is not to say that the rich should be "soaked" just because the economic effect is likely to be small. Rather, it says that how the well-to-do are taxed relative to the not-so-well-off should depend on a fairness criterion — albeit subjective — rather than on the allegedly more "objective" grounds that society's goal of economic growth may be compromised.

Using the Tax System to Raise Family Income

The major role of taxation is to transfer resources from the private to the public sector. But taxes also redistribute command over goods and services *within* the private sector through their redistributive effects. Can the tax system be made to do more to increase equality in the distribution of income? And if it can, should it do so? This was a major issue in the 1972 presidential election in the United States.

In the 1960's, many Americans became increasingly aware of the problem of poverty in the United States. It is now clear that poverty is not going to vanish quickly from the face of America, even if priorities are reordered and a massive effort is devoted to eliminating the basic causes of poverty. It is also clear that while the graduated income tax has to some degree lessened inequality in the distribution of income, there has been no steady progress toward lessening income inequality in the last two decades. The extent of inequality in the distribution of income has remained about the same since the late 1940's. While in relative terms the top 1 and 5 percent of families may have lost some ground, the loss has been to the middle- and upper-middle income groups, dominated by professionals, skilled workers, and multiearner families.[2] Meanwhile, the distribution of wealth — including property, stocks, and bonds — which was always much more unequally distributed than income, has shown no signs of changing. It is estimated that in 1962 the top 5 percent of wealth holders enjoyed 53 percent of the total wealth.

The urgency of the poverty problem would be sufficient in itself to justify a more direct redistribution of income through the income tax system. In fact, however, there are signs that income inequality would pose important social problems even if

[2]Edward Budd, "Postwar Changes in the Size Distribution of Income in the U.S.," *American Economic Review*, May 1970, pp. 247–260.

all poor families had their incomes brought up to poverty line levels (about $4,000 for a family of four, with $700 increments per person for larger- and smaller-sized families). For example, increasing demands that families have a *right* to good housing and medical care may indicate that many families in the lower half of the income distribution feel themselves increasingly priced out of the market for these goods and services. But these demands may also reflect expectations of the "good life" that have outpaced the real income growth of the society as a whole, or the poor geographical distribution of housing and medical services. Even so, it is not idle to inquire how the tax system might play a role in raising incomes at the lower end of the income scale.

The Negative Income Tax.   One proposal which has received increasing attention in recent years is the "negative income tax," though the basic idea also has other names, including "welfare reform." As the name suggests, the income tax system would be used to pay "negative taxes," or transfer payments, as well as to collect taxes. Families with incomes below a specified level would receive income supplements rather than pay taxes. Given family size and income, the size of the negative tax payment would depend on the plan's three basic variables or components: These are: (1) a basic income allowance or income guarantee, G; (2) a break-even level of income, B; and (3) a tax rate, r, on the family's income. The three variables are related to each other in a very definite manner: $G = rB$. To change one of the basic variables would require changing at least one of the other two.

Perhaps the simplest negative income tax plan would be one that linked payments to the exemptions in the "positive" income tax system. Table 15.2, column (2) shows what level of exemptions will prevail in 1973. In effect, the exemption level would be made the break-even point, B. Families whose income fell below their exemption level would be eligible for negative income tax payments. They would receive a cash payment from the government equal to some percentage of the amount by which their income fell short of their exemption level. If the negative tax rate were 50 percent, the family would receive 50 percent of the shortfall. If the family had no other income, it would receive the basic guarantee, which in this case is 50 percent of the exemption level. If it had some income of its own, it would receive a payment that was less than the basic guarantee. Column (3) shows the level of the basic guarantee for different family sizes, assuming that the negative tax rate is 50 percent. Column

Table 15.2

(1)	(2)	(3)	(4)
Size of Family	Exemptions (including the low income allowance of $1,300)	Income Guarantee when negative tax rate equals 50% [a]	Income Guarantee when negative tax rate equals 33⅓% [a]
1	2050	1025	683
2	2800	1400	933
3	3550	1775	1183
4	4300	2150	1433
5	5050	2525	1683
6	5800	2900	1933

[a] If family has no other income, this is what it should receive.

(4) shows that the income guarantee is one-third of the exemption level if the negative tax rate were 33⅓ percent. Thus, given the break-even level of income, the level of the income guarantee is inversely related to the level of the negative tax rate. To raise the basic guarantee, holding the negative tax rate unchanged, requires raising the break-even level of income. The original equation stands; we cannot have everything at once.

Another method of building negative taxes into the present income tax structure is the tax credit approach. The current system of personal exemptions would be replaced by refundable tax credits.[3] The proposal would work as follows. Suppose the $750 exemptions which will apply in 1973 were converted into per capita tax credits equal to, say, $500. A new schedule of income tax rates would be constructed in order to raise the revenues required to pay for the negative income tax plan as well as to finance other expenditures now financed from revenue raised by the income tax. Suppose, for the sake of simplicity, a proportional tax is adopted with a rate of 25 percent levied on the family's total income (less any deductions it is still allowed to take). A four-person family with $2,000 in tax credits (4 x $500) and an income of $3,000 will have a gross tax liability (assuming no deductions) of $750 (or .25 x $3,000). The family's net tax liability is minus $1,250 ($750−$2,000), allowing it to receive a $1,250 check from the government. The scheme is pictured in Figure 15.1. When the family's income is above the $8,000 break-even level of income, where gross tax liability equals total tax credits, it would pay taxes. When the family has no other income, it receives a tax credit of $2,000, which is equivalent to the basic income guarantee described above.

The negative income tax plans described above are modest ones. Certainly an income guarantee of $2,000 for a family of four does not assure that the family will escape poverty — or even that its net income will exceed that for which it is eligible

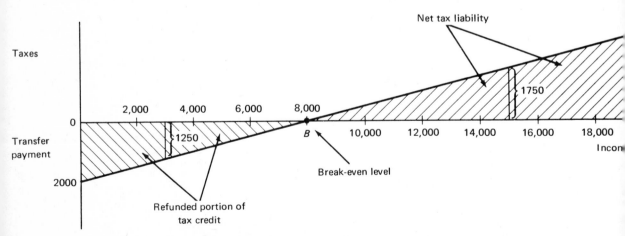

FIGURE 15.1 Negative income tax plan: tax credit type for a family of four.

---

[3]Earl Rolph, "The Case for a Negative Income Tax Device," *Industrial Relations*, Vol. 6 (February 1967), pp. 155–165.

under the present public assistance (welfare) system. The plans would, however, supplement the incomes of the "working poor" — families with low incomes due to low wages — almost all of whom are ineligible for present forms of public assistance.

Income Guarantees. To do more for the very poorest families would require raising the income guarantee. However, if the guarantee is raised while holding the break-even level constant at the exemption level, the negative tax rate must rise. (Remember G = rB.) As the negative tax rate is increased, the likelihood of undermining work incentives is increased. The negative tax rate is in one respect similar to a "positive" tax rate. It tells us how much of an increase in income will actually increase the family's disposable income. Thus, a "positive" income tax of 75 percent means that only 25 cents of each additional dollar earned or of other income will go to the earner; the remaining 75 cents will go to the Treasury. A negative tax rate of 75 percent tells us that a dollar increase in a poor man's earnings will decrease his negative income tax payment by 75 cents so that his disposable income increases by only 25 cents. Clearly, the higher the positive or negative tax rate, the smaller will be the net reward from, and the incentive to, work.

If the income guarantee is to be raised while keeping the negative tax rate low (a rate above 50 percent is believed by many who have examined the problem to be undesirable), the break-even level of income must rise. But raising the break-even level of income would substantially increase the cost of the plan to the government, and hence to the taxpayer, by making many more families eligible for negative tax payments. If the plan's objective is to concentrate payments on poor families, then raising the break-even level of income would compromise this objective by bringing into the plan's ambit many nonpoor — although low-income — families. Of course, if society were willing to redistribute more generally to low-income families, then raising the break-even level of income would be not only desirable but necessary. However, the high cost of plans with high guarantee and high break-even levels — costs running anywhere from $20 billion to $40 billion depending on the exact dimensions of the plan — make them much less politically acceptable than more modest plans costing $10 billion or less.

Clearly, then, there is some "inevitable arithmetic" at work, which is disturbing from a policy standpoint. If society takes the trouble to guarantee a minimum income, surely it would like to set a minimum that is consistent with the costs of meeting basic needs, and the minimum in a highly urbanized, technologically oriented society is no longer low. But society would also like to maintain work incentives, not only because of the diehard "Protestant Ethic" but also because undermining incentives will raise the cost of the plan if recipient families substitute leisure for work. But to accomplish both these objectives means raising the break-even level. This compromises the objective of concentrating payments on the very lowest income groups in the population, while substantially increasing the cost of the program. There is no escaping the fact that the various objectives are in conflict.

The tax system, then, can be restructured so as to redistribute income. There is more than one technique available, but all proposals have the same three basic variables and involve the same "inevitable arithmetic." How the arithmetic is dealt with will depend on a complex mix of value judgments and social objectives. But the basic issue is how far society wants to go in reducing income inequality.

SUGGESTIONS FOR FURTHER READING

Bator, Francis M. *The Question of Government Spending.* New York: Harper & Row, 1960.

Due, John F. *Government Finance.* 4th ed. Homewood, Ill.: Richard D. Irwin, 1968.

Eckstein, Otto. *Public Finance.* 2nd ed. Englewood Cliffs, N.Y.: Prentice-Hall, 1967.

Goode, Richard. *The Individual Income Tax.* Washington, D.C.: The Brookings Institution, 1964.

Groves, Harold. *Financing Government.* 6th ed. New York: Holt, Rinehart & Winston, 1964.

Pechman, Joseph. *Federal Tax Policy.* Rev. ed. New York: W.W. Norton & Company, 1971.

Phelps, Edmund, ed. *Private Wants and Public Needs.* New York: W. W. Norton & Company, 1965.

Tobin, James, Pechman, Joseph, and Mieszkowski, Peter. "Is a Negative Income Tax Practical?" *Yale Law Journal,* Vol. 77 (November 1967), pp. 1–27.

BASE PRICES

Phase II Economic Stabilization Program

A COMPLETE LIST OF BASE PRICES OF
ALL ITEMS SOLD IN THIS STORE WHICH
ARE SUBJECT TO THE
ECONOMIC STABILIZATION PROGRAM
IS MAINTAINED IN THE STORE OFFICE
AND MAY BE INSPECTED AT ANY TIME
UPON REQUEST.

16 *Inflation*

Inflation is probably more easily definable, more easily recognizable, and more easily fitted into economic theory than are many other more complex subjects. However, because its political and social ramifications are profound and because the cure often seems worse than the disease, coming to grips with inflation and taking the necessary steps to eliminate it inevitably result in such intense and bitter controversy that we may lose sight of its essentially simple origin. If we kept this simple origin clearly in view at all times, we might better succeed in staying out of trouble with inflation.

What Is Inflation?

Inflation is a word used to describe a broad and persistent increase in the prices of the goods and services we buy. If our daily expenditures involve the purchase of a hamburger, a bus ride to and from school or work, and an occasional drink and a movie, this package of goods and services might cost a total of $5. But if they all go up in price, even if at varying rates, then this same mix is going to require a larger outlay of money — or we will have to cut out one of the purchases to make our expenditures fit our pocketbook. We use the word inflation to describe this situation when all or most of the things we buy are increasing in price and when they keep right on going up even though we are hard put to keep enough money in our pocketbooks to pay for them.

But why do prices start going up in the first place? Since nobody ever *wants* to spend more money for the same quantity of goods and services, how can businessmen raise their prices and still manage to sell as much as they were selling at lower prices?

Economic theory tells us that prices rise when demand exceeds supply. More precisely, this describes a situation in which people are willing to continue buying the same physical quantity of goods and services even though prices are higher than they were before and even though their total money expenditure will have to be bigger than it was before. But that is only part of the story, because *demand* — the amount the buyer is willing to spend — is only one side of the process of price determination; the other side is what sellers decide to do. Frequently an increase in demand such as we have described here attracts new businesses into the market or encourages old ones to expand, so that then the *supply* increases: businessmen will be willing to sell more at a given price than they were willing to sell before. On many occasions, competition among businessmen who are attempting to gain a share of this profitable market will drive prices back downward again or keep them stable. In a free, flexible market economy, this is precisely the process that generates economic growth and stimulates the business sector to respond to consumer demands for a rising standard of living.

In an inflationary situation, however, note that prices rise and keep on rising. Note, furthermore, that rising prices appear in all, or at least most markets, not just in some. Inflation, in other words, describes a condition in which *total* demand in the economy exceeds or is rising faster than *total* supply. Hence, it starts up when people's purchasing power is expanding — when their incomes or the amount of money they have in their bank accounts and pocketbooks is rising — but for some reason businessmen and other suppliers are unwilling or unable quickly to respond to this by producing more goods and services for them to buy. Cattlemen, for example, cannot increase the supply of beef overnight.

The Battle of Bargaining Power. Before finding out why supply may fail to respond and why our market economy can behave differently from the way the textbooks say it should, let us digress briefly to look at some of the social and political consequences of the inflationary process. At this point, some noneconomic insights into inflation may add flavor and realism to the purely economic description.

As we said before, either you are going to have to go out each day with more money in your pocket when the price of hamburgers, transportation, and entertainment goes up — or you will have to cut something out of your budget. Since no one likes to see his standard of living go down, you will doubtless try to persuade your family to give you more spending money. But the members of your family will have to find that additional money for you, which means either that they will have to cut back on their budgets somewhere, or save less, or increase *their* incomes. If they ask their employers for a raise (because, of course, the things they buy are also costing more), each employer will either be squeezed or will have to get the extra money from *his* customers by raising his prices. And his customers' families will also go through an identical process.

Inflation, in other words, sets up an almost irresistible drive for us to step on one another's heads in order to stay in the same place! The effort to preserve and protect one's living standard of necessity involves getting something extra from the other fellow, whether he is your father, your employer, or your customer. Indeed, the fear of falling behind in the parade and losing purchasing power pushes people to ask for more than they need to keep pace, and that only makes matters worse.

It follows from this that inflation should really be called the Battle of Bargaining Power. Experience shows that bargaining power with respect to income is a lot more important in staying ahead of inflation than investing in assets like common stocks that may even decline in value during inflationary periods. If you are your father's pet, if he is an essential employee (or if his job is protected by a powerful union), and if his employer produces something that is in urgent demand and that people *have* to buy, then you, your father, and his employer will be able to keep pace with inflation. But if your family favors your younger brothers and sisters, if your father is an unskilled, unprotected worker who can easily be replaced by another man or by a machine, and if his employer sells into a highly competitive market or if he sells something that people have no urgent desire for, then you, your father, and your employer will get the short end of the stick.

What this means is that your ability to keep pace with inflation — to maintain your purchasing power in the face of rising prices — will depend upon your ability to increase the number of dollars in your pocket and your bank account. Two groups of people find this especially difficult, because both are tied to contracts that specify payment in a fixed number of dollars. The first is composed of retired persons who live off pensions set at the time they retired, when prices were probably much lower than they are right now; that is why pension arrangements have become such a burning issue in collective bargaining negotiations in both the public as well as the private sector of the economy. (Social Security payments made by the government now rise with the general price level, following a 1972 act of Congress.) The other group includes those who lend money, such as bankers and other financial institutions, and savers who turn their funds over to institutions of this type. If a farmer borrows to plant his crop when wheat is selling at $1.00 a bushel and then harvests and sells his crop when wheat is going for $1.25, he will obviously have more money left over than he expected to have, while the lender, the depositor, and the buyer of life insurance will all be able to buy fewer things with the money that is repaid to them.

For all these reasons, inflation is a natural breeding ground for intense social conflict as people jockey around for position to protect themselves; each can gain only at the expense of the other fellow.

But since inevitably people turn to the government to help resolve the Battle of Bargaining Power, and since each group wants the government to help improve *its* position, inflation is a natural breeding ground for political conflict as well. Indeed, the very effort to bring inflation under control involves some of the most painful dilemmas that any politician ever has to face.

If, as is frequently the case, physical limitations on supply exist, especially in the civilian sector of the economy, then the traditional way to stop inflation is to reduce demand. That means higher taxes or restricting money and credit, so that people will find it more difficult and more expensive to finance higher expenditures, or some combination of the two. But nobody likes to pay higher taxes or higher interest rates. In addition, if people have less take-home pay or are unable to borrow the money they need, they will probably spend less. That means bad business for somebody, profits squeezed, jobs lost, suppliers hurt. Who is to decide where the ax will fall, who will bear the largest part of the burden of stopping inflation, who will fall behind in the race? Once again, power — economic, social, and political — becomes the basic determinant of the final result.

This analysis also substantiates the point we made at the outset: while it is easy enough to see how inflation gets started and while it is also easy to see why nobody likes it, the cure is so painful that it is often postponed or applied only gingerly, thus creating deeper and deeper economic and social maladjustments in the process. We shall look at this sad story in detail, as it was played out in the United States between 1965 and 1971, later.

Causes of Inflation

As we return to the main thread of our economic argument, we must ask first how it is that the economy can work itself into a situation where total demand persistently exceeds total supply. How can it be that businessmen lack the physical capability of responding as usual to an expanding market situation?

We can answer this question by reference to a basic fact of life: by and large, throughout the history of mankind, our needs and wants have exceeded our capacity to satisfy them. In all economies at all times, therefore, an innate tendency toward inflation has existed. But this just hints at the essence of the problem. People can come into the marketplace and bid up prices only if they have the money with which to buy. In other words, inflation will develop only in circumstances where, somehow or other, money is put into people's hands in such quantities that they can express in the marketplace the great, unsatisfied desire for a better life that was potentially present all the time. In short, we find inflation where a nation is attempting to meet goals and objectives that are beyond the resources available to achieve them.

The most classic and frequent — but by no means only — cause of inflation is war. War is an insatiable consumer of resources, physical as well as human, which means that supplies of goods and services to meet civilian needs will usually be restricted and subordinated to the demands of Mars. At the same time, however, the people who produce the armaments and the men who serve in the armed forces receive pay for their efforts. They want to spend their money and improve their lot just as much as the fellow who is producing groceries or clothing. Here, then, in simple terms, is how we begin to move into a situation where demand is increasing faster than supply.

But inflation is also characteristic of countries whose major focus is on economic development and whose efforts to take off toward higher living standards exceed the resources available to them. The man who builds roads or electric power projects or who teaches people reading and other skills is not available to drive a truck or maintain power lines or to operate a computer. Later on, his efforts will result in higher levels of productivity in his country, but meanwhile his participation in the process of building physical and human capital restricts the supply of goods and services people need and want in the present. Just as in warfare, then, this process leads to a situation where people are paid to do things that make no immediate contribution to the flow of goods and services that people desire; unlike warfare, however, the process of economic development leads in the long run to a much greater supply of desired goods and should in time lead to a lower rate of inflation as a result.

There are other variations on the theme. Some countries have suffered from inflation as a *postwar* development, when defeat, destruction, disorganization, or revolution have so disrupted their capacity to produce and distribute goods and services that supply falls hopelessly behind demand. Some countries, like the Netherlands, on the other hand, have experienced inflation because they have been too prosperous, too successful and efficient. In these circumstances, foreign importers are induced to do their shopping in that country, but the goods produced by foreigners appear relatively expensive and unattractive to importers of the country concerned. Then goods will be shipped out of the country (and the people who produce them will be paid for doing so, nevertheless) while home demand is high. Once again, supply will lag behind demand.

Inflation and Money

Many people associate inflation with excessive quantities of money rather than with excessive levels of demand. We remember the stories about Germans after World War I who needed wheelbarrows to carry all their currency when they went shopping; history tells us of monarchs who debased the coinage by secretly cutting down on the amount of precious metal in each coin minted, thereby permitting themselves to mint more coins; the expression, "Not worth a Continental!" refers to the depreciated value of the currency our own Continental Congress issued during the American Revolution. Bankers and other keepers of the faith of sound money frequently warn of the dangers of "turning on the printing press."

Indeed, demand is meaningless without the money to finance it, so money is an essential part of the story. Where is the money to come from to pay the soldier or the gun manufacturer? Of course, the government could tax people in order to raise this money, but taxation is anathema to politicians (or even monarchs) whose survival depends upon winning friends and influencing people. The government could borrow the money, but if the war is big and expensive, its credit may be inadequate, or, even if its credit holds up, the level of interest payments required could be intolerable. Nevertheless, to the extent that governments raise money by taxation or by borrowing from their citizens, inflationary pressures, while still present, are likely to be subdued. It is when governments take the easier and more tempting route of simply creating new money out of thin air, and then using that new money to finance their expenditures, that we find demand increasing so much faster than supply. Unlike the situation in which people pay taxes or lend their savings to the government, everyone has as much money in their pockets as they had before, while the soldier and gun manufacturer have even more.

Although the basic principles involved have remained intact through history, the process of creating money to finance inflation has changed as people's financial habits have changed and as we have varied the forms that money takes. We have already referred to debasing the coinage. A country could also increase its supply of money by borrowing from other countries. The enormous quantities of gold discovered in the New World during the sixteenth century enabled the Spaniards to finance major imperialistic adventures, but also caused European inflation. Since paper currency has come into use, virtually every government at war has at some point literally resorted to the printing press to provide the means of paying its soldiers and suppliers.

In the twentieth century, the process has become more sophisticated, although its impact on the economy is identical to that of more primitive financing techniques. It is more complex than it used to be because our most popular form of money is the checking account, a claim on a commercial bank that can be shifted to somebody else on demand by handing him a check written by the depositor and ordering the bank to transfer a given number of dollars from the balance of the depositor to the designated payee. Even if the government were to issue a lot of new currency under present circumstances, about $75 out of every $100 would probably be deposited by the recipients into their checking accounts, where it could be kept more safely and used to make payments in much more convenient fashion than by retaining it in the form of currency.

The process of increasing the supply of checking account money is in fact more complicated — or at least less obvious — than the process of debasing the coinage or turning loose the printing presses. The basic principle is simple enough, however.

Money is what we use to buy things with and to pay our debts; using checking accounts in commercial banks to store our purchasing power and to make payments to others is by far the simplest method available; consequently, money seldom leaves the banking system because a withdrawal by one depositor to make a payment is offset by the fresh deposit that the recipient of that payment will make in his checking account. While this is admittedly something of an oversimplification, the essentials of this description are valid. We may sum them up merely by saying that one man's withdrawal usually ends up as another man's deposit and vice-versa.

Now, banks are in the business of making loans and, much the same thing, of buying bonds and other forms of debt obligations with the money that their depositors leave with them. The interest they earn in this manner is their major source of income. A bank that holds checking accounts is generally known as a commercial bank. When a commercial bank lends money, it usually increases the balance in the borrower's checking account on its books, thereby creating a new deposit that did *not* result from any other depositor's withdrawal.

Of course, borrowers borrow money in order to spend it, so the lending bank is likely to lose cash to other banks as borrowers withdraw the proceeds of the loan and pay it out to other people. Furthermore, sellers of securities will only by coincidence keep their checking accounts in the same bank that is buying the securities, so that the bank buying securities is also likely to lose cash to other banks as sellers deposit the proceeds of the security sale in their own banks. *But the crucial point is that while the bank that is lending money or buying securities may lose cash and deposits, those deposits and cash end up in another bank in the system; they neither disappear nor go out of existence.*

What happens as a result of this normal business process? New money has come into being, just as though the government had printed nice fresh crisp paper currency! The new checking account balances generated out of commercial bank loans and investments circulate throughout the system and are available for their owners to draw upon just like any other money held in anybody's checking account. They look the same and buy the same and function the same as all the other dollars we use to buy goods and meet our financial obligations.

Since about three-quarters of all the money we use is in the form of checking accounts and only one-quarter in the form of currency, does that mean that the government has no control over the quantity of money available to people to spend? If the creation of money is essentially the result of normal business dealings by commercial banks, it would appear that the government might have little say in the matter.

But such is not the case. Through the operations of a quasi-governmental agency known as the Federal Reserve System, the government can increase or decrease the cash assets that the banks use to determine whether they should be making new loans and purchasing more securities or whether they should be contracting their credit operations. Hence, the government can greatly influence (which is not quite the same thing as control) the credit functions of the banking system and, in that manner, the quantity of money in the economy.

The crude process of the printing press to increase the money supply has now been replaced by something a lot more elegant. The Federal Reserve, if it wishes, takes steps to encourage the banks to lend and buy securities; the government then sells debt obligations that are attractive to commercial banks; the banks issue checks in payment; and the government has new money to spend without taking it from anyone's pockets.

There is a crucial difference between the modern method and the old techniques. In the past, when money consisted exclusively of coin and currency, only the government could create money. Now, when we also use checking accounts — and use them to a far greater extent than we use money that can be bitten or felt — the commercial banks are the major creators of money. Under these circumstances, money is created no matter to whom these banks lend money, and no matter whose bonds they buy. If they are lending to business firms instead of to the government, or if they lend to consumers to finance the purchase of homes and automobiles, they are still creating new deposits and new purchasing power. Unlike earlier times, therefore, when government was the sole source of inflationary pressures, the private sector of a modern economy can now become a major monetary influence on the process of inflation, though the Federal Reserve can set limits.

Cost-Push Inflation

So far, we have seen that inflation comes about when people want to buy more — and can buy more — than the economy is able to produce to satisfy their needs. Some people like to refer to this process as "demand-pull" inflation.

The use of this shorthand description is important because we also have to deal with a phenomenon that looks similar but is actually different. Under some circumstances, prices may rise *even though demand appears to be well below the capacity of business firms to produce.* During 1970 in the United States, for example, production declined, unemployment increased, and productive capacity continued to expand at an impressive rate, but the prices of goods bought by consumers rose even *faster* than they had in 1968 and 1969, when the economy was much more fully employed than it was in 1970. Essentially the same sequence of events had occurred in 1958, when prices continued to rise in the face of a clearly weakening business situation.

Businessmen justified raising prices in the face of shrinking demand by insisting that higher costs, particularly higher wages, gave them no choice. Inflation that occurs under these conditions is usually called "cost-push" inflation to differentiate it from the demand-pull type. It reflects, to an even greater extent than demand-pull inflation, the influence of economic power. Strong unions can negotiate higher wages even in the face of unemployment, and business firms with monopoly or near-monopoly positions can raise prices in the face of weak demand for their products. Marginal workers — those who are unskilled, untrained, and inexperienced — and marginal firms — those in intensely competitive markets with limited financial resources — suffer as a consequence. For if prices rise during a period when customers feel a much more subdued sense of urgency about spending money (when the demand-pull phenomenon has exhausted itself or been repressed by government measures, in other words), then in all likelihood, people will buy a smaller physical volume of goods and services. The resulting cutbacks in output and employment will obviously affect the marginal worker and the weaker firms the most, though even a "concentrated" or near-monopoly industry such as the U.S. steel industry has suffered badly in its profits in periods of slack demand, despite its ability to keep raising prices.

The degree to which producers can raise prices under conditions of weak demand depends a great deal upon what the government is doing about the situation. All other things being equal, as we have just seen, customers will buy less when prices are high than when prices are low. If, however, the economy is flooded with money, thanks to government action, and everyone feels flush and liquid, customers may keep on buying even though prices go up. Vigorous efforts by the government to restrain purchasing power in the economy may result in unemployment and business failures but will eventually bring cost-push inflation to its demise; on the other hand, fear of what high unemployment and business failures may bring often leads the government to keep purchasing power up, and this will tend to perpetuate the cost-push process.

Thus, in both kinds of inflation, the decisions of politicians are crucial. In the end, the government either creates inflation or "ratifies" an inflation produced by private economic power.

Some politicians find their electoral base among well-established middle-class groups who have a high degree of employment security, who believe in saving money, and who may resent efforts to help the poor or to distribute money to people who do no work; such politicians will favor sternly repressive measures to squeeze inflation out of the economy. But other politicians find their electoral base among the poor, the minority groups, and the smaller businessmen. These people have a chance to find jobs and to get ahead only under boom conditions. Their needs are so urgent that they are always in debt and spend every penny as soon as it comes in. While people in these circumstances often find the going rough when prices are rising, the drastic process of curing inflation can mean total disaster for them in the form of no employment or personal business failure. Politicians with this type of base will clearly favor more expansionary economic policies, even at the cost of perpetuating cost-push inflation. Sometimes this dilemma is referred to as the trade-off between unemployment and inflation.

Inflation American-style

Although much of this may sound general or theoretical, all of it rests upon a solid basis of historical fact. Therefore, let us take a look at the broad span of American price history and at a few of the inflationary episodes that the country has experienced, Figure 16.1.

One of the most striking features of the long-term chart of our wholesale price index is that while sharp peaks and valleys alternate, there is, nevertheless, little or no indication of any innate or fundamental tendency toward continuous inflation. Prices have barely doubled over a period of 170 years; they have moved downward during almost as many years as they have moved upward; if we eliminate the five periods of wartime inflation and their aftermaths (1815–1822, 1860–1863, 1916–1921, 1940–1945, and 1965–1970), the price line is essentially trendless.

Since Figure 16.1 covers the history of the most extraordinary economic development of any nation in the history of the world, the virtual absence of peacetime inflation is especially significant. When we think back over our past, to the building of the cities and factories, to the construction of the great inland waterways, the railroads, and the enormous educational facilities, and to the advent of the automobile and electric power, our ability to build a great source of productive capital without inflation is in sharp contrast with the records of most other countries, certainly those that have attempted this task in the twentieth century. This is particularly striking during the period from 1870 to 1900, when industrialization in this country was most rapid and dramatic.

The explanation for this extraordinary experience goes right back to first principles. In our history, *supply has been able to expand rapidly in response to rising demand.* We have been blessed with a generally stimulating climate, with great wealth in raw materials and inland waters, with a labor force that grew very rapidly during the nineteenth century as a result of immigration, with major contributions by foreign capital, and with an ethic that encouraged and rewarded hard work, achievement, and mechanical and scientific ingenuity. We have also had a government that did not regularly "print" too much money, directly or indirectly.

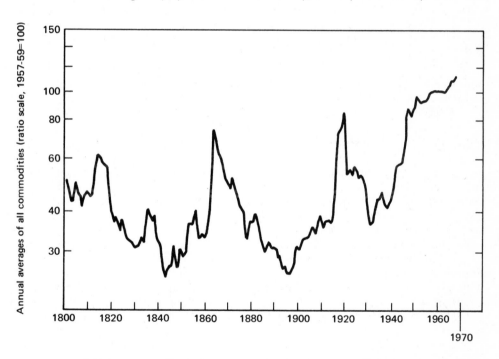

FIGURE 16.1   American wholesale price history, 1800–1970. (Ratio scale, 1957–59＝100.)

Other nations have shared some of these characteristics, but no other nation has enjoyed all of them. The rate of inflation in other countries relates directly to the degree to which these advantages have or have not existed. Indeed, to the extent that Americans choose to discard or use up some of these advantages in the years ahead — by exhausting our resources, polluting our environment, changing our attitudes toward work and education, or spending more government money than we raise in taxes — peacetime inflation is likely to be much more of a problem for us in the future than it was in the past.

Inflation Wartime-style

The past thirty years or so may be worth a closer look, not just because they constitute the most recent period, but also because the configurations of this period are different from our earlier experience. World War II was never followed by the steep drop in prices that followed all other major inflationary episodes.

The story properly begins in 1939, when World War II broke out in Europe; even before our own direct participation began 27 months later, the economic impact on us was significant. Defense spending rose from $1.2 billion in 1939 to $2.2 billion in 1940 and then to $13.8 billion in 1941. It subsequently zoomed upward in giant steps to a peak of $89 billion in 1944. Our total federal government expenditures during the five years of the war amounted to some $340 billion, of which only about one-third, $130 billion, was raised through taxation; the rest was borrowed.

Despite the sharp rise in government spending between 1939 and 1941, prices paid by consumers at the end of 1941 were less than 5 percent higher than they had been at the end of 1938 and were still lower than they had been 10 years before. Why? Because supply was able to expand almost as fast as demand. Although some recovery had occurred by 1939 from the trough of the depression, many factories and machines languished in idleness; furthermore, in 1939 over 9 million people — more than one out of every six men and women willing to work — were still without jobs. Unemployment two years later at the time of Pearl Harbor was still in excess of 5 million people, although it was subsequently to drop below a million by the peak of the war effort three years later.

After Pearl Harbor, as our idle productive resources were drawn into activity and as people who were formerly unemployed — or working part-time or struggling on subsistence wages — began to have much more money in their pockets, prices started upward and inflation got under way. Consumer prices jumped almost 10 percent in 1942 and continued onward at that rate in 1943 until price controls and rationing were brought into action to blunt the inflationary trend.

We must remember that inflation occurs when people are willing and able to buy more than the economy can produce. In simpler terms, it is a situation in which there just isn't enough to go around, and somebody is going to have to make do with less than he wants. If prices rise freely, then obviously those people with the largest financial resources or with the greatest bargaining power to increase their dollar incomes will make out fine, while the poor and the weak will be forced to go without.

Through rationing, the government can arbitrarily hold down demand to match the available supply at existing prices regardless of how much money people have or are willing to spend. Note, however, that rationing does nothing to reduce the overall cutback in civilian living standards from what they would have been under inflation; rather, it substitutes the ration book for the price level in determining how that burden is to be distributed.

Despite the development of some black markets and some misallocation of resources, the price control and rationing system of World War II did a good job: consumer prices rose by less than 5 percent from 1943 to 1945. This is all the more impressive in that personal incomes after taxes rose by 13 percent, while the money supply expanded by 35 percent over the same period.

What happened at the end of the war? At the conclusion of all previous wars, government spending had dropped off sharply; veterans and former workers in armament factories were unable to find jobs, but the capacity of business and farmers to produce was a lot bigger than it had been at the beginning of the war. In other words, the shoe was now on the other foot, with supply in excess of demand. Prices collapsed and inflation disappeared rapidly.

The situation after World War II was different, however. Government defense spending did drop sharply from over $96 billion in 1944 to $82 billion in 1945 and then to only $25 billion in 1947. It was the expectation of this cutback and the vivid memory of earlier experiences that led to the removal of controls in rapid succession during 1945 and 1946. But even some very wise men failed to appreciate both the enormous unsatisfied demands for goods and services that had built up during the depression and the war and the accumulation of such a tremendous pool of purchasing power during the war that people had ample financial means to satisfy those demands.

A torrent of spending burst forth from the civilian economy — both from individuals and from business firms rushing to reequip themselves to meet these great demands — and inflation broke loose once again. Between 1945 and 1948, prices rose 40 percent.

But then inflation suddenly stopped. Prices in 1949 were actually a little lower than they had been the year before. Supply had caught up with demand. Not only were consumers feeling somewhat less urgent in their demands — or even a little satiated — after the spending spree of the previous three years, but American business had once again demonstrated its extraordinary ability to expand output in the face of rising demand. Consequently, although we never had the collapse in prices that followed other wars, given the inflationary potentials in the situation after World War II, this was an impressive demonstration that the American economy *in peacetime* had few, if any, inflationary biases.

Another demonstration of this occurred in the latter part of the 1950's. Consumer prices rose about 7 percent between 1955 and 1958, which was a small increase compared with wartime increases, but distressingly large for a peacetime period. Curiously enough, government was innocent in this period, having run its budget at a surplus in 1956 and 1957 and with the national debt increasing by only 1 percent over the whole three years. The pressure on demand this time came from business managements, who rapidly increased their expenditures for expanding productive capacity; while this investment process was going on, the demand for goods and services was rising faster than the supply. However, as the investments were completed and began to bear fruit in a larger volume of production, the inflationary process rapidly phased out. The annual increase in consumer prices from 1958 to 1965, at 1.2 percent a year, was only half as great as it had been from 1955 to 1958.

Inflation Vietnam-style

But then came the escalation in Vietnam — another classic case of demand expanding far faster than supply. Unlike the situation in World War II, the American economy in the summer of 1965 had relatively limited supplies of unused physical and human resources. Yet between 1965 and 1968, government defense spending rose by $28 billion, more than 50 percent, and nondefense spending rose as well;

prices rose by more than 10 percent over the same period of time. The jump in government spending brought in its wake a surge of consumer spending and then, in the fear that new facilities postponed until tomorrow would surely cost much more than facilities bought today, corporations went on a massive spending spree for new plants and new equipment.

Despite the belated imposition of higher taxes, in the form of an income tax "surtax," in mid-1968, which managed to swing the federal government from a deficit running at an annual rate of about $10 billion to a surplus running about the same amount one year later, private demands continued to surge forward, helped along by a $25-billion increase in the money supply during 1967 and 1968, in the latter year partly because the Federal Reserve authorities reacted to fear of overkill from the surtax. Consumers spent more and saved less; business spent more and borrowed more. No wonder that prices each year increased at a rate faster than in the preceding year.

The inflationary process appeared to be gaining so much momentum by the end of 1968 that there seemed no alternative to cranking down the money supply. If individuals and businessmen would find it more difficult to finance a higher level of spending, then, hopefully, excess demand would be squeezed down, the economy would cool off, expectations of future inflation would abate, and prices would stop going up.

Consequently, the increase in the money supply during 1969 was held back down to $6 billion, virtually all of which was packed into the first half of the year. Federal spending was also curtailed and held approximately at 1968 levels during 1969 and 1970. Soon business activity began to respond: production flattened out in 1969 and declined in 1970. From a situation in 1968 when virtually anyone who wanted a job could find one, unemployment at the end of 1970 was 70 percent above 1968 levels, and affected about 6 percent of the labor force.

But the increase in unemployment was not the only uncomfortable consequence of the effort at disinflation. Stock market prices fell precipitously. Prestigious Wall Street firms teetered on the brink of failure. The Penn Central Railroad succumbed to bankruptcy and other major firms came close to the edge. Financial distortions caused by record-high interest rates, reflecting lenders' fears of further inflation, attracted funds away from the savings institutions that normally finance residential construction, so that home building was hard hit; without special government efforts to protect it, the disaster here might have been total. Furthermore, with financial markets in chaos, tax revenues declining as a result of lower levels of business activity and employment, and civil servants on a rampage for higher salaries and pensions, states and municipalities were forced to cut back on major essential services and to abandon hopes of early alleviation of the urban crisis.

But despite the tremendous clout of the combination of higher income taxes, cuts in federal spending, and a restrictive money supply policy, the increase in prices in 1969 and 1970 was just about as great as it had been in 1967 and 1968! The few hopeful signs that did appear were frail evidence indeed. As a result, expectations of a continued high level of inflation persisted, as exemplified by labor union demands for outsize wage increases, by a continued high level of business expenditure for plant and equipment even though production was well below capacity, and, perhaps most indicative of all, by an unwillingness of savers and savings institutions to lend money except at historically high interest rates that they hoped would compensate them for the loss of future purchasing power.

The Policy Dilemma

The failure of higher taxes and restrictive monetary policy to slow down inflation in the face of falling production and rising unemployment gave rise to intense controversy over these policy decisions. They had brought near-chaos into the stock and bond markets and had nearly knocked the residential construction industry into a cocked hat. They had unleashed demands for wage increases far in excess of what businessmen could absorb without raising prices, and this had spread into the public sector, where civil servants and teachers showed a militancy and willingness to go on strike that brought on social as well as economic turmoil in the cities.

Perhaps most disturbing, the hangover of continued inflation in an economy struggling to recover from the impact of orthodox anti-inflationary medicine in 1969 and 1970 left us with a cruel paradox. The recovery in business activity and employment that got under way in early 1971 fell well below the government's expectations, as the fear, uncertainty, and discouragement resulting from the failure of the policy mix resulted in growing hesitancy on the part of consumers and businessmen to spend. At the same time, the persistence of inflation here led to a distressing excess of imports over our ability to sell high-priced American goods abroad, and this also was a drag on economic recovery. *But the slow recovery contributed to the continuation of the inflation!* This occurred because the sales of business firms were rising more slowly than their costs, which meant that cost-push forces remained as virulent as ever. Yet the government was hesitant to take strong steps to drive the economy forward for fear that such steps would at the same time convert cost-push inflation into demand-pull inflation and just make matters worse.

Hence, some experts argued, and had been arguing for some time, that a more direct attack on inflation was necessary. Inflationary patterns had become so deep-seated, they claimed, and inflationary expectations showed so few signs of abating that the entire environment of negotiating wages and setting prices had to be changed. They urged the government either to apply direct price and wage controls, as in World War II, or at least to designate certain maximum rates for wage and price increases that would be considered acceptable. With the government bringing its influence to bear, either formally or informally (the informal use of official influence is sometimes referred to as "jawboning"), wage and price increases would be smaller and a more expansionary economic policy could be pursued, with lower levels of unemployment and a more rapid movement toward widely desired social goals.

Indeed, stimulating the economy toward a more rapid rate of expansion was likely to accomplish more than just a higher level of output and a lower level of unemployment. Since a major part of the inflation problem lay in the sluggish growth in sales that was insufficient to offset the far from sluggish growth in costs (which in turn forced businessmen to keep raising prices to maintain their already low profit margins), a faster upswing in sales would provide wider profit margins and, in fact, make it possible for businessmen to live with lower rates of price increase. Rather than causing demand-pull inflation, a more vigorous business expansion would actually *reduce* cost-push pressures and make it easier for the authorities to bring inflation under control. With so much slack in the economy, as exemplified by an unemployment rate of about 6 percent of the labor force and an output that was running only around 75 percent of capacity, there was clearly plenty of room for demand to rise before it would begin to outpace supply.

This line of reasoning finally led to the historic presidential decisions of August 15,

1971. They brought price and wage controls into effect and at the same time led to congressional action giving tax relief to individuals and corporations; and, by devaluing the international exchange rate of the dollar, they were destined to lead to a more rapid rise in exports than in imports. Hence, stimulus replaced restraint, while direct controls replaced orthodox policies as a means of subduing the inflationary wage-price spiral and the virulence of inflationary expectations.

Should We Try to Control Inflation? The experience with efforts to control inflation since 1965 hardly warrants much confidence that we can do a good, prompt, equitable, and effective job of it. The orthodox methods of tight money and higher taxes bring real dangers of overkill. Direct interference with the wage and price-setting mechanism involves a certain government arbitrariness that could result in serious errors of judgment, in inequities, and ultimately in shortages when demand begins to exceed supply at the ceiling price.

One might fairly ask, therefore, whether we should try to control inflation by any means, particularly since some of the cures seem to be so painful. Indeed, excess demand leads to low levels of unemployment and opens up job opportunities to marginal workers who might otherwise never have a chance. Expectations of higher prices encourage risk-taking and business expansion. Experience in other countries provides no certain evidence of consistent relationships between inflation and economic growth; some countries have made impressive progress despite a high rate of inflation, while others have lagged behind despite a low rate of inflation (and vice-versa, of course). Indeed, the evidence of 1945 – 1949 and 1955 – 1958 does suggest that in our highly productive economy we can safely leave supply to rise to meet demand and thus not worry too much about letting demand rise rapidly.

These are serious considerations, not to be dismissed lightly. In view of the inability — and occasional total failure — of public policy to deal adequately with inflation both here and abroad and in view of the distortions and inequities that even an effective fight against inflation can cause, the temptation to let nature take its course has its appealing aspects. This is particularly the case when only booming economies provide a real chance for minority and other marginal workers to find adequate employment opportunities.

But the risks are enormous, too. Most runaway inflations in the history of capitalist nations have led to catastrophe. Serious inflation attracts capital into areas where asset values increase — such as land, art, jewelry, and buildings — rather than into more productive areas where income and jobs can increase, because increased incomes are hard to come by when costs are skyrocketing. Because lenders are unwilling to part with money that will buy so much less when it is repaid, financial structures and systems are torn apart, and capital flees to countries that have their affairs under better control. The anticipation of future price increases makes it essential to cover tomorrow's needs today, but ultimately the accumulation of inventories or productive facilities will cover the requirements for the day after tomorrow and the day after that and after that; when we arrive at that point, demand will inevitably collapse.

Any one of these events can lead to total disaster.

An Ounce of Prevention . . . The conclusion to which all these arguments lead is that the way to stop inflation is to prevent it in the first place. Each of the cures implies throwing the baby out with the bath water, but the consequences of uncontrolled inflation can be just as terrifying.

The lessons of recent history provide an excellent illustration of this. When the Johnson Administration decided to escalate in Vietnam in the summer of 1965, at a time when domestic government spending was also rising, they either believed that the required effort would be sufficiently small and brief so that there would be no economic problems as a result, or they believed that any economic sorrows would be less serious politically than would a request for higher taxes and tighter money at that particular moment. But no one can postpone the inevitable. The inflationary impact of the escalation turned out to be enormous, psychologically as well as monetarily. By the time the authorities faced up to this, however, the process was rolling forward with great momentum. The direction in which it was leading the economy was chaotic; the subsequent effort to turn the tide also bordered repeatedly on the chaotic. The consequences will be around to haunt us for a long time to come: disruption to social programs, the near bankruptcy of the cities and their inability to keep pace with overwhelming problems, the tensions created by rising prices accompanied by rising unemployment, and the contorted financial statements of many leading corporations. Given the decisions taken with respect to the Vietnam war in the first place, a prompt decision to raise taxes and tighten monetary policy, unpopular as it would have been in mid-1965, might well have led to a far healthier economy and even a victory for the Democrats in November, 1968.

Our conclusion, in fact, stems directly from our beginning. We understand so well how inflation gets started, and can so readily identify its early symptoms, that we should have the strength of character to stop it at the very beginning. If we fail at that point, we will have to face increasingly complex policy choices later on — and the genuine possibility that none of them will save us from very great pain.

SUGGESTIONS FOR FURTHER READING

Bernstein, P. L. *A Primer on Money, Banking and Gold,* Parts II, III, and V. 2nd ed. New York: Random House, 1968.

————and Heilbroner, R. L. *A Primer on Government Spending,* Chapter 8. 2nd ed. New York: Random House, 1971.

Eckstein, O. and Brinner, R. *The Inflation Process in the United States.* Washington, D.C.: Joint Economic Committee, 1972.

Federal Reserve Bank of St. Louis. *The Impact of Fiscal and Monetary Policy on Aggregate Demand.* Working Paper #4. March 1969.

Ritter, L. S. and Silber, W. L. *Money,* Part I. New York: Basic Books, 1970.

Samuelson, P. A. *Economics,* Chapters 13, 15, and 19. 8th ed. New York: McGraw-Hill, 1970.

17 *Defense*

When President Franklin Roosevelt sought to end the Great Depression of the 1930's by applying with a vengeance the new-fangled economic theories of the Englishman John Maynard Keynes, many Americans thought that he would bankrupt the nation with the seemingly huge federal budget deficits deliberately incurred to stimulate "aggregate demand." But Pearl Harbor quickly led to budget deficits many times larger than those of the thirties to meet the vast outlays of World War II. And what was the result, economically speaking? National bankruptcy? Far from it; just the opposite, in fact. Gross national product in 1946 was double the predepression (1929) level (50 percent higher in "real" GNP — that is, after allowing for price rises), and the U.S. economy was poised on the brink of its greatest period of economic expansion and prosperity.

Or take the more recent case of Vietnam. The persistent inflation of the late sixties and early seventies was caused in large part by the sudden spurt in defense spending (by more than 50 percent from the pre-Vietnam plateau of $50 billion a year) at a time when nondefense demand, both private and public, was pushing the economy to its capacity.

The point is simply this: the sheer magnitude of defense spending is so great that it is bound to have far-reaching effects on the economy — for better or for worse. Furthermore, the impact is not evenly distributed; some segments of the economy are affected more than others. The lesson from the past is clear: the government cannot afford to ignore the impact of defense spending. It must do its best to employ in wise and timely fashion the economic policies appropriate to the situation if it wants to avoid major economic problems.

Here is where the economist enters the picture. It is he who develops and tests the theories upon which sound policies must be based. In this chapter we will define and measure the costs of defense, including what economists call the "true" costs. We will examine past trends in defense spending as the level of expenditure has moved up or down in response to changes in the perceived threat to the nation's security. We will look first at the "macroeconomic" aspect to gain an understanding of the macroeconomic policies at the disposal of the government to cope with such overall economic problems as inflation and unemployment engendered by changes in the level of defense spending; then we will take a brief look at the "microeconomic problems" that beset specific industries, regions, and occupational skills as a result of defense cutbacks.

Besides this generous legacy of *problems,* there are some *benefits* that accrue to the civilian economy from defense efforts, albeit unintentionally, particularly as a result of defense research and development. These are sometimes called "spillover" benefits.

In the final section of the chapter we will discuss five popular "myths," or misconceptions, concerning defense spending and its consequences for the economy, such as the myth that *only* through a high level of defense spending can we hope to achieve full employment and maximum economic growth.

Defense Spending: What It Includes

In studying the effects of defense spending on the economy, and especially in comparing the experience of one year with that of another, one must be careful (1) to note whether the data are for *calendar* years or *fiscal* years (the federal government's fiscal year, FY 1974, starts July 1, 1973, and ends June 30, 1974), and (2) to note just which government programs are included under the rubric "defense spending." Since passage of the National Security Act of 1947, there has been a single Department of Defense (DOD), which includes the Departments of the Army, Navy, and Air Force plus the Office of the Secretary of Defense. Data on expenditures by the three military services are available back to the American Revolution.[1] However, these data cover only the most direct and immediate costs of national security; they specifically exclude such important defense-related programs as atomic energy, foreign aid (both military and economic), and space.

To the economist, even a broad definition of national security, or defense, expenditures which includes "defense-related" expenditures does not fully reflect the "true" cost of defense. Since the basic fact of economics is scarcity — that is, that there are simply not enough resources to produce all the goods and services desired — the *true* cost of defense spending consists of the goods or services given up ("foregone") because the resources that might have been used to produce those goods (more housing, say) were used instead for defense. This is what is meant by the term "opportunity cost": by using resources to produce missiles and tanks, we deny ourselves the opportunity of using those resources to produce automobiles or other civilian products. For example, Professor Seymour Melman of Columbia University has estimated that the cost of each *month* of the Vietnam war during the peak of the U.S. war effort could have paid for a full *year* of the services of state and local police in all 50 states of the union.[2]

The economist is also aware of the fact that some costs cannot be quantified. What is the "cost" of a life lost in fighting a war? The federal budget expresses the

---

[1]Conference Board (CB), *The Federal Budget, Its Impact on the Economy, Fiscal 1972 edition* (New York: The Conference Board, Inc., 1971), p. 18.

[2]Seymour Melman, *Pentagon Capitalism: The Political Economy of War* (New York: McGraw-Hill, 1970), p. 185.

"explicit" costs of defense; but there are important "implicit" costs that are omitted there — for example, the difference between the pay actually received by a draftee and the pay that would have been required to induce him to enlist voluntarily.

Recent Trends in Defense Spending. Just how big *is* defense spending? Is it rising or falling? How heavy is the defense burden on the American taxpayer? Is the burden greater or less than in previous years? Is defense absorbing a larger or smaller share of our resources than in the past?

A glance at Figure 17.1 shows the persistent upward trend in defense spending (broadly defined) since 1939. Wars cause a sharp step-up, and at the end of each war defense spending never subsides to its prewar level. (Secretary of Defense Melvin R. Laird claims an exception, that in the FY 1972 budget "for the first time in this century military spending has returned to the prewar level."[3] But this is in constant dollars, and the figures are *budgeted* expenditures, not actual expenditures.) Remember, these are "current dollars," so that inflation, which accelerates in wartime, is part of the explanation of the rising trend. Another part is technological, involving the rising costs of increasingly sophisticated weapons systems.

From $2 billion in 1940, annual defense spending shot up 44-fold to a World War II peak of $87 billion in 1944; from a $9 – 14-billion-level in the late forties, expenditures quadrupled to $49 billion at the height of the Korean War (1953); and from a pre-Vietnam (1953 – 1965) plateau of $50 billion, defense spending rose to $78 billion in the peak year of 1969.[4]

Yet despite these large increases in the dollar amounts spent on defense, defense spending *as a percentage of GNP* has been falling, not rising (see Figure 17.1). That is, the *share* of our economy devoted to defense has actually shown a declining trend since 1953. In the World War II peak year of 1944, the war consumed 42 percent of total national product. At its peak, the Korean War took only 13 percent of GNP. The tremendous growth in GNP during the sixties (GNP in current dollars approximately doubled between 1960 and 1970) meant that in the peak Vietnam spending years of 1968 and 1969, defense expenditures took only 9.1 and 8.4 percent of GNP, respectively; and by 1971 the percentage had declined still further to 6.8 percent — the lowest percentage since 1950.

A similar pattern emerges if we compare defense spending with total federal government spending or with total *public* spending (federal, state, and local). The budget of the Department of Defense for FY 1973 was only 31.8 percent of total federal spending, compared with 42.5 percent in FY 1968 and 62.1 percent in FY 1953, at the peak of the Korean War.[5] What has happened is that although defense spending has been rising over the years, federal *non*defense spending has been rising even faster, causing the ratio of defense spending to total federal spending to decline. Also, the percentages have been strongly affected by changes which have broadened the scope of the federal budget: the so-called "unified budget" in current use includes important programs that were omitted from the pre-1965 "administrative budget." Furthermore, many of the newer programs comprise the fast-

[3]Melvin R. Laird, *Statement of Secretary of Defense Melvin R. Laird before the Senate Armed Services Committee on his FY 1972 – 1976 Defense Program and the 1972 Defense Budget,* March 15, 1971, p. 148.

[4]*Economic Report of the President, Transmitted to the Congress February. 1971* (Washington, D.C.: U.S., Government Printing Office, 1971), p. 197.

[5]Laird, p. 151, and *The U.S. Budget in Brief, FY 1973* (Washington, D.C.: U.S. Government Printing Office, 1972), p. 43.

Calendar year	Defense spending in billions of dollars	Defense spending as percent of GNP	Calender year	Defense spending in billions of dollars	Defense spending as percent of GNP
1939	1.2	1.3	1956	40.3	9.6
1940	2.2	2.2	1957	44.2	10.0
1941	13.8	11.1	1958	45.9	10.2
1942	49.4	31.3	1959	46.0	9.5
1943	79.7	41.6	1960	44.9	8.9
1944	87.4	41.6	1961	47.8	9.1
1945	73.5	34.7	1962	51.6	9.2
1946	14.7	7.1	1963	50.8	8.6
1947	9.1	3.9	1964	50.0	7.9
1948	10.7	4.2	1965	50.1	7.3
1949	13.3	5.2	1966	60.7	8.0
1950	14.1	5.0	1967	72.4	9.1
1951	33.6	10.2	1968	78.3	9.1
1952	45.9	13.2	1969	78.4	8.4
1953	48.7	13.3	1970	75.4	7.7
1954	41.2	11.2	1971	71.4	6.8
1955	38.6	9.7			

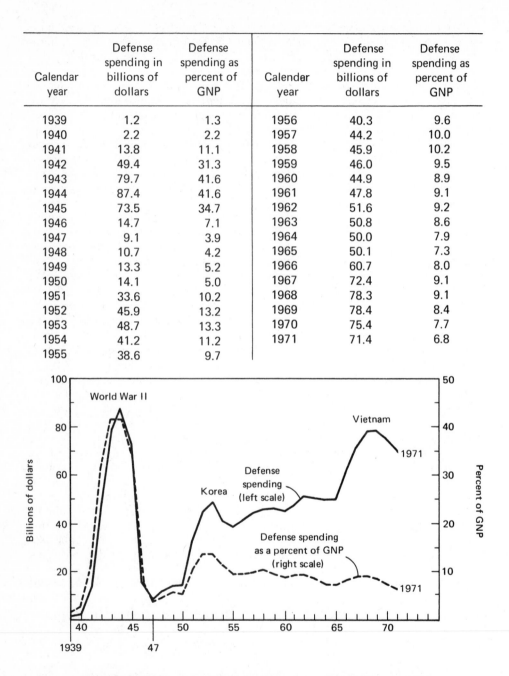

FIGURE 17.1   Divergent trends in defense spending: dollar trend is up, but defense's share of GNP has fallen to the lowest level since pre-Korea. [Source: *Economic Report of the President* (Washington, D. C.: U.S. Government Printing Office, January 1972), p. 195.]

est-growing part of the budget. Secretary Laird, in defending his FY 1972 budget, testified that (1) *non*defense federal spending and (2) state and local spending *each* grew by about $90 billion between 1964 and 1972, while defense spending was growing by $24.4 billion. As a percentage of total public spending, defense spending declined from 47.6 percent in FY 1953 to 20.9 percent in FY 1972.[6] In brief, only one-fifth of total U.S. federal, state, and local spending is now for defense.

In appraising the relative importance of defense spending as a component of government spending, the economist distinguishes between two classes of government expenditures: (1) government purchases of goods and services, and (2) "transfer payments." Transfer payments, such as Social Security benefits or unemployment compensation, are merely monetary shifts — a rechanneling of purchasing power; they do not directly use up productive resources, as do government *purchases*. Therefore, transfer payments are never counted as part of the GNP. (Transfer payments have grown tremendously in recent years, coming to more than 50 percent of total federal expenditures in 1970, as compared with 35 percent in 1955.)[7] National defense *purchases* in 1971 ($71.4 billion) comprise only 73 percent of total federal government purchases; this is significantly lower than the 85 – 90 percent ratio that prevailed during the fifties. A very high percentage of defense expenditures (around 95 percent) take the form of purchases of goods and services and, therefore, contribute directly to GNP. The small remainder covers mainly military retirement benefits and foreign aid.

Manpower and Employment Trends. Total defense-related employment increased from 6 million persons in mid-1964 to 8.3 million in mid-1968, the Vietnam peak. The 8.3 million included 3.5 million military personnel and 4.8 million civilians (including 3.5 million workers in defense-related *industry*). The Department of Defense estimated that defense manpower levels would be *below* the prewar (1964) level by the end of FY 1972. Military personnel were to be reduced to 2.5 million by June 30, 1972, compared with 2.7 million in both 1971 and 1964. Naturally, these manpower reductions have had a significant impact on the nation's unemployment rate. Job cutbacks averaged about 750,000 per year between 1968 and 1971, but are estimated to be less than half that, or about 300,000, during FY 1972.[8]

Macro Impacts and Economic Policies

Economists have long concerned themselves with economic fluctuations above and below the long-term growth trend — the booms and busts of the business cycle — and with what, if anything, can be done about them. In 1946, the federal government openly assumed responsibility for attempting to tame the cycle. In that year, President Truman signed into law the Employment Act of 1946. This was the government's response to the lessons taught by the Great Depression of the thirties and also to fears of a return to mass unemployment and depression as a result of the sharp cutbacks in defense spending at the end of World War II. Under the Employment Act, the government seeks to adopt economic policies that will

[6]Laird, p. 151.
[7]CB, p. 50.
[8]Laird, pp. 149 – 150.

promote economic growth without wide fluctuations in income and employment and without inflation. It is committed to "use all practicable means . . . to promote maximum employment, production, and purchasing power . . ."

Defense spending, even though it declined slightly in 1970 from the Vietnam peak and even though it has been declining as a percentage of GNP and of government spending, is still very large — certainly large enough to have an important impact on the overall economy, not to mention individual sectors of the economy. Keynesian theory (macroeconomics) stresses the key role of *aggregate demand* in determining the level of economic activity: where there is too little demand, depression will result; where there is too much, there will be inflation and the danger of a subsequent depression brought on by the excesses of a boom.

Aggregate demand is made up of private spending plus government spending. We have already seen that defense spending constitutes an important part of government spending. Over the years, U.S. defense expenditures have fluctuated quite violently in response to changes in the perceived threat to our national security, and especially to the actual outbreak or ending of a war. Naturally, these fluctuations tend to have a serious destabilizing effect on the economy. Whether the effect is stabilizing or destabilizing is largely a matter of luck. The sharp rise in defense spending at the start of World War II was economically beneficial because at that time the economy was still in a state of depression, with nearly 10 million people out of work and looking for jobs. But in 1965, with the economy at or close to "full employment," a much smaller increase in defense spending for Vietnam was enough to trigger a serious and persistent inflation. Reductions in defense spending, on the other hand, reduce aggregate demand and, unless offset, can lead to reduced incomes and rising unemployment — in short, to a recession or even to a depression.

What can the economist contribute to the solution of this problem? Using macroeconomic theory, he can predict the consequences of a given change in the level of defense spending, whether up or down. If the consequences are undesirable, he can suggest alternative policy actions that the government could take to *offset* the change in defense spending.

There are two main types of policy action which the government can employ to counteract the economic effects of shifts in defense spending: (1) fiscal policy, and (2) monetary policy. Under fiscal policy, the government uses its taxing and spending powers to raise or lower aggregate demand; under monetary policy, it uses its powers to expand or contract the money supply to the same end. First, let's see how these economic tools might be employed to offset the undesirable economic consequences of a sharp *increase* in defense spending.

What To Do About Increased Defense Spending.   The principal threat brought on by a sudden increase in defense spending is the threat of inflation. Assuming that the economy is operating at a reasonably high level of employment, any sudden further increase in aggregate demand will pose the threat of inflation. This occurred at the outset of both the Korean and Vietnam wars; World War II in its early stages presented a different situation in that there was a great deal of slack in the U.S. economy at the time Hitler invaded Poland in September 1939. Even in 1940, 14.6 percent of the civilian labor force was unemployed and factories were operating far below capacity. The increase in aggregate demand stemming from war orders from our allies during the more than two years before Pearl Harbor was actually helpful in reducing unemployment and raising GNP and national income.

Fiscal Policy. Economic theory indicates that if inflation is to be avoided in the face of sharply rising defense expenditures, the government must act quickly to channel resources away from normal peacetime civilian production and into military uses. Nondefense government expenditures should be reduced as much as possible to liberate resources needed for the defense effort. At the same time, taxes should be increased, not only to help pay for the increased defense expenditures, but also to remove purchasing power from the civilian sector of the economy. Economically speaking, the limit on tax increases is the point at which incentives to produce would be impaired; the *political* limit (the increase that is politically feasible, that Congress is willing to pass) is undoubtedly reached much sooner.

Proper timing is of the utmost importance. In the case of Vietnam, the Johnson Administration badly underestimated the rate of buildup and did not request Congress for a tax increase soon enough. Also, the amount requested was too small: the initial request (January 1967) was for only a 6 percent surcharge on the income tax levied on individuals and corporations, later (August 1967) changed to a 10 percent increase. In continuing to urge Congress to act on the tax increase more than a year after he had proposed it, President Johnson in February 1968 pointed to the "sharply rising Federal spending" as a "strong expansionary force in the economy" and said that "because of the already high level of defense outlays, total Federal expenditures are too large to be piled on top of *normal* private demand without overheating our economy."[9] Congress finally acted on the President's request, which became law in June 1968, some 18 months after the initial presidential request had been made and too late to prevent the disastrous FY 1968 budget deficit of $25 billion. The result: serious inflation.

Of course, it is far easier for the economist — the detached and objective scientist sitting in an ivory tower spinning out theories — to prescribe the right medicine (especially after the fact!) than it is for the politician — be he President or congressman — to apply exactly the right dose of economic medicine in a given real-world situation. There are honest differences of opinion even among professional economists, for example as to the exact state of the economy at any given moment. Then there is the governmental machinery, the way that power is distributed among the branches and agencies of the government. Take the Federal Reserve System, for example, which administers monetary policy.

Monetary Policy. The second great economic tool for applying macro theory is, by law, administered by the Federal Reserve System (FRS), not by the President or the Secretary of the Treasury. In creating the FRS in 1913, Congress deliberately gave it a large degree of independence precisely so as to keep political influences to a minimum. In the case of the Vietnam buildup, which we have already examined with respect to *fiscal* policy, the appropriate *monetary* policy for meeting the inflationary threat would have been a tight monetary policy — curtailing the money supply. Ideally, these two great policy tools — fiscal and monetary — should be carefully coordinated lest they pull in opposite directions and offset each other. In actuality, the Federal Reserve System saw the threat of inflation earlier than the President or his economic advisers did; as a result, it began to apply a tighter monetary policy as early as December 1965, more than a full year before the President saw fit to ask Congress to raise taxes to help finance the war. Tight money, in the absence of fiscal

[9]Lyndon B. Johnson, *Economic Report of the President, Transmitted to the Congress February 1968* (Washington, D.C.: U.S. Government Printing Office, 1968), pp. 9 – 10.

restraint, affected some sectors of the economy more than it did others (for instance, home building declined sharply in 1966, while business investment spending continued on its merry way), thus creating serious imbalances in the economy. The slowdown in some sectors brought on by tight monetary policy undoubtedly was a factor in the slow response of Congress to the President's call for a tax increase. The institutional arrangement continues basically the same to this day, but the conflicts of the period did give rise to a closer informal coordination between the President's top economic advisers and the Federal Reserve System's economists.

Direct Controls. Unlike World War II and Korea, direct wage and price controls were not used to contain the inflation brought on by Vietnam; that is, they were not used until August 15, 1971, when President Nixon reluctantly invoked a 90-day wage-price freeze. Phase II of Nixon's New Economic Policy began in mid-November 1971 and consisted of the administration of *flexible* wage and price controls to compel restraint in wage and price increases in compliance with standards set by the government.

A less stringent form of "incomes policy," "wage-price guideposts," had been tried during the early and middle sixties by Presidents Kennedy and Johnson on the urging of Walter W. Heller, Chairman of the Council of Economic Advisers from January 1961 until November 1964. Paul Samuelson states:[10]

> From 1961 to 1964, wages and prices were remarkably well behaved in the face of an unprecedented economic expansion. By 1965, 1966, and 1967, prices began to be pulled up by Vietnam spending, the Kennedy-Johnson tax cut [of 1964], and a plant-and-equipment boom. Wages began to rise by more than the guidepost numbers. . . . After 1967 Johnson's guideposts were a dead letter, and Nixon formally rejected them.

Most economists would agree with Samuelson's statement that an incomes policy — even legislated wage-price controls — cannot substitute for proper macroeconomic fiscal and monetary policies.

What If Defense Spending Should Decrease Sharply? In the early seventies, with the phasing out of a U.S. ground combat role in Vietnam and with mounting pressure (1) to cut U.S. troop strength in Europe and (2) to reorder national priorities in favor of more *non*defense government spending on pressing domestic social problems, it is important to examine what the probable macro impacts of *reduced* defense spending would be. Furthermore, although the results from arms control and disarmament negotiations have not been very promising to date, such negotiations as the Strategic Arms Limitation Talks (SALT) between the United States and the USSR have achieved one agreement (mid-1972) and may well lead to reduced defense outlays in the future.

As with our analysis of *increased* defense spending, aggregate demand also holds the key to dealing with *cutbacks* in defense spending. Macro theory tells us that a reduction in one component of national spending, such as defense spending, will cause a reduction in GNP and in employment *unless* it is offset by an equivalent *increase* in some other component of aggregate demand. What alternative options

---

[10]Paul A. Samuelson, *Economics* (8th ed.; New York: McGraw-Hill, 1970), p. 815.

are open to the government to offset a reduction in defense spending? Basically, the government has three choices (or some combination of the three): (1) to reduce taxes and thereby increase private spending by returning purchasing power to the taxpayer; (2) to maintain taxes and increase *non*defense government spending by an amount commensurate with the reduction in defense spending; or (3) to maintain taxes and use the "savings" from defense cutbacks to reduce the national debt by way of a budget surplus. This third alternative is universally condemned by economists, who predict dire deflationary consequences from such a policy. As President Johnson's Committee on the Economic Impact of Defense and Disarmament put it, "Experience during recent decades, both here and in other countries, suggests that an attempt to generate the kind of budget surplus that is needed to reduce the debt substantially would so retard the growth of aggregate demand as to prevent prosperous economic conditions and high levels of employment. Indeed, by reducing growth in output and income, such a policy would prove almost wholly self-defeating, since it would reduce the income base from which tax revenues flow."[11]

Either of the other two alternatives, or some combination of them, represents a feasible approach to solving the problem of reduced aggregate demand caused by reduced defense spending. The first alternative — cut taxes — has the appeal that the taxpayer would get to decide what to buy with the money released by defense cutbacks. John Kenneth Galbraith, on the other hand, argues that "social imbalance" already exists, that too large a proportion of our resources is even now (before the assumed defense cutbacks) being allocated to private goods and services at the expense of starving the public sector. Do we need more TV's, cars, and appliances or should we, through government, spend more on education, crime prevention, mass transportation, and the like?

In any event, as President Johnson's Economic Impact Committee concluded from its examination of a hypothetical 25 percent cut in defense spending, "There is no economic reason for the Nation to undergo a major economic decline or a slow stagnation if and when defense outlays are reduced. 'Full-employment' fiscal and monetary policies can, within reasonable bounds of error, assure an adequate growth of aggregate demand, within which the necessary shifts of resources from military to peaceful uses take place."[12]

Micro Impacts: The Redirecting of Resources

Maintaining aggregate demand through appropriate fiscal and monetary policies is essential to a smooth adjustment of the overall economy to major shifts in defense expenditures; but by itself, it is not enough. Whereas *macro*economics is concerned with economic aggregates and with the major problems of unemployment and inflation, *micro*economics is mainly concerned with the economic activities of *individual* consumers and producers, with the "markets" for individual products or resources. The microeconomic problem facing the government as a result of major

---

[11]Gardner Ackley, *Report of the Committee on the Economic Impact of Defense and Disarmament* (Washington; D.C.: U.S. Government Printing Office, 1965), p. 29.
[12]*Ibid.*, p. 29.

swings in defense spending is the problem of smoothly and swiftly redirecting resources — away from defense and into nondefense uses following the U.S. withdrawal from Vietnam. (Of course, similar micro problems can arise simply from major shifts in individual defense programs even within essentially the same level of overall defense spending.)

Defense purchases are not spread evenly over the economy. On the contrary, certain industries, and therefore the workers in those industries, depend heavily upon defense orders for their very survival. Likewise, the communities where these industries are concentrated are seriously affected by reduced defense spending. The seriousness of the problem is mitigated somewhat by extensive subcontracting on the part of firms which have been awarded "prime" contracts, as well as by the DOD policy of placing "a fair proportion" of its total purchases with "small" businesses (which constitute over 90 percent of all business firms and provide payrolls for more than 35 percent of all workers in manufacturing).

Department of Labor estimates of the amount of private employment attributable to defense spending for FY 1965 and FY 1968 show that aircraft, ordnance, and transportation together accounted for about 40 percent of the Vietnam-induced increase in employment. "These industries have consequently been most strongly affected by the cutbacks in defense spending occasioned by the withdrawal."[13]

Defense workers are generally more skilled than the civilian labor force as a whole and many of them have lost their jobs as a result of the Vietnam cutbacks. The most seriously affected skill categories were aeronautical engineers (59 percent of all jobs for aeronautical engineers were generated by defense spending in 1968), airplane mechanics (54 percent defense-dependent), and physicists (38 percent defense-dependent).

Defense spending is most heavily concentrated in the Pacific Coast states and in New England. In FY 1970, almost 50 percent of the total value of prime contracts awarded for military procurement went to firms in California, Connecticut, Massachusetts, New York, and Texas. By far the largest share of jobs eliminated by Vietnam cutbacks occurred in California, and within this group scientists and engineers in the aerospace industry were disproportionately affected.[14]

How can the economist help solve the kind of problem that is presented by micro, or structural, adjustments to shifts in defense spending? As Professor George Bach of Stanford University says, "In our economy the main job of transferring resources in response to changing demand falls on private initiative, the profit motive, and the marketplace."[15] Adam Smith would have left the task to "the invisible hand." In this case, since the mischief seems to be almost entirely of the government's making, the federal government has been supplementing the market mechanism by aiding the adjustment process for more than a decade.

To assist communities in adjusting to defense cutbacks the Department of Defense, in 1961, created an Office of Economic Adjustment. This office helps the affected community to attract new industry and helps the displaced workers to find new jobs. More recently, in March 1970, President Nixon created an Interagency Economic Adjustment Committee, under the chairmanship of the Secretary of Defense, to assure that *all* of the services and facilities of the federal government

---

[13]*Economic Report of the President, 1971*, p. 45.
[14]*Ibid.*, pp. 46 – 47.
[15]George L. Bach, *Economics* (7th ed.; Englewood Cliffs, N.J.: Prentice-Hall, 1971), p. 673.

would be available to assist communities seriously affected by defense cut-backs.[16] In June 1971 the President launched "Project Transition" to help "Vietnam-era" veterans in the job market by means of counseling, training, and placement. Also in 1971, in the private sector, the Jobs for Veterans Committee and the National Alliance of Businessmen sponsored more than 100 Job Fairs aimed at placing more than 100,000 veterans in jobs by June 1972. The result of the combined effort: civilian employment of Vietnam-era veterans rose by 500,000 during 1971. However, these programs have by no means "solved" all of the micro problems created by the recent defense and space cutbacks.[17]

Spillover Benefits of Defense Spending

Although defense spending is undertaken for the purpose of protecting the nation's security, it may have some important, though unintended, beneficial side effects on the private sector of the economy. Education and training provided to servicemen or veterans (including the "G.I. Bill") are good examples of expenditures by the government in connection with the defense program which have important "spillover" effects on the private economy when the individual leaves the service and takes a civilian job. Highways, airfields, or port facilities built for defense may provide a lasting benefit to civilian transportation.

"Perhaps the most important of these indirect gains, however, are the spillover benefits from military research and development," since new ideas from research frequently have numerous, unforeseen applications, according to Charles Hitch and Roland McKean.[18] More than two-thirds of all R & D spending in the United States since the Korean War has been financed by the federal government, nine-tenths of which was paid for by national security (including space) funds. Almost all *basic* research in the United States is funded this way.[19]

The "Planning-Programming-Budgeting System" developed and applied by the Department of Defense to make defense spending more efficient is widely used in other government departments and agencies (by order of President Johnson in 1965) and in private industry.

The point is simply that the *costs* of defense are obvious; some of the spillover *benefits* for the civilian economy may not be so obvious.

Some Modern Myths

By way of a summary we will examine five popular myths concerning defense spending, using the foregoing economic analysis and data to help discover the fallacies in them.

> *Myth I.* That economic prosperity and growth in the United States are dependent on a high level of defense spending, and that a major reduction in defense spending would cause a serious depression.

---

[16]*Economic Report of the President, 1971*, p. 48.
[17]*Economic Report of the President, Transmitted to the Congress January 1972* (Washington, D.C.: U.S. Government Printing Office, 1972), p. 109.
[18]Charles J. Hitch and Roland N. McKean, *The Economics of Defense in the Nuclear Age* (New York: Atheneum, 1965), p. 83.
[19]Bach, p. 674.

It is true that periods of war have been associated with periods of economic boom — and also inflation. It is also true that the Korean armistice and the de-escalation in Vietnam were followed by periods of recession. World War II appears to have been an exception; many Americans predicted a severe depression at the end of that war as defense spending dropped precipitously from nearly half of GNP to about 5 percent. Special circumstances associated with *private* demand — pent-up consumer wants, available wartime savings stemming from sheer inability to spend as much as desired because many goods were unavailable, plus industry's planning for reconversion — combined to contribute to a surprisingly smooth adjustment from war to peace.

What would be the economic consequences today if international negotiations resulted in total disarmament? The answer would depend upon how skillfully the government applied the economic policy tools at its disposal. Prosperity need not depend on defense spending. Disarmament need not lead to depression — *provided* the government takes timely and adequate measures to rechannel the released resources into *non*defense uses, as discussed earlier in this chapter.

>   ***Myth II.*** That the "peace dividend" — money saved by a U.S. with-
>   drawal from Vietnam — will provide enough released resources to make
>   a major contribution to the solution of our domestic social problems.

During the peak year of spending on the Vietnam war, FY 1969, the "*full* cost" of the war to the United States was officially put at $28.8 billion. But this included some costs that would have been incurred anyway, even if there had been no Vietnam war. The Department of Defense estimated the FY 1969 "incremental," or extra, costs of the war — the costs that would *not* have been incurred if there had been *no* such war — at $21.5 billion, some $7 billion less than the so-called full cost of the war. The incremental cost is the correct measure of the size of the "peace dividend" at its maximum. Three years later (FY 1972), this peace dividend had dwindled to a mere $7 billion, or ¾ of 1 percent of the GNP, according to estimates by the Confer-ence Board.[20]

What happened to the peace dividend? Where did that $20 – 22 billion a year go? No one can say exactly. By FY 1971, President Nixon was able to report some shift in resources from defense to "human resources" programs (education, health, income security, and veterans' benefits) as the share of the government's budget going to these programs exceeded national defense spending's share, which dropped to the lowest percentage since 1950. In FY 1972, however, budgeted spending for defense began to rise again in response to the forces of inflation, pay raises for servicemen, and the purchase of costly modern weapons systems whose procurement had been postponed because of Vietnam. Secretary of Defense Laird argues that two-thirds of the real increase in federal spending on civilian (that is, nondefense) programs be-tween FY 1968 and FY 1972 "can be viewed as having been financed by defense cut-backs"; his data have been adjusted to eliminate the effect of increased prices; on that basis, they show a drop of $23.9 billion in total defense spending during the four-year period, at the same time that there was an increase of $36.4 billion in fed-eral nondefense spending.[21] In this sense, the peace dividend has been declared, paid, and spent.

---

[20]CB, p. 27.
[21]Laird, p. 150.

To the extent that aerospace and other defense-oriented firms have not found commercial business to replace their defense orders for Vietnam, and to the extent that returning Vietnam veterans have been unable to find civilian jobs, it must be admitted that part of the peace dividend has simply vanished — in the form of reduced national output below the economy's potential at full employment.

It must be concluded that the *"growth* dividend" — the increased revenue that flows to the government (with *existing* tax rates) purely as a result of increases in GNP and national income — is a more promising source of funds for expanding government services than the elusive and illusory "peace dividend."

> **Myth III.** That the United States cannot "afford" an adequate defense.

According to this myth, the United States does not have sufficient resources to stay in the arms race with the Soviet Union; and if it tries to, it will, in some sense, "go bankrupt."

The simple reply to this myth is that in the early 1970's less than 7 percent of our GNP is being devoted to national security programs, the smallest percentage since 1950 (pre-Korea) and far less than at the peak of World War II (42 percent) or Korea (13 percent). The conclusion is inescapable that if the nation's security required it, the economy could support a much larger defense program than the present one.

A deeper analysis necessitates a careful definition of terms. What do we mean by "afford" or "not afford"? According to the National Planning Association's 1953 report, entitled *Can We Afford Additional Programs for National Security?*, in a period short of a major war "the U.S. cannot 'afford' a national security program if it absorbs, over a long period of time, so much of the productive resources of the nation that not enough is left for maintaining and expanding productive capacity."[22] To be sustainable over time the expanded military program should absorb only a part of the "growth dividend," leaving part for increased production of consumer and capital goods.

According to the NPA, the United States "cannot afford" a defense program so large (1) that taxes to support it would stifle work incentives; (2) that disruptive inflation would result; (3) that comprehensive direct controls (over prices, wages, and so on) would have to be established and maintained; or (4) that some combination of the three would occur.

The NPA, after examining the consequences of each of three hypothetical increases (of $10, $20, and $33 billion from the $53 billion level in 1953), concluded that a 60 percent increase in defense spending over a three-year period to $70 – 75 billion, or *about 18 percent of GNP* in 1956, "would lie within the nation's financial and economic capacity without necessitating wartime controls" and "would be practical without weakening the strength of the American economy, if such increase should be clearly needed."[23] Whatever the exact "outer limit" may be, it is obviously for higher than the less than 7 percent of GNP now being spent on defense.

> **Myth IV.** That "the military-industrial complex" (MIC) — the one President Eisenhower warned of in his farewell address of January 1961 — has already come to pass in the form of a giant conspiracy of Pentagon

---

[22]Gerhard Colm, *Can We Afford Additional Programs for National Security?* (Washington, D.C.: National Planning Association, 1953), pp. v – vi.
[23]*Ibid.,* pp. viii and 52.

planners, defense contractors, and "bought" congressmen all feeding upon one another for their mutual enrichment.

As George Bach says, " 'The military-industrial complex' means different things to different people."[24] Even some of its most strident critics disclaim any accusation of conspiracy and speak of the participants as "men of good will" or "mostly honest men." Seymour Melman speaks of "institutionalized power-lust" rather than of individual power lust as the driving force behind what, he feels, has become "the most powerful decision-making unit in the United States Government" — the "state-management," as he calls the MIC.[25] Professor Galbraith sees the problem as one not of conspiracy or corruption but of unchecked rule.[26]

If the MIC is not a conspiracy, then, what is it and how did it arise? It is simply the natural outgrowth of the experiences of World War II and Korea — of the discovery that defense is big business, that it consumes vast quantities of resources, and that the specialized skills (including research and development skills as well as production skills) for developing and producing complex modern weapons systems frequently can be had only through contracts with very large corporations (or at least medium-sized corporations). Over the period 1959 – 1967, prime contract awards by the Department of Defense to the 100 largest companies in the United States ranged between 65 and 75 percent of total DOD procurement, while the top *five* companies were awarded between 20 and 25 percent of the total.[27] The trend in concentration, however, has been generally downward. Furthermore, military business constitutes only a small fraction (less than 5 percent) of the sales of the top ten U.S. corporations, with only a handful of companies, mainly aerospace companies such as General Dynamics and Lockheed, depending for more than half their total sales on DOD contracts. As Bach puts it, "the widespread notion that the biggest American corporations depend primarily on military contracts for their business and profits is clearly incorrect." In addition, prime contractors subcontract a large part of the work (61 major defense suppliers surveyed in 1956 – 1959 paid other companies 50 percent of their military receipts). Between 20,000 and 40,000 different U.S. firms help produce military items.[28]

Some MIC critics claim that defense contractors make excessively large profits and that the desire for profits leads them to press for even larger defense budgets. President Nixon's Blue Ribbon Defense Panel reported on July 1, 1970, that the rate of profits enjoyed by defense contractors has been declining and that there are now instances where profits are abnormally low or nonexistent.[29] A number of other studies — by the government's watchdog agency, the General Accounting Office, and by private research organizations — have concluded that the defense industry is not making excessive profits, and that, in fact, the rate of profit on defense sales is only about half as large as on the normal commercial sales of the same companies.[30]

---

[24]Bach, p. 453.
[25]Melman, p. 2.
[26]John Kenneth Galbraith, *How to Control the Military* (New York: Signet Books, 1969), pp. 23 – 31.
[27]Harry B. Yoshpe and Charles F. Franke, *Production for Defense* (Washington, D.C.: Industrial College of the Armed Forces, 1968), pp. 23 – 25.
[28]Bach, p. 454.
[29]Gilbert W. Fitzhugh, *Report to the President and the Secretary of Defense on the Department of Defense,* by the Blue Ribbon Defense Panel (Washington, D.C.: U.S. Government Printing Office, 1970), p. 174.
[30]Barry J. Shilito, Assistant Secretary of Defense for Installations and Logistics, *Submission for the Record at the Joint Economic Committee Hearings on the Acquisition of Weapons Systems,* May 25, 1971.

Radical proposals for "bringing the DOD under control" are misguided, based on false premises, and would lead to more problems than they would solve — especially to the danger of seriously weakening our defense posture in a dangerous world. Murray Weidenbaum argues that closer scrutiny and supervision of defense contracts is likely to cost taxpayers *more* rather than *less*. Bach's recommendation perhaps best expresses the viewpoint of the dispassionate economist: "Substitution of economic incentive plans for government contracting, rather than increasingly detailed surveillance of operations, is likely to provide more defense output for the dollar. . . . The basic goal for the nation is the provision of needed national defense with a minimum use of economic resources, not the minimization of defense contractors' profits."[31]

   Myth V.   That the cost of an all-volunteer armed force would far exceed the cost of the present "mixed force" of volunteers and conscripts.

"Although the *budgetary expense* of a volunteer armed force will be higher than for the present mixed force of volunteers and conscripts, the *actual cost* will be lower."[32] This was the important and unanimous finding of President Nixon's Commission on an All-Volunteer Armed Force submitted in February 1970. Recall our discussion of "opportunity costs" early in this chapter. By forcing men to serve in the armed forces at artificially low pay (that is, below the free market price for that service), the government is actually making them pay a tax, albeit a tax in kind rather than in dollars. Since the benefit of having an adequate military force is received by *all* citizens, those who are *not* drafted are, in a very real sense, being *subsidized* by those who are forced to serve. The extra cost (the dollar value of the subsidy) is hidden; it does not show up in the DOD budget. But it is just as real as if it did. In addition, there are "the costs borne by those young men who do not serve, but who rearrange their lives in response to the possibility of being drafted. Taking these hidden and neglected costs into account, the actual cost to the nation of an all-volunteer force will be lower than the cost of the present force."[33]

To switch to an all-volunteer force it will be necessary to increase the pay of servicemen by the amount of the tax in kind paid by the inductee. The increase will then show up in the budget and will have to be met out of tax revenues. In short, the tax burden will be shifted from the draftee to taxpayers at large. The commission estimated that draftees bear a tax burden more than three times that of comparable civilians, quite apart from "the abridgement of individual freedom that is involved in collecting it." The commission finds conscription to be a "tax that is not only discriminatory, but regressive" (since it falls more heavily on those with low incomes).[34]

President Nixon's announced goal is zero draft calls by July 1, 1973. In March 1971, Secretary of Defense Laird compared the total pay of a private (including allowance for his quarters, subsistence, and tax advantage) who has just finished basic training, $2,700, with the $6,000 that is common beginner's pay for an unskilled blue-collar worker, or the $9,500 starting salary of a New York City policeman. He recommended an average basic pay increase of 36 percent for enlisted people with less than two years service and of 50 percent for new entrants.[35]

---

[31]Bach, p. 458.
[32]Thomas S. Gates, *Report of the President's Commission on an All-Volunteer Armed Force* (Washington, D.C.: U.S. Government Printing Office, 1970), p. 8.
[33]*Ibid.*, p. 9.
[34]*Ibid.*, pp. 23 – 33.
[35]Laird, p. 133 – 134.

The President's Commission estimated that the budget increase required to move toward an all-volunteer force would be $3.2 billion (in FY 1971), but that $0.5 billion would flow back to the Treasury in increased income tax collections, so that the net increase in the budget would be $2.7 billion.[36] On November 24, 1971, the largest military pay raise ever granted, a record $2.4 billion a year, became effective and brought military pay scales into a more reasonable relationship with the private sector.

SUGGESTIONS FOR FURTHER READING

GOVERNMENT PUBLICATIONS

Committee on the Economic Impact of Defense and Disarmament. *Report of the Committee on the Economic Impact of Defense and Disarmament.* Washington, D.C.: U.S. Government Printing Office, 1965.

Economic Report of the President, together with the Annual Report of the Council of Economic Advisers. Washington, D.C.: U.S. Government Printing Office, 1971 and 1972.

President's Commission on an All-Volunteer Armed Force. *Report of the President's Commission on an All-Volunteer Armed Force.* Washington, D.C.: U.S. Government Printing Office, 1970.

Rowen, Henry. *National Security and the American Economy in the 1960's.* Study Paper No. 18 for the Joint Economic Committee, 86th Congress, 2nd Session. Washington, D.C.: U.S. Government Printing Office, 1960.

Yoshpe, Harry B. and Franke, Charles F. *Production for Defense.* Washington, D.C.: Industrial College of the Armed Forces, 1968.

OTHER BOOKS AND PAMPHLETS

Bach, George Leland. *Economics. An Introduction to Analysis and Policy.* 7th ed. Englewood Cliffs, N.J.: Prentice-Hall, 1971.

Colm, Gerhard. *Can We Afford Additional Programs for National Security?* Washington, D.C.: National Planning Association, 1953.

Conference Board. *The Federal Budget, Its Impact on the Economy, Fiscal 1972.* New York: The Conference Board, Inc., 1971.

Hitch, Charles J. and McKean, Roland N. *The Economics of Defense in the Nuclear Age.* New York: Atheneum, 1965.

Melman, Seymour. *Pentagon Capitalism: The Political Economy of War.* New York: McGraw-Hill, 1970.

Samuelson, Paul A. *Economics.* 8th ed. New York: McGraw-Hill, 1970.

---

[36]Gates, p. 8.

Part **4**

The Global Concern

18 *Trade and Protectionism*

"We have been in many respects 'Uncle Sucker' to the rest of the world." "Protection is a losing game any way you play." As these contradictory statements by former Secretary of Commerce Maurice Stans and William Spencer, the President of the First National City Bank, illustrate, there is a little agreement as to the value of a "free trade" policy for the United States.

Whether American foreign trade should be unfettered of restrictions as far as is possible or whether particular domestic industries should be "protected" from the full force of competition by means of tariffs or quantitative restrictions on imports is a question that still draws heated debate. Whether one is for or against free trade is analogous to a poker game: it depends on where one sits and the cards one holds. Yet there is no right or wrong position with regard to free trade, as we shall see, but only valid and invalid arguments concerning the interests various parties are seeking to protect; in this sense, all parties to the debate are protectionists.

The Economists' Argument for Free Trade

The economists' fundamental argument on behalf of free trade was forcefully advanced by Adam Smith and David Ricardo almost 200 years ago in their successful battle against the *mercantilists*. The mercantilists argued that a positive balance of international payments was beneficial to a nation and that therefore it should do everything in its power to limit its imports of finished goods and promote the export of its manufactures, acquiring monetary gold as a result. Adam Smith argued brilliantly in *The Wealth of Nations* (1776) that the source of a nation's wealth lay not in the amount of gold it possessed but in "... the annual produce of its land and labour."

International trade benefits a nation in the same way that domestic trade does. It permits the products of one country, the United States, for example, to be exchanged for the products of another country which can produce them more cheaply. As Adam Smith observed, it is the division of labor which permits greater efficiency and lowers the cost of production. What determines the extent of specialization that will occur in the production of goods? Again, Adam Smith gave an answer that is still accepted today: "As it is the power of exchange that gives occasion to the division of labor, so the extent of this division must always be limited by the . . . extent of the market." The larger the market for a good, the greater the potential extent of specialization that can take place. The frontiersman was compelled by his isolation to become highly self-sufficient. Once transportation improved, however, he gladly gave up this self-sufficiency to trade his cattle, crops, or skins for goods produced elsewhere. He concentrated his efforts on the production of goods which he could produce relatively cheaper and exchanged his surplus for goods produced elsewhere.

The division of labor need not be confined within a national frontier. The possibility of international trade increases the size of the market and permits the degree of specialization in production to be extended further. It is the specialization in production both domestically and internationally that has permitted the tremendous growth in output per worker — and hence in real income per worker — over the past century. Oranges from Florida, wheat from Kansas, cheese from Holland, and transistor radios from Japan are all examples of the regional specialization of production that has lowered the cost of goods. The division of labor in the production of different goods in different regions of the United States and of the world can be partly explained by differences in climate, soil conditions, resources, skills, and the relative abundance of labor.

The greater the amount of exchange that takes place under conditions of free competition, the better off everyone is. This proposition is based on the simple idea that if two parties to an exchange did not feel they were better off after making the exchange they would not enter into the exchange voluntarily.

In short, specialization is dependent on the extent of the market. The larger the market, the more opportunities for specialization and trade, and therefore the greater the welfare of everyone concerned. It is on these widely accepted principles that free trade economists rest their case. What is true of the benefits of domestic exchange, they maintain, is equally true of international exchange. The free trader therefore claims that the burden of proof that free trade is harmful lies with the protectionist.

Adjustment to Economic Change.   Many of the problems that arise from international trade are those that arise from economic change in general. The migration of the textile industry from New England to the South that was made possible by new forms of technology, particularly cheap electricity, resulted in many depressed areas in the New England states. The failure of the Appalachian area to participate in the general growth of the rest of the United States widened the income gap between Appalachia and the rest of the nation. The mechanization of agriculture in the United States made millions of workers in rural areas unnecessary and forced them to seek employment in the cities, with all the personal costs that moving and learning a new occupation involve. None of these massive changes, and the associated pain, had anything to do with foreign trade.

The effects of some of these changes were beneficial to the country, but the cost to the dislocated workers often went uncompensated. The move of the textile mills to the South helped raise Southern workers' wages and reduced the gap between wages in the North and the South. Many of the surplus agricultural workers moved to the cities of the East and West to learn new jobs that paid higher wages, but others joined the ranks of the unemployed and became welfare recipients, often for life. Eventually New England, after a difficult period of adjustment, was able to attract new industries to take advantage of the skilled labor that remained after the textile mills departed. The subsequent movement of labor and capital, therefore, partially offset the personal costs imposed by the more efficient location of production, though by no means were all the personal costs borne by individuals fully offset. Some people were permanently injured by the economic changes that had occurred.

The costs imposed by the *international* relocation of production due to specialization may be more severe than those caused by a domestic relocation, mainly because the associated migration of labor and capital between countries is more difficult. In fact, they may be severely restricted by countries which otherwise advocate free trade. For example, most nations, including the United States, limit immigration. Almost all major countries exercise some type of control over capital movements, both into and out of their borders. International restrictions on labor and capital movements do not prevent adjustments to economic changes, but they do slow down the rate of adjustment.

The general point to be made here is that many of the economic changes that benefit society as a whole involve social costs; the persons who bear these social costs may not be fully compensated by the benefits obtained by society. These persons may, with a certain moral justification, object to the changes taking place and claim that they should be stopped or at least slowed down. The argument is even stronger when applied to economic changes that stem from changes in international specialization of production, first since two of the factors that smooth the process of adjustment, namely the interregional movement of labor and capital, may be impeded or even prevented from operating. Second, although we know that two nations participating in international trade under conditions of competition both benefit from the international exchange of goods, international trade theory tells us little about the division of the gains from trade as between the two countries. Neither does international trade theory tell us how long it will take the long-run benefits from international trade to outweigh the short-run social costs that are borne by particular groups and individuals injured in the adjustment process. All valid protectionist arguments concern either the division of the benefits among nations, or among economic groups within a nation, or the speed of the adjustment process. Let us now look at these protectionist arguments from the point of view of some of the interest groups concerned.

The Economic Argument for Trade Restriction. While it can be shown that under conditions of free competition free trade will maximize the *world's* income, the question as to how these benefits are distributed among nations remains. The free trade argument does not prove that a country cannot improve its own welfare relative to that of other countries by imposing a tariff or quota. On the contrary, there is a good case that under certain conditions a country *can* improve its welfare by imposing a tariff or quota. A tariff accomplishes this by increasing the domestic price of the imported good, thereby lowering the total demand for the imported commodity. If competitive markets prevail in the exporting country, the reduced demand in the importing country will result in a decline in the foreign supply price of the imported good, and eventually in a relative reduction in the ratio of the prices of imported goods to the prices of exported goods in the importing country. (This ratio is sometimes called the terms of trade.) It is an ironic case of first raising the price at home in order to bring about a price reduction for imports soon afterward. This is particularly likely to be the case if the country imposing the tariff or quota buys a significant proportion of the total world imports of the commodity in question and if the supply of that commodity in the exporting country is relatively insensitive to price changes, as is true of certain agricultural commodities such as sugar and cocoa. This gain, however, is achieved at the expense of the country producing the imported commodity, whose producers will then receive a lower price.

The possibility of increasing the gains from trade by raising tariffs or imposing quotas is contingent upon the absence of retaliatory action by other countries, since they too could play the same game to minimize the losses imposed upon them. If retaliatory action takes place, it is possible that a trade war, with each country competing as to how high it could raise its tariffs, might ensue. The result of such a trade war might be that all countries would end up worse off than they were before the initial rise in tariffs was introduced. This is the nightmare that all countries wish to avoid. The possibility of a trade war exercises restraint on a government's willingness to give in to particular interests at home. The increase in tariffs in the early 1930's imposed by most countries around the world contributed to a shrinkage in world trade from $69 billion in 1929 to $24 billion in 1933 and was a major factor in both causing and prolonging the worldwide depression of that period.

The Ambivalent Position of Labor

The position of the American labor movement with respect to free trade has been ambivalent because of its dual role both as producer and consumer. Before World War I, the American Federation of Labor maintained what President Samuel Gompers called a "neutral" attitude on the question of whether tariffs benefited labor. The AFL noted that protected industries were not necessarily high-wage industries and argued that union organization was the only way labor could improve its position. In the interwar period, although protectionist forces within organized labor were growing in strength, the AFL continued to maintain the "neutral" policy of allowing individual unions to follow their own interests concerning tariffs, then the principal form of trade restriction in use. In the postwar period, organized labor until the mid-1960's supported trade liberalization, subject to certain qualifications, and advocated aid to workers in injured industries. In the early seventies, however, organized labor moved toward a more protectionist policy as imports seriously threatened the textile, shoe, steel, and a few other industries.

Historically, the most common debate over whether tariffs or other forms of trade restriction benefit labor has centered on the "cheap labor" argument for protection. The main lines of this argument are that American labor must be protected from competition from imports made with cheap foreign labor. If these imports are not restricted, it is maintained, they will depress American wages to the point where American wage costs will equal foreign costs, or else imports will take over the market and American workers will simply lose their jobs.

Strong disparities in wages between countries would encourage emigration from the low-wage country into the high-wage country and tend to equalize wages in both countries. For this reason, high-wage countries such as the United States tend to limit immigration. It has been argued theoretically, however, that international trade can be a partial substitute for immigration. According to this type of reasoning, labor-abundant countries would tend to export labor-intensive goods, such as simple textiles, and import capital-intensive goods, such as airplanes and machinery, which would raise wages and lower the price of capital in those countries. The reverse would be true for a capital-abundant country. This theory would lend support to the "cheap labor" argument and would further suggest that increasing tariffs sufficiently against labor-intensive goods while reducing trade would not only maintain, but increase, labor's *share* of national income in the importing country, such as the United States. The reduction in trade resulting from higher tariffs would cause a reduction in total national income, but if the share of labor rose sufficiently as a consequence of the tariff, labor might offset this loss and enjoy an absolute gain in income.

As convincing as this argument is theoretically, it has not found empirical support. Professor Wassily Leontief of Harvard has found that for the United States, the most capital-abundant country in the world, exports are labor-intensive compared to imports; in 1947 American exports of manufactured goods contained approximately $14,000 of capital for each man/year of labor, while our imports contained $18,000 of capital for each man/year of labor. Japan, which has often been cited as a user of cheap labor, actually exports capital-intensive goods to the world while importing labor-intensive commodities; this pattern is reversed only with respect to Japanese trade with America. There are several other examples of what has come to be known as the "Leontief paradox," where exports and imports differ in relative factor intensity — labor versus capital — from what a country's relative factor endowments would lead us to believe.

Attempts to explain the pattern of trade by differences in the productivity of labor in various industries have met with much greater empirical success. There does seem to be a relationship between labor productivity in an industry and its ability to export. Furthermore, since the cost of similar goods in international markets tends to be the same in money terms, this would also offer a partial explanation of the relative difference in wages in different countries. For example, if a ton of sheet steel in world markets has a price of $150, a producer in Belgium may be able to sell at that price only if he pays wages lower than American wages, because his workers' productivity is lower. If this is the case, then "cheap labor," far from explaining a country's ability to export, is actually a reflection of its lower level of productivity. Thus, as long as American labor can keep its productivity at a level three to four times that of the Japanese, there is no reason why American wages should not remain three to four times higher than Japanese wages.

Unfortunately, in recent years the rate of increase in productivity in the United States has been less than that of our international competitors, so that even though foreign wages have, in general, been rising faster than American wages, U.S. unit labor costs have been rising even faster than foreign unit labor costs (see Figure 18.1). This has also caused U.S. export prices to rise faster than have foreign export prices (see Figure 18.2).

Since productivity is a function of both human and physical capital, the outlook for the relative wage of the American worker need not be endangered by international trade. In both these types of capital, the United States still has a considerable advantage over other nations.

Since 1965, the AFL-CIO has taken an increasingly protectionist stand on two grounds: (1) the rise in imports relative to exports has resulted in a loss of jobs, and

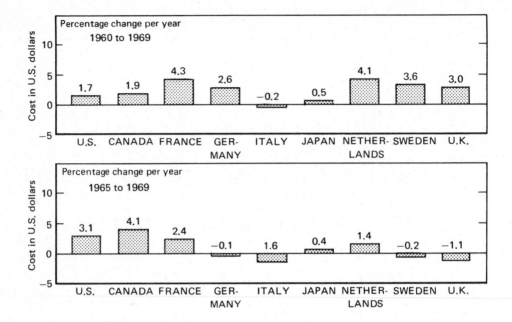

FIGURE 18.1 Annual rates of change in unit labor cost in manufacturing in nine countries, 1950–1969. (Source: U.S. Department of Labor, Bureau of Statistics.)

(2) imports restrain the rise in American workers' wages. Neither argument is as simple as it seems. There is no reason why full employment cannot be maintained with fiscal and monetary policies no matter what the level of deficit in our trade balance. Until 1971, the trade balance surplus was in our favor. What labor is really arguing is that workers cannot be asked to bear the social costs of readjusting to a new pattern of demand for labor, or, as the President of the AFL-CIO, George Meany, put it, "a worker [cannot be equated] with the retooling of a machine."

What concerns American labor is that if the competitive advantage of our exports lies in capital-intensive and technologically intensive industries, then these advantages are being dissipated rapidly. Capital has increased its international mobility greatly in the decade of the sixties as American business has been building and buying plants abroad — mostly to serve foreign markets but, in part, to serve the American market as well. In the past 25 years, about 8,000 subsidiaries of American companies have been established abroad, mostly in manufacturing. It is estimated that the annual sales of these foreign branches of U.S. firms to foreign and U.S. markets amount to approximately $200 billion — almost five times the amount of U.S. exports.

The Social Costs of Adjustment. The American government is committed under the Employment Act of 1946 to use all its powers to sustain high levels of employment, and most economists believe that it is within the economic power of the government to accomplish this, if it chooses to give this goal priority over other

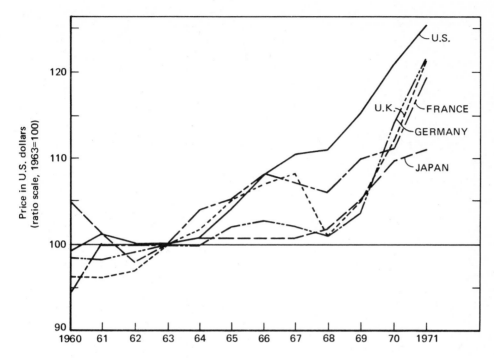

FIGURE 18.2   Export price indices, 1960–1971. (Source: International Monetary Fund, *International Financial Statistics.*)

goals such as price stability. If the government honors this commitment, and there are strong political pressures in the economy to see that it does, the crux of labor's argument that imports result in a loss of jobs is in reality a protest not against overall high unemployment but against the fact that specific workers alone bear the social cost of relocating, retraining, and possibly accepting a reduction in wages because they are no longer able to use the specialized skills that may have taken them many years to acquire. The problem is rather like telling a cellist that he must retrain as an office manager because there is no longer any need for orchestras. And this is not so farfetched an example as it may seem, since this is exactly what happened to musicians in the thirties and forties with the growth of electronic means of reproducing music.

American society has traditionally turned a deaf ear to personal problems of this type, accepting them as the cost of progress. The public conscience has been partly assuaged by the knowledge that unemployment insurance and welfare assistance exist and has not bothered to concern itself with the often irreparable personal psychological and financial losses incurred by displaced individuals during the "adjustment" process of finding a new occupation. Organized labor is questioning this traditional approach. Labor has thus far rejected the idea of compensation, such as special unemployment benefits, to offset the losses caused by labor "adjustment" to imports, and has instead argued for protection in order to slow down, if not completely halt, the need for the reallocation of labor. A final point, while it is of little economic significance, is of great political significance within organized labor. Up to now, the discussion of "adjustment" has been confined to injured workers and firms. No one has publicly discussed "compensating" an injured union which has suffered a drastic loss of membership and whose *officers* may find even more of a problem "adjusting" than the rank and file when they leave the import-affected industry.

The Benefits to Labor from Trade.   Economists argue that consumers, most of whom are workers, are the chief beneficiaries of trade since it is through trade that they obtain a larger assortment of goods at lower prices. This argument is strongly challenged by labor leaders who argue that the competitive markets that must prevail to bring about this result do not exist. Rather, they claim that there is little, if any, genuine price competition in many areas that are dominated by powerful corporations, and that the supposed benefits of import competition are thus illusory. In short, they argue that a large part of the American market is dominated by oligopolists who employ lower-cost imports of semifinished and finished goods to lower their costs and increase their profit margins. There is, however, no statistical information to support the proposition that firms buying a larger portion of imported goods earn higher profits than firms using a smaller proportion of imported finished and semifinished products. Nor is there agreement on the degree of competition that prevails in the American marketplace. However, even labor cannot deny that a cheap garment from Hong Kong or Korea widens the American consumer's choice.

While labor has attempted to measure the cost of trade in terms of "lost" job opportunities and the impact of imports on wages, few studies have been made to measure quantitatively the gains from trade. The net affect of trade on labor is not known, though the government has made several studies of the number of jobs "created" by exports.

A strong argument made by both labor and business is that foreign exports are not priced as they would be if competitive market conditions prevailed. Foreign governments often impose various forms of tariff and other restrictions on imports — and, more important, offer various forms of subsidies to exports which may influence both the amount of the gains to be obtained from trade and their distribution among countries. Many of these restrictions, particularly in the industrialized countries, have been imposed because foreign workers, just like American workers, are unwilling to accept the social costs of adjustment that unrestricted trade would impose. Belgian, German, and British coal miners are a good example. If one admits that the ideal solution of removing all barriers to trade in all countries as advocated by the free traders is politically unacceptable, then one can argue that a second-best solution would be the imposition of just enough tariffs by the United States to result in a price relationship between imported goods and domestically produced goods close to that which would prevail under freely competitive markets.

However, it is hard to visualize that other countries would accept any major increase in the level of U.S. protectionism without retaliating against American exports. The best that could be hoped for is that foreigners would accept limited protection by us for particular industries where the social or political cost of adjustment may be felt to be high. There is some precedent for this in the mutual acceptance of protectionism in agriculture, as well as in textiles, by the United States and Europe.

Industry's Arguments for Protection

Industry's arguments for protection parallel those used by labor. Industry often claims that imported goods made with "cheap labor" give foreigners an "unfair" competitive advantage in American markets. Imports made with "cheap labor" result in reduced profits either by forcing domestic industry to maintain lower prices than it would in the absence of imports or, if it chooses to maintain prices, to give up a large share of the domestic market.

Of course, the same argument could have been, but was not, made when the textile industry left New England to take advantage of the "cheap labor" available in the South. The reason why not is obvious. Manufacturers gladly abandoned their old plants in New England, absorbing the costs involved, and moved to the South to take advantage of the lower wages prevailing there. It may be seen, therefore, that underlying the "cheap labor" argument of industry in the international trade field lies an implicit assumption of the immobility of capital.

Mobility of Capital. One must ask why U.S. capitalists who are faced with competition from cheaper imports, which they cannot meet profitably, do not shift their production facilities abroad or, if this is not possible, why they do not invest their capital in other, more profitable, domestic industries. To some extent this is what has happened; for example, many television and automobile companies produce components of their products abroad and then import them into the United States. In some cases, the capital-intensive steps in manufacture are done in the United States; the product is then sent abroad — including to nearby Mexico — where the labor-intensive operations are accomplished, and then the finished product is sent back to the United States, where it can take advantage of the preferential tariff treatment given imported products that contain U.S.-made parts. In addition, many American firms have established subsidiaries abroad to produce products for foreign markets to which they formerly exported U.S.-made products. This procedure has many advantages for the producer, apart from lower labor costs; transportation costs may be lower; the subsidiary is not subject to tariffs and other trade barriers imposed by the foreign country; the product may be produced so as to more closely approximate foreign tastes; and, last but not least, the United States grants favorable tax treatment to these subsidiaries.

Still, there are many firms that are too small to undertake international manufacturing operations of the type described above and are therefore confined to domestic production. Other firms, as in the steel industry, may be prevented from establishing plants abroad by foreign restrictions placed on investment.

Assuming that these domestic firms, which are prevented from going abroad, are not able to increase their productivity and lower their costs, we must ask why they do not use their depreciation allowances and retained earnings to diversify into more profitable industries at home that either are not subject to import competition (for example, housing) or are able to compete profitably with imported products (for example, the automotive industry). Again, many firms have done exactly this, and the conglomerate corporation searching for profitable ways to employ its capital is a fact of American life. Still, many industries that compete with imports spend a large amount of their energies not only in trying to reduce costs or in seeking other uses for their funds, but also in lobbying for protection against imports.

The persistent clamor of import-competing industries for protection can be partially explained on three grounds. The first is that many industries have fixed costs, as represented by their existing plant and equipment, which can only be recovered over a period of years. Any rapid upsurge in imports, as has occurred in some industries, may result in losses for these firms if they cannot quickly shift their facilities to the production of other products that can withstand domestic and foreign competition. The rate of penetration by imports may exceed these firms' ability to reduce profitably their level of output, by allowing their plants to depreciate and thus saving on taxes.

A second factor is that the management of many industries is divorced from the ownership of the industry — the stockholders. In many corporations, the board of directors and officers of the corporation own little or no stock in the company they run. They may see their interest as maintaining the sales of the existing company, even though profit-maximizing considerations might dictate that it would be wiser for the stockholders to phase out the company and enter a new industry with brighter profit prospects.

A third group of firms operates in noncompetitive markets in which there are few sellers. To some degree, these firms control the domestic price of their products. They may be able to obtain higher profits than they would if the market were perfectly competitive. Import competition in this instance, by destroying their market power and control over prices, would result in lower prices and profits. The most outstanding example of this type of industry is the oil industry, which has successfully restricted the import of foreign oil into the United States.

In the case of industry, as in the case of labor, an argument can be made that even if free trade is to be favored, stockholders and owners should be protected from having to bear the costs of making a rapid adjustment to *sudden* increases in imports. However, the argument here is weaker because capital, unlike labor, is domestically very mobile and can be reallocated at a much lower social cost than can labor.

Noneconomic Arguments for Protection. The owners of industry, recognizing the political weakness imposed by their small numbers and the general unpopularity of their basic objective of trying to maintain or increase prices and profit margins, have attempted to clothe their arguments in more attractive colors. This has taken the form of supporting workers' demands for protection and of claiming that the preservation of their industry is necessary for the maintenance of national prestige or the defense of the country. In general, it is only when large numbers of organized *workers* have been willing to support trade restrictions that industry's efforts to obtain protection from imports have been successful. Again, a notable exception to this rule is the U.S. oil industry, which has a relatively small labor force. With very little popular support, it has maintained import quotas on oil since 1957 on the dubious grounds that there is a need for protection in order to encourage new exploration for national defense purposes. The use of quotas is particularly surprising in view of the fact that most economists and all government reports on the subject have recommended that, if protection is granted, tariffs are superior to quotas.

Many corporations that are dependent on exports for an important portion of their sales, or on imported raw materials and goods, have taken a free trade stance. There has been no quantitative attempt to assess what the net impact of a protectionist policy on business would be. What evidence there is does not indicate a strong presumption that either large net gains or great injury to business would result from protectionism. Business arguments for protection, therefore, appear to depend on what the social cost of adjustment to increased imports of *particular* products would be.

No discussion of the issues involved in free trade versus protection can be complete without mention of the crucial matter of currency exchange rates. We cannot in this chapter explore the intricate problem of the world monetary system. But in our context the issue can be put simply: a Japanese-made wool sweater or a Toyota car is far cheaper in the U.S. market if $1 buys 360 yen, as it did until August 1971, than if $1 buys 308 yen, as it does under the international currency agreement signed in December 1971. It is widely agreed among economists that a good part of the problem of the rapid increase of imports into the United States during the 1965 – 1971 period arose from what is called an "overvalued" exchange rate for the dollar, which in turn came about partly because inflation in the United States during that period was worse than it was in many other industrial countries. The overvaluation of the dollar has been eliminated, or greatly reduced, by the devaluation of late 1971. This particular cause of sudden and often excessive import competition has been dealt with; only events will tell us about the extent to which overvaluation of the dollar was the cause of many of the problems that labor complains about.

Protection to Increase Economic Growth

Soon after Adam Smith and his followers established free trade as the prevailing economic philosophy in England, its applicability to other countries was questioned. One of the early critics of the English classical economist was Alexander Hamilton, first Secretary of the U.S. Treasury. In his *Report on Manufactures* (1791), he advanced what has come to be known as the "infant industry" argument for protection. Hamilton maintained that new domestic industries could not compete with imports because of the limited size of the market and because of their inability to produce immediately an output large enough to achieve the economies of scale necessary to reduce costs to a level where domestic production would be competitive. He argued that a protective tariff would help new import-competing industries to establish themselves and to achieve a level of production that would enable them to become competitive in world markets, at which time the tariff could be removed.

While Hamilton's argument had considerable theoretical merit, the practical difficulties in implementing such a policy were enormous and Congress rejected Hamilton's proposal. However, it remained the principal argument of protectionists until the Civil War. The successful imposition of a tariff to promote infant industries requires that the tariff be continually lowered as the industry gains in efficiency; otherwise, new high-cost firms will emerge which can only make a profit with the help of the tariff. Historically, it has been most difficult to remove protection gradually so that marginal firms would not disappear suddenly.

The ideas of Hamilton were reborn in a more sophisticated form in recent times in the work of the Argentine economist Raul Prebisch, former head of the United Nations Economic Commission for Latin America.[1] Prebisch was concerned with the

---

[1]Raul Prebisch, *Towards a New Trade Policy for Development.* Report by the Secretary-General of UNCTAD (New York: United Nations, 1964), pp. 11 – 16.

implications of free trade for the development of the less developed countries in Africa, Asia, and Latin America, which he called the "periphery," relative to the development of the advanced industrial countries of the "center."

Prebisch argued that the gains from international trade were unequally divided between the center and the periphery. More precisely, there was a continuing tendency for the prices of the exports of the periphery to decline relative to those of the center. The reason for this, he suggested, was that the center chose to take increases in its national income in the form of higher wages at relatively constant prices. The periphery, on the other hand, because of the large amount of surplus labor that held wages down, took increases in income in the form of lower prices. This tended to deteriorate the "terms of trade" of the periphery relative to the center and imposed a disadvantage that was difficult to overcome.

However, simple redress of the terms of trade by way of international commodity agreements or other means of holding up raw material prices, Prebisch argued, is not sufficient to improve the growth rate of the periphery relative to that of the center. The level of savings and of investment in nations on the periphery is dependent on their level of income. Most of the nations of the periphery produce raw materials or primary products. The markets for these products lie primarily in the advanced industrial nations of the center. The major factor influencing the rate of growth of demand in the industrial nations of the center for primary products of the periphery is the rate of growth of income in the center nations. Prebisch maintained that because of these facts, the rate of growth of the nations of the center would *determine* the rate of growth of nations of the periphery. His chain of reasoning runs as follows:

1. Demand for the exports of the periphery is determined by the rate of growth of the center nations.
2. Exports are the major determinant of the rate of growth of income in the periphery and therefore the major determinant of the rate of growth of savings and investment in the periphery.
3. Since the rate of growth of investment is the major determinant of economic growth, and this is determined by the rate of growth of the center nations, the periphery can never grow faster than the center. Therefore, it cannot close the income gap that exists between the center and the periphery. The periphery is thus condemned to perpetual backwardness.

To break this chain, Prebisch argued for industrialization, even if it could only be accomplished by recourse to a high level of protection against imports and a loss of income in the short run. To obtain the capital to finance this industrialization, Prebisch advocated large-scale foreign aid, commodity agreements to improve the terms of trade of the periphery, reduction of trade barriers and the institution of preferential treatment by the center for the exports of the periphery, and the institution of common markets among the nations of the periphery until such preferential treatment is attained.

Prebisch's theories have had an enormous impact on the political and intellectual leaders of the less developed countries, far outstripping those of his Marxian rivals.

Empirical evidence supporting Prebisch's thesis is not unanimous. First, there are obvious exceptions. For example, oil-producing countries have had high rates of growth of exports and income, and the same is also true of several other mineral-producing countries. The long-run deterioration of the terms of trade of the periphery has not been established. Nor is the link between increased income, exports, and investment always clear. Yet in spite of these flaws, it would not be an overstatement to say that the theories of Prebisch underlie the economic policies of more nations in the world than those of any other man.

Recently, American business and labor, as we have seen, have also suggested that tariffs may be necessary to sustain American prosperity and economic growth. The theoretical basis for such an argument in a developed country must rest either on a doubt that the economic authorities will be able to maintain full employment or on the assumption that labor and capital are sufficiently immobile that any loss of employment as a result of imports may well persist for a considerable period of time, resulting in a reduced rate of economic growth. This argument was more valid before, than after, World War II because of the government's strong current commitment to maintain high levels of employment.

Types of Restrictions on Trade

Once the desirability of restricting trade has been decided upon by the national authorities — whether for valid or invalid reasons — it still remains to decide on the *form* the trade restriction will take. There are four general types of trade restrictions that can be imposed: tariffs, import quotas, currency exchange restrictions, and non-tariff barriers. Each type of restriction presents special problems with respect to whether it can achieve the desired degree of restriction and whether it can be enforced.

Tariffs versus Quotas. In general, tariffs and quotas are substitutes for one another. Any degree of restriction that can be achieved by a tariff can also be achieved by a quota. However, since the economic authorities possess only imperfect knowledge of the supply and demand schedules in the importing and exporting country for the commodity whose import it is desired to restrict, the two in practice cannot be regarded as equivalent. Quota restrictions precisely limit the quantity of goods to be imported. The price effects of quotas, however, are difficult to forecast. Quotas will probably raise prices domestically, but the extent to which they raise prices will depend on the slope of the demand curve and the degree of monopoly power possessed by domestic producers. Imports, when not covered by international agreements among producers (cartels), serve as a restraint on the exercise of monopoly power by domestic producers.

The price effects of tariff restrictions normally can be predicted with greater precision. In no case would one expect the price of the imported commodity to rise by more than the amount of the tariff. The quantity of goods imported under tariffs, however, is less predictable. Only in the case where the tariff is so high as to prevent all imports can the effect on the volume of imports be predicted with perfect accuracy.

Exchange Control. The rationing of the means of making foreign payments was widely used in the postwar period by most countries until the late 1950's. The effect of exchange control on trade is much the same as the effect of quotas, with the additional characteristic that it permits precise control not only over the amount of imports permitted but also over which domestic importers shall be permitted to import which products. The administration of exchange controls requires a large bureaucracy and a definite idea as to the economic priorities of the nation if it is to be economically efficient. It is interesting to note that exchange control as we know it today was largely developed and perfected by Nazi Germany in the early 1930's. Since the introduction of exchange control, it has been used for a wide variety of purposes, not merely to restrict imports and protect domestic industries.

Nontariff Barriers to Trade. In addition to quotas and exchange controls, there exist a large number of other nontariff barriers to trade. These include subsidies for exports, the use of state trading organizations with a monopoly over the importation of some or all commodities, administrative regulations which make it difficult for foreign products to enter (for example, maximum truck width and axle loads which are specified by many European countries), and taxation, which, although legally nondiscriminatory is in fact discriminatory against imports. This is only a partial listing of the multiplicity of devices that are employed by nations to restrict trade. Even health or environmental regulations can keep out imports. The existence of nontariff barriers to trade often diminishes the importance of international agreements to reduce tariffs and emphasizes the limitations of a purely legalistic approach to the liberalization of trade. Experience has shown that when nations do not genuinely desire to reduce their level of trade restrictions, they will be sufficiently ingenious to devise legally valid methods of circumventing international agreements requiring them to do so. The use of political pressure to force nations to sign trade liberalization agreements that they do not really support has often resulted in empty victories.

Trade restrictions cover a very wide spectrum of specific measures, many of which are not subject to international agreement or negotiation. Economists, in general, if they favor restrictions at all, prefer tariffs to other types of restrictions because they give the greatest play to market forces to allocate resources efficiently. It is specifically because of this, however, that protectionist forces dislike tariffs and prefer more precise controls over the entrance of imports. Because of the large number of means of restricting trade, nations interested in liberalizing trade cannot place undue emphasis on the removal of any one type of restriction such as tariffs or quotas, since these may be replaced by other forms of trade restriction if the parties to the negotiation are not agreed in principle concerning the underlying desirability of liberalizing trade.

The Political Dynamics of Protectionism

The actual trade policy followed by a nation is a political synthesis resulting from the balancing of domestic political considerations, foreign policy goals, and national defense objectives. U.S. trade policy therefore cannot be analyzed in economic terms only or to the exclusion of the trade policies of other nations. We shall try to look at the foreign trade policy of the United States as it relates to the trade policies followed by Western Europe, particularly the Common Market countries, by the less developed countries, and by the Communist bloc countries. In this multilateral context we shall also look at international cooperative efforts to remove barriers to trade.

U.S. Trade Policy. In an unsuccessful attempt to ward off the deepening recession of the 1930's, the United States passed the Smoot-Hawley Tariff in 1930 — the highest tariff in our history. The United States was not alone in this policy, as other countries raised their tariffs too, with the result that world trade plummeted. New Deal supporters, believing that trade expansion was one way in which economic recovery could be hastened, passed the Reciprocal Trade Agreements Act of 1934. The original reason given for this measure reflected the incorrect belief that most of the goods we import are goods that we cannot produce ourselves. The Roosevelt Administration sought to reduce tariffs on goods we did not produce in exchange for concessions on goods we exported. The act gave the president authority to negotiate reciprocal reductions in tariffs. Labor's opposition to more liberal trade disappeared as it placed its faith in the domestic policies of the New Deal to increase employment. The original act of 1934 was to last only three years. It was, however, renewed 11 times, and the average level of duties fell from 53 percent in 1934 to 12 percent at the time it finally expired in 1962. In response to the creation of the Common Market, composed of Belgium, France, Germany, Italy, Luxembourg, and the Netherlands, the Congress passed the Trade Expansion Act of 1962, which gave the president broad power to negotiate further reductions in trade barriers. These laws, basically aimed at reducing tariffs, also gave the president the authority to raise tariffs under certain conditions:

1. *Injury to domestic producers.* If the Tariff Commission determines that serious injury is being caused or threatened to domestic industry as a result of increased imports due to trade agreement concessions, the president may revoke all or part of the concessions granted. If he fails to act, Congress may, if it wishes, compel him to act by a majority vote.
2. *National security.* The president is directed not to decrease tariffs or other import restrictions on any products if he determines that this would threaten to impair the national security, and he can even impose new import barriers.
3. *Retaliation.* A third reason for withholding trade concessions or raising trade barriers is for the purpose of inducing foreign countries to remove restrictions against United States exports. In addition, there are several laws on the books to prevent the "dumping" of foreign goods in the United States at prices below their fair value.
4. *Agricultural quotas.* The president retains the right to impose restrictions on the import of agricultural commodities subject to domestic price-support programs.

   Up to now, the president has not made great use of these options to increase the level of restrictions. The Tariff Commission has rejected most of the requests for a finding of injury. The national security clause is currently in effect only in the case of petroleum, where most economists outside the oil industry believe it has been misapplied. The United States has used its retaliatory powers only in several minor instances, and these have generally been successful in removing the newly imposed foreign trade barriers. In 1970 and 1971, the Nixon Administration made a new effort to improve the enforcement of the antidumping laws, and the number of cases has risen sharply.

   Over the years the president has extensively used his authority to impose quotas on agricultural commodities that are subject to price-support programs. This has not created any reaction because of the even more restrictive policies on agricultural imports followed abroad, particularly in the European Common Market.

Adjustment Assistance. The Trade Expansion Act of 1962 contained one important new feature. Business firms or workers can apply for "adjustment assistance" if the Tariff Commission reports that their industry has been injured as a result of trade concessions. Adjustment assistance to firms may take the form of technical, financial, or tax assistance in order to make the firm more competitive with imports or even to help it to switch to another line of products. Adjustment assistance to workers may take the form of training, extra unemployment compensation benefits, or relocation allowances, in an effort to permit workers to acquire new skills and move to new jobs. Little use has been made of adjustment assistance thus far because of the difficulty in obtaining a finding of injury from the Tariff Commission. Although labor was the original sponsor of this provision, it has felt that, as presently administered, the provision provides little job security, and this conclusion has tended to support labor's requests for protection for import-impacted industries. Labor's term for adjustment assistance is now "burial benefits."

The Stalemate in U.S. Trade Policy. In the early seventies, U.S. trade policy faces an impasse. The general level of tariffs both in the United States and Europe is low. The average Common Market tariff was 8.4 percent and that of Japan 10.9 percent in 1969. The U.S. tariff averaged only 8.3 percent in 1969, although many individual products are protected by high tariffs. The purely tariff problems now involve only those items on which there is a wide disparity between European and American tariffs. It is precisely in those industries that are protected by high tariffs that the economic repercussions of reducing the disparities produce the greatest political reaction since this might entail acceptance of a sharply reduced share of the domestic market for the protected industry and a consequent reduction in its labor force, which may be highly specialized.

But the impasse goes deeper than just the tariff problem. There is, first, the deep disagreement within our own country as to whether the basic direction of trade policy should continue to be in the direction of liberalization. But even if that issue is decided in the affirmative, the negotiation problem with other countries will be exceptionally difficult. Agriculture is the chief case in point. For a host of reasons, nearly all countries support farm prices or otherwise subsidize farm incomes, and these programs cannot work if free import competition is permitted. In addition, as the treatment of textiles, steel, and oil reveals, where the basic principle of freer trade has been sacrificed to import restrictions, sometimes for political reasons, it will not be easy to change course again.

President Nixon announced early in 1972 the intention of the United States to engage in a major new set of trade negotiations with the aim of further reducing trade barriers. While no one can yet say how this effort will turn out, nor even whether Congress will grant the President the necessary authority to reduce the remaining U.S. barriers, it is clear that future negotiations will have to deal in different ways with the different parts of the world.

European Economic Community. There is one instance in which the United States has willingly encouraged trade discrimination against itself — that of the European Economic Community (EEC), commonly called the "Common Market."

The Common Market consists of Belgium, France, Germany, Italy, Luxembourg, the Netherlands, the United Kingdom, Denmark, and the Irish Republic. These countries have pledged themselves to achieve complete economic integration, which would permit the free movement of goods, capital, and persons within their collective borders. The United States did not object when these countries agreed to eliminate their tariffs among themselves while maintaining a common tariff toward third countries. This discrimination was permitted in the belief that if Western Europe was to serve as a bulwark against the expansion of Communism, it would require a strong economic base. To implement our foreign policy objectives, we tolerated a short-run discrimination against our imports in favor of members of the Common Market. The United States hoped that, in the longer run, greater economic efficiency in Europe would encourage a lowering of the Common Market external tariff below the average level of tariffs which member countries had maintained before they joined the Common Market. This, in fact, has occurred, with the result that the nontariff barriers to trade, such as health and safety regulations and "buy national" government procurement policies, have become more important than tariffs and have been particularly difficult to eliminate. This is true above all of the Common Market's complex restrictions on imports of agricultural products, in which the United States, as a major agricultural exporter, is vitally interested. As this is written, it would appear that unless a drastically different approach is taken, little advance will be made in the further liberalization of trade. If further progress is to be made, a more effective and comprehensive program must be developed, one that will include adjustment assistance to both workers and businesses which are dislocated by changing trade patterns.

Less Developed Countries' Trade Policy.   The less developed countries (LDC's) of the world have generally adopted highly restrictive trade policies, based on the belief that unless they did this they could never industrialize their economies. We have noted, for example, the theories of Prebisch. The developed countries have generally tolerated these policies, largely because they have not been prepared to offer an alternative policy. The less developed countries, for their part, have made two general demands of the developed countries with respect to trade policy. One is that they offer special preference — by way of a zero tariff — to manufactured products imported from the LDC's, and the second is that they support commodity agreements designed to maintain primary (agricultural and mineral) product prices at satisfactory levels. The former French colonies together with Greece, Turkey, and several other countries were able to obtain preference in the Common Market to the detriment of the other LDC's, although recently a more general preference plan for the poorer countries has been adopted by the Common Market. Britain has for a long period of time given small tariff concessions to Commonwealth members and entered into long-term agreements with Commonwealth countries for the purchase of certain foodstuffs such as sugar. The United States has offered preferential treatment to the less developed countries, but only if this principle were accepted by all the industrialized nations. In 1971 the European Common Market and Japan accepted this principle and have begun to implement it, and President Nixon has promised that the United States would follow, subject to congressional approval. To back up their demands, the less developed countries brought pressure to create the United Nations Conference on Trade and Development (UNCTAD), which it was hoped would further the objectives mentioned above. But except for the agreement on tariff preferences, UNCTAD has thus far been a failure, partly because the LDC's are too divided among themselves to exert the type of political leverage necessary to attain action from the developed countries. In the realm of commodity agreements, only one, the Coffee Agreement, can be regarded as a success. The others — dealing with cocoa, sugar, wheat, and tin — have had only mixed success, and protracted negotiations had still not produced a new cocoa agreement by 1972. The LDC's, feeling a sense of frustration in their trade policy, have tended to turn inward in an attempt to rationalize their own restrictive trade policies rather than continuing to seek preferential treatment abroad.

Communist Trade Policy. The Communist bloc countries have not been able to devise either a rational trade policy among themselves or one with Western countries. In general, the Soviet Union has attempted to devise a trading system whereby the bloc members would be largely autarkic (self-sufficient) as a group, while the satellites have favored a more liberalized policy toward the West. Western trade policy toward the Communist bloc has also been divided. The United States until very recently has favored a more restrictive trade policy toward the Communist bloc nations, on the theory that one should not assist one's potential enemies economically. European nations have taken the view that profitable trade is desirable in itself, and some have believed that by offering the bloc members an alternative to trade with Russia, they would weaken the monolithic character of the Communist bloc and encourage individual member countries to take more independent action. The United States' reluctance to follow Europe's more liberal trading policies has to some extent placed it in a puritanical position since our restrictive policy has had almost no economic impact, in view of Europe's more liberal policies. Furthermore, it seems inconsistent of the United States to offer friendship to Russia and China while at the same time denying trade. As this is being written, there is a relaxation in American trade policy toward both Russia and China making our policies more consistent with those of Europe.

International Organs for Trade Liberalization. The United States in 1948 scuttled the attempt of the United Nations to create an International Trade Organization (ITO) which would have had jurisdiction over all aspects of international trade policy. In its place, the General Agreement on Tariffs and Trade (GATT) was created in 1947 and became the general international forum for the discussion of trade matters.

The heart of the GATT is the "most favored nation clause," which provides that each member must receive the benefit of any tariff reduction made by another member. The GATT prohibits trade discrimination and the use of quantitative trade controls except for balance of payments difficulties, or if the same controls are imposed on domestic industry, as in agriculture. In addition, it permits LDC's to protect their "infant industries," but they, like any other country invoking an exception to the code, must periodically justify the continued use of import restrictions.

The GATT contains two "escape" clauses. It permits a country to raise its tariffs if a domestic industry is injured by imports. However, it allows countries whose exports are injured by these higher tariffs to suspend equivalent concessions unless they are compensated by other tariff reductions. The second escape clause permits GATT members to release a country from its GATT obligations under special unspecified circumstances. Almost all members of GATT have resorted to such waivers for various reasons.

The cumbersome bargaining machinery provided by GATT for reducing tariffs has often been bypassed in discussions among the principal trading nations, meaning the industrial countries. The great advantage of GATT is that it prevents a breakdown of communication among nations. One of the weaknesses of the GATT agreement in the past was that it concerned itself principally with tariffs, but GATT has recently established working parties to discuss nontariff barriers to trade as well. Congress has steadfastly refused to approve proposals to strengthen GATT or to replace it with a broader organization.

Trade Policy for the Seventies

The outlook for the increased liberalization of trade, which made significant strides in the fifties and sixties, is cloudy in the seventies. It is probable that any further substantial reduction in tariffs, either in the United States or in Europe, will result in injury to significant parts of the industries affected. This is a consequence of the success of the trade expansion policies followed in the sixties. We are now left with the "hard core" problems. While it is likely that the mounting pressure for new protection witnessed in the United States in the early seventies will abate with the restoration of high levels of employment and the resumption of economic growth, it is unlikely that organized labor will return to the free trade stance it adopted in the postwar period.

The great advantage of increased trade is that the gains of one country are not the losses of another. The welfare of all countries can be improved through increased trade. It is recognition of this fact that must provide the stimulus for further attempts at increased trade liberalization. If the potential benefits of trade are to be reaped by the United States and the other nations of the world, a new orientation must be given to American trade policy. The new trade policy will have to take advantage of the experience of the sixties if it is to be a success.

In brief, five things must be done: (1) future negotiations should be comprehensive in scope, not confined to tariffs or even to trade problems but rather extended to include the problem of foreign investment and the whole complex of issues relating to currency exchange rates and the balance of payments; (2) new efforts must be made to provide prompt, effective, and equitable adjustment assistance to workers and firms that are adversely affected by increased trade liberalization; (3) greater emphasis must be placed on the liberalization of trade in agricultural products, even though progress in this area, as in the past, may be a great deal slower than that experienced in trade in manufactured goods; (4) efforts must be made to facilitate — hopefully, on a nondiscriminatory basis—the access of manufactured and agricultural products from the less developed areas, while the less developed areas should be encouraged to follow a more rational policy of industrialization; (5) the expansion of East-West trade should be encouraged because it offers great hope of substantially improving the welfare of both areas.

In conclusion, the seventies hold great promise that further benefits for the United States may be obtained through the extension of world trade, but new directions must be sought out to obtain them. It is impossible to separate the political effects from the economic effects of trade. Fortunately, the steps that need to be taken to expand the benefits from world trade appear consistent with our foreign policy objectives of strengthening Europe, encouraging the growth of the LDC's, and improving our relations with the Communist nations. Domestically, many of the obstacles to increased trade liberalization will disappear with the reemergence of economic prosperity. Maintaining a strong internal economy is perhaps the most important contribution America can make to the expansion of world trade.

SUGGESTIONS FOR FURTHER READING

Balassa, Bela (ed.). *Changing Patterns in Foreign Trade and Payments.* Rev. ed. New York: W. W. Norton & Company, 1970.

Commission on International Trade and Investment Policy. *United States International Economic Policy in an Interdependent World: Report to the President.* 3 vols. Washington, D.C.: U.S. Government Printing Office, 1971.

Krause, Walter. *International Economics.* Boston: Houghton Mifflin, 1965.

Mitchell, J. B. Daniel. *Essays on Labor and International Trade.* Los Angeles: University of California, Institute of Industrial Relations, 1970.

19 Poor Nations in a Wealthy World

Poverty of nations, just as poverty of individuals, has existed since the beginning of mankind. The primitive man of many thousands of years ago, regardless of where he lived, had to struggle hard to provide food, shelter, and clothing for himself and his group. Primitive man did not know how to exploit the natural resources around him, nor did he have the ability or knowledge to fashion tools to help himself to produce more in order to improve his material conditions.

In the language of the economist, primitive man did not possess the technical knowledge or capital equipment to help himself satisfy his wants. In that long past history of the human race, the only inputs for the production of goods were land and labor. By combining them, prehistoric man could only produce what he needed for his consumption; that is, he consumed everything that he could produce. The breakthrough from that cycle of subsistence and continual struggle for survival came only when he could produce some surplus, that is, when he could produce a little more than he consumed. That did not come easily. In order to do this, he had to sacrifice some of his consumption.

The history of the economic progress of man could be written in this fashion. For a long time, man could hunt and kill with his bare hands three animals a week; from these animals he used the meat for food and the fur for clothing and shelter. Eventually he learned that by sacrificing his well-being in the short run, he could improve his chances for survival in the long run. That is, by putting aside time to hunt only two animals per week to meet his needs for food, clothing, and shelter, he could in the time left over break up stones into handy sizes and make himself a knife or other tools with which to hunt or tan hides more efficiently in the future. That knife enabled him to increase production; with it, he could hunt for perhaps five animals a week. In the economist's language, that knife was capital — a good which he produced but which he did not use all at once; it was used rather for further production; this added to labor and land, allowing for a substantial increase in production.

Over thousands of years, more and more knowledge was acquired on how capital goods could be created, with the result that more capital accumulation took place. But capital did not accumulate equally among individuals, communities, or nations. While other factors bear heavily on economic progress, no other factor has been so important as capital accumulation. This is why today we see the world divided into wealthy nations and poor nations. This division has always existed, but the nations so labeled have not necessarily remained on the same side. For instance, once upon a time, Egypt was the wealthiest nation in the world. Today it is one of the poorest. While Egypt flourished some 4,000 years ago, northern European countries were still in a primitive state with very little capital or wealth. Today, northern European countries are among the wealthiest in the world.

In 1970, the approximately 90 countries classified as poor represented three-quarters of the world's population but only about one-fifth of the world's income; they accounted for less than 10 percent of world public expenditure on health care and for 10 percent on education.

Characteristics of Poor Nations

Economists usually classify countries as being "developed" or "underdeveloped" according to the level of per capita income they have reached. The per capita income criterion has changed over time and can be meaningless in terms of United States dollars. In the 1940's, a nation was considered poor when its per capita income was below $200 – 300 per year. In the 1950's the criterion was $300 – 400, in the 1960's, $400 – 500, and in the 1970's, probably $500 – 600.

Per capita income is an important economic indicator, but taken by itself it can be deceiving. For example, per capita income in both Venezuela and Libya is over the standard of $600. Yet these countries are considered underdeveloped. One reason is that while per capita income on the average is high, income is not distributed equally on the average. However, the maldistribution of income alone does not make a country underdeveloped. In more advanced countries, income is also quite unequally distributed. Other characteristics can indicate that the country is underdeveloped.

Since the primary needs of people all over the world are for food, clothing, and shelter, it is not surprising that underdeveloped countries are mainly agricultural. Because these countries are agricultural, but even more because over the last generation great advances have been made in medicine, population in the underdeveloped areas has grown faster since World War II than in any previous period. Population growth per se does not necessarily have to be a handicap since the population densities (number of people per square mile) of developed countries like Belgium, Holland, England, and Germany are much higher than in underdeveloped areas such as China, Brazil, or Africa. The optimum size for a population depends on the availability and use of resources.

In the underdeveloped countries, social structure tends to be stratified according to class, tribe, or caste. Little social mobility also characterized medieval Europe. We all know that for a thousand years in Europe economic progress was very slow. On the other hand, the political structure of poor countries today is different from that which prevailed in Europe during the Middle Ages. Most of these countries are at least unified at the national level. In fact, freedom from colonialism together with a new impulse toward nationalism or national pride might help stimulate their development. Yet the establishment of power hierarchies in most of these countries stultifies initiative. One cannot expect democracies to develop here. Universal democratic participation in a society requires a kind of sophistication that is lacking in underdeveloped areas. This is due not only to the centuries of repression of individual initiative but also to the widespread lack of education or even literacy. Modern industrial societies require citizens who are literate and who possess a certain minimum of technical knowledge to cope with the intricacies of industrial interdependence.

Poverty, whether of individuals or of nations, is not a natural happening. That is, there is nothing in the law of nature that requires some nations to be poor and others rich. In more recent times, some nations have become wealthier than others for a combination of reasons. The causes of poverty are always manifold. They may include, as mentioned earlier, *lack of capital* — although even countries that have accumulated capital over the years, like certain Middle Eastern oil-producing countries, are still very poor; *large population* — though the richest nations in Europe have higher man-land ratios (densities) than those typical of most of sparsely inhabited Africa; and *lack of natural resources* — though, here again, many Middle Eastern countries which remain poor have abundant natural resources, such as oil, while Israel, which lacks almost any natural resources, ranks among the wealthy nations today.

Some economists maintain that poor countries have an available, if not a sufficient, surplus to use for capital; but such countries usually have little control over this surplus. The accumulated surplus in agriculture is either transferred to merchants, money lenders, and intermediaries in the cities or is appropriated by foreign firms. This is consistent with the "imperialism" theory,[1] which claims that foreign investments in poor countries do more harm than good. The positive features of foreign investment are evident in new economic enterprises and more nonagricultural employment opportunities. On the other hand, foreign investment in poor countries is concentrated mainly in primary activities such as mining and agriculture. These enrich not only the foreign investors, who export their large profits, leaving no surplus for use in the poor country, but also the economically advanced nations, which can then use these raw materials for the production of manufactured goods. Some of these finished goods are later sold at high profit to the poor nations. When foreigners do invest in manufacturing enterprises, these are usually of the "assembly" type and depend on capital-intensive methods; that is, more capital than labor is used in the production process. The first casualty in this process is cottage industry, which is labor-intensive and can not stand the pressure of higher productivity and better management. Therefore, this type of foreign investment ends by destroying more employment opportunities than it creates. As this process goes on, the world as such becomes wealthier, with more resources at its command; yet the poor countries continue to stagnate.

Dual Economies.   Many former colonies are locked into trade patterns that first developed under their colonial masters. Not only trading partners and trade relationships but also production patterns remained the same after these countries achieved their independence. Most poor countries have dual economies, composed of a small industrial enclave tucked away in a much larger traditional agricultural

---

[1]See discussion on this point in Paul A. Baran, *The Political Economy of Growth* (New York: Monthly Review Press, 1968), Chaps. 2 – 4.

sector. These dualistic conditions may continue for close to a century, as they did in Japan. However, unlike Japan, most poor countries today have a traditional sector catering to domestic use and an export-oriented sector. Some economists contend that the size and the strength of the export-directed sector determine development. Yet when we examine the record of the underdeveloped world over the past two decades, we find that countries with strong export-oriented sectors did not necessarily achieve conditions of development. Their exports usually consist of agricultural (plantation) products or subsoil raw materials. As exports, these sectors have no forward linkages (that is, output is not used for the domestic production of other goods), and as primary products, they have no strong backward linkages (that is, little of the output of other sectors is needed for production in primary sectors). It is well known that linkages are a key ingredient for achieving economic growth. Backward linkages are propelled by those sectors that use many domestic inputs at various stages of production.

Petroleum for about 20 countries in the world, mainly in the Middle East, has been the main export-directed sector over the last two decades. By nationalizing the industry and by demanding a larger share of the revenue from foreign companies engaged in oil operations, each oil-producing country has succeeded in increasing its total oil revenue. In none, however, have the general conditions of underdevelopment completely disappeared. True, the growth rate measured in monetary value of the gross national product or revenue has increased considerably because of the increasing returns from petroleum, but the general standard of living has not increased commensurately.

Terms of Trade. The tendency to concentrate in one or a few products, usually primary products such as certain agricultural or mining products, makes these countries vulnerable to international price and demand fluctuations.

Countries that produce only bananas, sugar, or tin have no elbow room. They must compete with other countries in the same line. Vagaries of weather as well as of international politics greatly affect how much and at what price such products are sold, if they are sold at all. The dependence of Cuba on sugar and of Jamaica on bauxite are the best examples of struggling, one-export-commodity, poor countries.

These problems of poor countries are known as "terms of trade." This is the relationship between the prices for primary products generally exported by poor countries and the prices for manufactured goods generally imported by poor countries. When the price of sugar is 10¢ per pound and the price of a tractor $20,000, it takes 200,000 pounds (100 tons) of sugar to buy one tractor, but when the price of sugar goes down to 5¢ a pound, then twice as much sugar (200 tons) is required to buy one tractor. Some economists, notably Raul Prebisch of South America, claim that the terms of trade for poor countries have been deteriorating over the last 20 years.

International prices are set through the interaction of demand and supply according to the elasticities of demand and supply. Price elasticity of demand refers to the response of a buyer to a change in price. Demand is generally elastic when the response is strong, and inelastic when there is little or no response, that is, when the quantity purchased does not change much with a change in price. Demand for primary products is quite inelastic, but so is supply. Figure 19.1 shows the interaction of supply and demand based on market supply and demand schedules for a commodity. The price P is obtained with a supply schedule as represented by S. When crops are large or new sellers enter the market, the supply line tends to move to

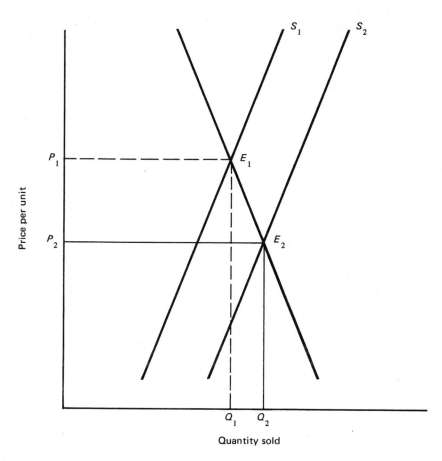

FIGURE 19.1   International price setting as it reflects the interaction
of supply and demand schedules for a commodity. The quantity sold
increases at a lower price and decreases when the price is raised.

the right to S_2, denoting that at every price more of that commodity can be supplied.
Indeed, the total quantity sold is increased (Q_1 to Q_2), but at a much lower price.
This can have a detrimental effect on the total revenue (price per unit, P, times quantity sold, Q) of the producing countries. This larger quantity sold produces a smaller
total revenue (represented by the square 0, P_2, E_2, Q_2) than would selling quantity
Q_1 (represented by the square 0, P, E, Q). This happens because of the specific
price elasticities of demand and supply. With a more elastic demand or supply with
respect to price, less change in total revenue for a change in supply would occur.

Prices of manufactured goods imported by poor countries do not behave alike.
They are usually controlled by a few firms and the supply is not greatly affected by
whether or not new firms enter the market. Therefore, any time the supply of commodities shifts to the right (uniformly at every price), poor countries have to pay
more for manufactured goods. This is why poor countries have asked that prices be

established by international agreement rather than through the market. A few such agreements (for instance, the Coffee Agreement) have been signed over the last few years, thus helping at least some poor countries.

Growth and Development

Growth and development depend predominantly on productive capacity. A country's productive capacity in turn depends on its endowment in natural resources, the quantity and quality of its labor supply, the amount of investment and technological knowledge available, plus the use of all these resources. Poor countries usually have some of these resources, but they do not use them efficiently. While labor may be quantitatively abundant, it usually does not have the necessary training. But the aim of poor countries is to increase capacity in order to raise the standard of living. We call this a supply problem. Supply is the ability and willingness to produce and sell a good at a certain price. In poor countries, the willingness may exist, but the ability is very limited.

Developed economies, with the technology available at present, can produce almost everything that is needed. In these countries, there is usually a problem of demand (ability and willingness to purchase a good at a certain price): how to sell more rather than how to produce more. The goal of developed economies is to generate enough demand both at home and abroad to maintain production at high levels. Even if per capita income is high, the distribution of income or allocation of resources can be such that the majority of people in developed countries have a low per capita income. When this happens, there is not enough demand to maintain total production. This is not to say that there is no problem of demand in poor countries. But since not enough capacity to produce exists in the first place, little income is generated, and therefore little demand arises.

One of the tenets of eighteenth- and nineteenth-century classical economic theory was that supply created its own demand. In other words, the problem was to produce more; production would then be bought up automatically. The reasoning behind this theory is that individuals contribute to production with inputs such as labor, capital, or land; they receive payment for their contributions in the form of wages, interest, and rent. When they receive this payment, they will spend it, that is, they will have the ability to buy, willingness being assumed. Another assumption of this theory is that nobody will withhold any payment; one way or another, they will spend it either on goods for consumption or by putting it back into the business as an investment. However, this closed loop has some basic faults because income is not distributed evenly or even necessarily equitably. When people contribute an input such as labor but their payment in the form of wages does not represent their entire contribution to production, then they will not be able to purchase enough goods and services. When people do not have enough income to purchase goods and services, less of their services will be needed to produce them and thus more people will be unemployed. That is, supply does not necessarily create its own demand.

Disadvantages of Poor Countries. The problems of poor countries today are different from the problems of economies which were on the verge of development a century or two ago. First of all, Western European countries did not then have much competition elsewhere; there were no other developed economies to compete with them. Second, per capita income and literacy are lower in poor countries today than they were in the United States and Europe 100 or 150 years ago. This is why the Western European countries and the United States could afford at that time to have so-called spontaneous development. Government interfered with and encouraged development indirectly rather than directly. In England, international trading companies were chartered and protected by the Royal Navy; in France, industries and agriculture were subsidized; in the United States, land was given to homesteaders, but also 10 percent of the national land heritage was given to the railroads. Agricultural experimentation stations and universities were also developed with the help of, or· by, government.

Today's poor countries need even more prodding and more deliberate governmental direction. Market forces alone, even when combined with encouraging state policies such as existed in Western Europe and the United States over a century ago, are not sufficient to lift these countries out of poverty. International dualism exists today, with the wealthy countries on one side and the poor on the other. Poor countries, because they lack resources, quality production, marketing sophistication, or for a composite of reasons, are not in a position to compete with the production of more highly developed countries. This is why overt governmental policies are needed to help them not only to sustain competition but to create their own production base.

Stages of Economic Growth.   According to Walt Rostow, an economic historian, all countries go through certain stages of economic growth. These stages are: (1) the traditional society; (2) the precondition to takeoff; (3) the takeoff; (4) the drive to maturity; and (5) the age of high mass consumption.

The traditional society is similar to what existed in medieval Europe. The main societal form then was the manor. In a sense, the manor was a closed economic, social, and political system which had little interaction with other manors; exchange was difficult not only because no surplus was being created but also because the use of money as a means of exchange was limited. People used truck or barter, trading one good for another. Money is a measuring rod among products; it is difficult to exchange a tenth of a cow for a pair of shoes; yet money allows exactly this to be done. While money in itself does not produce anything, its use is very important in breaking away from a subsistence economy.

In the second stage, money comes to be used more widely. With the help of money as a means of exchange, some surplus appears in agriculture. The increasing food supply in turn abets the development of cities, because when agricultural production goes beyond what is needed for subsistence, some people can then be employed in other endeavors and be fed by the people who remain in farming. At that stage, agriculture can satisfy the demand of urban areas. Also because the agricultural sector can sell its products to the cities, urban dwellers can then produce a little more efficiently some of the goods that were previously produced on the farm, such as clothing or farm utensils. Therefore, some specialization appears and the supply of goods for the agricultural sector is generated. Production at above subsistence levels in agriculture also provides a surplus that can be used for capital accumulation, either for investment in farm buildings and machinery or for investment in nonagricultural endeavors.

With an increasing surplus in agriculture, the time is ripe for the "takeoff" stage. Historically, this stage is connected with an industrial revolution and rapid structural change. Landlords and serfs are replaced by capitalists and industrial workers. The system of production changes from homespun or cottage industry (a small-scale type of production done at home and not highly specialized) to the factory system, where all factors of production are under the same roof. The factory system depends on hired and more specialized labor. The laborer does not receive payment *directly* for what he produces but *indirectly* for the time and effort he puts into production, and he sells his labor anonymously. The laborer works increasingly with the aid of machinery (capital).

The fourth stage is the drive to maturity. At this point, technological knowledge is widespread, and a country can produce almost everything it desires. Creating capacity (supply) ceases to be a goal. At this stage, the economy becomes demand-oriented. The fifth stage is best exemplified by the United States, where the age of mass consumption started, according to Rostow, when the first Model T Ford car rolled off the assembly line in Dearborn, Michigan.

Growth or Development?   There is still much controversy concerning the "right" way to achieve development. Generally, economic growth means an increase in per capita income — total national income divided by the number of people in a specific country. Economic development is more inclusive; it requires structural changes in the socioeconomy, that is, institutional changes, as well as different relationships among productive factors and an improved standard of living. An area could accomplish economic *growth* without necessarily achieving *development:* total income or average per capita income could increase without an accompanying improvement in the standard of living. Conversely, some areas could achieve some degree of economic development without achieving economic *growth*. For instance, in China per capita income has not substantially improved over the past two decades, in part because of rapid population growth, but also because income has been distributed more equally. Before the Communists came to power in 1949, a few people possessed most of the wealth and income in the country. The vast majority were on the verge of starvation, but this allowed for a surplus. After the revolution, apparently few have gone hungry and living conditions have improved considerably. But a greater equalization of income distribution has not allowed for the accumulation of surpluses.

A surplus appears when not everything of what has been produced is consumed. This surplus is usually called capital. Capital helps people to produce more than they could have produced with their bare hands alone. To this end, growth is an important part of development, because when productivity increases, people can enjoy more material goods. But if the returns of this productivity are lopsidedly distributed among the population (that is, when most of the population still lives in poverty) or if this increase in productivity does not increase the well-being of people (for example, when it goes mostly for the production or purchase of weapons), then economic growth will not necessarily contribute to development.

Furthermore, to achieve economic growth by capital accumulation (surplus), sacrifices are necessary: people must give up something for the present in the expectation of having more in the future. In wealthier countries, where more resources are available for everybody, a decision to sacrifice the present for the future is not so significant. But in a poor country, where people live just above or close to the subsistence level to begin with, they can sacrifice but little. There is no general solution to this dilemma between welfare and growth, that is, between the need to satisfy present wants and the need to create some capital in order to improve future conditions. There is no doubt, however, that the poorer the country is, the fewer the choices it has. The choices relatively open to poor countries involve the size and composition of the population, the structure of the labor force and organization of agriculture, the process of industrialization, the role of government in the productive sector, planning, type and size of education and welfare, regional policies, and international policies.

Organization of the Population

Population pressure exists when individuals consume more than they produce. This is generally true of poor countries, since those added to the population seldom contribute the capital which would make increased production possible. That is why economists talk about the neo-Malthusian problems developing in poor countries. The Reverend Thomas Malthus, an economist of the early nineteenth century, postulated that while population increases in geometrical progression, resources increase in arithmetical progression. Thus, according to him, the time will come when widespread famine will set in because there will not be sufficient resources to satisfy the continuous increase in population.

The Malthusian analysis, however, does not take into consideration technological change. Malthus did not realize that with the aid of technology and capital, people would be enabled to produce more than they consumed; that resources might actually increase faster than population. On the other hand, the Malthusian analysis applies to today's poor countries because a surplus is very difficult to achieve under conditions of continuous population growth. In fact, the population increases even faster today than it did in the past, not because there are more births but because people now live longer. Increased longevity was the result of improvements in sanitation, medicine, and diet. Health progress in poor countries may have some positive effects because more people survive childhood, when they are only consumers, to become producers, or at least potential producers. But the negative effects are overwhelming because, in general, more people must then be fed and cared for and few jobs are created outside agriculture.

Governments could impose, induce, or plead for population reduction or stabilization through a variety of means. One method would be to tax large families rather than to give couples an incentive to have large families through tax rebates for additional children, as is done now in the United States and many other nations. In some countries, the minimum age at which people are permitted to marry is still as low as 10 – 13 years of age. This was reasonable when life expectancy was only 30 years of age, but now, with the increase in longevity, there should be an increase in the minimum age for marriage to 18 or 20, so that the childbearing span of women could be reduced. Also the government could dessiminate birth-control techniques. For instance, the coil costs only a nickel, which makes it appropriate for use in underdeveloped countries. But the populations of underdeveloped countries are generally wary of any interference with their reproductive lives. Alternatively, governments could legalize abortion or give bonuses to those who did not have children. These suggestions have been taken up by India on a small scale, but so far they have not yielded very positive results.

The Labor Force.   Greater population implies a larger labor force. In wealthier countries, the labor force is composed mostly of wage earners. It is very difficult to define a labor force in less developed areas because often entire families are involved in some part of production on the farm. In fact, in most of the underdeveloped areas, 70 – 90 percent of the labor force is in agriculture, with the balance in trade or in small cottage industries. These industries, like agriculture, are characterized by having very little capital (machinery or electric power) to work with. Because of this, productivity (output per worker) is very low. Therefore, more workers do not necessarily mean more production. Also, in many countries, because life expectancy is still low, much of the population is very young. Together with the very old, this dependent population becomes a drain on the working population.

In poor countries, rather than there being a large mass of unemployed people, there are masses of underemployed people. Unemployment means that people are completely out of work for a period of time. Underemployment means that people are working only part of the time or are seasonally unemployed. In general, primitive agriculture is seasonal so that workers are occupied only part of the year. To solve the problem of underemployment, some observers believe that productivity in agriculture could be raised by encouraging an exodus of labor from agriculture. But in underdeveloped agriculture labor is underemployed in part because of seasonal discrepancies between supply and demand and in part because of the limited use of modern technology. Under these conditions, farm labor cannot be transferred to other activities on a permanent basis. The agricultural hiatus produced by China's "Great Leap Forward," when agricultural laborers were kept through the season on other public works, showed that even when population pressure is substantial, the decline of labor availability during the season may bring about an absolute decline in agricultural output. A study of Turkey's agriculture showed that in 1967, 90 percent of the farm laborers were needed in season, and it is expected that almost all will be needed in 1972.[2] Therefore, there is little expendable labor. These examples indicate that the marginal productivity of labor (extra production for each laborer added) in agriculture is far from zero. Removal of any labor during the high season, unaccompanied by any changes in technology or organization, could decrease total agricultural output.

The Agricultural Sector.   The release of agricultural labor for other endeavors requires structural changes in agricultural production. These changes could be achieved through the adoption of modern farm technology and organization. Since peasants usually have limited acreage and since fear of famine is ever present, they tend to grow grains even in places like southern Europe and North Africa where much of the soil is eroded and unfit for these crops. This implies subsistence living: cultivation is for consumption rather than for the market, thereby excluding the peasantry (the majority of the population) from the money economy. No benefits from the division of labor and specialization are possible under these conditions.

During the last century, Japan, through the use of modern technology and intensive farming, succeeded in doubling its agricultural productivity (yield per acre) over a period of 30 years. More recently, Taiwan has almost tripled its productivity in the

---

[2]Gustav Schachter, *Regional Dualism in Turkish Development,* RR No. 23 (Boston: Research Center, Northeastern University, August 1970), pp. 17 – 19.

same period of time. But the successes of Japan and Taiwan, as well as of Denmark and New Zealand, in achieving rapid agricultural development are exceptions rather than the rule.

Agricultural development is very difficult to achieve in today's poor countries, and not merely because of the primitive techniques used. Farm organization is as important as technology for the less developed areas — if not more so. Many economists believe that the reorganization of peasant farming on the basis of owner-operated holdings would be one of the most efficient ways. Owners give tender care to their land and have a greater incentive to improve production. The failures of collective farming in Eastern Europe and the success of owner-operated farms in the United States might be taken as pointing in this direction. However, the reversal in Poland from collective to peasant farming did not bring a marked improvement in production. The success of American agriculture — technology aside — is that it is not and never has been peasant farming but rather a commercial venture, organized along factory lines, based on the specialization of labor and production.

The advantages of commercial farms, operating with hired labor, over peasant-owned holdings are similar to the advantages of the industrial factory over home-spun production. The success of the industrial and agricultural revolutions in Western Europe during the nineteenth century was based on just this type of organization. It is remarkable that thus far the only successful agricultural units in socialist countries have been the "state farms," which are organized on the same basis as are commercial farms in the American West.

Problems of Industrialization

In the 1950's and 1960's remedies for poor countries were sought that were based on models designed to further the development of already highly industrialized nations. Economists and policy-makers from the more advanced countries tended to believe that these models could also be applied to poor countries and that poor countries were capable of becoming copy-images of their own more developed lands. This did not work. First of all, they ignored the initial disparate level of development, and, in the second place, their "Westernizing" goals were resented. Each country has its own cultural and historical heritage, its own institutional framework, its own social and climatic conditions. But the economists of wealthy nations often have difficulty grasping the uniqueness of each area's problems. That is why the models they offered were for rapid industrialization and the development of the same structures that existed in wealthy nations. Economists and advisers are not entirely to blame, however. Often, "Westernizing" is pressed by the leaders of these less developed countries. There is a strong desire to emulate the advanced countries.

In the early stages of the development process, poor countries face more than the choice between primary agriculture and industry. They must also choose between consumption and saving, among various types of industrialization, and between balanced and unbalanced processes of growth. At the same time, the poorer a country is, the less room to maneuver it has. A wealthy nation can choose between building cars or railroads and can sometimes do both (as in Western Europe today). The essential problem is that all countries have a production possibility frontier. With the existing resources and available technology, there is a limit to production and a

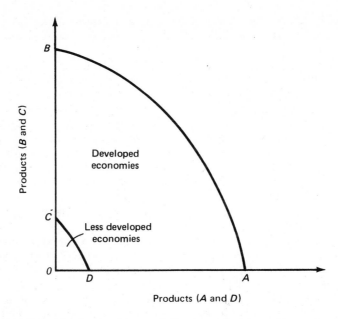

FIGURE 19.2   Production possibility frontiers for wealthy and poor nations. The poorer nation has less area in which it can maneuver its growth.

trade-off occurs. Figure 19.2 attempts to show graphically that a wealthy nation has many choices: the entire area covered by *BOA*. The poor country's area of maneuverability is almost nonexistant in *COD*; for example, not much more output, *C*, could be obtained by giving up *D*.

For the last two decades not much headway has been made in solving the problems of industrialization in poor countries. First, labor tends to move to whatever places of better accommodation exist abroad. Second, small firms have difficulty in acquiring good management, low-interest loans, and adequate channels of distribution. Third, even low interest rates subsidized by the public sector have not attracted moderate-sized enterprises that use labor, rather than capital, intensively. Fourth, local initiative and enterprise are weak. Fifth, outside entrepreneurs lack adequate experience for making investment decisions in less developed areas. No induced investment is possible in these areas because there is no past local experience with a particular investment. In a sense, in less developed areas all investment is autonomous for both outside and indigenous entrepreneurs. An investment is called induced when it depends on a change in demand. When people want more shoes, factories will have to buy more machines to produce the shoes. This investment (production of shoe machinery) is induced by an increase in the demand for shoes. In contrast, autonomous investment occurs when a firm puts up a plant or buys machines or improves its machinery or type of production regardless of sales or the demand for shoes. Since in poor countries income is low, demand for goods and services also tends to be low; therefore, investors cannot benefit from usual market signals of demand. Investments are autonomously derived from some program to achieve a certain goal or are based simply on wishful thinking.

In general, policies for industrial development encourage the establishment of a few large capital-intensive industries. These policies are based on the premise that capital-intensive industries have strong linkages. The creation of an industry creates demand for inputs from another industry (for example, steel, coal, and iron ore). In turn, the output of that industry, steel for example, could be used in other industries such as construction or machinery. That is why these policies promote investment in those branches that supply heavy industry with raw and semimanufactured goods and in those branches whose production depends on heavy industry.

In poor countries, the replacement of labor by machinery may produce a higher yield per man-hour, just as it does in more developed areas. But in poor areas labor is abundant, and capital-intensive techniques displace labor, thus further adding to the already substantial unemployment and underemployment problems. Therefore, the cost of rapidly substituting machines for human labor is often too high to make it economically feasible. Potential labor resources remain underemployed, with a net implicit loss to the economy. For this reason, public policies must encourage those industries which will take into account "labor creation."

Market Discrepancies in Poor Countries

Looking at things more creatively, poor countries have before them the entire gamut of available technology and can make deliberate decisions as to the specific development path best suited to them. The decision must be deliberate because often there are strong discrepancies between the private and social costs involved. For instance, an individual might decide to build a factory to produce electric toothbrushes for domestic consumption. It is questionable, however, that this would be the wisest thing to do with the limited resources available in a poor country (without electricity) even if the product were intended for export.

The marketplace is a poor indication of the choices open to poor countries because of the peculiar behavior of prices: wages (labor prices), exchange rates (prices of foreign exchange), and interest rates (prices of loans or capital).[3]

Wage Rates. In advanced economies, the price of labor is adjusted according to the demand for and supply of laborers. Demand depends on how many workers are available for jobs and how many jobs are available for workers. The price of labor is more or less fixed by the market — as well as by the collective bargaining that takes place between trade unions and corporations. In underdeveloped countries, there is a large pool of underemployed and unemployed labor. Also, laborers are not well organized in unions, as they are in advanced countries. There is a large pool of laborers with an inelastic supply, because for any price (wage) change, the supply of labor (the number of laborers available) remains pretty much the same. Since the demand is also inelastic (because not many more laborers are required at lower wages than at higher wages), there are no demand and supply forces at work. Consequently, wages can go to the bottom, even to below subsistence level.

---

[3]See discussion of this in J. Tinbergen, *The Design of Development* (Baltimore: Johns Hopkins Press, 1958), pp. 39ff.

Exchange Rates. A second discrepancy lies with exchange rates, that is, the value of one currency calculated in terms of another or gold. Usually, the currencies of poor countries are overvalued (they are worth less than officially proclaimed) for reasons of national prestige, which prevents any such national currency from being used in international markets. These are called soft currencies. A hard currency is usually accepted by everybody in trade transactions or deferred payments, that is, for credit. Therefore, poor countries cannot use their own currencies in international transactions.

Interest Rates. Also, interest rates (the price for using funds) in poor countries do not depend as much on the market as they do in advanced countries. For the last 20 years, interest rates in the developed economies have fluctuated between 4 and 10 percent; in underdeveloped countries, they have fluctuated between 10 and 60 percent. This has happened because there are no capital markets (trading in funds) and because there are not many people who want to lend or who want to borrow. Since capital funds are scarce, the rate of interest, or the price for capital, is very high.

Planning and the Role of Government

These discrepancies make the decision-making process for poor nations different from what it is for wealthy nations. Since market forces are not operative, more governmental coordination is required. This is why almost every country in the world has an "economic plan." Such a plan is a kind of balance sheet used by policy-makers to allocate resources in the short run or the long run; it is based on hindsight and/or derived analytically. Such a plan must be comprehensive and consistent. To be comprehensive, it has to cover all aspects of the socioeconomy. To be consistent, allocation of resources must at least equal the availability of resources. For instance, a country cannot decide to operate a steel mill if it has no available funds (in some cases, about half a billion dollars) with which to build the plant.

Planning has for long been "maligned" as a socialist tool of development. It might be socialistic, but it is not Marxist. Karl Marx saw socioeconomic contradictions resolving themselves in new forms of socioeconomic organization and looked upon this process as a "natural" determinant. But this "determinism" is not substantially different from the "invisible hand" concept advanced by his classical precursor Adam Smith. The "invisible hand," as visualized by Smith, consists of natural forces in the marketplace which make for a continuous equilibrium between supply and demand through the price mechanism. Smith could not free himself from scholasticism, including determinism. Yet determinism is the negation of free choice, while planning is an exercise in free choice because it involves *deliberate* action to forge the type of society that citizens (or, more often, their leaders) want.

Planning can be directed in various ways. Soviet and Turkish planning, for instance, are poles apart. The former is centralized, with all decision-making originating in the policy-makers; even at the plant level, day-to-day operations follow a general plan. This type of planning is *operational*. Then there is the *indicative* type of planning, such as is practiced in Turkey, Yugoslavia, and Italy, where policy-makers submit only guidelines, while day-to-day decisions at the plant level are left to local personnel. There are many variations lying between these extremes, but essentially all types of planning control the quantity and often the composition of investment.

In less developed countries over the past two decades the role of the public sector has been considerably larger than it was during the nineteenth century, when the presently developed nations were going through similar stages of economic growth. For the underdeveloped areas, various estimates hold the public sector responsible for nearly 50 percent of total investment. In the less developed economies, because there are no alternatives, the public sector is driven to play an important role in all sectors, including those traditionally reserved for private enterprise in the more advanced economies of the West.

"Balanced" and "Unbalanced" Growth.   It is indeed difficult to specifically pinpoint the prerequisites for growth or development. When more resources are used on roads and housing, fewer resources could be available for manufacturing. On the other hand, in order to have a viable industrial sector, some roads are needed. Some economists believe that a lag between the endowment of social overhead capital, such as roads, water mains, and electricity, and direct productive activities, such as manufacturing, may actually help development. This is an "unbalanced growth" approach, which may act as a springboard: more industries would require more roads and vice-versa.[4] But this does not necessarily have to be symmetrical. Factories and commerce would require a minimum of roads, but one could build roads to eternity without effecting industrial growth or a change in the standard of living.

Generally, the "unbalanced growth" approach makes better sense for poor countries. "Balanced growth" (that is, accelerating economic activity in all sectors) is applicable to wealthier nations where indeed many sectors are already blooming. In poorer countries, with their limited resources, only a few sectors can be primed at one time. Those sectors that are primed act as leaders and create disequilibria in the economy, with the lagging sectors catching up to the leading sectors. Unbalanced growth offers a series of disequilibria to prime socioeconomic change. This replaces the wonders of "innovation" used by advanced countries, where new technologies have been developed. For poorer countries, the "wonder" of discoveries is lacking because the technology exists already. This operates as "induced investment," even though at times actual cash disbursement is not necessary. It acts "psychologically" rather than materially.

Other economists show that there are notable benefits to be derived from the balanced growth approach. For example, one might invest in producing bicycles because a demand for bicycles exists. In poor areas, people may want bicycles, but bicycles have never before been produced or sold there. The investor therefore could not benefit from previous experience. When many sectors are primed at one time, each sector becomes the client of another — both demand and supply are present — and all benefit from external economies; the presence of one industry benefits all the others. For example, a hotel near a railroad terminal benefits from this terminal's existence and vice-versa; once passenger service is abandoned, this hotel most probably will have to close.

In general, external economies arise when social services (such as roads, railroads, education, health services, and so forth) are made available to everyone. External

---

[4]See discussion on this point in Albert O. Hirschman, *The Strategy of Economic Development* (New Haven: Yale University Press, 1959).

economies supplied by the public sector are deliberately intended to promote growth. The source of external economies, however, can be public as well as private. This is so because the additional output of a firm is due not only to its own input but also to the output of all firms existing in the region. Thus, the private sector creates spontaneous external economies via interdependence. External economies appear whenever strong market interdependence among firms exists or is created. External economies are a social concept. Since the public sector assesses economic means from a social rather than an individual (profit) point of view, this sector must be called upon to supply external economies. Advanced countries are endowed with better and more widespread public services and benefit from the external economies provided by an established complex of industries. This could also work for poor countries when the resources are there.

A mixture of balanced and unbalanced growth has been attempted within limited areas ("growth poles") in some countries. The equilibrium between balanced and unbalanced growth is accomplished by the need to have many activities located at one particular place with a small territory. Each enterprise benefits from the external economies furnished by the complementary activity and concentration of the infrastructure. At the same time, an external imbalance is created because other locations do not benefit from these external economies. However, scarce resources in poor countries would in this way be concentrated and the results of these activities could spread to other localities in time. To date, no real success with growth poles has been obtained in poor countries, though some degree of success has occurred in the United Kingdom and the Netherlands.

"When in Doubt, Educate."   It is generally recognized that education creates important external economies. Indeed, most development economists have up until recently stressed the importance of education to the process of economic development. One of the main causes for the backwardness of nations is believed to be lack of education. It is repeatedly pointed out that funding for education is investing in human capital. In other words, accumulated knowledge in a person has the potential to produce further output. From a *development* point of view, education is very beneficial in improving living conditions and in expanding horizons. From an *economic growth* point of view, that may not necessarily be so. It is doubtful that peasants who are going to continue in peasant farming need to be literate. While some credence can be given to the claim that literacy may break the traditional pattern of peasant farming and help bring about a more efficient type of agriculture, if peasants do not apply what they have learned through the organized educational system, they will unlearn even faster than they have learned. Funds used for this type of education are wasted. These funds could be applied more effectively toward improving living conditions. Funds in the underdeveloped countries are limited; there can be alternative uses for them. Frequently, when a choice must be made between educating peasants and some industrial project, political leaders will prefer to encourage literacy simply because they can never be proven wrong. "When in doubt, educate." Yet it still has to be proven that in traditional agriculture there is any correlation between level of literacy and level of output.

Many governments in underdeveloped areas realize the importance of vocational training, but the results to date are not encouraging. On the other hand, the process of "overeducation" is widespread, and at a cost that is not sustainable by poor countries. In India, for instance, tens of thousands of engineers and physicists have been turned out in the last two decades. But the economy has not expanded sufficiently to absorb them. For a while, when the economy of the United States was booming, many of them emigrated here, providing a net gain to the United States and a net loss to India. While India trained them to the age of 22 or 25, they did not contribute at all to India's economy; they were only consumers. Rather, they have contributed to the United States' economy, serving as a sort of foreign aid in reverse. Over the last few years the situation has become even worse because the United States also has unemployed engineers and physicists; the result is that India is producing a horde of unemployed and unemployable specialists.

While education in general effects a widening of horizons, it can be detrimental to the development of a country, not only because fewer goods and services will be produced while the educational process is going on but also because it creates new frustrations among the people who have worked hard at acquiring complex skills in the hope of being able to improve themselves. When an engineer or a physicist has to work as a mechanic or street cleaner in Delhi or Calcutta, this has a psychologically degrading effect on him, not because being a mechanic or a street cleaner is degrading, but because he cannot put to use the skills and knowledge he has acquired.

Sociocultural Problems.

The amount and type of education that is desirable for poor countries remains debatable. Yet the importance of the question is overwhelming in terms of what social changes are conducive to development. Nobody is ever sure what these changes should be. Is "elitism" necessary? What kind of class structure would various changes bring about? In general, many institutional characteristics are detrimental to industrial expansion. Usually in poor countries there is a complete absence of a middle class. Instead there is a large peasantry and a small elite of *intelligentsia* and politicians. Sometimes, especially in the new nations, the army constitutes the elite and is the main political factor. These classes differ from the peasants in that they do not work with their hands.

Religion and Development. Other handicaps originate with religion. For instance, in Moslem countries, it is customary for believers to go to the mosque five times a day. In a modern industrial society, this is impossible because, if tradition were followed, every assembly line would have to stop five times a day. The sacred cow of India supplies manure to fertilize the land but it also consumes large amounts of food without benefiting the population commensurately.

The Problem of Contract. Two other cultural factors impinge even more immediately on economic expansion. First, where contracts are concerned, the cultural pattern in most underdeveloped countries is such that each partner to a transaction feels that he is losing something by the deal. Each side asks himself: "Why should the other party want to conclude this transaction if it were not beneficial to him?" This is why so much bargaining occurs in the bazaars and markets of less developed areas. People simply do not believe that every party can benefit from an exchange or a transaction. To be sure, in a primitive society, not very much exchange occurs because not very much surplus exists; barter or truck take the place of exchange. In a more developed society, where specialization exists, money becomes a means of exchange and a transaction can bring benefits to both parties. But because people in underdeveloped areas do not perceive that benefit, fewer transactions and exchanges occur; therefore, less specialization is possible.

Exaggerated Liquidity Preference. Second, there are few opportunities for investment in poor countries. Also, the possibility of transferring investment funds from one place to another is very limited. This is why individuals who have funds prefer to keep their money in Swiss banks or under the mattress rather than investing it in some productive endeavor. They are afraid of missing out on future opportunities; but by being afraid of missing some chance in the future, they lose out in the present because they do not receive any returns. In addition, the economy suffers because funds which could have been used for productive investments are removed from circulation.

This is known in economics as exaggerated liquidity preference. One prefers liquid assets to anything else. An asset is liquid if it is readily convertible into something else. Cash is the most convertible asset because with it one can readily acquire goods, services, or other assets. An equity stock is less liquid because one has to sell it before one can use it for purchasing something else; real estate or direct investment in a plant are even less liquid because of the time span required to convert such assets. In poor nations, as might be expected, there are only a few such assets but also very few potential buyers. In more advanced countries, one gives up some liquidity for some future opportunities. In poor countries, the same thing could happen, but culturally individuals are not prepared to do this. It means risk-taking and foregoing future idealized opportunities.[5]

The Idea of Change and Group Loyalties. In poor countries, changing cultural patterns is even more difficult to accomplish than changing investment practices or output. In these countries, *the idea of change* is limited because for generations, or even centuries, stagnation has prevailed. Since the experience of the past did not include change, people cannot envision the possibility of change. Their "change" time period is *yarin* or *crass*, which translated from the Arabic or Latin may mean either "tomorrow" or "never." Procrastination is a way of life because nothing seems urgent or possible; people take a static rather than a dynamic view of life.

There is no way to solve sociocultural problems rapidly. Often in poor countries, people feel loyalty only to their restricted families or clans. Indeed, a larger social group like a community, village, city, or nation may be quite incomprehensible to them. The outlook in these countries is parochial. In many ways, the forging of nations out of former colonies has given new impetus to breaking down this attitude and to creating different and wider loyalties. In China, the traditional extended family was replaced in the 1950's by the nuclear type of family common to Western countries. Loyalty to the "head of the family" was transformed into loyalty to the Party or State, thus enlarging the basic social organization.

---

[5]See an excellent analysis of liquidity preference in poor countries in Hirschman, *The Strategy of Economic Development*, Chapter 1.

Nationalism and Foreign Aid

Nationalism may prime the building of a society by bringing about greater inter-dependence and by increasing the general welfare through the contributions and exchanges among large groups of people. Nationalism can be forged by building palaces, pyramids, unneeded airports, or steel mills — because all of these serve as cohesive symbols. From a strictly *cash* economic point of view, such projects may seem wasteful to outsiders; but for the people affected, these works constitute a new source of pride and function as a catalyst for socioeconomic transformation which cannot be measured in dollars and cents alone.

Unfortunately, nationalism has its ugly side in that further waste is created by war or weapons purchases. In 1968, poor countries spent about 5 percent of all their resources (about $22 billion) for military expenditures, more than the total spent on education and public health combined (about $16.5 billion). Under these circum-stances, foreign aid cannot really help. The advanced nations' aid constitutes about one-third of 1 percent of their gross national product, but this is only one-third of the amount that less developed countries spend on military matters. It is also true that foreign aid is often just more military aid. For example, about half the foreign aid given by the United States is military.

In general, foreign aid does not greatly affect the receiver countries. Most of the aid has strings attached; for instance, the receiving country can spend the money it receives only in the donor country. Furthermore, financial aid is neither particularly appreciated nor helpful. It mitigates the balance of payments (foreign payments less receipts) problems of poor countries, but it does not induce enough structural change. Technical assistance and trade are more welcome and useful.

Poor countries are at a disadvantage in international trade. Usually their produc-tivity — output per man-hour — is lower for each single product, though they have a comparative advantage with respect to products depending on labor-intensive techniques. Still, the difference in trade potential between advanced countries and poor countries remains. Under free trade, poor countries could never compete in the world market and develop national industries. The greatest boon, from their point of view, would be to have one-sided tariffs against advanced countries but no tariffs on products sold by the less developed countries.

Conclusions

There is no significant disagreement among economists regarding the need for developing the poor countries. They differ only with regard to the best means of achieving it. It is still questionable whether the free movement of goods and factors of production in an open economy will achieve development in poor countries, when outstanding international differences exist. Classical theorists believe that free trade may lead to factor price equalization. Because of the free exchange of goods, cost of labor-wages, and cost of capital, interest will be the same in all areas. Free movement of resources will cause commodity price equalization (prices of goods and services will tend to be equal everywhere). The location of development will be determined by the attractiveness of resources (or their combination) to private en-trepreneurs. Industries will flock to poor areas to benefit from the low labor costs available there and to rich areas to take advantage of the comparative abundance of capital and external economies. This, of course, will narrow income differentials and close international gaps in a relatively short period of time.

However, historical evidence from many countries demonstrates that market forces alone will not close the international disparity among nations with respect to economic growth. An area left behind economically can never reach a sustained level of development unless adequate measures are taken to counterbalance the advantages enjoyed by the more advanced areas. In other words, development policies favorable to poorer areas are needed to stop the process of spontaneous polarization in areas of already high economic activity. For this, financial aid is less important than technical aid and tariff concessions.

SUGGESTIONS FOR FURTHER READING

Baldwin, Robert E. *Economic Development and Growth.* New York: John Wiley & Sons, 1966.

Baran, Paul A. *The Political Economy of Growth.* New York: Monthly Review Press, 1968.

Bhagwati, Jogdish. *The Economics of Underdeveloped Countries.* New York: World University Library, 1966.

Galbraith, John Kenneth. *Economic Development.* Boston: Houghton Mifflin Co., 1965.

Horowitz, Irving Louis. *Three Worlds of Development,* pp. 271 – 448. New York: Oxford University Press, 1972.

Mishan, E. J. *Technology and Growth: The Price We Pay.* New York: Frederick A. Praeger, 1970.

Myrdal, Gunnar. *The Challenge of World Poverty.* New York: Vintage Books, Random House, 1970.

———. "Political Factors in Economic Assistance," *Scientific American,* Vol. 226, No. 4 (April 1972), pp. 15 – 21.

Pearson, Lester B. *Partners in Development.* New York: Frederick A. Praeger, 1970.

Schumpeter, Joseph A. *The Theory of Economic Development.* New York: Oxford University Press, 1961.

Ward, Barbara. *The Lopsided World.* New York: W. W. Norton & Company, 1968.

20 *World Hunger*

World hunger is by no means a recent problem. Crop failures from drought, flood, blight, or poor farming methods as well as cattle-killing epidemics have been common throughout recorded history. Ancient famines were recorded in the literature of many Asian countries and in the Biblical texts. Every continent has experienced periodic loss of crops and resulting mass starvation. It is said that during the Chinese famines of 1810, 1811, 1846, and 1849, 45 million people starved to death.[1] Of the great famine of 1877 in northern China, historians record that 9,500,000 died from food shortage. The results were proportionately as bad in the Irish famine of 1845 – 1849. Again, in 1892 and 1894, drought in the Chinese provinces of Shansi, Shensi, and Hopei in Mongolia is reported to have caused millions of deaths. India, too, has experienced great famines in the past, as have parts of Africa. During the 1930's, something close to famine stalked many regions of the United States as families stood in line, sometimes for days, awaiting handouts of grain from government supplies.[2] Even today, there is malnutrition and hunger in some of the poverty-stricken rural areas of the United States, particularly in the South, though this has nothing to do with agricultural crop failures.

The Problem

It is obvious that hunger has been one of the world's problems for a long time; but what kind of a problem is it? The causes and cures are neither obvious nor simple. Isn't it true that the United States produces great surpluses of food? If so, then hunger is not the result of a production problem. However, since some regions of the country, and of the world, are in short supply, it may be a distribution problem. It may also be a soil management problem — often combined with a weather problem — as it was

---

[1]George, Cressy, *Land of the 500 Million* (New York: McGraw-Hill, 1955), p. 11.
[2]Studs Terkel, *Hard Times: An Oral History of the Great Depression* (New York: Pantheon, 1970), pp. 232, 233.

when the great Dust Bowl droughts of the South and West produced widespread famine in the United States in the 1930's, or when vast areas of the Middle East eroded into desert in centuries past due to the devastation of forests and natural growth. Yet even with good soil management and reasonable distribution, the rural — and urban — malnutrition that exists today appears to be due more to a lack of income with which to buy food than to an inability to produce food.

Hunger in Asia is said to be due to overpopulation; it is also attributed to the underuse of fertilizers, modern technology, highly productive seeds, and pesticides. A different set of solutions is required for each one of these problems.

Thus hunger is a many-faceted problem. It is partly economic in that there is a need for improved economic incentives to bring about the production of better yields and better distribution patterns, but it is also sociological and educational in that there is a need for new cultural outlooks, more advanced training, and a wider knowledge of technology. The problem can be partly political too according to whether the government fixes low prices (as in India) or high prices (as in the United States), or whether it legislates output quotas or obstructs distribution. Low prices for food in India, designed to keep the masses content, penalize the farmer and give him little incentive to improve his yield and income, whereas high-support prices in the United States have tended to favor the giant and prosperous farmer rather than the small, poor farmer who most needs help. Mechanization makes farming highly productive, but creates rural unemployment; and, later, when families move to cities, it creates urban unemployment and high welfare costs for cities.

All these considerations and paradoxes will enter into this examination of the problem of hunger. Since the problem itself is many-sided, solutions to it will inevitably be equally so.

The Historical Perspective: Prophets of Doom

There have long been sincere and intelligent people who were certain that the world would eventually run out of food, not to mention other natural resources generally deemed "essential."

Just after World War II, when the industrialized world — and at least part of the less developed world — was about to launch its period of greatest prosperity, one best-selling author of 1948, William Vogt, concluded his book, *Road to Survival*, with the dire threat that "Unless man readjusts his way of living, in its fullest sense, to the imperatives imposed by the limited resources of his environment, we may as well give up all hope of continuing civilized life. Like Gadarene swine, we shall rush down a wartorn slope to a barbarian existence in the blackened rubble." However, the decade of the 1950's actually turned out to be more prosperous, at least for the Western world, than had the previous decade of high-level economic activity generated by the war and its aftermath.

The 1960's produced still another crop of pessimists warning of disaster ahead. William and Paul Paddock, for example, in their 1967 book *Famine 1975!* were predicting that the battle to feed humanity was over and that many millions of human beings would die from famine by 1975 because of the world's inability to produce adequate food supplies. The Paddocks were joined by W. Osborne, Paul Ehrlich, C. P. Snow, and many other gloomy prognosticators who repeated the same theme.

All of this is recent history; yet the threat of world, not just regional, starvation has bothered mankind for centuries. Thomas Malthus was perhaps the earliest — and certainly the most famous — proponent of a subsistence theory of survival. As far back as 1798, when his best-selling *Essay on the Principle of Population* first appeared, Malthus had concluded that the ability (or inability) of man to increase the output of food would provide the ultimate check on population growth. According to Malthus, the earth could only yield food increases at an arithmetical rate (2,4,6,8,10), while population growth was doomed to progress geometrically (2,4,8,16,32).

What is the lesson in all this? On the one hand, for decades and even centuries, there have been warnings of impending world hunger, while the world's capacity, by some combination of circumstances, seems thus far to have proven the predictors of mass famine quite wrong.

Or has it? In this chapter we shall examine the productive potential of agriculture in the United States and the rest of the world for satisfying man's most basic requirement — food. Special consideration will be given to the United States because of its importance as a world supplier of food and because of its leadership in the technological revolution in agriculture. Areas of the world where hunger appears to be most threatening will be given special attention.

In the United States — Abundance

The enormous capacity of the United States to produce food is well known. For example, U.S. farmers produced nearly 1.5 billion bushels of wheat in 1969, though Americans consumed only about one-half that quantity. According to the Department of Agriculture's Economic Research Service, the U.S. stockpile of wheat in 1970 was 2.3 billion bushels, even after over 700 million bushels had been exported.[3] This immense productivity can be attributed to (1) the extensive acreage of fertile soil in this country; (2) the mechanization of agriculture; (3) the use of quality seeds, ample fertilizers, and pesticides; and (4) improved cultivation and other techniques.

In 1870, there were 408 million acres of land devoted to farming, but a hundred years later there were 1.1 billion acres under cultivation — despite the popular impression that total farmland has been decreasing. Over the period mentioned, the value of farm machinery used increased from $271 million to over $30 billion, while the use of commercial fertilizers increased more than a hundredfold — from a total of 321,000 tons in 1870 to about 40 million tons by 1970. The increased use of machinery on the farm reduced cost per worker and greatly increased output per man-hour, making possible a sharp decline in the need for laborers on U.S. farms, from about 15 million farm workers in 1870 to less than 4 million by 1970.

The effectiveness of the use of quality seeds, machinery, fertilizers, improved cultivating techniques, and other inputs is dramatically measured in the phenomenal rise in the value of the output produced on America's farms. U.S. farmers produced $2.5 billion worth of goods in 1870, but the value of farm output had soared to well over $50 billion by 1970 — again a hundredfold increase. Put another way, the value of output per worker increased from $167 in 1870 to $21,500 per worker in 1970. This growth in productivity per worker is a reflection of the miles of planting and harvesting accomplished when farmers apply modern, giant-sized machines to farming.

[3]U.S. Department of Agriculture, Economic Research Service, *Wheat Situation*, May 1971, p. 2.

Less Labor, More Output.   The miracle of farming in the United States is in that key word, productivity — getting more and more out of the farmland for less and less human input. As indicated before, the number of laborers on the nation's farms has decreased by well over 10 million in the past 100 years, while the value of the output of farms has increased a hundredfold during the same period. What has happened to all the laborers who left the farms? Those forced to abandon farming have taken up other occupations and, in many cases, settled in or near the large metropolitan areas of the country where job opportunities are, generally, more abundant.

It does not follow from these facts that *all* the families or laborers who remained on American farms increased their productivity and thereby earned more income. A significant proportion of U.S. farms — over 20 percent — consist of 50 acres or less, and 60 percent of the farms are 100 acres or less in size. Although much depends on what is grown (huge farms are not needed for profitable vegetable-growing, for example), often this size farm can barely make ends meet, let alone provide a surplus for investing adequately in equipment or commercial fertilizer. Moreover, because of their size, these small farms do not usually qualify for the U.S. subsidy programs. This is paradoxical because one would assume that the so-called farm problem had to do with alleviating poverty. Instead, the purpose of the subsidy programs is to minimize disastrous price and income fluctuations for farmers, and quite often it is the largest of them who benefit the most.

This is not the place to discuss the merits and demerits of the United States farm program, which is a subject by itself. It has long been a matter of controversy, but several observations can be made without fear of contradiction.

First, no matter what modifications of the program have taken place over the years — as between high government price supports and partial cash subsidies to farmers, for example — U.S. agriculture has continued to increase its productivity and to satisfy all domestic needs and much more besides.

Second, the cost of the farm subsidy program is rapidly declining as a portion of the total federal budget. For fiscal year 1973, for instance, it ran about $4 billion out of a total budget of almost $250 billion. Whether it is, or is not, the best possible program, it is undoubtedly a factor in keeping many farmers in the business of farming and making some profit.

Third, one part of the program has long involved an effort to reduce surpluses by retiring land from production: the so-called "soil bank" program and others with the same purpose. Yet these programs are an admission of the fact that the United States could readily produce much more food than it presently does.

The longer-term future for food output in the United States — looking into the twenty-first century — could be either good or bad depending on how the rest of the world's food needs are met. If food output in the rest of the world lags far behind the growing demand, U.S. stocks and idle acres will be used to meet the essential needs of starving people elsewhere. If the rest of the world generates higher production levels, the pressure on U.S. supplies will ease.

Present indications are that the U.S. food industry will move ahead for many years to come, yielding remarkable abundance and variety in the mix of foods it is able to produce for the marketplace. Already, there is a plentiful diversity in foods of every category to suit all tastes and needs. For example, there are 350 different food suppliers, over 200 baking mix and flour suppliers, and even more than 100 suppliers of different pet foods. Food processing now caters to the tastes and recipe preferences of each state in the union, while concentrated additives to various foods provide the dietary balance and nutritional fortification needed to combat fatigue, disease, and various blood deficiencies. There is every expectation among the experts that the trend toward sophisticated preparations and packaging, as well as toward concentrated food fortifications which give more physical and mental energy per ounce, will continue into the next century, and that such advanced countries as the United States, Japan, or West Germany will lead the way in this dynamic process.

We have given special attention to the food-producing capacity of the United States partly because of its relative significance in the world's trade in food crops. For example, the United States accounts for over 75 percent of the entire world's noncommercial — sold on "easy" terms — wheat exports to developing countries. In the early 1960's, it accounted for as much as 98 percent. The commercial exports of the United States are now about equal to U.S. noncommercial exports, as Figure 20.1 shows. Noncommercial exports are provided for under the Public Law 480 loan

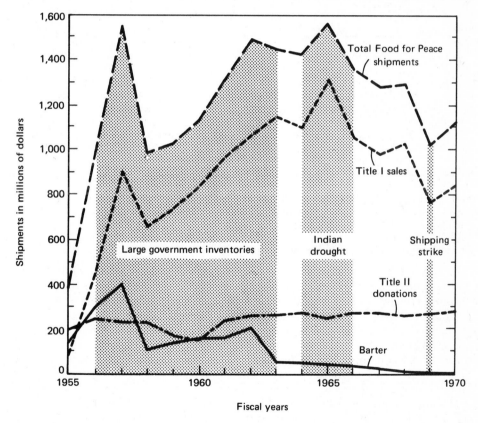

FIGURE 20.1 U.S. agricultural shipments under PL 480. U.S. low-cost food shipments are substantial but have been declining since 1965. Title I sales include long-term credit sales for foreign currency, dollars, and convertible foreign currency. Title II donations include government-to-government donations through American voluntary relief organizations and multilateral organizations such as World Food Program. Data for 1970 is estimated. [Source: Quentin M. West, *War on Hunger* (A Report from the Agency for International Development), Vol. 4, No. 5 (May 1970), p. 15.]

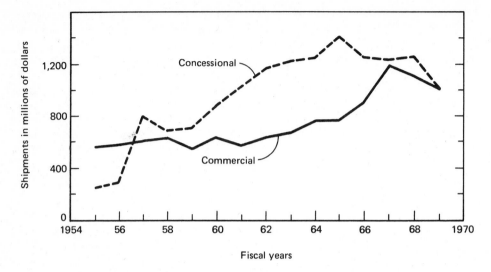

FIGURE 20.2 Commercial and concessional value of U.S. agricultural exports to less developed nations. While low-cost (concessional) farm exports have been declining, commercial sales have caught up. [Source: Quentin M. West, *War on Hunger* (A Report from the Agency for International Development), Vol. 4, No. 5 (May 1970), p. 15.]

and grant food programs for countries and voluntary agencies in need. Figure 20.2 shows the trend in these shipments since 1955.

In the Rest of the World — Threat of Hunger?

Outside the United States, there are, of course, other developed countries which have high food productivity. Canada's wheat stocks achieved such a high level in 1970 (one billion bushels) that wheat acreage was reduced by 50 percent to cut the inventory stockpile. Australia had to set lower marketing quotas and reduce guaranteed prices in 1969 because of record stocks of wheat. The *Financial Times* of London stated on March 25, 1971, that, ". . . it can be taken for granted that there are too many farmers in Europe."[4] To induce farmers to leave the land, European governments provide subsidies, enforce small farm amalgamation schemes, and establish training programs to help young farm people make the transition to industry.

In sum, for many years the most advanced areas of the world have had a food crop *surplus* problem, which has led to drastic cutbacks in land use for crop output, sharp reductions in the number of families and workers living on farms, and the promotion of schemes to coax owners of small farms to leave the land in favor of other means of making a living.

Thus far, this does not sound much like a world hunger problem. Yet we know that in certain regions, even in the developed countries, hunger and malnutrition exist. We also know that famines have occurred in recent years in India, Pakistan,

---

[4]"The Angry Farmers of Europe," London *Financial Times,* March 25, 1971.

Biafra, and elsewhere. It is clear from the description of the enormous food productivity and surplus situations in the developed, or advanced, areas of the world that there is, at least, a serious distribution problem in the world's food system. It does not seem rational that one-quarter of the world's people should be vigorously pursuing policies to reduce their surpluses while the other three-quarters endure periodic or regional famine or chronic undernourishment. Yet this is the essential paradox of the world food system.

Historic Trends and Modern Miracles.   What does the long view tell us about agriculture? We can start with an example. The fact is that throughout the 50-year period preceding the end of World War II, India and Pakistan were experiencing a deadening downward drift in annual food crop production. The average annual production of food crops in India in the years 1893 – 94 to 1895 – 96 was 74 million tons.[5] The average for the 10 years before World War I was about the same, while the average for the 20-year period beginning in 1926 was less than 70 million tons. During this whole period, the population had increased nearly 40 percent. The result, therefore, was a significant decline in food crop output per capita, exceeding 30 percent.

Fortunately, since World War II, the gradual accumulation of new techniques, the years of research on new seed varieties, and the education of farmers in many parts of the world have all combined to produce a modern revolution in world agriculture.

The new "miracle" high-yield seeds, inputs of fertilizer and pesticides, ingenious use of new water sources, and improved knowledge of cultivation have helped bring about the so-called Green Revolution. Only a few years ago, Pakistan's use of fertilizer was negligible. In 1960, it was 30,000 tons; by 1967, it was 185,000; and in 1969, 420,000 tons. The story is similar in India. Before 1960, fertilizer use was rare, but by 1964 it had reached 600,000 tons; by 1967, it was 1.3 million tons; and in 1968, 2 million tons. In other countries, the record is similar. The farmers themselves pay for many of these new inputs, but the United States and other countries have joined the local governments in subsidizing the effort. The United States, for example, financed $200 million worth of U.S. fertilizer exports to India in 1969, while the Indian government provided another $120 million from its own scarce "hard" foreign currencies to buy fertilizer, high-yield seeds, and pesticides. India has also undertaken to build new fertilizer plants so that it can supply its own needs. U.S. firms have invested heavily in new Indian and Pakistani fertilizer plants, together with Indian and Pakistani businessmen, in the full expectation of making a profit.

The importation of new high-yield varieties of wheat, rice, and other food grains has produced increases in output of from two to four times that attained by the old seeds and methods. By 1972, the new varieties were planted on about 15 million acres in India, on nearly 5 million acres in Pakistan, and on close to 500,000 acres in Turkey. The word is spreading rapidly among farmers of the impact of these new seeds, so that soon impressive increases in output will probably be noticeable in areas hitherto unaffected. Meanwhile, research continues to investigate ways of improving the yields from corn, millet, and sorghums as well.

---

[5]Daniel Thorner, "Long Term Trends in Output in India," in S. Kuznets et al, *Economic Growth* (Durham, N.C.: Duke University Press, 1955), pp. 121, 124. Also, Richard J. Ward, "Long Think on Development," *International Affairs,* January 1970, p. 12.

In some areas, the Green Revolution has produced such phenomenal results that problems of storage, distribution, and buffer stock-building, as well as second-generation problems related to new plant diseases immuned to pesticides; are of more concern today than are shortages of supply. A former importer, Japan, has accumulated large stocks of rice. Pakistan exported 120,000 tons of rice in 1968 and more than that in 1969 — hardly a practice to be indulged by a starving nation. Self-sufficiency in food grains has become a realistic target for Iran, Afghanistan, India, Ceylon, Nepal, and other Asian countries.

A report made in the London *Financial Times* in March 1971 indicated that because of the substantial increase in world rice supplies, particularly in Asia (which produces 90 percent of the world's rice), sharp price declines in rice have been averted only because of acreage restrictions applied to the commodity by the United States and Japan.

The Disincentives Paradox.   Thus far, we do not seem to have been discussing world hunger so much as world abundance. Before qualifying some of the optimistic trends we have noted, or predicting the longer-term future, it is important to know what other factors — besides new high-yield seeds, increased use of fertilizers and pesticides, and better usage of water — have contributed to the transformation in agriculture that has been going on outside some of the advanced high-productivity countries.

For years prior to the mid-1960's, some countries, through government planning, maintained low prices on their food crops. They did this not only to keep the basic food items cheap enough so that the poor could buy them but also to avoid the political unrest that higher prices might cause. Basically, it was a social policy. It was assumed to be humane, good for the masses, and economical. Then economic advisers from the World Bank, the U.S. Agency for International Development, and other donor countries urged abandonment of this price policy in favor of allowing the price to drift upward, in order to give farmers an incentive to buy better seeds, more fertilizers, and other inputs to increase their yields. In sum, it was thought that the former price policy discouraged production and productivity, while the higher price policy would encourage it.

At the same time, the U.S. program for providing grains as grants under Public Law 480 to countries showing food grain shortages was scrutinized for its dampening effect on local grain prices in the countries receiving these commodities. If the United States was pumping its surplus grains into India, Pakistan, Turkey, or Indonesia, how could the local prices rise and how could local farmers be stimulated to increase output to meet the supply shortage?

Thus, the paradox of food aid was that U.S. grain crop and/or flour grant programs were far from economical in the long run. By hindering rather than helping the local farmer in his effort to produce more efficiently and for a larger market, these imports literally destroyed motivation to improve productivity.

Gradually, the PL 480 programs have changed. Most of the commodities provided are no longer received under grants, but must be paid for under loan agreements, with the exception of food grains for emergency situations, which remain donations, as Figure 20.2 indicates. With completely "free" food (from the United States) less available, recipient countries now have more incentive to increase their own output.

To illustrate: in five years, West Pakistani farmers had invested, out of their own resources, $50 million to build tube wells which would give them a dependable source of water for their crops. To earn such sums, these farmers had to rely on good markets for their crops. If PL 480 commodities had flooded the world markets with wheat, rice, and other staples, these Pakistani farmers could not have received a price for their harvest sufficient to enable them to save enough to purchase the tube wells.

Bottlenecks to Progress

Traditionally, there have been cultural as well as economic obstructions to rising farm productivity in developing countries. For instance, where a system of absentee land-ownership has prevailed for generations, owners are not always progressive in their outlook; but where farmers are given a stake in their own acreage, productivity almost inevitably increases. Many countries in the Near East and South Asia have carried out land reform programs in order to give the farm laborer an incentive to produce more efficiently for better profits. Africa and Latin America, too, have introduced land reform programs designed to change the cultural milieu in favor of incentives to share in the rewards of successful farming.[6]

Another serious drawback to farmers who cannot afford to buy better seed varieties, fertilizers, or pesticides without borrowing is the high interest rate on credit. When local money lenders charge interest rates of 20 to 50 percent or more on their loans, farmers either refuse to borrow or, in paying back, never get sufficiently ahead to benefit from borrowing. The high cost of money for farm improvement has traditionally been a disincentive to improved farming in many less developed lands. The creation of low-interest agricultural cooperatives and banks, together with the better price outlook for crops, has contributed to the agricultural revolution of increased production that has been taking place in these areas.

The so-called extended family has also been a deterrent to increased farm productivity because it has placed a heavy obligation on the senior member of the family to "take care" of all his relatives, no matter how tenuous or remote the relationship. In such a system, common to Asia, a bumper crop usually meant that each member or unit of the family tribe would simply receive a somewhat heartier repast than before. The farmer's immediate family would not reap the whole, or possibly even a substantial part, of the benefit. This contributed to the perpetuation of a low level of aspiration. This system has by no means disappeared, but there is increasing evidence that such burdening obligations are declining, so that farmers may save out of their surpluses — by selling for cash — and invest in the inputs needed to increase productivity.

Finally, the set of circumstances described above which has helped to perpetuate subsistence conditions in the rural areas of the less developed world, combined with the philosophical belief in a passive dependency on God for all favors, or lack of them, has fostered a pervasive *fatalism* in much of Asia which, in the deepest rural enclaves, is slow to yield to modernizing influences. But it is yielding where the opportunity to benefit from enterprising practices has been demonstrated.

---

[6]William Barber, "Land Reform and Economic Change Among African Farmers in Kenya," *Economic Development and Cultural Change*, October 1970, pp. 6 – 24; A. H. Bunting "Research and Food Production in Africa, in Daniel Aldrich, ed., *Research for the World Food Crisis* (Washington, D.C.: American Association for the Advancement of Science, 1970); Montague Yudelman, *Agricultural Development in Latin America* (Washington, D.C.: Inter-American Development Bank, 1966).

In spite of all the hopeful signs conveyed by these facts, the world is still subject to occasional famines and, what is even more germane, to extensive malnutrition. One cannot be complacent about the outlook for world food *consumption* patterns, as distinct from trends in *production* patterns. In view of the encouraging assessment of the world's productive capacity, some blame for famines and malnutrition must be placed on *poor storage and distribution systems*. The picture of India's bumper crops piled up in village centers, where they were exposed to weather and to rat and insect infestation, perfectly illustrates what can result from deplorable storage and distribution arrangements. The serious Indian famine of 1966, though nothing like those of a century ago, significantly enough took place in the province of Bihar, even while stockpiles of food existed in other provinces of the country. This situation came about because provincial leaders would not agree to release their own hard-won surpluses for fear of losing the security that such stocks gave the inhabitants of their own provinces. Moreover, storage and distribution facilities were woefully inadequate and inefficient.

The starvation in the Nigerian province of Biafra, so thoroughly covered by the communications media during the civil war that took place there in 1969 – 70, was due not to world shortages of food, but to local political ineptness as well as to storage and distribution inadequacies. Why should citizens of Bihar or children of Biafra starve when the developed world has well over 2 billion bushels of wheat in storage? It would seem that it is not the productivity side of the equation that is at fault, but the management of the world's abundance.

It is, therefore, important to realize that most famines in the world are caused not by deficient farm output in general but by droughts, blights or pests; by wars and civil disturbances and natural catastrophes such as floods or earthquakes; and by the inadequacies of distribution practices. Natural catastrophes are difficult to plan for, yet even here, distribution is a key factor. In March 1971, Dr. Jean Mayer, Professor of Nutrition at Harvard, wrote in *War on Hunger*:

> In spite of the efforts by some of the leaders of FAO [Food and Agriculture Organization of the U.N.], a World Food Bank or regional food banks for emergency situations have not come into existence. Where there is thus no universal and automatic pathway for famine relief, the continued availability of large surpluses of cereals in the United States, Canada, France and other countries makes relief possible; but in spite of the creation of such national organizations as Food for Peace, the actual process of relief is often slow and cumbersome.

Aside from these basic famine situations, the world problem of malnutrition or dietary deficiency is far more critical. This is partly so because of the fact that undernourished individuals seem to carry on, working, though not efficiently, and surviving to middle age. The cumulative effect of mass malnutrition on a country like India is to reduce the incentive and the ability to work for or even to aspire to a better life. Instead, it produces stunted bodies and minds, which in turn yield low returns in whatever occupations or roles these people find themselves. Such malnutrition can be partly attributed to the ineffective distribution of food grains, but it is also caused by inadequate balance in the diet, in the form of a deficiency in meat, fish, or vegetables.

Future Prospects

These pockets of famine or malnutrition aside, the *productivity potential* of the world in output of food is undoubtedly very great. The developed countries could markedly increase their capacities if they so chose. Already, the less developed areas of the world are finding the way toward food self-sufficiency. Crop diversification programs are being implemented to provide improved and balanced diets. Research is actively uncovering new opportunities and techniques for Asian, African, and tropical agriculture.

The long-run prospect for certain agricultural categories has been developed by the Food and Agriculture Organization of the United Nations, as indicated in Table 20.1.

Table 20.1   Per Capita Food Output Will Continue to Grow: Composition of Gross Value of Agricultural Production 1962[a] and 1985, by Regions[b,c]

	Africa south of Sahara		Asia and Far East		Latin America		Near East and Northwest Africa		Zone C (study countries)	
	1962[a]	1985	1962[a]	1985	1962[a]	1985	1962[a]	1985	1962[a]	1985
	Thousand million dollars									
Crops	5.44	11.06	22.12	52.96	8.89	17.71	3.62	8.08	40.06	89.81
Livestock	0.82	2.53	3.55	9.64	5.19	12.26	1.84	4.36	11.39	28.80
Crops and livestock	6.25	13.59	25.67	62.60	14.08	29.97	5.45	12.44	51.45	118.60
Fisheries	0.12	0.38	1.12	2.60	0.24	0.54	0.09	0.16	1.56	3.67
Forestry	0.46	0.83	0.50	1.25	0.85	1.98	0.08	0.16	1.89	4.22
Total agriculture	6.83	14.80	27.28	66.45	15.17	32.48	5.62	12.76	54.90	126.49
	Growth rates 1962[a] to 1985 (percent per year)									
Crops	3.1		3.9		3.0		3.6		3.6	
Livestock	5.0		4.4		3.8		3.8		4.1	
Crops and livestock	3.4		3.9		3.3		3.7		3.7	
Fisheries	5.3		3.7		3.6		2.8		3.8	
Forestry	2.6		4.1		3.7		2.9		3.5	
Total agriculture	3.4		3.9		3.4		3.6		3.7	

Source: Food and Agriculture Organization, *A Strategy For Plenty: The Indicative World Plan for Agricultural Development* (Rome: FAO, 1970), p. 8.

[a] 1961 – 1963 average.
[b] Totals and growth rates calculated from unrounded figures.
[c] 1985 data include additional pork and poultry alternative "A."

If world population is increasing at an average of 3 percent a year or less, it is clear from the table that food output per capita will be increasing, at least until 1985. This is hardly a forecast of widespread starvation. The chances are that such trends will continue on into the twenty-first century unless unforeseen events or catastrophes distort the expected trend. In all categories of food output, including livestock and fisheries, the trends are above the average world population growth of 3 percent a year (except for fish in the Near East and Northwest Africa).

Moreover, all the farm inputs discussed are projected by the FAO to continue to play a growing role in promoting future productivity, as Figure 20.3 indicates.

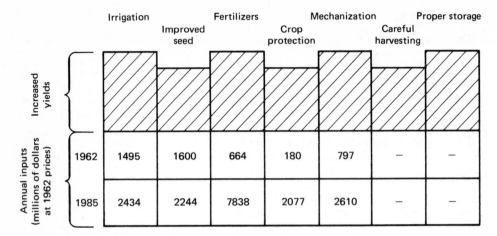

FIGURE 20.3   Modern technology is the key to greater crop production. (Data not available for Items 6 and 7.) [Source: Food and Agriculture Organization, *A Strategy for Plenty: The Indicative World Plan for Agricultural Development* (Rome: FAO, 1970).]

The increase in these inputs, however, cannot occur without cost. The FAO estimates that the cost to less developed countries of all seeds, feeds, pesticides, mechanization, irrigation, land improvement, and fishery equipment will be $5 billion a year up to 1985, as Table 20.2 shows. However, the rate of increase in the cost of inputs will about equal the rate of increase in food output at 3.5 percent a year.

Table 20.2   The Cost of Increasing Farm Output: Identified Current Inputs and Investment Requirements [a] of Zone C Study Countries

	Value		Change	Growth rates
	1962*	1985	1962* to 1985	1962* to 1985
Identified current inputs	Million dollars at 1962* prices		Percent	Percent per year
Seed	1,673.1	2,473.6	+ 48	1.7
Feed	3,028.8	6,993.8	+ 131	3.7
Fertilizers	671.4	8,362.4	+1,146	11.6
Crop protection [b]	180.0	2,076.9	+1,054	11.2
Mechanization	797.1	2,610.2	+ 227	5.3
Irrigation	1,494.7	2,433.7	+ 63	2.1
Total crops and livestock	7,845.1	24,950.6	+ 218	5.2
Fishery	358.9	983.7	+ 174	4.5
Forestry	183.9	413.0	+ 125	3.6
Total identified inputs	8,387.9	26,347.3	+ 214	5.1
Total output (gross value)	54,900.1	121,640.4	+ 122	3.5
Ratio input/output	15.3	21.7		

	Cumulative 1962 to 1985	Distribution
Identified investment requirements	Million dollars at 1962* prices	Percent
Land improvement and development	47,100	42
Equipment, machines, etc. [c]	39,064	35
Livestock inventory and buildings	18,229	16
Fisheries: vessels, etc.	4,329	4
Forestry and logging	3,743	3
Total identified investments	112,465	100

Source: FAO, *A Strategy for Plenty* (Rome: FAO, 1970), p. 48.

[a] As taken from regional studies.
[b] Excluding Central America.
[c] Excluding Africa, south of the Sahara.

Notwithstanding the general rise in per capita food output that is expected to be maintained around the world, the problem of achieving nutritionally balanced diets for the world's peoples will remain for a long time. This is reflected in Table 20.3, which shows the low per capita incomes in many countries around the world.

Table 20.3   Africa: Population (mid-1968), GNP Per Capita (1968), and Average Annual Growth Rates (1961-1968)

No.	Country	Population (1,000)	GNP Per Capita (US $)	Growth Rates Population (%)	Growth Rates GNP Per Capita (%)
1	Nigeria	62,650	70	2.4	-0.3
2	United Arab Rep.	31,693	170	2.5	1.5
3	Ethiopia	24,212	70	2.0	2.6
4	South Africa	19,781	650	2.3	3.7
5	Congo, Dem. Rep. of	16,730	90	2.1	-0.3
6	Sudan	14,770	100	2.9	-0.4
7	Morocco	14,580	190	2.9	0.4
8	Algeria	12,943	220	2.3	-3.5
9	Tanzania	12,508	80	2.5	1.2
10	Kenya	10,209	130	2.9	1.4
11	Ghana	8,376	170	2.7	-0.7
12	Uganda	8,133	110	2.5	1.1
13	Mozambique	7,274	200	1.3	3.6
14	Malagasy Republic	6,500	100	2.4	-0.2
15	Cameroon	5,590	140	2.2	1.1
16	Angola	5,362	190	1.3	2.1
17	Upper Volta	5,175	50	2.2	0.1
18	Southern Rhodesia	4,940	220	3.2	-0.1
19	Mali	4,787	90	2.1	1.3
20	Tunisia	4,660	220	2.3	2.7
21	Malawi	4,270	50	2.6	2.2
22	Ivory Coast	4,100	260	2.8	4.8
23	Zambia	4,065	220	3.0	3.6
24	Niger	3,806	70	3.6	-1.6
25	Guinea	3,795	90	2.7	2.7

No.	Country	Population (1,000)	GNP Per Capita (US$)	Growth Rates	
				Population (%)	GNP Per Capita (%)
26	Senegal	3,685	170	2.1	-1.4
27	Chad	3,460	60	1.5	-1.5
28	Burundi	3,406	50	2.0	0.0
29	Rwanda a	3,405	70	3.1	1.5
30	Somalia a	2,747	60	4.0	0.2
31	Dahomey	2,571	80	2.9	1.1
32	Sierra Leone	2,475	150	1.3	1.5
33	Libya	1,803	1,020	3.7	19.4
34	Togo	1,769	100	2.6	0.5
35	Central African Rep.	1,488	120	2.4	-0.6
36	Liberia	1,130	210	1.7	0.7
37	Mauritania	1,120	180	1.8	11.3
38	Lesotho a	910	80	2.9	1.2
39	Congo, People's Rep. of	870	230	1.5	2.2
40	Mauritius a	787	230	2.5	-1.8
41	Botswana a	611	100	3.0	0.8
42	Portuguese Guinea	529	230	0.2	4.3
43	Gabon	480	310	0.9	0.7
44	Reunion	426	610	2.9	4.4
45	Swaziland a	395	200	2.8	5.4
46	Gambia a	350	100	2.0	-0.1
47	Equatorial Guinea	281	260	1.8	4.6
48	Comoro Islands	260	120	3.7	4.5
49	Cape Verde Is.	245	110	2.6	-1.8
50	Ceuta and Melilla a	162	300	0.9	3.5
51	French Territory of Afars & Issas	84	620	1.4	6.8
52	Sao Tome and Principe	65	290	0.2	-0.1
53	Ifni a	55	160	1.5	3.0
54	Seychelles Is. a	50	70	2.2	-0.3
55	Spanish Sahara a	48	240	2.0	4.1

Source: International Bank for Reconstruction and Development (World Bank) *Atlas,* September 1970.

a Estimates of GNP per capita and its growth rate are tentative.

Table 20.4   Asia: Population (mid-1968), GNP Per Capita (1968), and Average Annual Growth Rates (1961-1968)

No.	Country	Population (1,000)	GNP Per Capita (US$)	Growth Rates	
				Population (%)	GNP Per Capita (%)
1	China (*Mainland*) b	730,000	90	1.5	0.3
2	India	523,893	100	2.5	1.0
3	Pakistan	123,163	100	2.6	3.1
4	Japan	101,090	1,190	1.0	9.9
5	Philippines	35,883	180	3.4	0.8
6	Thailand	33,693	150	3.1	4.6
7	Korea, Rep. of	30,470	180	2.7	5.6
8	Iran	27,150	310	3.0	5.0
9	Burma	26,353	70	2.1	1.6
10	Vietnam (*North*) b	20,700	90	3.2	3.3

No.	Country	Population (1,000)	GNP Per Capita (US$)	Growth Rates Population (%)	GNP Per Capita (%)
11	Vietnam, Rep. of	17,414	130	2.7	1.9
12	Afghanistan	16,113	80	2.0	-0.3
13	China, Rep. of	13,466	270	3.0	6.5
14	Korea *(North)* [b]	13,000	250	2.6	5.9
15	Ceylon	11,970	180	2.4	2.3
16	Nepal	10,652	80	1.8	0.3
17	Malaysia	10,386	330	3.1	4.3
18	Iraq	8,634	260	2.8	2.9
19	Saudi Arabia	7,112	360	1.7	7.2
20	Cambodia	7,087	120	3.4	0.6
21	Syria	5,701	210	2.8	3.5
22	Yemen [a]	5,440	70	2.1	2.0
23	Hong Kong	3,927	710	3.1	8.1
24	Laos [a]	2,825	100	2.4	0.2
25	Israel	2,745	1,360	3.3	4.7
26	Lebanon	2,580	560	2.6	2.4
27	Jordan	2,103	260	2.7	4.8
28	Singapore	1,988	700	2.5	3.8
29	Mongolia [b]	1,210	430	3.0	0.8
30	Southern Yemen [a]	1,195	120	2.3	-4.9
31	Ryukyu Islands	965	580	1.2	9.3
32	Bhutan [a]	810	60	2.0	-0.1
33	Muscat and Oman [a]	565	250	0.0	15.4
34	Kuwait	540	3,540	8.7	-3.3
35	Macao	274	270	6.2	5.3
36	Bahrain [a]	200	390	3.7	3.1
37	Sikkim	187	70	2.0	-0.3
38	Trucial Oman [a]	133	1,920	3.9	37.3
39	Brunei [a]	112	910	3.7	-0.5
40	Maldive Islands [a]	106	80	1.8	1.1
41	Qatar [a]	80	3,490	7.5	1.8

Source: International Bank for Reconstruction and Development (World Bank), *Atlas,* September 1970.

[a] Estimates of GNP per capita and its growth rate are tentative.
[b] Estimates of GNP per capita have a wide margin of error mainly because of the problems in deriving the GNP at factor cost from net material product and in converting the GNP estimate into U.S. dollars.

When per capita income is less than $300 per year, the bulk of a person's diet is in starchy foods; animal fats, proteins, and sugar energy are relatively meager simply because he cannot afford them. In most African countries, the annual per capita income is $200 or below, while the vast majority of people in Asia (when mainland China is included) live on per capita incomes of about $100 or less. These low incomes, and consequent low nutritional intake levels, seriously erode the ability or capacity of laborers to produce effectively. As Table 20.5 indicates, it requires a minimum intake of 3,500 calories for a worker to perform very heavy labor, or 2,500 calories to perform moderate labor. When incomes are $100 per capita or less, these levels are not attained, and productivity from available manpower for purely physical reasons is, therefore, very low.

Table 20.5   Caloric Allowances in Famine Area

Age, sex and occupation	Emergency subsistence [a] (calories)	Temporary maintenance [b] (calories)
0 to 2 years	1,000	1,000
3 to 5 years	1,250	1,500
6 to 9 years	1,500	1,750
10 to 17 years	2,000	2,500
Pregnant and nursing women	2,000	2,500
Normal consumers (sedentary):		
Male	1,900	2,200
Female	1,600	1,800
Moderate labor	2,000	2,500
Heavy labor	2,500	3,000
Very heavy labor	3,000	3,500

Source: Jean Mayer, "Famine," *War on Hunger*, Vol. 5, No. 3 (March 1971), p. 2.

Not by Bread Alone

Superficially, the problem of world hunger would appear to boil down to first ascertaining the world's capacity to produce food and then calculating this against the needs of the world's growing population. There is, after all, just so much arable land in the world, the productive yield of which is such and such, depending upon how many of the inputs which affect productivity have been applied. Similarly, population growth projections should be reasonably reliable. Therefore, the world's food situation should be seen clearly either as a debit or credit account, with no need for controversial debates as to whether an "optimistic" or "pessimistic" view is the more realistic.

However, this simple choice has never been complacently accepted by scholars. In this chapter, we have presented principally the views of agriculturalists — in government, in foundations, or in organizations such as the United Nations' Food and Agriculture Organization or the World Bank. We have avoided dwelling at length on the more extreme assessments, which, on the one hand, predict mass famine, and, on the other, limitless abundance.[7] In what we have presented, there are certainly hopeful signs. It is always within the realm of possibility for catastrophes to occur, but despite centuries of such predictions, the world food situation has continued to improve. Utopians, for their part, have for centuries predicted Garden of Eden prospects for mankind in relationship to the world's resources. Nor have these come to pass on a worldwide scale, either.

Yet one senses from the works of such brilliant philosopher-scientists as Buckminster Fuller, and from the tremendous potential lurking just around the technological corner in energy production, oceanography, food substitutes and adaptations, and in

---

[7]For example, the noted statistician and economist Colin Clark, in his book *Starvation or Plenty?* calculates that the world could readily feed over 10 times its present population at current U.S. standards of consumption.

man's continuing ability to respond to the serious challenges of the environment, that the real problem of the future will have less and less to do with food and more and more to do with the quality of the intake not only of the body but also of the mind and character as well.[8] From the evidence, it would appear that, with due qualifications and concern for the nutritional quality problem, the world will continue to produce an adequate supply of food. At the same time, food will probably continue to be stored or distributed badly or inadequately in specific times and places. The infinite capacity of the earth to produce food is probably a myth, but we are by no means certain of that, and Fuller's Utopia may indeed be a viable prospect. Beginning in the time of Malthus and on down to the present, humans seem always to have found new ways to thwart the iron laws of subsistence postulated by some of the classical economists of the "dismal science" school.

Still, we cannot be complacent. Increases in productivity must be planned as though lives depended on it. Starvation will always haunt the lives of segments of the world's population, but if it should become an increasing threat to still more of the world's masses, it will be due not to the niggardly yields of nature, but to man's recklessness, his irresponsibility, or his sudden abandonment of the vision that has produced so many forward leaps in production over the last generation.

SUGGESTIONS FOR FURTHER READING

Brown, Lester. *Seeds of Change*. New York: Frederick A. Praeger, 1970. Treats in full detail those elements of the Green Revolution that can be attributed to the discovery of "miracle" high-yield seeds, which generated higher protein sources and the possibility of self sufficiency in many areas.

Bryant, John. *Health and the Developing World*. Ithaca, N.Y.: Cornell University Press, 1969. Covers health standards in 21 Asian, African, and Latin American countries and discusses problems of malnutrition resulting from inadequate diet.

Helfman, Elizabeth. *This Hungry World*. New York: Lothrop, Lee & Shepard, 1970. By using examples drawn from many parts of the world, this book reveals the struggle against hunger and malnutrition that is being waged in different cultures. Uses many pictures to demonstrate.

McNeil, William J. *Marine Agriculture*. Corvallis: Oregon State University Press, 1970. This book provides scientific perspective on how food production can be increased through marine cultivation. Many graphs, charts, and diagrams.

Turk, Kenneth. *Some Issues Emerging from Recent Breakthroughs in Food Production*. Ithaca, N.Y.: Cornell University Press, 1971. Describes problems resulting from the Green Revolution, including problems relating to the production of food crops, to storage, distribution and marketing, and the need to apply technology to crops other than rice and wheat.

---

[8]R. Buckminster Fuller, *Utopia or Oblivion: The Prospects for Humanity* (New York: Bantam Books, 1969).

Appendix A
Abbreviations
Used in Text

ABM	antiballistic missile
AC	average cost
AFDC	Aid to Families with Dependent Children
AFL – CIO	American Federation of Labor – Congress of Industrial Organizations
AID	Agency for International Development (division of the U. S. Department of State)
AMA	American Medical Association
Amtrak	American National Railroad Corporation
AR	average revenue
ARC	Appalachian Regional Commission
AT&T	American Telephone and Telegraph
CAB	Civil Aeronautics Board
CB	Conference Board (formerly, National Industrial Conference Board, NYC)
Comsat	Communication Satellite Corporation
DOD	Department of Defense (popularly known as the Pentagon)
EEC	European Economic Community (called the Common Market)
FAO	Food and Agriculture Organization of the United Nations
FCC	Federal Communications Commission
FFRDC	Federal Funded Research and Development Centers
FHA	Federal Housing Association
FHLB	Federal Home Loan Bank
FHM	Federal National Mortgage Association
FRB	Federal Reserve Board
FRS	Federal Reserve System
FTC	Federal Trade Commission
FY	fiscal year
GATT	General Agreement on Trade and Tariffs
GNP	gross national product
HUD	Department of Housing and Urban Development
IATA	International Air Transport Association
IBRD	International Bank for Reconstruction and Development (commonly known as the World Bank)
ICC	Interstate Commerce Commission
ITO	International Trade Organization
ITT	International Telephone and Telegraph
LDC	less developed country
LPA	labor's average product
LPN	licensed practical nurse
MC	marginal costs
MIC	Military-Industrial Complex
MLC	marginal labor cost
MR	marginal revenue

MRP	marginal revenue product
NEP	New Economic Policy of President Nixon with wage-price controls
NNP	net national product
NPA	National Planning Association (a private research organization, Washington, D.C.)
NSF	National Science Foundation
OASDI	Old Age Surviving and Disability Insurance
OPA	Office of Price Administration
PL 480	Public Law Number 480 (originally, Agricultural Trade Development and Assistance Act of 1954)
R & D	Research and Development
RN	registered nurse
SBA	Small Business Administration
SLA	Savings and Loan Association
SSA	Social Security Administration
SST	supersonic transport
TVA	Tennessee Valley Authority
UNCTAD	United Nations Conference on Trade and Development
VA	Veterans Administration

Appendix B
Glossary

Absolute Advantage: Exists when a nation or region, with superior endowment of resources and/or acquired technical knowledge can provide a good or service at lower factor inputs or lower absolute costs in terms of factors than other nations.

Accelerator: An increase in employment and income due to a change in consumer demand.

Accounting Profit: The difference between total revenue and total cost.

Active Population: All persons over 16 years of age who are able to work, including housewives, but excluding students.

Ad Valorem Subsidy: A fixed percentage subsidy related to the price of the good involved.

Ad Valorem Tax: A fixed percentage tax on the value of the price of a good.

Agency for International Development: A division of the Department of State which administers financial and technical assistance programs to less developed countries.

Aggregate Demand: The total value of output that all sectors of an economy are willing and able to buy at any given time.

Aggregate Supply: The total value of output that sellers are willing and able to sell at a given time.

Agricultural Adjustment Act: A federal law which authorizes price supports for certain farm products and controls the production of certain crops.

American Federation of Labor-Congress of Industrial Organizations (AFL-CIO): The federation of labor unions formed in 1955 by the members of the AFL and the CIO. It is the trade union with the largest membership in the United States.

American National Railroad Corporation: Mixed corporation created in 1971 to run intercity passenger trains.

American Telephone and Telegraph: Operates the major portion of telephone service in the United States and U.S. territories and serves as an interconnection between the U.S. telephone system and those in other parts of the world.

Annually Balanced Budget: When in a government budget total government expenditures equal total revenues.

Antitrust Laws: Laws aimed at preventing monopolies, concentration of economic activity, and conspiracies in restraint of trade.

Arbitrage: Buying a thing in one market and selling it at the same time in another market in order to take advantage of price differences.

Arbitration: When two parties to a dispute agree to the appointment of a third party to decide the issue, the disputants agreeing to abide by the decision rendered.

Assets: Tangible or intangible resources which have market value.

Atomism: The concept that the sum of the parts is equal to the whole. Applied to classical economics to show that maximizing individual welfare would necessarily mean maximizing society's welfare.

Autonomous Investment: Investment that is not induced by changes in effective demand (consumption), output, and income (expectations), but is a function of public policy and/or technological change.

Automatic Stabilizers: Nondiscretionary (built-in) government policies that are written into laws covering the graduated income tax, unemployment benefits, old age benefits, and corporate dividend policies to help avoid erratic economic fluctuation. Fluctuations are diminished because when the economy is on a downswing, taxes decline and transfer payments increase; therefore, people's income declines less. The reverse happens during an upswing.

Average Cost: The average input cost of producing one unit of output. It is obtained by dividing total costs by the number of units of output.

Average Fixed Cost: The average cost per unit of output for fixed inputs. It is obtained by dividing the fixed cost by the number of units of output.

Average Propensity to Consume (APC): Proportion of income spent on consumption. It is measured as:

$$APC = \frac{\text{Total Consumption}}{\text{Total Income}}$$

Average Propensity to Save (APS): Proportion of income not spent on consumption.

$$APS = \frac{\text{Total Saving}}{\text{Total Income}}$$

Average Revenue (AR): Revenue obtained per unit of output sold, that is, total revenue (TR) divided by the number of units sold. It is measured as:

$$AR = \frac{TR}{\text{Quantity Sold}} = \frac{\text{Price x Quantity Sold}}{\text{Quantity Sold}}$$

Average Variable Cost: The total cost of all variable inputs per unit of output.

Backward Linkage: See *Derived Demand.*

Balanced Budget: When total expenditures equal total revenue.

Balanced Growth: Distribution of resources among several economic sectors (for example, industry and agriculture) to attain simultaneous expansion in all sectors.

Balance of Payments: Record of the dollar value of all transactions between one country and the rest of the world during a given time period. It includes exports and imports of goods and services, movement of short-run and long-run loanable funds, investments, gifts, currency and gold.

Balance of Payments Disequilibrium: When a nation's receipts from foreign trade *do not* equal its expenditures on foreign trade.

Balance of Trade: The difference between exports and imports. For a particular country, the balance of trade is favorable (surplus) when exports exceed imports and unfavorable (deficit) when imports exceed exports.

Balance Sheet: A condensed list of assets and liabilities.

Banker's Acceptance: A draft or bill of exchange accepted for payment by a bank.

Barter: The direct exchange of one commodity or service for another without the use of money.

Benefit-Cost Analysis: A method of assessing alternatives through the comparison of present values of all expected benefits with all expected costs.

Benefit Principle: An individual should pay taxes according to the benefits he receives from public expenditures.

Bill of Exchange: A sight or time draft arising from payments to or from a foreign country.

Bimetallic Standard: Where the monetary unit is defined in terms of two metals, presumably gold and silver.

Black Capitalism: An effort to expand Negro ownership of business.

Black Market: A term indicating transactions that are in violation of fixed prices and rationing laws.

Board of Governors: The seven-men group which supervises the operation of the Federal Reserve System.

Bonds: IOU's sold on the market by corporations or the government.

Boycott: Concerted action by a group involving the refusal to do business with other groups (buying or selling).

Brannan Plan: A proposal by which farm parity payments to farmers would be eliminated and replaced by direct payments.

Breakeven Point: That level of output at which a firm's total costs equal its total revenues.

Budget: Estimate of future revenues and expenditures.

Budget Deficit: When total expenditures exceed total revenues.

Budget Surplus: When total revenues exceed total expenditures.

Business Cycles: Periodical increases and decreases in output and/or employment.

Cameralism: A variety of mercantilism that appeared in Germany in the mid-eighteenth century the chief goal of which was to increase the revenue of the state.

Capital: Goods not used for present consumption but to aid future production.

Capital Consumption Allowance: See *Depreciation.*

Capital Deepening: The increase of capital in relation to other resources, most often labor.

Capital Formation: Net increase in the stock of buildings, equipment, and inventories.

Capital Markets: Those centers where long-term credit instruments are transacted.

Capital Output Ratio: The ratio of the total stock of capital to the level of output.

Capital Productivity: Output per unit of capital.

Capital Stock: The permanently invested capital of corporations contributed by the owners. The major classes are common stock and preferred stock.

Capitalism: An economic system characterized by the private ownership of the means (factors) of production. Production and distribution of goods and services are determined through the market mechanism and profit is the central motive for the owners of capital, or capitalists.

Cartel: A contractual association of independent business organizations, located in one or more countries, for the purpose of regulating the markets and prices of the goods produced by the members.

Celler Antimerger Act (1956): An antitrust act forbidding a corporation from acquiring the stocks or assets of another corporation in order to lessen competition or to achieve a monopolistic position.

Certificate of Deposit: A document showing that a deposit has been made in a bank. Usually carrying some restriction or penalty for withdrawal before a specified date.

Change in Amount Consumed: A change in the amount of consumption expenditures due to a change in disposable income. In a technical way, this is represented as moving along the same curve.

Change in Consumption: A change in consumption represented by a shift in the consumption-function curve.

Change in Demand: This is represented by a shift in the demand curve due to changes in other factors such as the consumers' income, tastes and preferences, prices of related goods, future expectations, and entrance of more buyers into the market. For example, increases in the buyers' income will shift the demand curve upwards to the right since more will be demanded at each price level.

Change in Quantity Demanded: Occurs when the demand for a commodity increases or decreases due to a price change. It is represented by a movement along the demand curve.

Change in Quantity Supplied: A change in the quantity of a specific good supplied due to a change in its relative price.

Change in Supply: A shift of the supply curve to a new position; for each price the quantity supplied changes.

Checkoff: The deduction by an employer of labor union dues and assessments from the pay of his workers and the payment of such dues directly to the union.

Circular Flow: The general movement of resources from the production sector to the consumer sector and vice-versa.

Civil Aeronautics Board (1938): Regulatory agency with powers over civil aviation within the United States.

Classical Economics: A school of economic thought of which laissez-faire was the characteristic feature, originating in England with the works of Adam Smith and his followers Ricardo Malthus, Say, and J.S. Mill.

Class Struggle: A doctrine which asserts that modern industrial society is characterized by an inevitable and constant struggle between the owners of the means of production and the workers.

Clayton Antitrust Act (1914): An act of Congress aimed at the prevention of monopolies.

Closed Shop: A company or place of business where only union workers are accepted for employment.

Cobweb Theorem: The conditions for the convergence of price and quantity at a stable equilibrium.

Coefficient of Relative Effectiveness (CRE): Name given in the Soviet Union to the expected payoff note on a capital investment.

Coincident Indicators: Specific time series that move in the same way as the aggregate economy and can be used to measure economic activity.

Collective Bargaining: The meeting of employers and representatives of their employees for the purpose of discussing and agreeing upon wages and working conditions.

Collective Demand: Society's demand for a good that no individual could promote alone, for example, streets, police protection, fire protection, and so forth.

Collective Farms: Agricultural cooperatives formed by communities of farmers who pool their resources and divide the total output.

Command Economy: An economic system in which an authoritarian government exercises total control over the production and decision-making processes.

Commercial Bank: A bank whose major function is to receive demand deposits and to make short-term loans.

Common Market: An association of trading nations that agree to facilitate trade among them and to set common external barriers against nonparticipants. See *European Economic Community.*

Common Stock: Share of a firm's capital; it entails ownership of a corporation with the liability limited to the amount of stock.

Communication Satellite Corporation: A mixed public-private organization which provides international video communication via artificial earth satellites.

Communism: An economic system where all means of production are state-owned and everyone contributes according to his ability but is awarded a payment according to his needs.

Community (Social) Rate of Return: The excess of benefits over costs which accrues to society from some investment either public or private.

Company Union: A labor union whose membership is made up of workers employed by one company only, and usually not affiliated with any other labor union.

Comparative Advantage: Principle that states that if every nation or region specialized in the products in which it had the greatest relative efficiency, all nations would have more goods through trade. For example, the cost of production of wheat and steel is lower in the United States than in Germany. If the ratio of the cost of producing wheat in the United States and Germany is lower than the ratio of the cost of producing steel in the same countries, then it can be said that the United States has a comparative advantage in wheat, and Germany in steel. Comparative advantage provides the basic reason for free international trade.

Comparative Statics: Method of analyzing an economic variable in two or more points in time.

Compensatory Transactions: Transactions between nations that directly affect the balance of payments position of the countries involved.

Competition: The condition that exists in a market when a large number of traders all deal in the same product so that no one of them can affect the price or quantity of the goods supplied.

Complementary Goods: Two goods that are usually used together (related) so that a change in the quantity demanded of one will result in a *direct* change in the quantity demanded of the other (for example, coffee and sugar).

Compound Interest: Interest calculated on a principal sum and also on all accumulated interest earned by that principal sum as of a given date.

Concentration Ratio: The percentage of the output of one industry accounted for by its four or eight leading firms.

Conspicuous Consumption: The competitive consumption of goods others have or want ("keeping up with the Joneses").

Constant-Cost Industry: An industry where cost remains the same per unit of product regardless of variations in total production.

Constant Dollars: A term used to represent actual prices in a given year in terms of a previous year's average of actual prices.

Consumer Goods: Finished products that consumers buy for final consumption.

Consumer Possibility Curve: Graphical representation of possible allocations of household income distribution, as, for instance, for rent, electricity, gas, and so forth. It is also called budget line.

Consumer Sovereignty: The concept that consumers control the quantity and quality and type of products offered for sale in the market.

Consumption: The utilization of services or material goods for the gratification of human desires.

Consumption Function: The relationship between consumption expenditures and income.

Corporate State: A capitalist economic system controlled by the collusion of big business and big unions acting on behalf of a minority of the people, widely known as *fascism.*

Corporation: An organization created by law and consisting of one or more persons; within the scope of its charter, liability of participants is limited to the amount invested.

Correlation Analysis: Econometric analysis to determine the "degree" of relationship between two or more variables.

Cost (C): Payments made for an input incurred in the production of a good or service.

Cost Effectiveness Analysis: A technique for determining the least costly method of achieving a predetermined goal.

Cost-Push Inflation: When price levels rise because of the increased cost of factors of production, for example, wages, interest, and profits.

Craft Union: A labor union composed of workers in one skilled trade, plumbing, for example; also called a *horizontal labor union.*

Crawling Peg: A system of exchange rates where the par value of a currency is alleged to fluctuate freely within a specified range.

Credit: The rise of resources in the present in return for the payment of some resources at a future date.

Creditor: A person or institution due to receive a sum of money from others at a future date.

Creeping Inflation: A slow and persistent rise in the general level of prices over a long period of time.

Cross Elasticity of Demand: One type of elasticity concept used to describe the degree of interaction between two complementary or competing goods. That is, it measures the impact of a price change of a good (in percentage) on another commodity. For example, an increase in the price of coffee will increase the demand for tea. Mathematically, this is expressed as:

$$\text{Cross Elasticity} = \frac{\text{Percentage change in the quantity of coffee good}}{\text{Percentage change in the price of the other good}}$$

Mathematically, it measures the percentage change in a dependent variable resulting from a 1 percent change in the independent variable. For example, our willingness, or ability, to buy TV will be influenced by a change in its price. This is represented as:

$$\text{Elasticity (E)} = \frac{\text{Percentage change in quantity demanded}}{\text{Percentage change in price}}$$

Currency: A medium of exchange in the form of coins or notes.

Current Assets: Cash plus other assets readily transformable into cash.

Current Dollars: An expression reflecting the actual prices of goods and services for each year.

Current Liabilities: Debts that are due in one year.

Customs Union: An agreement between two or more nations to abolish customs, duties, and other trade restrictions among themselves and to adopt a common policy regarding their trade with nations outside the union.

Cyclically Balanced Budget: Revenues and expenditures in the government budget should be allowed to differ in the short run but must balance in the long run.

Cyclical Unemployment: Unemployment attributed to the ups and downs of the business cycle.

Death Taxes: Taxes on estates and inheritances.

Debit: A transaction that results in an outflow of money.

Debitor: A person or institution owing a sum of money to another person or institution.

Decreasing Cost Industry: An industry where the cost of production becomes lower as it expands its output.

Deduction: A process of logical reasoning starting with a premise generally accepted as true and arriving at one or more conclusions based on such a premise.

Deflation: Decrease in price levels.

Deflationary Gap: The amount by which aggregate demand (spending) must be increased in order to obtain full employment.

Demand: Willingness and ability to purchase goods and services at certain prices at a given period of time.

Demand Curve: A graphical representation of the amounts of a good people would be willing to buy at different given prices at a certain time.

Demand Deposit: Deposits in a bank which can be withdrawn at request, widely known as checking accounts.

Demand, Law of: A principle stating that as prices move in one direction, the quantity of the good demanded will vary inversely.

Demand Price: The maximum price a consumer will pay for a given quantity of a particular good.

Demand-Pull Inflation: When price levels are rising because of a rate of increase in demand that is faster than the rate of increase in supply.

Demand Schedule: A table showing what quantities of a particular commodity will be demanded at different prices.

Demonstration Effect: The desire to own high-quality goods and services when one comes in contact with them.

Dependent Variable: Variable that is conditioned by the other variables. For example, consumption is dependent mainly on income.

Deposit Expansion Multiplier: Because of fractional reserves, commercial banks based on loans and demand deposits of customers increase the money in circulation a few times over the amount of deposit.

Depreciation: Annual "consumption" of capital goods. A building or a machine is worth less of its original value every year because of wear and tear, obsolescence, and so on.

Depression: A time when production and employment are at a low level.

Derived Demand: Refers to the demand for the factors of production because the demand for (inputs) productive factors indirectly depends on the final demand for goods and services.

Determinism: Philosophical view that events *have to* follow a certain path; that is, there is no liberty of action for man.

Dialectic: A mode of philosophical analysis where one entity is passed into and retained by its opposite.

Dialectical Materialism: Marxian theory stemming from idealistic dialectics giving priority to matter over mankind; it claims that all events (not only ideas) operate in nature through their own negation out of which new events are then forged.

"Dictatorship of the Proletariat": The ultimate goal of a Communist revolution, along with the elimination of private property.

Diminishing Marginal Utility: The extra or marginal satisfaction obtained per unit decreases as more is consumed within a time period.

Diminishing Returns: With fixed factor inputs (such as a machine), additional variable factor inputs (such as a laborer) will bring an increase in output smaller than the increase in output brought about by the previously used variable factor inputs. For example, with one machine, 10 workers produce 50 shirts per day or 5 shirts per worker; 11 workers produce 54 shirts a day; thus, the first 10 workers produced 5 shirts each but the addition of the eleventh worker adds only 4 shirts to total output.

Direct Production Activities: Activities performed by firms engaged in the production of goods and services for individuals or other firms.

Direct Taxes: Taxes explicitly attached to income or property, for example, the personal income tax.

Discount Rate: The rate of interest that the Federal Reserve Bank pays for commercial paper (loans) that the banks want to turn into cash.

Discretionary Stabilizer: Deliberate policies undertaken by the government to moderate swings in the business cycle, for example, the lowering or increasing of taxes or government expenditures.

Disguised Unemployment: A condition of less than full employment, when workers are employed seasonally, part-time, or are put on short hours.

Disinvestment: When the amount of depreciation is larger than the amount of gross investment.

Disposable Personal Income: Income available to households after taxes have been withheld and transfer payments received.

Dissaving: When expenditures are larger than income.

Dividend: A return to an equity stock (common stock) paid by the corporation out of profits.

Division of Labor: When the separate parts of a productive process are assigned to different categories of workers, each specializing in a particular process.

Domestic Product: Total market value of all final goods and services produced in a country regardless of the citizenship of the producers.

Double Taxation: Occurs when a firm or an individual is taxed by two governments for the same income.

Downward Sloping Demand (Curve): Graphical representation of the demand schedule depicting the inverse relationship between quantity and price; that is, when the price of a good is raised, while all other things such as income, prices of other goods, and tastes are held constant, less of it is demanded.

Draft: A commercial paper ordering an institution to pay a certain amount to a third person.

Dumping: Selling goods on the international market below international prices.

Durable Goods: Commodities which are not completely consumed in a single period, such as machinery, equipment, household appliances, and cars.

Econometrics: Quantitative methods designed to test economic hypotheses.

Economic Cost: An opportunity cost; that is, the cost of a resource is determined by its best alternative use.

Economic Development: Structural change in an economy, the usual inference being a change from a traditional agricultural society to a modern industrial society.

Economic Dualism: An economy in which various levels of economic development exist, especially one in underdeveloped countries where traditional economic activities and modern sectors exist side by side.

Economic Good: Scarce commodity or service which is exchangeable.

Economic Growth: Increase in the real output or income of an economy over time. Usually expressed in terms of the rate of growth of GNP or NNP (at constant prices) over a period of time. *Economic growth* is not synonymous with *economic development.*

Economic Index: Relationship over time for certain variables of the economy starting at some base period. For instance, the "consumer price index" indicates by how much prices of consumer goods increase every year beginning with a base year; when a consumer price index shows 125 in relation to, say, 1958, it means that prices have increased by 25 percent.

Economic Planning: A deliberate process by which resources are allocated to an area or unit of the economy for a period of time. National or regional economic planning is usually based on some national or regional goal and indicates how resources should be allocated. See *Operational Macro Planning* and *Indicative Macro Planning.*

Economic Profit: Earnings of a business entrepreneur for the services he performs.

Economic Rent: A payment to a factor of production in excess of the amount required to bring the factor into the production process. Any factor may earn an economic rent.

Economics: The study of the production and distribution of goods and services with the use of limited resources (land, labor, and capital) for present and future consumption. The study of how limited resources (land, labor, and capital) are employed to produce and distribute goods and services for present and/or future consumption.

Economic System: The set of institutional laws, rules, and customs under which limited resources are combined by various components of the economy (households, firms, government, and so forth) to satisfy individual or public needs and desires.

Economic Welfare: The well-being of the individual. Generally assumed to be whatever the individual perceives it to be.

Economies (Diseconomies) of Scale: Increased or decreased efficiency due to the larger scale of productive activities.

Elasticity: Used to measure the degree of responsiveness of a variable when a change occurs in another variable.

Employment: Accounting of individuals who are gainfully occupied in an economy.

Employment Act of 1946: Federal legislation directing the president to receive the advice of a Council of Economic Advisers for the purpose of maintaining high levels of employment.

Endogenous Change: Changes that can be attributed to factors within the system; for instance, in a particular economic system, changes in production, income, demand, credit, and so forth are endogenous changes.

Engel's Law: Originated by a nineteenth-century Prussian statistician, Ernest Engel, to express the relation (behavior) between expenditures for basic needs such as food and family income. It states that the percentage of income spent on basic needs declines as family income increases.

Entrepreneur: Businessman who assembles and organizes the productive resources for the production of goods and services.

Equation of Exchange: $PQ = MV$, or the price (P) times quantity (Q) of production is equal to the quantity of money (M) times the turnover of money (V), or the amount paid for production equals the amount received for production.

Equilibrium: A condition of balance among factors such that production equals consumption, supply equals demand, or savings equals investment.

Etatism: An economic system based by and large on the market economy but one in which the state takes those actions necessary to achieve set goals.

European Economic Community (EEC): Known also as the "Common Market." Founded in 1958, it is composed of Italy, France, Germany, Belgium, the Netherlands, and Luxembourg; it aims to eliminate trade impediments among these nations and to integrate them ultimately into one political entity.

European Free Trade Association (EFTA): A loose economic association founded in 1960 by seven Western European countries for the purpose of eliminating tariffs among the seven members.

European Recovery Program (ERP): Known also as the "Marshall Plan," it consisted of a coordinated effort by the United States and Western Europe to reconstruct Europe's economy after World War II.

Excess Reserves: The amount of cash or assets that a bank has in excess of its legal reserves.

Excise Tax: A sales tax imposed on various manufactured goods.

Exogenous Change: Changes that are caused by factors outside the economic system such as population growth or war.

Explicit Costs: Costs that appear in the accounts of a particular firm for particular outputs.

Exports: Goods sold abroad.

External Economies (Diseconomies): Nonmarket interrelationship between firms and/or consumers. They are beneficial effects which firms or individuals have on other firms or individuals for which the party generating the benefit is uncompensated. Diseconomies are the converse, where, instead of benefits, firms or individuals produce undesirable effects, such as pollution.

Factors of Production: Productive resources (inputs) such as land, labor, capital, and entrepreneurship used in the production of goods and services.

Family Allowance Plan: Government allowances to families based on number and age of children.

Fascism: See *Corporate State.*

Featherbedding: Employed labor not needed for production, that is, labor for which marginal physical product equals zero.

Federal Communications Commission (1934): Agency charged with regulating interstate and foreign communications by wire and radio in the public interest.

Federal Open Market Committee: Part of the Federal Reserve System. This committee makes decisions on trading of government securities on the open market.

Federal Reserve Bank: One of the 12 district banks of the Federal Reserve System. It deals only with banks and not directly with individuals or firms. It is a "banker's bank."

Federal Reserve Board: Regulates commercial banks, money supply, and credit, as well as rates of interest.

Federal Reserve System: Banking system created in 1913 to regulate banking operations, credit, money issues, and other national financial aspects.

Federal Trade Commission Act (1915): Commission charged with maintaining free competitive enterprise as the keystone of the American economic system by preventing free enterprise from being stifled or weakened by monopolies or corrupted by unfair or deceptive trade practices.

Financial Intermediaries: Financial institutions outside the banking system (such as savings and loan associations, credit unions, and so on) which receive only time deposits and make loans.

Firm: An organization involved in an economic activity aiming to maximize profits.

Fiscal Dividend: Distribution of federal government surpluses to states or programs.

Fiscal Drag: High levels of unemployment and low levels of economic activity due to accumulated surpluses caused by the progressive tax structure unaccompanied by any automatic adjustment in government expenditures.

Fiscal Policies: Governmental tax and expenditure policies aimed at maintaining economic stability and changing total product demand and employment to desired levels.

Fixed Costs (FC): Costs that in the short run can not be varied directly as production changes. They exist regardless of the size of production — for example, rents, interest payments, and property taxes.

Floating Exchange Rates: When the relationship between national currencies is allowed to fluctuate according to supply and demand.

Flow: Movement of resources and economic activities over time.

Food and Agriculture Organization of the United Nations: Carries out extensive research and developmental programs and projects in the field of agricultural technology and improved productivity. The head office of this organization outside the UN nucleus in New York is in Rome.

Forced Savings: A situation in which individuals and households cannot spend as much as they desire because of government policies or inflation.

Foreign Exchange: Currency or assets used for international payments.

Foreign Exchange Rate: Relationship between two currencies used in international payments.

Foreign Investment: Direct (investment) or portfolio investment made in a country by foreign citizens or governments.

Foreign Trade: The exports and imports of a nation; external trade between one nation and the rest of the world.

Forward Exchange: Foreign exchange bought at a certain price to be delivered and paid at a future date.

Forward Linkage: Output of an industry that can be used as an input by another industry.

Free Good: Commodity or service that is not scarce and not exchangeable, for example, air.

Free Trade: Trade of goods and services over national boundaries unrestricted by such devices as tariffs and quotas.

Frictional Unemployment: Unemployment of workers between jobs, as in construction work.

Full Employment: A situation that exists whenever all resources are gainfully employed. In a more restricted sense, it refers to the ability of the entire labor force to find jobs at any wage level.

Full Employment Budget: Federal government system of accounting in which the forecasted revenue is assumed to be at full employment conditions.

Functional Income Distribution: Distribution of national income in the form of wages, interest, rents, and profits rising from the relative contribution of such factors of production as labor, capital, land, and entrepreneurship.

General Agreement on Tariffs and Trade (GATT): An agreement among most of the world's nations to pursue fair practices in international trade and to attempt to lower international trade barriers.

General Equilibrium Theory: A model of the comprehensive interrelationships between prices and outputs that outlines the processes leading to overall equilibrium.

Gift Tax: A tax imposed on gifts over certain amounts.

Gold Bullion Standard: A system of international exchange in which payments are made in gold or in currency representing gold. Gold is the international money.

Gold Exchange Standard: Gold is represented by one country's currency (such as the dollar or the pound), but international transactions are carried out in other currencies that can be converted into a convertible exchange (such as the U.S. dollar until 1968) and ultimately into gold.

Goodwill: Nonquantifiable asset of a firm such as a patent or the possession of a widely known brand.

Government Expenditures: Dollar value of all goods and services purchased by the government.

Graduated Income Tax: See *Progressive Tax.*

Grants-in-Aid: Financial assistance rendered by the federal government to states or localities or by the states to localities.

Great Leap Forward: A policy pursued by the People's Republic of China between 1958 and 1960 to achieve the level of industrialization of more advanced countries in a short period of time.

Gresham's Law: A postulate by Gresham that bad (cheaper) money drives away good (more expensive) money from the market.

Gross Investment: Total investment made in a given time period, including the replacement of worn capital (the replacement of capital allowances).

Gross National Income: Total income received by those contributing to the national production of goods and services within one year.

Gross National Product: The market value (dollars) of all final consumer goods and services produced in a given year in a particular country (total market value of the production of final goods and services in an economy).

Growth Pole: Concentration of resources in a limited area with the goal of achieving economic expansion in a larger region. It is balanced growth applied to a small area and unbalanced growth between that area and the rest of a region or nation.

Guaranteed Annual Income: A contractual agreement between management and labor specifying that labor will receive a minimum annual salary.

Hard-Core Unemployed: Unemployed persons who due to technological or structural change in the economy cannot find employment for long periods of time.

Hoarding: Part of disposable income that is not spent and not made available for investment (such as putting one's money under the mattress instead of depositing it in a bank). See also *Savings.*

Horizontal Merger: The merging of two firms which produce similar products or services.

Human Resources: A group of people with various skills and capabilities.

Hyperinflation: See *Runaway Inflation.*

Hypothesis: A statement formulated for which proof is necessary to accept.

Idealistic Dialectics: Use of dialectics in the analysis of ideas. See *Dialectic.*

Imperfect Competition: General conditions in capitalist economies due to lack of all requirements for perfect competition. See *Competition.*

Import Quota: Legislation that sets the maximum quantity of a certain good that can be imported during a given time.

Imports: Goods purchased from abroad.

Income: Earnings received by a person, household, or institution.

Income Effect: The effect on demand of changes in prices viewed from the change in income owing to that price change. Each price change has two effects on demand: a "substitution effect" and an "income effect."

Income Elasticity of Demand: Concept used to describe (or measure) the degree of responsiveness (in terms of percentage changes) of quantity changes to a change in income. Algebraically, income elasticity is measured as:

$$\text{Elasticity coefficient } E = \frac{\text{Percentage change in } Q}{\text{Percentage change in } Y}$$

Income elasticity has three alternative categories such as elasticity, unitary elasticity, and inelasticity. See *Price Elasticity* for the relevant explanation.

Income Tax: A tax set on the income of an individual, household, or institution.

Income Velocity of Money: The number of times dollars are spent to purchase all goods and services that are included in gross national product.

Independent Variable: Variable whose variations are not explained by other variables.

Index Number: A number denoting a change of a value from a certain base; for example, when in year t_o, GNP is $500 billion, and in year t, it is $600 billion, if t_o = 100, then t = 120.

Indicative Macro Planning: Usually a forecast on how a government expects to allocate its resources in order to achieve set goals.

Indifference Curve: A diagrammatical representation showing the combinations of two different goods that yield a person the same satisfaction.

Indirect Taxes: Taxes that are imposed on the productive enterprise for its actual output and thereafter can be shifted either partially or entirely onto the buyers. Indirect taxation is added to net national product (national income) at factor cost to arrive at NNP at market prices. Examples: sales taxes and excise taxes.

Induced Investment: Investment that is directly related to changes in the income, output, and employment level of the economy. That is, an increase in national product may induce a higher level of net investment.

Industry: A group of firms producing the same type of goods or services.

Infant Industry: An industry in a less developed country which is just beginning to develop and which must compete with similar products imported from foreign countries. (See also *Prenatal Industry*.)

Inflation: When there is an increase in prices without a commensurate increase in the quantity or quality of the goods or services transacted.

Inflationary Gap: The amount by which actual spending must be reduced to bring the economy to the full-employment level (at stable prices), that is, excess aggregate demand over aggregate supply at full-employment level.

Innovation: New methods used in economic activities to increase the productivity of resources.

Input-Output Analysis: Analysis of the flow of inputs, final goods, and services among different sectors of an economy. Used in economic planning to determine the structure and interdependence of the economy.

Interest: Payment for the use of capital. Usually stated as a rate, as a percentage of the amount of capital used.

Interlocking Directorate: A situation created by having the same person(s) on two or more boards of directors of firms producing similar goods or services.

Internal Economies (Diseconomies): Increasing or decreasing costs for a firm that appear explicitly on the account of the price. See also *External Economies.*

International Air Transport Association: Sets international fares and conditions of labor and settles disputes by unanimous agreement.

International Bank for Reconstruction and Development (IBRD - World Bank): A nation's bank created by the United Nations in 1944 to provide technical assistance and loans or grant financing for worthy projects in countries unable to generate foreign exchange in sufficient volume to finance all of their own import requirements.

International Monetary Fund (IMF): An institution created by the United Nations in 1944 to facilitate international financial transactions.

International Telephone and Telegraph: A private conglomerate with worldwide holdings and influence.

Interstate Commerce Commission (1887): Regulates carriers which are engaged in interstate commerce or in foreign commerce to the extent that it takes place within the United States.

Inventory: The amount of goods a firm has on hand at a certain time.

Investment: The purchase or construction of machinery, buildings, equipment, and other capital goods for the production of further goods and services. It includes increases in inventories (unsold goods), but excludes transfer of bonds and stocks.

Invisible Hand: Expression coined by Adam Smith in his *Wealth of Nations* (1776) to refer to the beneficent effects of a laissez-faire economy. He argued that the best good for society would be produced if every individual pursued his own self-interest without any government interference. The invisible hand presumes a state of perfect competition while ignoring the possibility of government interference and monopolistic competition.

Knights of Labor (1869-1917): A labor confederation accepting as members workers, farmers, and certain professionals. Its downfall was due partly to its heterogeneity but also to the advent of business labor unions, such as the American Federation of Labor, which organized on a craft basis.

Labor: Any form of human effort devoted to the production of goods and services.

Labor Force: In the United States, this includes all persons 16 years of age and older who are gainfully employed plus all those who are unemployed, but actively looking for jobs.

Labor-Management Relations Act (1947-Taft-Hartley): Legislation meant to protect employers from certain forms of union behavior such as secondary boycotts, organizational strikes, and jurisdictional strikes. Among its provisions are a 90-day cooling off period which can be called for before a strike is implemented.

Labor Productivity: Output per unit of labor, per unit of time.

Lagging Indicators: Time series for certain economic activities that have the general tendency to move behind the time series of other economic activities.

Laissez Faire, Laissez: ("Let it be done, let it pass") Expression coined by a French businessman when asked by Colbert in the seventeenth century what role the state should play. Generally, it means that economic affairs should be run by the private sector (business) without government interference.

Land: Primary factor of production which includes urban sites, agricultural land, and subsoil resources (mining).

Land Reform: Change in the distribution and ownership of land in order to increase the efficiency of agricultural production and/or to spread the distribution of land holdings.

Leading Indicators: Time series for certain economic activities that have a general tendency to be ahead of the time series of other economic activities.

Legal Reserves: A minimum share against deposits that a commercial bank is required to keep either with the Federal Reserve Bank or as cash in its vaults.

Liability: The amount of money owed by one firm to another firm, person, or institution.

Limited Liability: The maximum amount for which a person can be held responsible in an economic activity. For example, a stockholder of a corporation is liable only up to the amount of the stock he owns.

Liquidity Preferences: Keynesian theory showing that individuals prefer to hold liquid assets and willing to forego interest earnings at low levels of interest.

Loanable Funds: Funds which are available for loans, such as bank deposits, savings accounts, and insurance premiums.

Location Theory: The location of economic activities depends on demand and supply factors, demand for output plus transportation costs.

Lockout: When a firm shuts down its operations to keep the workers out and then uses this as a bargaining tactic against labor.

Long Run: A period long enough to add new capital or, according to convention among economists, a period longer than one year.

Lorenz Curve: Graphical exposition comparing cumulative percentage relationships between two variables. Often used to measure the distribution of a society's income.

Macroeconomics: (Macro, "big") The part of economics which deals with the economy as a whole in terms of aggregate production, income, employment, investment, savings, and general price levels.

Malthusian Theory: A theory developed in 1796 by the British Reverend Thomas Malthus in which he predicted famine because by his reckoning population increases in a geometrical progression (1, 2, 4, 8) while food resources grow in an arithmetical progression (1, 2, 3, 4).

Marginal Cost (MC): The cost of production of one extra unit of output.

Marginal Efficiency of Capital (MEC): The relationship between the cost of an extra unit of capital and the revenue afforded by the addition of an extra unit of capital.

Marginal Labor Productivity (MLP): Additional output due to the addition of an extra unit of labor.

Marginal Physical Product (MPP): Measurement of extra output in physical terms.

Marginal Product (MP): Extra output resulting from an additional use of variable input. Usually expressed as:

$$MP = \frac{\text{Change in total output}}{\text{Change in input}}$$

Marginal Propensity to Consume (MPC): (Proportion) fraction of each extra dollar of income that is spent on additional consumption.

$$MPC = \frac{\text{Change in total consumption}}{\text{Change in income}}$$

Marginal Propensity to Save (MPS): Proportion (ratio) of each extra dollar of income that is saved.

$$MPS = \frac{\text{Change in total saving}}{\text{Change in total income}}$$

MPC and MPS should always add up to one

Marginal Rate of Substitution: The rate at which a person is ready to exchange one product for another in order to maintain the same satisfaction.

Marginal Revenue (MR): A firm's additional (extra) revenue extracted from the sale of one additional unit of output. It is measured as:

$$MR = \frac{\text{Change in total revenue}}{\text{Change in quantity sold}}$$

Marginal Revenue Product (MRP): Value of the extra output resulting from one additional unit of input.

Marginal Tax Rate: The tax rate corresponding to a change in the level of income.

Marginal Utility: The extra satisfaction derived from the consumption of an additional unit of a commodity or service.

Margin Regulation: Legislation allowing the Federal Reserve System to set the minimum percentage cash to be paid for transactions on the stock market.

Market Concentration: The extent to which control of a sector of the economy is exercised by a few people or firms.

Market Economy: An ideal system where allocation of resources is based exclusively on the operation of competitive demand and supply.

Market Price: The price of a good or service as determined by the market demand for and supply of that good or service.

Market Rate of Interest: Equilibrium rate of interest as determined by the interaction of the demand for and supply of capital; often the rate of return (yield) on government bonds is thought to be the market rate.

Market Yield: The actual return for a bond according to its market price; thus, if a $100 bond at 4 percent sells for $80, its yield is 4 x 100/80 = 5 percent.

Marxism: Theory developed in the last century by Karl Marx according to which the overthrow of capitalist societies and the take-over by the proletariat were inevitable. Almost all Communist nations today claim to operate according to Marxist principles, but in no place does the proletariat reign.

Mean: Average. The mean for 3, 10, 6, 9, and 7 is 7.

Median: The middle number of a series of numbers. The median for 3, 10, 6, 9, and 7 is 6.

Member Bank: A bank subjected to direct regulation and with full benefits of Federal Reserve System operations. By law, all nationally charatered banks have to be members; state-chartered banks become members if certain conditions are fulfilled.

Mercantilism: Set of economic and political doctrines and practices common to Western Europe from the sixteenth century until the Industrial Revolution which aimed at raising national power and prosperity by accumulating bullion through colonial exploitation and a favorable balance of trade. Mercantilism is usually identified as the stage of precapitalism. The doctrine was attacked by laissez-faire advocates such as Adam Smith.

Merger: When two or more firms buy each other and operate as a single firm.

Microeconomics: (Micro, "small") The part of economics which deals with the decision-making of specific economic units such as households, firms, and industries.

Mixed Economy: An economic system in which decisions are partly private and partly public. All systems are "mixed" to a certain degree.

Model: Formal presentation of a theory or system.

Monetary Policy: Exercised by the Federal Reserve Banking System to attain price stability and to bring production and employment to desired levels. It regulates the supply of money through open market operations, changing reserve requirements and discount rates.

Money: Anything that is accepted in exchange for other things. It is used 1) as a medium of exchange for the transaction of goods and services; 2) as a measure of value; 3) as a standard of deferred payments for lending or borrowing; and 4) as a store of value to save for the future.

Money Market: Market where transactions in short-term IOU's such as treasury bills are coined out.

Money Wages: Wages received at current prices unadjusted for inflation or deflation.

Monopolistic Competition: A market structure with both monopolistic and competitive characteristics. That is, new firms can enter, but products are not homogeneous and price leadership develops easily.

Monopolistic Profit: Profits that occur because of the producer's ability to price a good at a point where average revenue and average cost are not equal. May be equated with economic rent.

Monopoly: One type of market structure in which a specific product with no close substitute is produced (or sold) by a single firm.

Monopsony: A market in which there is only one buyer of a specific input such as labor.

Most-Favored-Nation Clause: A clause in an international trade treaty by which one party agrees to give the same preferential treatment to the other party as the best treatment given to other parties in the future.

Multiplier: Keynesian principle postulating that an increase in investment induces a larger increase in output and/or income.

National Income at Factor Cost: The difference between national income at market prices and indirect taxes. The national sum of all payments to factors of production: wages, rents, interest, and profits.

National Income at Market Prices: Equivalent to net national product. It represents the total income of the country, including indirect taxes. It is the sum of final goods and services produced within a period, for example, one year.

National Labor Relations Act (NLRA, 1935-Wagner): Legislation which legalized collective bargaining and established governmental mechanisms for the protection of labor's right to organize.

Natural Monopoly: Also called a legal monopoly when established by the government to enable the production of goods and services operated on increasing returns to scale by a single public or semi-public agency. Public utilities such as water supply, gas, electricity, telephone, and postal services are all natural monopolies operated by public or private firms.

Near Money: Liquid assets which can easily be converted into money, for example, government bonds, different kinds of savings accounts like cash values, insurance policies, and so forth.

Negative Income Tax: A way to achieve greater income equalization through the government's paying a subsidy to an individual whose total income is below a certain level.

Neoclassical Economics: School of economics based on the operation of the free movement of resources; its main representative was Alfred Marshall who with others developed marginal analysis in the study of microeconomics.

Net Investment: Change in the stock of capital in a given time period. The difference between gross investment and depreciation.

Net National Product: Total dollar value of the net production of goods and services in an economy. It is also defined as the total of all factor earnings (wages, interest, rents, and profits) paid for the production of final goods and services. NNP can be obtained by deducting depreciation from GNP.

Net Worth: The difference between the assets and the liabilities of a firm or an individual.

Nondurable Goods: Commodities whose economic life is short, such as food and clothing.

Nonprice Competition: When firms compete on service or other factors rather than on price.

Normative Economics: Analysis of what *ought* to be rather than what *is*. See also *Positive Economics*.

Norris-La Guardia Act (1932): Labor legislation outlawing the yellow dog contract and limiting the use of court injunctions to prevent strikes, a forerunner of the National Labor Relations Act of 1935.

Notes Payable: An IOU or a promissory note by which a holder can claim an amount of cash.

Obsolescence: Technical depreciation, when a good or process is technically outdated.

Oligopolistic Market: A market in which homogeneous or differentiated products are sold by a few firms. There are two types of oligopolistic markets: 1) pure oligopoly in which a few firms sell a homogeneous product, as, for example, the copper or steel industries; and 2) imperfect oligopoly; in which a few firms sell differentiated products, as, for instance, the automobile or detergent industries.

Open-Market Operations: The purchase and sale of government bonds by the Federal Reserve System in order to maintain, enhance, or modify the actual trend of the economy. One of the major monetary policies of the Federal Reserve System is to change the money supply through the purchase or sale of government securities.

Open Shop: Legislation allowing firms to hire laborers who do not belong to a union under contract to the firm.

Operational Macro Planning: A deliberate set of actions pursued by the government to allocate resources to achieve a set of goals.

Opportunity Cost: The real (alternative) cost of resources that are used in the production of goods and services, that is, the implicit cost of the foregone opportunity. For example, the opportunity cost of the Vietnam war expenditures are (the foregone) civilian goods and services which might otherwise have been provided.

Paradox of Thrift: In the aggregate, more savings could mean no additional savings because more savings mean less spending, when less is spent, fewer workers are needed to produce goods and thus less income is generated. A larger traditional savings multiplied by a smaller income may yield no increase.

Parameter: The constant quantity determining the slope and shape of a curve.

Parity: The rate of exchange between the currencies of two countries which fixes the purchasing power of one currency in terms of the other.

Partial Equilibrium Theory: A model or theory which considers only one market in isolation, assuming the other markets to be in equilibrium.

Patent: An exclusive right given by the government for an invention for a limited period of time.

Perfect Competition: An abstraction of market conditions under which there are many sellers, homogeneous products, free movement of resources, full knowledge of the market by everyone, and no government interference.

Permanent Income Hypothesis: A hypothesis advanced by Milton Friedman stating that consumption in one period depends on past and expected future income rather than on current income alone.

Personal Income: The part of national income received by all individuals in an economy.

Phillips Curve: An analysis that relates the level of inflation to the level of wages and the rate of unemployment. Generally, it states that the smaller the unemployment rate, the higher the rate of inflation.

Physical Product: Output in physical terms.

Physiocracy: Philosophy of political economy developed by François Quesnay in eighteenth-century France. Physiocrats believed that agriculture was the main source of wealth and that the economic process should be based on laissez faire in agriculture.

Planned Economy: An economy where the what, how, and for whom decisions are deliberately made by a planning board rather than through the marketplace.

Plough Back: The amount of profits a corporation decides to retain rather than to distribute in the form of dividends.

Polarization: Spatial concentration of economic activities in one area.

Positive Economics: Analysis of *what is* rather than *what ought to be.* See also *Normative Economics.*

Poverty Line: Arbitrary minimum below which level the government considers a household's or individual's income to be inadequate.

Preferred Stock: Equity share of a corporation implying ownership but not control. Usually, owners of preferred stock have the right to receive fixed dividends rather than dividends based on profits, but do not have voting rights.

Prenatal Industry: An industry in a less developed country which is just starting to develop but which does not have to compete with similar imported products. See also *Infant Industry.*

Price: Payment for a unit of a good or service.

Price Discrimination: When different customers are charged different prices for the same product or service with no corresponding variation in costs.

Price Elasticity: Measures the sensitivity of the quantity demanded or supplied relative to a change in price. That is, it describes the degree of response of changes in quantity supplied or demanded associated with a change in price. There are three alternative elasticities: 1) If the percentage change in quantity demanded or supplied exceeds the percentage change in price, it is elastic. In this case, total revenue of the firm will increase with a price cut; 2) if the percentage change in quantity is equal to the percentage change in price, it is called unitary elastic — total revenues of the firm being unchanged; 3) if the percentage change in quantity is less than the percentage change in price, it is inelastic, and total revenue of the firm will decline with a price reduction.

Price Leadership: A situation in which one or a few firms, because of their size and control of the market, can dictate prices for the entire industry, for example, as U.S. steel does for the steel industry.

Price System: An economy where the what, how, and for whom are decided in the marketplace through supply and demand. The equilibrium between supply and demand is achieved through changes in prices.

Primary Factors of Production: Productive resources (inputs) which do not require any human effort; these resources are used as found in nature, as, for example, land and subsoil resources (mining).

Prime Rate: The interest rate charged by large banks to their best and most credit-worthy customers.

Private Property: Exclusive ownership of an asset by an individual, household, or institution to which they have a legal right.

Producer Goods: Intermediate or finished goods used in the production of further goods and services. These are mainly machinery, equipment, and buildings.

Production Function: A relationship between an output and an input. Most frequently used is a so-called Cobb-Douglas type: $Q = AK\alpha L\beta (\alpha + \beta = 1)$ where Q = output; A = constant of proportionality; K = capital; L = labor; and α and β = parameters.

Production Possibility Curve: Graphical representation of all possible combinations of total output for an economy under conditions of scarce resources and a given technology. Any point on the production possibility curve assumes the full and efficient use of resources. It depicts the allocation of different amounts and kinds of scarce resources to the production of alternate commodities.

Productivity: Relationship between an input and its contribution to total output.

Profit: In economic terms, payment for services performed by entrepreneurs. In accounting terms, profit is the difference between total revenue and total cost (including a payment for the entrepreneur's services).

Profit-Push Inflation: Inflation caused by excessive profits made by firms.

Progressive Tax: A type of taxation which results in the proportion of income paid increasing as income rises. It is also called a graduated income tax because the percentage rate increases at higher income brackets. The U.S. personal income tax is an example.

Property Tax: A tax on real estate or other assets.

Proportional Tax: A tax that is charged at the same rate for everyone regardless of income or wealth.

Psychic Income: Nonmaterial satisfaction derived from economic activities.

Public Law Number 480: Provides for the sale abroad of surplus agricultural commodities by the Department of Agriculture's Commodity Credit Corporation. Payments for these commodities could be made in foreign currencies, which helped less developed countries with scarce foreign exchange resources. Most of the proceeds from these sales were then loaned to the foreign government for development purposes. The remainder would be used to pay for United States government expenditures in the foreign country. This law was originally known as the Agricultural Trade and Development Act of 1954.

Public Works: Government programs creating social overhead capital, such as roads, river basins, parks, and so forth.

Pure Competition: A market structure characterized by (1) many buyers and sellers of homogeneous (identical) products; (2) no control over prices by buyers and sellers; and (3) free entry or exit by sellers. It is usually synonymous with perfect competition, which in addition requires perfect resource mobility and perfect knowledge.

Quantity Theory of Money: Classical theory stating that there is a definite relationship between the money supply and the price level.

Rationing: A method of allocating scarce goods to individuals and households when shortages occur; used in the United States during World War II.

Real Income: The purchasing power of money income, that is, income measured by the total goods and services it can purchase, accounting for price changes over some base year period.

Real Wages: The purchasing power of money wages accounting for price changes for goods and services over some base year period.

Recession: A situation in which aggregate national output decreases and an increasing number of people are unemployed.

Recovery: A marked improvement from conditions of recession, during which national aggregate output increases and more working people are employed.

Regression Analysis: An econometric analysis that estimates the relationship between two or more variables.

Regressive Tax: A tax that is a relatively heavier burden on low-income groups than on higher-income groups.

Relative Income Hypothesis: States that when a household's income declines, consumption will decline relatively less than the decline in income. The consumption of a family unit is dependent upon its position in the overall income distribution.

Rent: Payment made to landowners.

Reserve Requirements: Minimum percentage against deposits that (commercial) banks are required to keep in the form of cash or as reserves in Federal Reserve Banks. This is one of the weapons with which the Federal Reserve Bank controls the amount of demand deposits in the economy.

Resource Allocation: Distribution of the factors of production among various uses such as consumption and investment.

Returns to Scale: The larger the size of operation, the larger the output per unit of input.

Revenue Product (RP): Output in monetary terms. RP = price x quantity.

Right to Work Laws: State legislation, operative in some southern states, making it voluntary for workers to join unions. Their aim is to limit the growth of labor unions, but the attempt has proved relatively unsuccessful.

Robinson-Patman Act (1936): Antitrust legislation aimed especially at price discrimination practices.

"Rule of Reason": An interpretation of 1911 antitrust legislation stating that mere size was not cause for antitrust action; it was monopolistic practices that came within this law. This was applied to Standard Oil in 1911 but reversed in 1945 in the case of the Aluminum Corporation of America (ALCOA), in which antitrust action was based only on size.

Runaway Deflation: Rapid decrease in prices.

Runaway Inflation: Rapid increase in prices.

Sales Tax: A tax imposed on finished goods when they are sold to consumers.

Savings: The part of income (disposable) that is not spent but made available for investment, for example, in a bank account. See *Hoarding.*

Say's Law: The law of markets, which states that supply creates its own demand.

Scarcity: Refers to the fact that human desires and wants (for economic goods) are not completely satisfied by the limited amounts of goods produced on the earth; that is, the demand for economic goods exceeds the supply. That is why economics deals with the production and distribution of these limited (scarce) goods.

Seasonal Fluctuations: Short-run ups and downs in economic activity due to weather, traditions, or other respective factors.

Secondary Boycott: A device used by a labor union against the products of a firm (or industry) which purchases goods from another firm (or industry) against which the union is on strike. This practice was deemed illegal in 1947 by the Taft-Hartley Act.

Sherman Antitrust Act (1890): First antitrust legislation in the United States. It was aimed against conspiracies in restraint of trade. It was a very ineffective tool up to 1914 when the Clayton Antitrust Act was enacted.

Short Run: According to conventions in economics, it is usually one year or less. In theory, it is a period in which fixed inputs, that is, capital, do not change.

Single Tax: As proposed by Henry George (1839-1897), this was a land tax to be levied instead of any other tax. As land was a gift of nature, it belonged to society and therefore anyone enjoying its fruits or ownership should pay society for this.

Slope: Steepness of a line, or the rate of change of a factor in relation to the rate of change of another factor.

Small Business Administration: A federal agency charged with financially assisting small businesses.

Social Benefit-Cost Analysis: Comparison of costs and returns on an activity affecting a community.

Socialism: A system based on Marxian philosophy wherein all or some of the means of production are owned by the state, and the operation of the economy is based more on the directives laid down by policy-makers than on the forces of demand and supply.

Social Overhead Capital (SOC): Economic activities provided by the public sector for the use of everyone, for example, roads, parks, schools, and so forth.

Social Security Act (1935): Federal legislation 1) making it compulsory for certain individuals to contribute to a fund to be used to pay a monthly pension to these individuals and 2) providing other welfare measures for the deprived, unemployed, sick, and injured. This law has been expanded and amended many times since 1935.

Special Drawing Rights (SDRs): A bookkeeping trick to create extra intentional reserves to replace gold. The International Monetary Fund allocates an extra quota of reserve to participating countries depending on their gold reserves.

Specialization: The distribution of tasks among individuals in areas according to their best capabilities.

Spread Effect: Economic activities in one location or industry that affect other locations or industries.

State Farms: Farms organized on a commercial basis (using hired labor) and publicly owned.

Static Analysis: Analysis done at one point of time.

Stock: Goods on hand at a certain moment in time; for example, capital stock is the amount of buildings and machinery a company has at a specific date.

Strike: Joint action by a group of workers who refuse to work until certain conditions are fulfilled.

Structural Inflation: A perennial price income situation caused by monopolistic practices which raise the price of products without reference to supply and demand.

Structural Unemployment: A type of long-term unemployment resulting from structural problems prevalent within the economy such as racism, illiteracy, regional imbalance, technological lag, lack of skills, and geographical location.

Subsidy: Funds allocated by the public sector to certain private activities for economic or political reasons.

Substitute Good: A good which could be exchanged for another good with similar utility, for example, oil heating and gas heating, or molasses and honey.

Sunspot Theory: A theory of Stanley Jevons claiming that business fluctuations are due to the 11-year cycle of sunspots which affect crops, thus agricultural output and total national income and employment.

Supply: The willingness and ability of producers to sell goods and services at certain prices during a given time period.

Syndicalism: An economic system based exclusively on the organization of society, both employees and employers, in trade unions. The fascist movements in Italy and Spain attempted this type of organization.

Tariffs: Tax or customs duties imposed on goods imported or exported.

Tax: Compulsory payment to the government to help finance its operations (expenditures). Also a tool used in adjusting aggregate demand in an economy.

Tax Base: Income, wealth, property, or other factors considered in setting tax levels.

Tax Evasion: Illegal ways of avoiding tax payment.

Tax Incidence: The burden of a tax on a certain group or factor.

Tax Shifting: Changing the burden of taxation from one group to another or from one factor to another.

Technology (T): Systematic way of using alternate resources in the production of goods and services. (It is the art of combining various resources with know-how to produce goods and services.)

Tennessee Valley Authority: A United States public corporation which generates and distributes (wholesale only) electric power in the Tennessee River Valley states.

Terms of Trade: Value of a good sold by a country in terms of the value of a good imported by a country, for example, how many bags of coffee equal a canning machine in the marketplace.

Theory: A set of hypotheses attempting to explain in a general way certain phenomena, facts, or activities.

Time Deposit: Deposits made in financial institutions (for example, savings banks) on which one usually receives a return (interest) but for which one must give notice to the institution to withdraw. Such funds are not transferable to a third party "on demand," as are demand deposits.

Time Series: Changes in the quantities of a variable over time.

Total Cost (TC): The sum of both variable and fixed costs.

Total Revenue (TR): The total receipts of a firm obtained from the sale of goods; that is, TR = price x quantity sold.

Trade Expansion Act (1962): Legislation aimed at cutting tariffs and generally expanding trade between the United States and other nations.

Transfer Payments: Government programs such as Social Security payments, old age pensions, funds for the disabled, interest payments on government bonds, veterans' loans, and so on. In general, payments made by individuals to the government in one period and payable to same or/and other individuals at another time.

Treasury Notes: Short-term IOU's issued by the U.S. government.

Tying Contract: A contract with a clause obligating the buyer to buy another good (or meet some other condition) to fulfill the basic contract; for instance, U.S. foreign aid requires countries receiving it to spend it on purchases made in the United States.

Unbalanced Growth: Growth strategy prescribed by Albert O. Hirschman to the effect that lags among economic sectors during development would achieve faster economic growth for the less developed countries.

Underconsumption Theory: Marxian theory claiming that recessions are caused because workers receive wages that are lower than what is warranted by their input; therefore, their income and per capita income is lower, fewer goods are produced, and fewer workers are needed, all of which creates unemployment and a decline in the gross national product.

Underdeveloped (Less Developed) Countries (LDC): Countries with a low level of economic activity and a per capita income much lower than that in the United States or Western Europe.

Underemployment: A situation that exists whenever resources are not being used in the most efficient way.

Unemployment: A situation that exists whenever part of the labor force (resources) cannot or does not find steady gainful occupation.

Union: An organization of laborers whose aim is to obtain for their services increasingly equitable (that is, "more today than yesterday") wages and improved working conditions.

Union Shop: A place of work at which the employer is allowed to hire workers only from the union with whom he has signed a contract, or workers who must join that union shortly after they are hired.

Upward Sloping Supply (Curve): Graphical representation of the supply schedule showing the direct relationship between market prices and the amount of a commodity that sellers are willing to supply at certain prices, all other things being constant.

Utility: Satisfaction derived from the consumption of goods and services.

Utopian Socialism: Nineteenth-century reaction to growing industrial capitalism. Its aim was to place control over the economy in the hands of everyone. This philosophy assumed various forms, its most famous exponents being Proudhon, Charles Fourier, and Robert Owen.

Value: Monetary worth of goods and services.

Value Added: Factor costs (payments for inputs) involved at each stage in the production of a good. This is a method used to estimate national income at factor cost by summing up all value added for all goods and services.

Variable Cost (VC): Cost that varies directly with output; that is, it increases as the output increases, as, for example, labor and raw materials.

Vertical Merger: When a firm purchases other firms which either produce goods that are used by the purchasing firm or use goods that are sold by the purchasing firm.

Wage-Fund Theory: Proposed by John Stuart Mill in 1848, according to which the total funds of a firm are fixed so that when more of this fund is used for wages, less is available for return to capital.

Wage-Push Inflation: Inflation caused by wages increasing faster than labor productivity.

Wages and Salaries: Payments made for services performed by labor. Frequently expressed in money terms per hour, day, week, or month.

Wealth: Assets which have value.

Yellow Dog Contract: A contract between an employer and employee in which the employee specified that he would not join a labor union. Such contracts were outlawed by the Norris-Laguardia Act of 1932.

Yield: Rate of return on an input.

Appendix C

Basic Principles — Chapter Cross Reference

Principle	Chapter number
Aggregate Demand	16, 17
Agricultural Economics and Development	5, 19, 20
Antitrust Laws	14
Automation	13
Balance of Trade and Payments	16, 18, 19
Budget Deficit and Surplus	15, 16, 17
Business Cycles	8, 16, 17
Capital (Accumulation; Cost, Mobility; Domestic, International Markets)	2, 9, 13, 18, 19
Capitalism	14
Comparative Advantage	18, 19
Competition	14, 18
Consumer's Sovereignty	9, 14
Cost (Opportunity Cost, Comparative Cost)	2, 3, 5, 10, 12, 15, 17
Cost — Benefit Analysis	9
Decentralization	6, 9
Demand	2, 7, 8, 9, 11, 16
Depreciation and Obsolecence	13
Derived Demand	9
Devaluation	16
Diminishing Returns	7
Discrimination	1, 2, 3, 5
Economic Dualism	2, 19
Economic Growth	2, 6, 7, 13, 15, 18, 19
Economic Planning	4, 5, 19
Economies of Scale	7, 14
Economic Opportunity	1, 2, 3, 19
Economic Power	2, 14
Elasticity	8, 9, 11
Equilibrium of Supply and Demand	5, 8, 9, 16
Exploitation	1, 3, 19
Externalities	7, 8, 10
Factors of Production	3, 9
Financial Markets (Domestic and International)	8, 14, 15, 16, 18
Fiscal Policy	1, 11, 15, 17, 20
Foreign Aid	19, 20
Foreign Exchange	18
Free Trade	18
Full Employment	2, 5, 12, 17
Government's Economic Role	4, 5, 6, 7, 10, 12, 13, 15, 16, 17

Index

369